Success in Twentieth Century World Affairs

Success Studybooks

Success in
TWENTIETH CENTURY WORLD AFFAIRS
since 1919

Jack B. Watson, M.A.
Senior Lecturer in History
Preston Polytechnic (Poulton-le-Fylde Campus)

John Murray

Foreword

This book attempts to outline and explain some of the major developments in contemporary history since the First World War. It is intended for the general reader who seeks understanding of how the problems of our day have come about; it also aims to provide a framework for students who wish to pursue a first course of study in preparation for examinations in schools and colleges. The author of any book on contemporary history, especially one which rashly takes for its title *World Affairs*, must feel that his feet tread only through quicksand. Whenever he approaches the present day and tries to imprison it in the written pages of history, he is fully aware that the events of today can be perceived only dimly, and that the events of tomorrow may well overturn whatever judgment he has been reckless enough to venture. Yet he *must* make judgments and he *must* be selective, for no single volume can embrace more than a fragment of the history of a century when men and events move faster than ever before. Inevitably much must be omitted.

The historian's problem is to select events which seem, at the time of writing, to be of the greatest importance, and which will continue to be regarded as important in the future, when looked at again in retrospect. The perspective is always changing and this is one of the major hazards that confronts anyone who has the temerity to commit himself to paper on the subject of contemporary history.

In this book my selection of material has been governed by two aims: first, to throw light on events which have already happened, and second, to go some way towards explaining the problems which confront the world in the final quarter of the twentieth century. Thus the book moves steadily outwards from Europe, into the world of the super powers and the world of the developing nations; from the problems of European frontiers, reparations and unemployment to the problems of under-development, minorities and race relations.

No historian can be totally objective; he is human and his own point of view is bound to show in anything he writes. However, he can try. Here I have tried to maintain as objective a view as possible not only in listing and describing important events, but also in offering comment and explanation which will help the reader towards a fuller understanding of these events. But understanding can only come from individual thought and inquiry and my aim throughout the book is to provoke thought. Students of contemporary history must always hesitate before making assertions too strongly; therefore this book may, at times, seem to be tentative, almost as if asking questions instead of answering them. Too many revolutions in attitudes have already occurred in our century for easy explanations always to lie at hand. On such ground a wise student will readily confess that he does not know all the answers, but he will do his best to arrive at some understanding of the problems we face and how these problems have emerged.

Students who are working for any of the sixteen-plus examinations for which this book is appropriate (including the present 'O' and 'A' levels), or who are studying at pre- or first-year university level, will find a number of aids to study incorporated in the text. The maps and tables are especially important, as is the detailed index. The cross-references throughout each Unit help the reader to revise or look forward at will, to grasp connexions and acquire confidence to move about in time and space. The exercises are designed to encourage not only thought and understanding, but further discovery; they also provide the opportunity to practise writing answers to questions which are typical of modern examination papers. This work requires a personal contribution which goes beyond mere feats of memorizing. Students need first to read the question with care, and then to think out an answer which is relevant. Public examinations today seek, above all, evidence from candidates of their understanding and of their ability to draw on factual information with which to illustrate their answers. In the early part of the book I have given some guidance on tackling questions; later the student should plot his own course, drawing where necessary on the index and on the suggested further reading lists.

Contemporary history, of course, goes on. This book deals with the world since 1919. It is essentially a story without an end, but a story which every reader may update daily by referring to the news media, a good newspaper or a work of reference such as *Keesing's Archives*. In time, with the benefit of greater hindsight and the knowledge of events which have occurred after the writing of this book, the reader may wish to revise some of its judgments. If he is willing and able to do so, this book will have succeeded in one of its chief aims, that of encouraging the reader and student to develop his own informed opinions on the modern world.

J.B.W.

Acknowledgments

Any author who can rely on the candid comment and constructive advice of well-informed colleagues is fortunate. In this respect I have been especially fortunate and I am happy to be able to acknowledge the debt I owe to those who have read this work in the course of its preparation and whose criticisms have undoubtedly done much to improve it. I must thank Sean Garrett who has given me invaluable assistance, not least in relation to the Far East where pitfalls abound to await the unwary westerner; and Edgar Rayner whose ability to take the broad view and at the same time to scrutinize the most minute detail commands the utmost respect of those who have the good fortune to work with him, and who has given me the benefit of his great experience both as a teacher and as a historian of the contemporary world. My thanks go also to Roger Moore who first thought that this work was possible and encouraged its beginning; and to my wife who endured its construction with patience and, with even more patient work on the index, ensured its end.

I must particularly thank Carolyn Nichols of John Murray whose diligence and expertise has made this book presentable and whose work in editing and researching illustrations has made the load so much lighter for me. I also owe a special debt of gratitude to Irene Slade, editor of the 'Success' series, without whose enthusiasm and guidance less would have been attempted and without whose cheerful confidence not much would have been achieved.

But whatever the faults and omissions of the finished book, the responsibility is mine alone. All those mentioned above have undoubtedly done their best to exercise over me that 'restraining influence' upon a 'tendency to over-confident assertion' once referred to by L. C. B. Seaman. If this book provides but a fraction of the pleasure and benefit that I have received from the historical writings of others—not least Bernard Seaman's—the work will have been worth while.   J.B.W.

We are grateful to the following for their kind assistance in providing illustrations:
National Monuments Record (Fig. 1.1); Radio Times Hulton Picture Library (Figs. 2.1, 3.3, 3.5, 4.2, 5.4, 8.4, 12.4); Barnaby's Picture Library (Figs. 2.5, 9.3, 11.4, 16.4, 18.1, 20.1, 22.1, 22.3); *Philadelphia Daily News* (Fig. 4.3); Keystone Press Agency (Figs. 4.4, 5.2, 10.1, 10.2, 12.2, 14.1, 15.1, 17.3, 20.3, 20.6); Cartoons by David Low by arrangement with the London *Evening Standard* (Figs. 6.2, 8.2); Associated Newspapers Group Ltd. (Figs. 7.2, 11.3, 19.2); *New Statesman* (Fig. 15.3); Camera Press (Fig. 15.4); *The Guardian* (Figs. 17.4, 19.4, 21.4); Syndication International (Fig. 21.2); Stanley Gibbons Ltd. (All stamps); Valtman—Rothco Cartoons (Cartoon, page 371); Les Gibbard, *The Guardian* (Cartoons, pages 365 and 384).

List of Maps

Contents

Unit One
The World in 1919

1.1   1917–19

At two o'clock on the morning of 7 November 1917, the Bolshevik Revolution began in Russia. By daybreak the Bolsheviks (revolutionary communists) had a firm grip on Petrograd, the capital of Russia. Half-disguised in a wig and an old cap, Lenin, the Bolshevik leader, directed the remaining operations from the Smolny Institute, a fashionable girls' school. By nine that evening the Tsar's Winter Palace had fallen to the Bolsheviks, and the world's first communist government had come to power.

A year later, at the eleventh hour of 11 November 1918 an armistice ended the First World War. Germany admitted defeat after a conflict which had raged with devastating results for more than four years. On 18 January 1919, delegates from thirty-two states met in Paris for the Peace Conference which followed the war. They had high hopes of creating a settlement which would clear away Europe's outstanding problems and establish everlasting peace in a world sickened by war.

At the time the most significant of these three dates seemed to be that of the armistice, 11 November 1918. For years afterwards, millions remembered it with an annual two minutes' silence, remembering the very hour when the terrible toll of human life had ceased. But, looking back, the date of the armistice was perhaps the least significant of the three, important though it was in ending a war which had taken over twelve million lives. Many expected the communist success in Russia to be short-lived. It was only when 'backward' Russia was able to challenge the United States of America as a super-power that 7 November 1917 gained acceptance as an outstanding date in world history. The opening of the Peace Conference in January 1919 attracted plenty of attention, but preliminary agreements seemed to have prepared the way for the settlement. People thought the First World War had been 'the war to end wars', 'the final war for human liberty'. It did not seem possible that the world could ever again resort to war, or that the politicians could fail to produce a settlement which would solve Europe's problems and lay the foundations for future progress. It was only later that men saw January 1919 as the date when *new* problems began to emerge.

The First World War began in Europe in 1914, developing out of the quarrels of Europeans, and it remained predominantly European. Most of the fighting took place in Europe where the *Central Powers* (Germany, Austria–Hungary and their allies) were locked in conflict with Britain, France, Russia and their allies. Many of the European states possessed great overseas empires and these too were inevitably caught up in the struggle. So too was Japan, bound to Britain by the alliance of 1902. The war thus sprawled like a plague across the world, reaching into Africa, the Middle East and the Far East and dragging in combatants from India and Australasia. The USA joined the war against Germany in 1917, angered by the activities of German submarines and German intrigue in Mexico. But Americans regarded it as a war to be settled 'Over There', that is in Europe.

Fig. 1.1 The Royal Artillery War Memorial, Hyde Park Corner, London

When the war ended in 1918, the main problems certainly seemed to be European ones. The stability of Europe had been in doubt for some years before the war, yet Europeans still regarded their continent as the centre of importance in the world. Few nations existed outside Europe which could compete with European states in wealth. Although the United States possessed both wealth and power Europeans consoled themselves that most Americans were of European descent. Elsewhere, it still seemed proper that Europeans should control large overseas empires. Europeans (and even Americans) thought it reasonable to assume that the settlement of European problems would lead automatically to the settlement of world problems.

1.2   Europe

The search for solutions to Europe's problems at the end of the First World War began among the presumed reasons for the beginning of that war. It was soon fashionable to believe that all would be well in international relations if, in addition to setting up a *League of Nations* (an association of countries which settled problems by agreement), there could be yet another adjustment to the balance of power in Europe and an extension of nation states, republics and democracy.

The *balance of power* was an old problem. It meant that no power must remain strong enough to threaten another, and no alliance of powers should dominate other alliances. In practice, a satisfactory balance of power meant that one's enemies should not be strong enough to be dangerous. In 1918 it was assumed that the victorious powers would settle the problem of the balance of power by weakening their defeated enemies, because it was the Central Powers who had caused the First World War to occur.

People also believed war had been brought about by discontent among nationalities trapped in the empires of Austria–Hungary and Turkey. It followed that if each nationality was allowed to set up a *nation state* (one people, with a government of the people's choice), Europe would become more stable. It became fashionable to believe in self-determination although politicians used a variety of words to explain what this meant. Woodrow Wilson, President of the USA, laid down *Fourteen Points* as a basis for the negotiation of peace and referred to 'frontiers along clearly recognizable lines of

Fig. 1.2 Europe in 1914

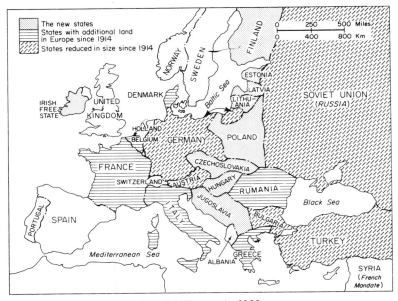

Fig. 1.3 Europe in 1923

nationality', 'autonomous development' and 'self-development'. He explained that his objective was 'justice to all peoples and nationalities'. David Lloyd George, Prime Minister of Britain, had earlier outlined his plan for a new Europe 'based on such grounds of reason and justice as will give some promise of stability'. Spelling out the details he too had spoken of 'self-government' and the 'recognition of separate national conditions'. Thus the Austrian and Turkish Empires were broken into fragments and many new states appeared on the map, among them Czechoslovakia and Jugoslavia. Some of the new nation states were also created from the empire which had once belonged to the Tsar of Russia, among them the Baltic states of Latvia and Lithuania. Although Russia had not been on the losing side in the recent war, the upheavals of 1917 had forced her to make an early peace with Germany, and had deprived the Russians of the power to resist major changes to their western boundaries.

The development of many new nation states made the map of Europe (and the Middle East) more complicated. Nevertheless, there was hope that, by removing the old European empires which had been the setting for so many crises before 1914, the nationalities of Europe would now rest content in their own nation states.

Many of the new nation states were *republics*. If greedy kings and emperors had contributed to bringing about the First World War, their removal from power seemed justified. Of the principal victorious powers in the war, France and the USA were already republics and the British would have argued that their monarchy, long since subdued by parliament, was not a greedy one.

Among the defeated, the royal Hohenzollerns ceased to rule Germany where the Weimar Republic was established. The Habsburgs, who had once ruled the vast, multi-racial Empire of Austria–Hungary, went into exile. By 1918, the Russians had already deposed their Tsar. The Sultan of Turkey survived only until 1922. Almost everywhere, the colourful pageantry of pre-war monarchy gave way to the humdrum gatherings of republicans and parliamentarians in sober suits and bowler hats. Where kings remained, in Britain and Belgium for example, they kept their thrones but had long since lost their powers. The lounge suit became the symbol of a Europe freed from the greedy ambitions of Hohenzollerns and Habsburgs, a Europe, it was hoped, 'made safe for democracy'.

The British, French and Americans had great faith in democracy. They could think of no more modern system of government than one in which the people elected their leaders and shared in determining their policies. The soberly-dressed politicians whom the people elected might well lack glamour but they seemed to guarantee stability and decency. The defeated Central Powers and the new nation states were urged to follow the excellent example of the victors and establish democracies. But revolutionary Russia was an embarrassment, because it could not fit neatly into the new arrangements being made for Europe.

The Bolsheviks gained power in Russia under the leadership of Vladimir Lenin. He did not scorn democracy but, at least in the short term, Russia was to be ruled by 'the dictatorship of the proletariat' (see Section 5.1). The Bolsheviks, for their part, confidently expected communist revolutions to occur elsewhere, most probably in Britain and Germany. Industrial unrest had reached dangerous levels in pre-war Britain; the war added further strains to capitalist society and it had brought defeat to Germany. The Bolsheviks thought that their own revolution was the first of an inevitable series of communist successes, but they were wrong. Only in Hungary did communists come to power, and even there their success lasted for just four months before their leader, Bela Kun, was driven into exile.

Actually, neither democracy nor communism was to provide the basis for a stable Europe, but in 1919 Europeans were optimistic. The war was over. Alcock and Brown flew across the Atlantic, as if symbolizing a new link between America and Europe for the pursuit of peace and prosperity. The age promised technological miracles. There was hope of increasing wealth. In Britain, politicians talked of 'a land fit for heroes to live in' and the heroes who had survived the war were returning to their families.

Europeans, like Americans, looked for a speedy return to normality. In their optimism, they too readily assumed that normality would bring back the best but not the worst of former times. Britain looked back to the apparently golden days of 1913. But she was quickly reminded that the pre-war years had not been golden and that the war had made her social and economic problems worse. In pre-1914 Britain, slums and widespread poverty had existed alongside apparent national prosperity. Grave inequalities had soured industrial relations. The slums, poverty and sourness remained. New economic difficulties arose and difficulties in selling exports led to unemployment. Such problems were by no means confined to Britain: the problems of peace threatened to be as serious as the problems of war for almost all countries. An epidemic of influenza which swept across the world claiming over six million lives made it increasingly difficult to remain optimistic.

As yet, however, Europeans were only dimly aware that the rest of the world also had serious problems and that these problems would become increasingly important in the twentieth century. Among the peace-makers in Europe in 1919 there were vague ideas of doing justice to these areas and peoples in the future, but the matter did not seem to be a particularly urgent one. The immediate problem for Europeans (and therefore for the world) was the settlement of Europe.

1.3 European Colonial Empires

A map of overseas colonial empires in 1914 shows instantly that few areas of the world had escaped European attention. The strength and prestige of the powers of Western Europe were sometimes judged by their overseas possessions. Austria-Hungary, Turkey and Russia sprawled across vast areas of Europe and Asia and their empires were huge blocks of land. For countries like Britain, France and Holland, empire had a different meaning. It meant possessions scattered across the whole world.

The British claimed a quarter of the world's territories and population. They had settled the almost uninhabited areas of Australia and Canada and imposed their authority on the crowded lands of India. In the last, almost frantic age of empire-building at the end of the nineteenth century, Europeans had carved up Africa and Britain had insisted on a major share. In 1914, therefore, subject peoples from almost every corner of the world joined her in the struggle against the Central Powers. To the British, as to all Europeans, the first duty of subjects in the colonies was to obey the instructions of the mother country.

By 1914, the only African states which remained free from European control were Abyssinia and Liberia. The rest of the huge continent had fallen to the British, French, Germans, Italians, Belgians, Portuguese and Spaniards. South-East Asia had been seized earlier, by the British, French and Dutch, and earlier still, Western Europeans had monopolized the West Indies and much of South America. However, in these last areas the tide had already turned, and independent South American nations had emerged, such as Brazil and Argentina. In the West Indies, too, some states had already seized independence, Haiti from France and Cuba from Spain. Elsewhere, China had recently become a republic and had preserved some independence against European ambitions, though not without losing many of her ports, including Hong Kong. Nevertheless, at the beginning of the twentieth century, the European passion for empire-building showed little signs of weakening.

In 1919, the colonies of the defeated powers were transferred to other rulers, although this was not simply a device to enlarge the empires of the victors.

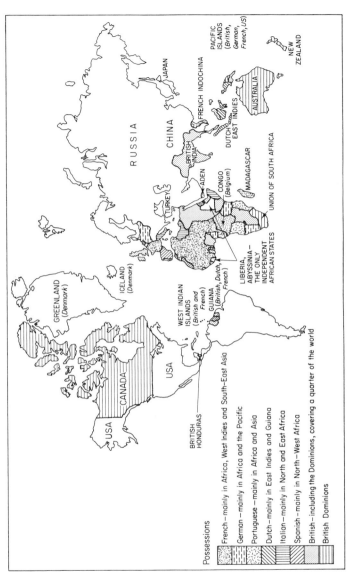

Possessions

French – mainly in Africa, West Indies and South-East Asia

German – mainly in Africa and the Pacific

Portuguese – mainly in Africa and Asia

Dutch – mainly in East Indies and Guiana

Italian – mainly in North and East Africa

Spanish – mainly in North–West Africa

British – including the Dominions, covering a quarter of the world

British Dominions

Fig. 1.4 European Overseas Empires, 1914

Such colonies were known as *mandated territories* of the League of Nations (see page 36). The League would be responsible for their welfare; meanwhile their new masters would prepare them for independence. In almost all cases the new masters were Europeans. Although mandated territories were to be prepared for independence (and other colonies might also expect independence at some time in the future), hardly any of these territories were considered close to it in 1919. Europeans who were victorious in the First World War expected to rule their empires for many more years. Those who had lost in that war argued that they had been robbed, prematurely, of their colonies. Nevertheless, Montagu, the British Secretary of State for India, had cautiously declared that Britain's policy would be 'the gradual development of self-governing institutions, with a view to the progressive realization of responsible government in India as an integral part of the British Empire'. This was far from satisfactory for those Indian nationalists who wanted instant independence. It meant no more than that Indians would gradually be allowed to share in governing their country with a vague suggestion that they might eventually take control, although still within the British Empire.

Britain, however, had a special problem. Within the British Empire were four states into which there had been extensive European immigration. Australia and New Zealand were peopled mainly by the British and their descendants. The same was true of Canada, which also contained many of French descent. None of these states had a large native population. In South Africa, native Africans heavily outnumbered white settlers but the whites were numerous enough to dominate the country. Already, Australia, New Zealand, Canada and South Africa were known as the *Dominions*, and they possessed extensive rights of self-government. One of the most urgent problems for the British was to clarify the status of these Dominions. Soon after the war, their claims for independence were accepted, and a new name was adopted to replace the British Empire (although the old name continued to be used too). Britain and the Dominions were said to be linked in the *British Commonwealth of Nations*, suggesting a partnership of equals (see Sections 6.1–2). Thus Europeans were admitting the equality of *some* peoples outside Europe. These peoples, however, had close ties with Europe and they were white.

1.4   The United States of America

Europeans were uncomfortably aware that the USA was the richest country in the world in 1919. In spite of their involvement in the First World War, the Americans had increased their gold reserves by almost £300 million since 1914. Britain had borrowed £959 million and France £634 million from the United States; Europe was, therefore, in debt. Europe had also suffered far heavier casualties than the USA, and while American industries had expanded their production and were now well placed to achieve even greater success in world markets, European states were war-ravaged and their economies unhealthy.

No European country could now hope to exert the same influence in the world as the USA. The balance of industrial power was obviously shifting.

Table 1.1   What governments spent on the First World War*

Allies	£m	Central Powers	£m
Britain	7 800	Germany	8 400
France	5 400	Austrian Empire	4 600
Russia	5 000	Bulgaria and Turkish	
USA	5 000	Empire	500
Italy	2 700		
British Empire	1 000		
Total	28 000	Total	13 500

* Figures adapted from Purnell's *History of the Twentieth Century*, Vol. 2, page 882.

Even by 1911, the USA's steel production was almost equal to the combined production of Germany, Britain and France. Her coal production was at that time over one-and-a-half times that of Britain, the world's leading industrial power in the nineteenth century. By 1920, American coal production was approximately twice that of Britain and Germany combined. In the twenty years before 1914, American exporters had increased their total sales almost six-fold. The USA, after 1918, seemed certain to be the most powerful economic force in the world.

Before 1914, Americans had shown increasing interest in the Pacific and the affairs of China but Europe had been of little interest to them. Many Americans were of European origin, but they had turned their backs on Europe and its problems. In 1914, they tried to keep out of Europe's war. President Wilson saw America's role as that of mediator and peace-maker, not as that of a belligerent. Neutrality was attractive but it failed to last and in 1917 the USA declared war on Germany.

When, at the end of the war, Wilson led an American delegation to the Peace Conference it seemed to mark for the first time a positive American intention to be involved in Europe's affairs. But those people who thought the USA would now play a major and permanent part in European affairs were mistaken. Many Americans were unwilling to risk further involvement in European quarrels: when the First World War ended they, too, wished to return to normality. For them, close involvement ended when Wilson returned from the Peace Conference. Europe was thus deprived of the USA's powerful influence when new problems arose. Those problems could be referred to the League of Nations but the United States refused to become a member. Britain and France were left as the major powers in the League and although the USA could not remain entirely aloof from Europe's economic problems, the American government after 1920 made it plain that Europe must solve her own political problems.

1.5   The Far East

Japan's part in the First World War involved little more than the occupation of German islands in the Pacific and German holdings in China. During the war, she increased her gold reserves by nearly £200 million, and her shipping losses were negligible. While European rivals threw their energies into production for the war, Japan made steady progress in developing her foreign trade and expanding industrial output. At the end of the war, her textile industry not only supplied domestic needs but was poised to make inroads into other British markets, including those in India. Europeans, in future, would face formidable competition from Japan. Moreover, Japan was without a serious Asiatic rival. Large areas of the Far East were still European colonial possessions. Russia had been routed by Japan in the Russo-Japanese War of 1904–5 and, in 1919, was quite unable to exert any influence in the Pacific. China was equally feeble.

Japan's involvement in the First World War, on the winning side, gave her a place at the Peace Conference. In spite of being allowed to keep many of the Pacific islands, the delegation was dissatisfied. Japan was quick to resent what seemed to be an indifference to non-European nations at the Conference, an indifference perhaps to those who were not white. On the other hand, Europeans and Americans were suspicious of what appeared to be Japanese aggressiveness, both in her attitude towards China and in her enthusiasm for intervening in the Russian civil war. After 1919 Japan was to establish herself as a major power, dominating the Pacific and making more demands on China.

Further Reading

Elliott, F.: *A Dictionary of Politics*. Penguin (Harmondsworth, 1970). This is a useful reference book from which to gain more detailed definitions of words such as *Communism, Democracy, Fascism.*

Gibbons, S. R. and Morican, F.: *World War One*. Longman (Harlow, 1965).

Martell, J.: *The Twentieth Century World*. Harrap (London, 1969). Chapter 1 provides another introduction to the period.

Watson, J. B.: *Empire to Commonwealth, 1919 to 1970*. Dent (London, 1971). Chapters 1 and 2 provide further information about the British Empire before and after the First World War.

Exercises

1. Using reference books (such as a dictionary or *A Dictionary of Politics* (above)) and the Index to this book, work out for yourself the meaning of the following terms:
   Democracy; Communism; Nationalist; Nation State; Empire; Overseas Empire; Republic; Balance of Power; Gold Reserves.
2. Compare the maps of Europe in 1914 and 1923 (Figs 1.2 and 1.3). Which of the above terms may be used to account for changes in these maps?
3. What evidence can you find from this Unit to support the following arguments?
   (*a*) That Europeans in 1919 still thought Europe the most important area in the world.
   (*b*) That 1919 seemed likely to be the start of a more hopeful period in world affairs.
4. Practise using the cross-references in this Unit, and the Index, to find out more about the Bolsheviks (page 5), mandated territories (page 8) and the British Commonwealth of Nations (page 8).

Unit Two
The Peace Settlement of 1919–20

2.1 The Dead in the First World War

Those killed in the armed forces of the principal countries engaged in the war were:

Allies:		
Russia		1 700 000
France		1 357 800
British Empire		908 371
Italy		650 000
Rumania		335 706
United States		116 516
Central Powers:		
Germany		1 773 700
Austria-Hungary		1 200 000
Turkey		325 000
All belligerents:		8 528 831

These figures do not include those who survived to emerge from the war blind, maimed or mentally deranged. The First World War was the most bloody that the world had ever experienced. The horrors of the conflict, not least the terrible war of attrition on the Western Front, made such a profound impression that to most people a repetition of such barbarism seemed unthinkable. When the statesmen gathered for the Peace Conference the war was horribly fresh in their minds. Their basic aim was everlasting peace. The world, and especially Europe, had had its fill of misery: such a war must never occur again.

2.2 The Peace Conference, Paris, 1919

There was no disagreement about the basic aim when the Conference opened in January 1919. There had been much preliminary agreement among the victors, and even long before the armistice, war aims had been defined and points of detail agreed. Nevertheless, fundamental differences remained about the best ways to secure future peace and stability.

The Treaty of Versailles, which dealt with Germany, was presented to the German delegation in May. For four months the victorious powers had hammered out the details. It seemed proper to them that they should work out the terms of the Settlement and then present it to the defeated. The Germans said that they were dictating the terms, that it was hardly a peace agreement at all: it was a *Diktat*, an imposed treaty.

Behind this controversy lay the fundamental dilemma of the entire Settlement. The peace-makers genuinely wanted future peace, but they also wanted to punish the guilty. Europe's problems would be settled in a manner which seemed fitting to the victors, and the victors found it difficult to distinguish on occasions between that which would make future peace more likely and that which brought them revenge for their recent suffering. The French argued that the harsh treatment of Germany was itself essential to future peace. The balance of power must be adjusted so that Germany could never again threaten her western neighbours. The British and Americans disputed the degree of harshness which was necessary, but the principle was accepted. Thus the Settlement tried to combine idealistic solutions to old problems with an element of retribution. Self-determination, republicanism and democracy (see Unit One) would create a new Europe; the League of Nations would be a new world authority to bring about international harmony, but, at the same time, old scores against the defeated Central Powers would be paid off.

Paris was chosen to be the centre for the Settlement. The area around the city could offer a variety of convenient palaces, which gave their names to the separate treaties dealing with the defeated powers. Austria was dealt with at St Germain, Hungary at Trianon, Bulgaria at Neuilly and Turkey at Sèvres. Germany was dealt with at Versailles, the most glorious palace but also the scene of France's humiliation after the Franco-Prussian war of 1871, when the Germans had held there the ceremony at which the new German Empire was established.

Paris in 1919 was not the ideal place in which to make a fair-minded Settlement. All the delegates were under pressure. Lloyd George reported the difficulties under which they worked: 'Stones clattering on the roof and crashing through the windows, and sometimes wild men screaming through the keyholes.' Most of the advice which flooded over the peace-makers was 'to make Germany pay'. Even in Britain it was popular to affirm that Germany should be 'squeezed until the pips squeaked'.

Non-Europeans like Jan Smuts of South Africa found this passion for vengeance exasperating and difficult to reconcile with hopes of future goodwill. But the Settlement was firmly in the hands of Britain, France and the United States. Its course was directed by the Council of Ten, to which each of the five principal Allies (the USA, Britain, France, Italy and Japan) contributed two members. Neither Italy nor Japan, however, exerted much influence on the Council. Most of the decisions, in fact, emerged from agreements between the Prime Ministers of Britain and France and the President of the USA.

David Lloyd George was re-elected Prime Minister of Britain at the end of 1918. During the election campaign it became obvious that there was a widespread belief that Germany should be punished, and there was much talk of hanging the Kaiser, William II, who was held personally to blame for the war. As a wartime Prime Minister and as a politician seeking popularity and votes, Lloyd George had contributed to the hatred which many felt for the Germans. Wartime propaganda could not now easily be forgotten, but in so far as there was a voice of moderation among the Big Three at the Peace Conference, it was the voice of Lloyd George.

Lloyd George went to the Conference with many ideas for future peace. He had made known his war aims at least a year previously. 'We want peace,' he said. 'We want a peace which will be just but not vindictive. We want a stern peace. . . . The crime demands it. But its severity must be designed not to gratify vengeance but to vindicate justice.' Reparations were imposed upon Germany to make her pay for the war. Lloyd George wished to scale them down, but he got little assistance from the Americans and met downright hostility from the French. Here and there, in Silesia, for example, he was able to obtain slightly better terms for Germany, but on Germany's western frontiers Lloyd George could make little headway against the determination of the French. Once the principle of punishment had been accepted, it was difficult to be too pernickety about its extent.

The myth developed that Lloyd George was in some ways a go-between who tried to adapt the ferocity of the French to the idealism of the Americans. Lloyd George was always a controversial figure with a capacity for attracting a bad press. Although, in Paris, he raised his voice for moderation, urged the peace-makers to act as 'impartial arbiters, forgetful of the passions of war' and appealed to 'all reasonable opinion', goodwill towards the defeated was not widely popular and Lloyd George met bitter criticism both in press and parliament for his lack of ruthlessness.

Woodrow Wilson, however, managed to emerge from the Peace Conference with a better reputation. European intellectuals regarded him as a high-minded idealist who came to Paris almost as a neutral. In fact, Wilson, too, agreed with the need to punish Germany, and although he came to be considered the founding-father of the League of Nations, he took up that idea rather late, when others had prepared much of the ground. He was first elected President of the USA in 1912, with an unprecedented majority, but when he arrived in Europe in 1918 the Democrats had already suffered losses in the recent elections, and his support in the American Congress had been undermined.

Wilson might more easily have stood aside from the revengeful passions which influenced Europeans. He genuinely sought a just Settlement and he contributed many constructive ideas, but he had a talent for making enemies. He seemed self-righteous, obsessed with his own views and intolerant of others. The essential soundness of Wilson's aims was sometimes obscured by the manner in which he defended them. If the American President had been able to work in closer harmony with Lloyd George a more moderate as well as a more coherent Settlement might have been produced.

Both, it turned out, had frequently to give way to Clemenceau, the veteran Prime Minister of France who presided over the Peace Conference. He had thorough-going ideas for the humiliation of Germany. He had already earned the nickname 'the Tiger'. If Clemenceau had his way Germany would never again be strong enough to harm France. The Prime Minister was an old man, and twice in his lifetime he had seen German troops on French soil. He wanted immediate compensation for French losses in the recent war and guarantees

Fig. 2.1 Clemenceau, Woodrow Wilson and Lloyd George at the Paris Peace Conference, 1919

that Germany could never strike again. Neither Britain nor America had been invaded by the Germans; it was difficult, therefore, to persuade the French to moderate their demands. Indeed, the lack of co-operation between Lloyd George and Clemenceau nearly caused a breakdown of the treaty negotiations at one point.

Not one of the Big Three survived long in office after the Peace Conference. Frenchmen thought that Clemenceau had not done enough, that Germany had been left alarmingly strong. In retirement, before his death in 1929, the old man brooded on the German problem and wrote his memoirs under the title *The Grandeur and Misery of Victory*. Lloyd George, after a troubled ministry from 1918 to 1922, lost the support of the electors and never again held office, although he continued to produce new ideas which lesser statesmen contrived to ignore. Wilson returned to America to campaign for active American involvement in world affairs, but by the end of 1919 he had collapsed and remained an invalid until his death in 1924. Meanwhile, the American electorate rejected his party. Electors in all three countries had expressed their lack of confidence in their representatives at the Peace Conference.

Elsewhere, there was equal dissatisfaction. Neither Italy nor Japan thought that her rightful claims had been met. The defeated Central Powers saw the Settlement as one which added humiliation to defeat and hardship. The optimism which had followed the armistice found it difficult to survive the peace.

2.3   The Basis of the Settlement

In spite of the apparently harsh verdict of electors almost everywhere, the Peace Settlement contained much to recommend it, and many of its ideas were constructive. It aimed, ambitiously, to do far more than merely share out the spoils of the recent war. In spite of the pressures of the need to work quickly, appease public opinion and grapple with urgent domestic problems at the same time, the statesmen produced a remarkably comprehensive Settlement in view of the vastness of the problems. Undoubtedly, it could have been more coherent. The principles on which it was based were not always consistently applied; parts of the Settlement were vindictive, and above all, it failed to bring a period of stability and prosperity even to Europe. But amendments to the Settlement began almost as soon as it was written, and if organizations such as the League of Nations did not work as successfully as the peace-makers hoped

Fig. 2.2 War Widow stamp, France. French suffering in the First World War had much to do with the outcome of the Peace Settlement

they would, the fault lay less with the peace-makers than with the next generation of statesmen. Hitler's aggressive disregard of the Treaty of Versailles stemmed more from Hitler's aggressiveness than from the alleged faults in the Treaty.

Unit One has already mentioned some of the basic ideas on which the Settlement was founded. When the peace-makers arrived in Paris there was already general agreement on basic principles. In January 1918 both Lloyd George and Woodrow Wilson had made statements of their war aims. Lloyd George announced *Britain's War Aims* (see Section 1.2) to trade unionists in London, and Wilson announced America's aims, the *Fourteen Points*, to the United States Congress. There was little disagreement about the aims in principle, though many of the Allies had reservations about precise meanings and detailed application. When they surrendered, the Germans agreed to accept a Settlement on the basis of the Fourteen Points. But the peace-makers also had other agreements to honour, and sometimes there was conflict. When Italy agreed to join the war against the Central Powers in 1915 a Treaty of London was signed which promised Italy territories such as Trieste and South Tyrol. Such promises had now to be matched with the later statements. Wilson had stated that Italy's frontiers should be 'along clearly recognizable lines of nationality', and he protested that the Treaty of London, previously secret, did not uphold this principle.

It remained clear, however, that much of the Settlement would be on the basis of nation states, created from the old European and Turkish Empires. Both Lloyd George and Wilson had stated this as part of their aims; both had insisted, for example, that an independent state of Poland should be established; both had marked the Austrian and Turkish Empires for breaking up.

There was also agreement that individual states such as Belgium and France should be restored completely. Lloyd George spoke of 'reparation' to Belgium, although Wilson used the words 'evacuated and restored'. Both agreed that Alsace-Lorraine, taken by Germany from France in 1871, must be returned to France.

Lloyd George and Wilson also agreed that the settlement of overseas colonial problems must be just. Both mentioned the interests of the inhabitants of these colonies as being of importance.

In some ways, Wilson went further than the British Prime Minister. Whereas Lloyd George spoke briefly of international law, the sanctity of treaties and an international organization, Wilson began his Fourteen Points by insisting on open diplomacy, freedom of navigation, freedom of trade and the reduction of armaments, and the last of the Points looked forward to an association of nations.

It remained, at Paris, to translate all these general statements into specific and detailed agreements. This difficult task must also be accomplished without the presence of representatives from Russia. In January 1918 Lloyd George had found it impossible to state precisely Britain's War Aims with regard to Russia. At that time the Bolshevik government was trying to get out of the war by making a separate peace with Germany. From its beginning Lenin had condemned the First World War as one in which 'hired slaves' in one country fought against 'hired slaves' in another. He argued that the working classes should fight not against each other but against capitalism and the bourgeoisie. If Russia now abandoned the war her western allies feared that Germany would be free to switch her troops to the Western Front, and Russia would be guilty of a sort of treachery. Lloyd George ended vaguely by remarking that 'Russia can only be saved by her own people'. Wilson was equally vague, although he looked forward to 'the evacuation of all Russian territory', to leaving the Russians to sort out their own affairs, and he recommended 'unselfish sympathy' towards them.

Russia had made a separate treaty with Germany, at Brest-Litovsk (see Section 2.8), where the Germans showed little of that charity which they later claimed should be extended to themselves. Civil war then developed in Russia. The Western powers forgot their intentions of leaving the Russians alone and tried to intervene, against the Bolsheviks (see Section 5.1(b)). They could hardly, at the same time, invite the Bolsheviks to the Peace Conference in Paris, and so the victors made the Settlement without their Russian ex-ally. Some discussions were eventually held, well away from Paris, with the Bolsheviks, but little came of them. It was generally believed in the West that the Bolsheviks would not survive. There were protests against having dealings with them at all.

The Settlement, therefore, attempted to produce treaties based upon the Fourteen Points. This involved remaking the map of Europe and of other parts of the world and trying to create, through the League of Nations (see Section 2.9(*b*)) the machinery for more civilized behaviour in international affairs. Combined with the Fourteen Points, however, was an attempt to punish, although it was not one of the aims of the Settlement that the victors should simply collect booty. Lloyd George had argued that 'the destruction or disruption of Germany or the German people' was *not* a war aim. The Allies' aim was more constructive than that. By weakening Germany in Europe, they hoped to protect France and Belgium and to make the continent more stable; by imposing reparations, they hoped to compensate those to whom the war had been costly in lives and property; by dismantling the German overseas Empire, they intended to secure a better future for the peoples in the ex-German colonies. It was one of Hitler's delusions that Germany was robbed in 1919 by international pirates preying upon the defeated.

2.4   How Germany was Treated: the Treaty of Versailles

Lloyd George had asked for 'a stern peace'. The Treaty of Versailles, which the Germans were required to sign in June 1919, was certainly 'stern'. But it did not justify the frenzy of hatred and self-pity with which Hitler taught Germans to regard it. Article 231 of the Treaty rapidly became notorious:

The Allied and Associated Governments affirm, and Germany accepts, the responsibility of Germany and her allies for causing all the loss and damage to which the Allied and Associated Governments and their nationals have been subjected as a consequence of the war imposed upon them by the aggression of Germany and her allies.

This was the 'War Guilt Clause'. It developed from the undertaking which Germany had accepted at the armistice to pay compensation to Allied civilians. In the Treaty it appeared to have become an over-simplified explanation of how the war began and an extension of Germany's obligation to pay compensation. Although in many ways the rest of the Treaty was often remarkable for its moderation, Germans insisted on extracting from Article 231 the maximum humiliation. The Allies were guilty of slipshod wording. It was absurd to suggest that Germany alone had brought about the First World War. It was equally absurd of the Germans to take the 'War Guilt Clause' in isolation and pretend that on this alone the Settlement of Europe was based. Nevertheless, what Germany lost and what Germany was made to pay came to be regarded as the foundations on which the whole Peace Settlement was built.

The list of the provisions of the Treaty of Versailles (see page 34) and the map of Germany (Fig. 2.3) show the European territories which Germany lost. Two large areas, Alsace-Lorraine and the Polish Corridor, were seized outright. For the French, there could be no further argument about Alsace-Lorraine. The provinces must be restored to France which had mourned their loss to Germany since 1871. The city of Paris had sorrowfully veiled its monument to the city of Strasbourg (in Alsace) since that time and the French quickly pointed out that, by demonstrations, the people of Alsace had already frequently shown their hostility to German rule. French honour must now be satisfied.

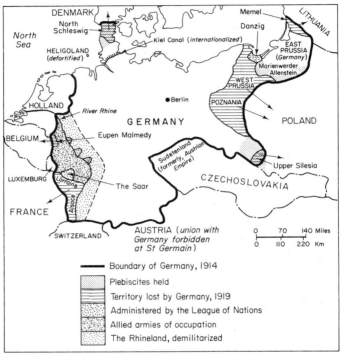

Fig. 2.3 Germany: the Treaty of Versailles

Poland, it was decided, must have access to the sea and so most of Poznania and West Prussia were taken from Germany to provide Poland with a corridor of land to the Baltic. This corridor divided East Prussia from the rest of Germany. Germans bitterly resented its existence and it was this area which was in dispute when the Second World War began in Europe, in 1939.

Comparatively small areas of land were transferred to Belgium, Denmark and, eventually, Lithuania. Germany was deprived of the port of Danzig and, for the time being, of the Saar. The new state of Poland gained part of Silesia. In many of these areas, *plebiscites* were held, partly owing to the arguments of Lloyd George, so that the local people could determine where the boundaries should be drawn. Thus the principle of self-determination was upheld.

The plebiscites saved for Germany some two-thirds of Upper Silesia, a small area of southern Schleswig, the Allenstein and Marienwerder districts of East

Prussia and, in due course, the Saar. Most of the plebiscites were held in 1920–1 but the Treaty stated that the Saar would be controlled by the League of Nations for fifteen years. Only then could its inhabitants vote upon their future. In the meantime, Saar coal mines would be in the hands of the French. (In 1935, the Saar plebiscite was held and 90 per cent of its people voted for reunion with Germany, which was promptly agreed.)

The plebiscites made it difficult to argue, unless one claimed, unconvincingly, that the votes were 'rigged', that the victors had gone all out to grab German land. Germany lost about 13 per cent of her European territory. These areas, however, contained some important economic resources. Lorraine was rich in iron ore, Upper Silesia and the Saar in coal. Alsace had a thriving textile industry. Danzig, of which the League of Nations took control, was an important port. Germans therefore pointed out that their true losses were:

Iron production	48%
Coal production	16%
Agricultural output	15%
Industrial output	10%

And to this list were to be added other grievous losses. The German overseas Empire was wiped out: Germany lost all her territories in Africa, China and the Pacific, most of them, such as German East Africa (Tanganyika), German South-West Africa, the Cameroons and Togoland, becoming mandates of the League of Nations (see page 36). German trade was handicapped by the loss of many treaty rights such as those which existed in China.

The German war machine was also crippled. West of the Rhine, and in some small areas east of the river, the Allies placed armies of occupation, to remain for fifteen years. Without time limit, Germany was to demilitarize all lands east of the Rhine for a distance of over thirty miles. This area was to be free from German troops and German fortifications, a safety buffer to protect France. The French would have liked to go further and make the whole area independent of Germany but that was totally unacceptable. The German army was limited to a force of 100 000, her air force abolished and her navy, with some limited exceptions, was to be handed over to the Allies. Never again should Germans build submarines. The naval fortifications on Heligoland were to be destroyed.

At the time, the disarmament of Germany was intended to be a step towards much wider disarmament and it was justified by referring to the tremendous damage which Germany's enemies had sustained in the war. Britain had lost nearly eight million tons of merchant shipping. France had seen great areas of her land ravaged to the point of almost total destruction. In the areas occupied by the Germans, over a quarter of a million houses had been destroyed, thousands of industrial plants wrecked and looted, mines devastated, agricultural land blasted and polluted to the point of uselessness and 500 000 cows and as many sheep carried off to Germany. Such evidence of devastation, much of it brought about by indiscriminate looting and vandalism as the Germans retreated, was used also to justify the sections of the Treaty of Versailles which dealt with economic matters and reparation.

Article 231 (see page 17) had asserted Germany's responsibility. The exact amount of compensation to be paid was left to be worked out by an Allied Reparation Commission. The Commission did not complete its calculations until April 1921. Meanwhile, the Allies had already taken steps to seize some of the more easily-removed German properties, such as railway engines, and the Treaty of Versailles gave them authority to seize the private property of Germans which lay outside Germany. The amount eventually fixed for Germany to pay was 136 000 million marks (£6 600 million) (see Fig. 4.1), plus interest. Much of the first instalment was paid in coal. The intention was that the Allies would take a regular share of the wealth Germany produced until the debt was paid. The Germans argued that this was a double punishment. The Treaty of Versailles deprived them of lands and resources making wealth more difficult to produce; it then required a share in that wealth for reparation.

In all, the Treaty of Versailles included 440 Articles. As with all the peace treaties the first twenty-six Articles set out the Covenant of the League of Nations (see page 36). It was another German grievance that they were not allowed immediately to join the League.

2.5 How Austria–Hungary was Treated

Two treaties were signed with what had formerly been the Austro-Hungarian Empire. Austria agreed to the Treaty of St Germain in September 1919. Hungary agreed to the Treaty of Trianon in June 1920.

(a) The Treaty of St Germain

The Austro-Hungarian Empire had broken up under the stresses of the last months of the war. Czechoslovakia already had a seat at the Paris Peace Conference. Republics had been set up in Austria and Hungary. By the Treaty of St Germain, the republic of Austria formally accepted the splitting up of the former Empire. The list of the provisions of the Treaty of St Germain (see page 34) and the map (Fig. 2.4) show what had become of this once-great Habsburg Empire.

Although the Austrian republic agreed in theory to make some reparation, no money was paid. Payments in kind were on a small scale because the new republic was obviously not wealthy. In March 1919, Austria sought to become a part of Germany but this was forbidden at St Germain. Austrians also complained that, although self-determination was used to justify the breaking up of the Habsburg Empire, the principle was ignored when Germans in the South Tyrol became subjects of Italy and those in the Sudetenland became subjects of Czechoslovakia. Almost all Austrians spoke German and many felt that it would be difficult for a tiny Austria to survive alone; so a union with Germany would be helpful. They therefore doubly resented the loss of their own German subjects and their enforced isolation from the new republican

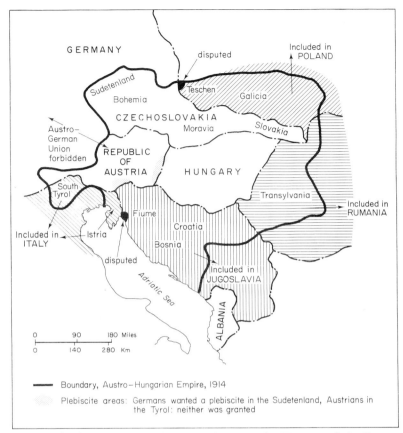

Fig. 2.4 The former Austro-Hungarian Empire: the Treaties of St Germain and Trianon

Germany. It was a slight consolation when a plebiscite in southern Carinthia enabled Germans in that area to remain in Austria and resist the claims upon them of Jugoslavia.

(b) The Treaty of Trianon

The Treaty with Hungary was delayed until 1920 owing to internal upheavals in that country. By the provisions of the Treaty (see page 35), the Hungarians then accepted, under protest, the reduction of the state which the Habsburg Emperor had formerly ruled as King of Hungary. In vain, they protested that plebiscites should be held in areas now declared to be parts of Czechoslovakia, Jugoslavia and Rumania. Over three million Magyars (Hungarians) now found themselves the subjects of foreign governments. Over half of them were in Rumania which had been persuaded in 1916 to assist the Allies in the war;

Rumania therefore expected a reward. The population of Hungary was now less than half of what it had been before the war.

2.6 How Bulgaria was Treated: the Treaty of Neuilly

Anxious to improve her position as one of the minor Balkan states, Bulgaria had joined the war on the side of the Central Powers in 1915. Under the provisions of the Treaty of Neuilly (see page 35), Bulgaria was now to share in the setbacks of the defeated. Like them, she suffered limitations on her armed forces and losses of territory and a figure was eventually worked out for reparation. The penalties imposed were by no means severe, however, and Bulgaria even gained a small area of land, from Turkey. The loss of access to the Aegean Sea, and thus to the Mediterranean, was the most serious of the injuries done to Bulgaria.

2.7 How Turkey was Treated

(a) The Treaty of Sèvres

There was no hope that the Turkish Empire, long-renowned for inefficiency and corruption, could escape the fate of the Austro-Hungarian Empire. The Allies had already made a variety of agreements about how they intended to deal with parts of this Empire. The principle of self-determination alone would be enough to ensure that it was broken up. By the provisions of the Treaty of Sèvres (see page 35) this came about. But the settlement of the Turkish problem was not a straightforward one.

Many of the Turkish possessions were populated by Arabs who hoped after the First World War to gain independence, but Europeans thought this would be premature and, in Palestine, Britain had already made conflicting promises to Arabs and Jews. Europeans were also worried about the effects of Arab nationalism on their economic interests at the eastern end of the Mediterranean. Among these was the Suez Canal, while Turkey herself bestrode the Dardanelles, an almost equally important international waterway. Moreover, both Greeks and Italians, successful though not decisive Allies in the First World War, hoped to profit at Turkey's expense.

The most striking feature of the settlement with Turkey in 1920 was the ending of all Turkish authority over North Africa and the Arab lands. A number of these Arab lands became mandates in the hands of Britain and France. Other parts of the former Turkish Empire became independent while Britain, Greece and Italy made good their claims to territories formerly Turkish. An international commission took charge of the Dardanelles and Bosporus to ensure free passage through the Straits.

The effect of this Treaty was to reduce Turkey to the barren and mountainous area of Anatolia (Asia Minor). She had been almost completely expelled from Europe; her capital city was separated from the rest of the country by Straits under international control and, even in Anatolia, the Greeks held the important city of Smyrna and the Italians held Adalia. The Treaty dealt the Sultan his death blow. Turkish nationalists, under the leadership of Mustapha Kemal, had been steadily undermining his authority. The Treaty was a surrender of which a nationalist, even one as realistic as Kemal who thoroughly understood his country's weakness, was forced to disapprove.

Kemal and the nationalists rejected the Treaty. The powers showed some readiness to give way. In summer 1921, the Italians left Anatolia and the French showed a willingness to negotiate. Lloyd George was in favour of standing firm but the Greeks made an already-difficult situation worse. While the Turkish nationalists gathered their strength at new headquarters deep inside Anatolia, the Greeks set about extending their area of occupation around Smyrna. They invited defeat and when they tried to penetrate to the nationalist stronghold at Ankara, they were checked. The major powers offered concessions but Kemal saw no reason to stop now. When the hostilities began again, the Greeks were routed at Afyon and, in September 1922, chased out of Anatolia. Even Turkish citizens who had Greek connexions felt that it was safer to flee from the vengeance of the Turkish nationalists.

There then developed the *Chanak Crisis* which proved to be a serious embarrassment to Lloyd George and the British government. Kemal was ready to extend nationalist authority to Constantinople and to depose the Sultan. From Constantinople, he could go on to chase the Greeks from East Thrace. But he would need to cross the Straits where international forces were stationed. The French and Italians promptly withdrew, and some of the forces from the Dominions, who shared the duties of the garrison with Britain, also left. Lloyd George felt that a stand should be made against Kemal. The Treaty of Sèvres could be renegotiated but it showed a dangerous lack of confidence in the postwar world to give in to the first violence which broke out. When the nationalists approached, the British garrison at Chanak was ordered not to give way. The danger passed only when the British commander, General Harrington, reached agreement with the Turks at Mudania. This agreement, signed in October 1922, was the basis of a new treaty with the Turkish nationalists, to revise the Treaty of Sèvres.

A month later, the Sultan of Turkey was deposed and the Chanak Crisis helped to bring about the defeat of Lloyd George in a British general election. In July 1923, Kemal and his followers signed a new treaty with the Allies, the Treaty of Lausanne. The Turkish nationalists had been the first seriously to challenge the new order which had been created at the Paris Peace Conference. Britain had stood against them almost alone but even in Britain the Prime Minister had been condemned as reckless and irresponsible.

(b) The Treaty of Lausanne

At Lausanne, Kemal achieved most of his immediate ambitions. The Treaty (see page 35) returned East Thrace to Turkey and left to the Turks the control of the Straits. Anatolia remained free from foreign troops and the Turks were required neither to limit their armed forces nor to make reparation. The parts of the Treaty of Sèvres which dealt with the Arab states were confirmed and only minor changes were made concerning the ownership of islands. Greeks and Turks exchanged some populations to lessen the risks of Greek retaliation against Turks and vice versa, but old hatreds between them remained. These hatreds would find a stage on which to contend, in the second half of the twentieth century, in Cyprus (see Section 20.4).

2.8 How Russia was Treated: the Treaty of Brest-Litovsk

The Tsar of Russia lost his throne in March 1917. In November 1917, the Bolsheviks came to power (see Section 5.1(*a*)). The war against Germany was going badly and the Bolsheviks intended speedily to end it. 'The soldiers have voted against the war,' Lenin said, 'they have voted with their feet by running away.' The Germans had the upper hand and they drove such a hard bargain that Trotsky, the Russian negotiator, thought the terms unacceptable. Lenin persuaded the Bolshevik government to over-rule him and the Treaty of Brest-Litovsk was signed in March 1918. Within nine months, Germany herself was defeated and was therefore unable to profit much from the Treaty, but, not represented at the Peace Conference in Paris, Russia was unable to recover much of the land she had lost. Lenin later remarked, 'We gained a little time and sacrificed a great deal of space for it.' Not until the closing stages of the Second World War did Russia extend as far westwards again (see Section 9.5(*b*)). The map Fig. 5.1 shows the extent of Russia's losses.

By the Treaty of Brest-Litovsk (see page 36), Russia lost nearly 20 per cent of her territory and nearly 25 per cent (46 million) of her population. The losses included lands important for their coal and iron deposits. Germany also extracted from Russia a promise to pay 3 000 million roubles. Lenin had asked for a peace free of annexations and indemnities but he was over-optimistic in imagining that the Germans would agree to peace without annexing territory or imposing penalties. When the Germans lost lands at Versailles and were required to pay indemnities under their new name, reparations, they preferred not to remember their treatment of Russia.

When the Peace Conference at Paris began, many of the states which Russia had lost had already become new nation states. The peace-makers, therefore, upheld the principle of self-determination and welcomed the freedom which Finland, Estonia, Latvia, Lithuania and Poland had won. They also approved when Rumania seized Bessarabia from Russia.

Bukharin and three other members of the Bolshevik government had resigned when Lenin accepted the Treaty of Brest-Litovsk. Lenin had argued that peace was essential if communism was to survive in Russia: for the moment, Russia had no alternative but to pay the price of that peace. Her former Allies saw no reason, at Paris, to make reductions in that price, although the Bolsheviks renounced the Treaty of Brest-Litovsk when Germany was defeated and were able to withhold the indemnities which Germany had imposed and to recover much of the Ukraine.

2.9   The Constructive Work of the Settlement

A great deal of territory thus changed hands in the years 1918–23. Most of the changes involved the creation of new nation states. The essential purpose of these changes was to apply the principle of self-determination in the hope of satisfying old grievances. The Peace Conference at Paris also set up the League of Nations and carried the basic idea of self-determination into the non-European world by means of the system of mandated territories. In all of this, the Conference intended to be constructive, to improve the likelihood of lasting peace.

(a) New Nation States

Czechoslovakia and Jugoslavia may be taken as examples of the nation states created in Europe after the First World War.

(i) **Czechoslovakia** was created in 1918 to satisfy the demands of the Czechoslovak National Council for a state free from Austrian control and an independent home for Czechs and Slovaks. It was made up of provinces formerly attached to Austria and Hungary within the Austro-Hungarian Empire. Eduard Beneš represented the new state at the Paris Peace Conference and from 1918 to 1935 was the Czechoslovak Foreign Minister. Together with Tómàŝ Masaryk, the country's first President, he secured the support of the victorious powers and, already possessing prosperous industry, the republic was regarded as an excellent example of how self-determination could bring a new look and a new stability to Europe. The political system was democratic;

Fig. 2.5 Tómàŝ Masaryk, the first President of Czechoslovakia, helped to give stability to the new nation state

the state had no aggressive ambitions against its neighbours; the resentment which had long smouldered, especially in Bohemia, against the rule of the Austrian Habsburgs could now be channelled into making the republic prosperous. Masaryk remained President until 1935 when he was succeeded by Beneš. Thus the state achieved political stability. Czechoslovakia also achieved a degree of international stability, developing close relations with Jugoslavia and Rumania in the Little Entente to preserve stability where once had been the Habsburg Empire. The Czechs who, from the outset, were popular with France, on whose system of government the Czechoslovak constitution was modelled, also made a new ally in the east when friendship was developed with Russia. Not everyone approved of ties with the communists but Czechoslovakia was in many ways a model of what the peace-makers had hoped to achieve in the new nation states.

The republic was not, however, free from handicaps. There was a week's fighting with Poland at the beginning of 1919 over a frontier problem. The squabble was settled by a Conference of Ambassadors when Poland gained the town of Teschen, but the quarrel left behind it some hostility between the two states so that co-operation when it was needed—against Hitler for example—was not forthcoming. Moreover, Czechoslovakia, with a population of only about 14 million people seemed a fragile neighbour alongside Germany. In 1919, Germany was weak but in some ways the peace-makers built trouble into Czechoslovakia for the time when Germany grew strong again, by giving her difficult minorities problems. Of the 14 million, over 3 million were German, mainly inhabitants of the Sudetenland which ran along Czechoslovakia's boundary with Germany. Another group, nearly three-quarters of a million, were Magyars. The Sudetenland had never been part of Germany (it was formerly in the Austro-Hungarian Empire), but Germans argued that the logic of self-determination was to include it in Germany. Hungary argued similarly that the Magyars should be subjects of Hungary but, as defeated powers, Germany and Hungary received no satisfaction. It was Hitler who later made the Sudetenland the subject of a major international crisis (see Section 8.3(c)).

(ii) **Jugoslavia** was designed to satisfy the demands of South Slav peoples for a state of their own, uniting those who, before 1914, had been trapped in the Austro-Hungarian Empire with those who had already broken free from the Turkish Empire. In 1914, many of the latter were inhabitants of Serbia, at that time a free kingdom. In the war, Serbia had been on the side of the Allies and so could now properly be rewarded. During the war, the Serbian government had retreated to the island of Corfu and there, in 1917, the idea of a new state of Jugoslavia, in effect an enlarged Serbia, was worked out. Until 1929, the state bore the cumbersome title of the Kingdom of Serbs, Croats and Slovenes —Jugoslavia was its later name. The original name was, however, revealing for, like Czechoslovakia, Jugoslavia was not exactly a nation state and tensions developed between the various races who made up the South Slavs. The principle of national self-determination was an attractive one and had much to recommend it, but it was not by any means easy to define nationality, and to make sure that in every nation there was only one nationality was impossible. (Even in Britain, different nationalities exist in England, Scotland and Wales; but they have ceased to fight about it and limit their rivalry to football matches.)

In Jugoslavia, Croats and Slovenes complained that the state was too much dominated by Serbs. Democracy crumbled under the strain and in 1934 King Alexander was assassinated by Croatian extremists.

Meanwhile, Jugoslavia was less prosperous than Czechoslovakia and further disturbances were caused by religious differences. Disputes also developed with Italy about the boundary between the two, particularly about the port of Fiume, and with Hungary about the northern frontier of Jugoslavia. Jugoslavia was, in 1924, forced to abandon Fiume to Italy but the Italians then gave up their more ambitious claims to much more of Jugoslavia's coastline (see Fig. 7.1).

Like the dispute over Teschen (see page 26), the dispute over Fiume developed from the loose ends left by the Paris Conference. It was enlivened by the exploits of Gabriele d'Annunzio, an Italian hothead, poet and airman. With three hundred volunteers, he determined to right some of the wrongs alleged to have been done to Italy and, in September 1919, he took possession of Fiume and held it for over a year. Many of the town's inhabitants were Italian but Jugoslavia claimed that the port was vitally important to her. On Christmas Day, 1920, an apparently ungrateful Italian government bombarded d'Annunzio's headquarters and the poet surrendered. He had, nevertheless, whetted Italy's appetite. For a time, the League of Nations took over the town but what a poet could do, Mussolini could do. Fiume was taken over by the Italian Fascists and this time Jugoslavia gave up the struggle.

(b) The League of Nations

(i) **Origins.** When speaking of Britain's War Aims, Lloyd George referred to 'some international organization to limit the burden of armaments and diminish the probability of war'. The last of Wilson's Fourteen Points referred to 'a general association of nations' to guarantee independence and security to all states.

The idea was not new. After the Napoleonic Wars, which ended in 1815, Congresses had been held to try to secure international stability by agreements among the great powers. The Congresses failed to last but the idea was revived from time to time and was discussed when conferences were called to consider disarmament, at the Hague in 1899 and 1907. A few international organizations had been created in the nineteenth century for specific purposes, among them the International Red Cross and the Universal Postal Union. The First World War quickened the search for an organization to keep the peace.

There were plenty of plans. The British Foreign Office and Grey, who had been Foreign Secretary in 1914, Taft, ex-President of the USA, and Jan Smuts of South Africa, together with a host of others, put forward ideas. When the war was ending, they were taken up by Lloyd George and Wilson.

There was some difference of opinion, however, about the sort of association to be set up. Some favoured a narrow league, rather like the Congresses after 1815, which would simply deal with crises as they occurred and delay war until a settlement was reached. Others wanted a broad league which would do much more. A broad league could extend international co-operation and might deal with disarmament, colonies, even social and labour problems. Jan Smuts enthusiastically brought such ideas to Paris, and at the end of 1918 published *The League of Nations: A Practical Suggestion.*

Woodrow Wilson accepted the idea of a broad league and insisted that it should have priority in the peace talks. It was later argued that he then concentrated his attention on getting the credit for the idea instead of tackling the details of how it could be applied. Many of the details were worked out by the British whose first preference had been for a narrow league, although Lloyd George was prepared to go along with the broader one. From its beginning, the League suffered from some woolly thinking about the details of its machinery. These details were included in the *Covenant* (see page 36), hastily agreed among the victorious powers and written into all the Paris Treaties. They were careful to build into the system a predominant place for themselves. They also assumed that threats to peace would come from lesser powers and therefore glossed over the biggest problem of all: how could the League prevent war if a major power was determined to be aggressive?

(*ii*) **The League at work.** The League began its work with a membership of 42 states. By 1923, the membership had grown to 54 and the first of the defeated powers, Austria, Bulgaria and Hungary, had already become members. These first years were taken up mainly in expanding the League's machinery. The diagram (Fig. 2.6) and the summary of the Covenant at the end of this Unit show how this machinery fitted together and how the League was intended to work. The settlement of disputes would fall mainly to the Council and Assembly. The Permanent Court of Justice and Commissions for Disarmament, Mandates and Minorities would deal with problems of a special character. Other organizations would be responsible for social, economic and humanitarian matters. Servicing the entire structure was the Secretariat whose officials undertook to put loyalty to the League above their separate nationalities.

The *Assembly* worked on the basis of equality. All members had an equal vote. Almost all of the League's activities came under their review. They controlled the League's budget. Every state could express its opinion and, such was the goodwill, the right which every state had to veto a decision was seldom used. With an optimism which proved to be not unjustified, those who framed the Covenant ruled that decisions should be unanimous. In theory it was thus easy to obstruct them. In practice, matters were frequently thrashed out in committees and when the final votes were taken those in a minority preferred to abstain rather than block the will of the majority. Meeting annually, the Assembly made a real contribution to international goodwill.

The *Council* met more frequently, at least every three months and at all times of crisis. It was designed to be a smaller body than the Assembly and one which could quickly get to grips with a difficulty. The five major victorious powers were to have permanent seats (but the USA failed to join the League);

	MAIN ORGANS		STAFF OF CIVIL SERVANTS	PERMANENT ADVISORY ORGANS	COURT OF JUSTICE	AGENCIES	'AD HOC' COMMISSIONS For Special Duties
	(Consultative)	(In Crises)					
		Central					
LEAGUE OF NATIONS (based on The Covenant)	THE ASSEMBLY (often worked through Committees) Original Membership: 42	THE COUNCIL Original Membership: 4 Permanent 4 Elected	THE SECRETARIAT at Geneva First Secretary-General: DRUMMOND, 1919–33	COMMISSIONS for DISARMAMENT MANDATES, MILITARY AFFAIRS, MINORITIES	PERMANENT COURT OF JUSTICE at The Hague Originally: 11 Judges 4 Deputy Judges	*Auxiliary* COMMITTEES: Health Organization International Labour Organization Organization for Communications and Transit Intellectual Co-operation Organization Economic and Financial Organization SPECIAL COMMITTEES FOR: Drug Traffic, Women's Rights, Refugees, Child Welfare. Universal Postal Union Support for Red Cross	COMMISSIONS OF ADMINISTRATION: The Saar; Danzig COMMISSIONS OF INQUIRY: Manchuria (Lytton) 1931
		Principal Organs				*Auxiliary*	
UNITED NATIONS ORGANIZATION (based on The Charter)	THE GENERAL ASSEMBLY (often working through a complex structure of Committees) Original Membership: 51	THE SECURITY COUNCIL Original Membership: 5 Permanent 6 Elected	THE SECRETARIAT at New York First Secretary-General: TRYGVE LIE, 1946–52	TRUSTEESHIP COUNCIL ECONOMIC AND SOCIAL COUNCIL Social Commission Economic Commission Human Rights Commission (Universal Declaration of Human Rights 1948) Regional Commissions for Europe, Latin America, Asia, Far East	INTERNATIONAL COURT OF JUSTICE at The Hague 15 Judges	SPECIALIZED AGENCIES: ILO – International Labour Organization FAO – Food and Agriculture Organization IRO – International Refugee Organization WHO – World Health Organization ITU – International Telecommunications Union WMO – World Meteorological Organization UNESCO – United Nations Educational, Scientific and Cultural Organization UNICEF – United Nations International Children's Emergency Fund IMF – International Monetary Fund INTERNATIONAL BANK UPU – Universal Postal Union Support for Red Cross	UN Peace-Keeping Forces in Cyprus UNEF – United Nations Emergency Force UNCTAD – United Nations Conference on Trade and Development Korean Reconstruction Committee Technical Assistance Committee Commission on Narcotic Drugs

Fig. 2.6 The machinery of the League of Nations and the United Nations Organization compared

four others were to be elected from time to time by the Assembly. The four became six in 1922 and nine in 1926 and so, if the great powers intended to dominate the Council, they were unable to do so. Most of the Council's decisions concerned political problems and those problems over which, through Commissions, the Council had a special control. Territories which the League looked after in the years following the Peace—Danzig and the Saar for example—and matters to do with the level of armaments and the mandates came under the Council's authority. Again, it was necessary for decisions to be unanimous. To obtain decisions, it was often necessary to compromise and thus the Council tended to be less decisive and to act more slowly than might have been hoped. Moreover, when real crises arose, the Council found itself without teeth. Over-optimistic and wary of setting up a machine which could be damaging to themselves, the peace-makers had made no real provisions for enforcing the will of the League. The Council could only with difficulty, and as a last resort, raise an army. Articles 10–17 of the Covenant barely faced up to the problem of major powers which refused to accept the League's rules. They were vague about non-members and too readily assumed that breaches of the peace could be dealt with by sanctions, a sort of economic boycott. Parties to a dispute were not allowed to vote on it in the Council but this was not enough to make sure that parties to a dispute would abide by a Council decision. In the 1930s, the League found itself helpless when states such as Japan simply ignored the League and walked out.

The *Secretariat* rapidly built up a large and dedicated staff of civil servants. They were soon to realize that a major handicap to the League was its poverty. Members of the Assembly co-operated most readily in cutting down the costs of the League's work and few nations contributed willingly to the organization's expenses. The world wanted peace. But it did not want to pay much for it.

In spite of this, however, many of the smaller bodies in the League did excellent work. The *Permanent Court of Justice* was set up at the Hague, in 1921. It had fifteen judges of various nationalities to deal with legal rather than political disputes and to advise the Council on judicial matters. As a safeguard against wasting time, cases were only accepted when disputing parties agreed in advance to accept the verdict. The *Mandates Commission* kept a watchful eye on the good government of the mandated territories and the *Minorities Committee*, though sometimes disappointing, performed some services in protecting minority groups against ill-treatment by majorities. The *Disarmament Commission* ran into difficulties. It was easy to accept the idea of disarmament. It was much more difficult to put the idea into practice (Section 7.4).

Other committees had many successes which frequently went almost unnoticed. Newspapermen were quick to report an international crisis and a storm in the Council. They found developments to improve world health (the Health Organization), communications (the Organization for Communications and Transit) and education (the Intellectual Co-operation Organization) rather boring, of little value as news. Among the many bodies which dealt with prisoners of war, white slaves, drugs and economic problems, only the ILO (*International Labour Organization*) achieved widespread publicity. This was partly due to Albert Thomas, the passionate French socialist who became the first director of the ILO, in 1919. Thomas threw his energies into a campaign to improve wages, working conditions, pensions and the status of trade unions, throughout the world. When he died in 1932, the ILO had influenced many backward governments towards more enlightened attitudes. Membership of the ILO was not limited to membership of the League of Nations so that even the USA joined it. Of the four representatives each member sent to the annual conference of the Organization, only two represented the government, the others representing employers and workmen. Millions of ordinary people had reason to be grateful to Thomas and the ILO.

(*iii*) **Keeping the peace.** The success of the League would be judged, however, not by the achievements of Albert Thomas but by its success in keeping the peace. In the 1930s, world war broke out again and it was said that the League had failed. Such a verdict was not entirely fair, but the League's record as a peace-keeping body was never very impressive. It began life with less than perfect machinery and, at birth, it was dealt a savage blow by the United States. Woodrow Wilson had foolishly refused to admit any Republicans to the delegation he took to Paris. Led by the Republicans, the Senate refused to ratify the agreements he brought back from there. The USA refused to join the League of Nations and, since the Covenant of the League was written into them, refused to confirm the treaties. The blow was mortal to Wilson and it did serious harm to the League which must now try to keep the peace without the help of America.

Before the League was really functioning, squabbles developed in which it was to prove almost powerless, for example over Teschen (see page 26), and the Straits (see page 23), over Memel, which Lithuania grabbed from the League's hands in 1923 and over Vilna which Poland had seized from Lithuania in 1920. Poland was a founder member of the League but showed little inclination to abide by its rules, launching a war against Russia in the same year that she seized Vilna. On the political problems which came before the Council in the League's opening years, and on those which passed it by, the Council could record few successes although it did assist Austria to survive grave economic difficulties by promoting a large loan. These were perhaps teething troubles. The history of the League as a peace-keeping body will be continued in Unit Seven.

(*c*) **The Non-European World**

We have already referred to the work of the Mandates Commission (see page 30 and Article 22 of the Covenant on page 36) and to the ex-German and ex-Turkish colonies which became mandates (see pages 19, 34 and 35). Not until after the Second World War did the European nations really come to grips with the problems of independence in the former colonial world and the problems of poverty and under-development which remained in many of these areas after independence. But a creditable and constructive feature of the peace-making of 1919 was that the great powers began to show an awareness that problems would exist. The mandates system, based on 'a sacred trust', gave expression to this awareness.

Among the first members of the League, moreover, were a number of South American states such as Brazil and Uruguay, the African state of Liberia and the Asiatic state of Siam, each with a vote in the Assembly equal to that of Britain or France. Brazil was one of the first members of the Council. Inevitably, most of the attention of the peace-makers centred upon Europe but their outlook was not so blinkered that they failed to recognize that Europeans had wider obligations, that developments in transport were rapidly extending men's horizons.

2.10   Assessments of the Work of the Peace of Paris

The Allies left Paris hopeful, but not confident. In a short space of time, they had attempted an enormous task of resettlement and construction. Their basic principles had been sound ones. The treaties and the League of Nations stood as monuments to their energy and hopes. But Wilson, the Democrat, returned to an America swinging to the Republicans and increasingly isolationist. Britain, too, seemed half to wish that it could be possible to ignore European affairs and to concentrate on domestic problems. France was uneasy. Germany had kept the Rhineland and the French seemed obsessed with fears of a German revival which the British thought tiresome. In truth, the French had depended on American membership of the League and American guarantees of the treaties for their security. When the USA renounced both the League and the treaties, France began a morbid brooding on her own weakness which seemed bound to end in disaster. Italy maintained that she had been cheated and before long Mussolini was compiling his shopping-list of what should have been, in his view, Italy's rightful property. China retired from the Conference dissatisfied with her own ineffectiveness and the apparent superiority of Japan. Japan retired dissatisfied with her apparent lack of superiority and brooding on the differences between white and yellow. Only Jan Smuts remained cheerful, returning to South Africa to become Prime Minister and to pursue his passion for international goodwill in the League of Nations and the British Commonwealth of Nations. But even he noticed that Europeans were already squabbling again, about places it was difficult to find on the map and about tiny frontiers which seemed absurd when measured against the vastness of Africa.

The Central Powers could at least disclaim responsibility for whatever mistakes had been made. They had been required only to sign the treaties, which they did under protest. They counted their losses, lamented that self-determination had not been wholeheartedly applied so that, for example, the Sudetenland Germans were locked inside Czechoslovakia, and convinced themselves that the treaties were vindictive. Only the Turks were able to do anything about it in the immediate future but in a Europe apparently full of dissatisfied nations, the Germans soon appointed themselves the most dissatisfied of all. They had particular grievances to the east of their country and, indeed, the further east one went from Paris the more unsatisfactory the Settlement seemed until, in Russia, it had nothing left to say. As they had no part in it at all, the Russians could regard the Settlement as almost completely irrelevant.

The treaties contained many good features (all the more remarkable in view of the size of the task the peace-makers undertook), but even in 1919, J. M. Keynes, the economist, wrote his vigorous attack upon them in *The Economic Consequences of the Peace*. He concentrated his fire particularly on reparations; and it was on reparations, above all else, that future criticism of the Settlement centred. Keynes argued that Germany would be unable to pay and that reparations would bedevil European economies for years to come. The latter claim certainly proved correct. When reparations ceased in the financial crisis of 1931, however, Germany had paid only about a quarter of the £6 600 million demanded and she had, in the meantime, received more than she paid in foreign loans, most of which were never repaid. The League of Nations had also arranged loans to aid Austria and Hungary, so that the defeated powers in the end received more aid than they paid in reparations. It may still be argued whether reparations were justifiable compensation for war damage or savage penalties to punish the defeated. It cannot be maintained that they crippled the defeated. Unfortunately, however, they prolonged the bitterness of the recent war, brought new controversy and made it more difficult to reconcile Germany to the new Europe which the peace-makers had toiled to construct. (The subject of reparations will be examined again in Unit Four.)

2.11 Appendix

British War Aims outlined by Lloyd George, January 1918:
1. The restoration and independence of Belgium
2. The restoration of Serbia and of the occupied lands of the Allies
3. The restoration of Alsace-Lorraine to France
4. 'Russia can only be saved by her own people'
5. An independent Poland
6. Self-government to nationalities in Austria–Hungary
7. The union of all Italians in Italy
8. Justice for Rumanians
9. Separate national conditions for subjects of the Turkish Empire
10. Self-determination in German colonies
11. Reparation for injuries in violation of international law
12. The sanctity of treaties
13. Some international organization to limit armaments and reduce the risk of war.

Wilson's Fourteen Points outlined in January 1918:
1. Diplomacy shall be open
2. Freedom of navigation on the seas
3. The removal of economic barriers
4. The reduction of armaments

5. The settlement of colonial problems with reference to the interests of colonial peoples
6. The evacuation of Russia. Goodwill towards her
7. The restoration of Belgium
8. The restoration of France and her recovery of Alsace–Lorraine
9. Italian frontiers along lines of nationality
10. Autonomous development for the peoples of Austria–Hungary
11. Territorial integrity for the Balkan states
12. Free passage through the Dardanelles and autonomous development for the peoples of the Turkish Empire
13. An independent Poland
14. An association of nations.

Summary of the Treaty of Versailles, 28 June 1919:
1. The Covenant of the League of Nations
2. German losses of territory:
   to France: Alsace–Lorraine
   to Belgium: Eupen–Malmedy (after plebiscite, 1920)
   to Denmark: Northern Schleswig (after plebiscite, 1920)
   to Poland: Poznania and West Prussia. Also part of Upper Silesia (after plebiscite, 1921)
   to direct League of Nations control: the Saar, Danzig
   to Allied control and then Lithuania: Memel
   to Allied Powers as mandated territories of the League of Nations: East Africa (Britain); South-West Africa (South Africa); Cameroons and Togoland (divided between Britain and France); Samoan Islands (New Zealand); New Guinea (Australia); Marshall Islands and Pacific Islands north of the Equator (Japan)
3. The loss of German concessions and trading rights in China, Egypt and elsewhere
4. The reduction of German military power. The Rhineland and Heligoland demilitarized. Restrictions on armed forces
5. An army of occupation west of the Rhine and in bridgeheads east of the Rhine at Cologne, Coblenz and Mainz
6. Germany undertook to make reparation and accepted responsibility for certain war damage
7. The Treaty of Brest–Litovsk became void. Germans were required to withdraw from the Baltic provinces as from all other occupied territory.

Summary of the Treaty of St Germain, 10 September 1919:
1. The Covenant of the League of Nations
2. The former Austro-Hungarian Empire was broken up:
   (a) the new state of Czechoslovakia was recognized
   (b) Austria and Hungary became separate states with no control over other lands which had formerly belonged to the Austro-Hungarian Empire
   (c) the new state of Jugoslavia was created, partly from lands formerly in the Austro-Hungarian Empire
   (d) parts of the former Empire were given to Poland (which gained Galicia), Rumania (Transylvania), Italy (southern Tyrol, Trentino and Istria)
3. Boundaries of Austria defined with a plebiscite in southern Carinthia

4. Austria was forbidden to unite with any other country without League of Nations approval
5. Limitations on Austrian armed forces
6. Austria accepted responsibility for certain war damage.

Summary of the Treaty of Trianon, 4 June 1920:
1. The Covenant of the League of Nations
2. Hungary accepted the break-up of the Austro-Hungarian Empire (see St Germain above)
3. Hungary was reduced in size
4. Limitations on Hungarian armed forces
5. Hungary accepted responsibility for certain war damage.

Summary of the Treaty of Neuilly, 27 November 1919:
1. The Covenant of the League of Nations
2. Bulgarian losses:
   to Jugoslavia: areas along Bulgaria's western boundary
   to Greece: western Thrace including Bulgaria's only access to the Mediterranean Sea at Dedeagach.
3. Bulgarian gains:
   from Turkey: land on Bulgaria's south-eastern boundary
4. Limitations on Bulgarian armed forces
5. Bulgaria agreed to make some financial reparation.

Summary of the Treaty of Sèvres, 10 August 1920:
1. The Covenant of the League of Nations
2. Turkey's losses:
   as mandates: Syria (France); Palestine, Iraq and Transjordan (Britain)
      several states gained independence, e.g. Hedjaz and Arabia
   to Greece: Eastern Thrace. Greek claims to many islands such as Chios were recognized. Greece would occupy Smyrna and a surrounding area for five years when a plebiscite would be held
   to Bulgaria: land on Bulgaria's south-eastern boundary
   to Italy: Rhodes and the Dodecanese islands, and Adalia
   to Britain: Cyprus (which Britain had occupied since 1878)
3. The Straits (Dardanelles and Bosporus) placed under an international commission
4. Britain, France and Italy retained troops in Turkey.

Summary of the Treaty of Lausanne, 24 July 1923:
1. Hardly any changes were made in the Treaty of Sèvres concerning the Arab countries and Mediterranean islands
2. Turkey regained East Thrace from Greece. Both sides of the new Greek–Turkish frontier were demilitarized
3. Turkey was left free from foreign troops (the Greeks had already left Smyrna and the Italians had already left Adalia)
4. The Straits would be demilitarized but under Turkish control
5. No restrictions were imposed on Turkey's forces and no reparations were required.

Summary of the Treaty of Brest-Litovsk, 3 March 1918:
1. Russia was to pay 3 000 million roubles to Germany
2. Russian losses:
    Estonia, Latvia, Lithuania and Poland (independent), Kars and Batoum (to Turkey)
    influence over Finland (independent)
    the Ukraine (independent of Russia but under German domination).

Summary of the Covenant of the League of Nations:
1 (Article): Membership—originally the Allies who signed the Paris Treaties and thirteen states neutral in the First World War; new admissions to be approved by two-thirds of the Assembly
2–6: Basic machinery:
  (a) The Assembly of all member states with one vote each
  (b) The Council composed of the USA, Britain, France, Italy and Japan (permanently) with four additional members elected by the Assembly; one vote each
  (c) Unanimous agreement of all members present in Assembly or Council required for decisions except where otherwise agreed
  (d) The Secretariat led by a Secretary-General, financed by members of the League
7: League headquarters at Geneva
8–9: Members undertook to reduce armaments. A Disarmament Commission would advise the Council
10–12: Members undertook to preserve all members against aggression, to refer disputes to the Council and not to go to war for three months after a Council decision
13–15: Members agreed to submit disputes to arbitration and accepted various methods of arbitration including a Permanent Court of International Justice
16: Members undertook to take action against a member who resorted to war and broke the Covenant. This action would take the form of economic sanctions (i.e. boycott). If further action was needed, the Council could request contributions from members for military action. Offending members could be expelled.
17: Non-members involved in disputes could be invited to accept the above rules of the League
18–21: All treaties should be made public and should be consistent with the principles of the League
22: The colonies of the defeated countries became mandated territories (mandates) where 'the well-being and development of (the) peoples form a sacred trust of civilization'. Selected powers undertook to look after these territories, reporting to the Council which would be advised by a Mandates Commission
23–25: Members undertook to co-operate for the common good (e.g. concerning conditions of labour, colonial subjects, traffic in drugs and the control of disease), to bring existing organizations in these fields under the League and to encourage the Red Cross
26: The ways in which the Covenant could be amended.

Further Reading

Ayling, S. E.: *Portraits of Power*. Harrap (London, 1965)—Lloyd George.
Gibbons, S. R. and Morican, P.: *The League of Nations and UNO*. Longman (Harlow 1970).
Mowat, C. L.: *Lloyd George*. Oxford University Press (London, 1966).

Documentary

Bettey, J. H.: *English Historical Documents 1906–1939*. Routledge & Kegan Paul (London, 1967). This includes Lloyd George's War Aims, Wilson's Fourteen Points and the Covenant of the League.

Exercises

1. What reasons are suggested in Units One and Two for the breaking up of the empires of Austria–Hungary, Turkey and Russia by the peace treaties?
2. What evidence can you find in this Unit to support the argument that each of the following treaties was harsh: Brest-Litovsk; Versailles; Sèvres?
3. Referring to the text, maps and appendices in this Unit, list, first from a French-man's point of view, and then from a German's:
   (a) the attractive features of the Treaty of Versailles
   (b) its weaker points.
4. How would the statesmen of 1919 have explained their eagerness to set up the League of Nations?
5. Find out how far Lloyd George's War Aims and Wilson's Fourteen Points were included in the *Settlement* of Versailles, i.e. the Peace Treaties made at Paris.
6. Using this Unit, Unit Three and other material about Lloyd George, find out why Lloyd George soon lost his popularity in Britain.

Unit Three

A World Safe for Democracy?

3.1 Enthusiasm for Democracy

Democracy was assumed to be the best form of government by the powers who were victorious in 1918. But definitions of democracy have not always been the same. In 1918 it was still a novel idea that women should be allowed to vote and take part in politics. New Zealand and Australia were the first to give women political rights, in 1893 and 1902 respectively, but many countries were slow to follow them. Women over thirty who were deemed to be 'responsible' were given the vote in Britain in 1918. In 1920 votes for women became

Fig. 3.1 UK stamp commemorating the campaign of Mrs Pankhust and the Act of 1918

general in the USA, but in France, Italy and Japan women had to go on fighting for the right to take part in politics and did not win the vote until after the Second World War. Equality between the sexes was an essential feature of communism, however, and Russia gave women the vote in 1917. Germany, moreover, was more enlightened than France, for universal suffrage (the right of all adults to vote) was a central feature of the German Weimar Republic in 1919.

However, there was general agreement in 1919 that democracy required governments to be based on elections and that governments should be answerable to the people (that is, people would be able to vote at regular elections to remove unpopular governments from power and to keep some control over what governments did with their power). Democracy, it was argued, offered a stable form of government. The system had worked effectively in the USA for over a century. Democratic Britain was remarkably stable in comparison with other countries in Europe. France pursued democracy with enthusiasm if not always with success and Italy, since the creation of a united state in 1861, had persevered similarly. In 1919 there was a widespread respect for democracy, even among the defeated powers. Democracy had apparently enabled the Allies to win the war, and the Allies were now eager to encourage it. Demo-

Table 3.1 Votes for women achieved

Country	Year
Norway	1913
Denmark	1915
Russia	1917
Britain	1918 and 1928
Austria	1919
Germany	1919
Holland	1919
Poland	1919
Czechoslovakia	1920
Sweden	1921
Turkey	1934
Hungary	1945
Italy	1945
Jugoslavia	1945
France	1946
Rumania	1946
Switzerland	1971

cratic constitutions were rapidly worked out in new nation states and in states where old monarchies, like those of the Habsburgs and Hohenzollerns, had fallen.

In 1917 Wilson had told the American Congress, 'The world must be made safe for democracy'. In 1919, democracy seemed to have the power to make the world safe. Basing governments upon the wishes of the people was thought to be a foolproof recipe for the future welfare of the world. Hereditary monarchies and systems based on privilege were swept away. 'One man, one vote' became a popular twentieth-century slogan, and the League of Nations was founded on the principle, 'One nation, one vote'.

3.2 Successful Democracies

(a) The United States of America in the 1920s

No country talked more about the virtues of democracy than the United States. But between 1920 and 1939, the USA did very little to preserve democracy outside America. The presidential election of 1920 brought to power the first of a succession of Republicans. Top of their list of priorities was the vigorous encouragement of ever-growing riches in the USA, *not* international co-operation to assist infant democracies. Warren Harding (1921–3)* won the

* American Presidential elections occur in the November of leap year (e.g. 1920). The President takes office at the beginning of the following year (e.g. 1921). See Table 13.1.

first postwar election on the policy of 'Back to Normalcy'. The word was newly invented, but the idea behind it was an old one. Life for Americans would not be complicated by foreign involvement: they would concentrate on growing more prosperous. Wilson lamented, 'We had a chance to gain the leadership of the world. We have lost it.'

Harding died in office and was succeeded by Calvin Coolidge, who then won the election of 1924, persuading the voters that business was booming, that this was 'permanent' and that Republicans were good for them. He retired in 1928 and Hoover became President. There was not another Republican President until 1952.

Herbert Hoover thought the strength of the American system lay in 'rugged individualism'. Throughout the 1920s Americans, individually and ruggedly, pursued material comforts, a rising standard of living and a larger income per head than was to be found anywhere outside the USA. Their success owed little to the positive actions of their government, for Republicans interfered as little as possible. Such a policy seemed to be highly effective, at least up to 1928.

(*i*) **Legislation and government policy.** Central to what little legislation was introduced were laws which dealt with tariffs and immigration. In 1922 the Fordney-McCumber Act imposed higher tariffs (custom duties) than ever before on foreign goods coming into America; and in 1930 they were raised even higher. Sheltered by high tariffs from European competition, already prosperous American industry became more prosperous, and other nations found it difficult to sell their exports to what, potentially, was the world's richest customer. A series of Immigration Acts cut down the rights of foreigners to enter the USA and limited the numbers of those who could share in America's booming prosperity.

The Republicans conducted the government in a businesslike way, encouraged technological improvements in industry, and fed vital information to American businessmen so that they could sell their goods abroad and increase their profits. Taxation was reduced, for the Republicans had no desire to undertake ambitious schemes which would require public money. Occasionally they were pushed into passing laws designed to bring about social and economic improvements, for example assisting poor farmers with loans, but such activity was unusual. Many Republicans were extremely conservative and believed that it was quite wrong to handicap private enterprise by state regulations, or build welfare schemes* on the basis of government action. They despised socialism and communism which interfered with personal freedom. They disliked trade unions which interfered with a businessman's freedom to make profits. In the early 1920s the courts were used to smash strikes in coalmines and in transport, and troops called in to disperse those who protested.

---

* A later Republican President, Richard Nixon (in 1972), still associated the 'welfare ethic' with weakness and dependence, the 'work ethic' with strength and independence.

'The business of America is business,' Coolidge declared in 1925. There was little room for sympathy with the weak, whether they were American citizens who found it difficult to keep up in the rat-race or luckless foreign states struggling to pay their debts to the USA. 'They hired the money, didn't they?' Coolidge asked. They must therefore pay it back at a proper businessman's rate of interest.

(*ii*) **Economic prosperity.** For those able to prosper in this system of 'rugged individualism', life in America in the 1920s was exciting. Henry Ford brought mass production to the car industry, flooding the country with fifteen million Model 'T' Fords by 1927. One came hurtling off the assembly line every twenty seconds. They could be bought on hire purchase, as could almost everything else: it was a matter of 'hiring money' and paying it back later. Never before had there been so many things to be bought: motor cars and radio sets, household gadgets, hats and clothes and cigarettes, tickets to travel and tickets for

Fig. 3.2 Ford and the Model T—symbols of American prosperity

cinemas and even shares on the stock exchange. Frenzied and syncopated music, skirts which became steadily shorter, the fashionable use of make-up, the tango and the Charleston all heightened the illusion that people had never before been so free and so rich, and that never again could they ever be poor. Few had much time to spare for those who contrived to remain poor amidst the plenty.

(*iii*) **Prohibition and violence.** One thing, in theory, money could not buy. In 1919, legislation was introduced in the USA to prohibit the manufacture and sale of alcoholic drinks, and in 1920 the whole of the country became 'dry'. During the war a long-powerful temperance movement had taken the opportunity to argue that alcohol was unpatriotic, apparently because it was frequently sold by Americans of German descent. *Prohibition* lasted from 1920 to 1933 and involved the authorities in an endless struggle with the numerous people who sought to break the law. Since Prohibition agents were comparatively few, evasion of the law was widespread.

Illegal 'booze' was seldom difficult to obtain. Illegal places mushroomed in which to drink it and Chicago alone had ten thousand of these 'speakeasies'. Businessmen who had no objection to gaining their profits by breaking the law set up criminal gangs to obtain and distribute alcoholic drinks, to bribe the police and to keep rival gangs from getting a share of their profits. Gangs had private 'armies', well-equipped with firearms, including portable machine-guns, and found the motor car ideal for conducting mobile warfare. Supplying the drinks trade ('bootlegging') thus became a major factor in spreading crime. Gang leaders such as Al Capone became as notorious as Jesse James and the wild men of previous American generations. Capone's annual earnings were an estimated 60 million dollars: when the law finally sent him to prison it was not for murder, violence or 'bootlegging' but for evading income tax—and that was not until 1931. It was not a matter on which the government wished to spend much money: the staff of the Bureau of Prohibition never exceeded 4 500. They were poorly paid, quite likely to be shot and it did little for their morale when they were required, in 1927, to take civil service examinations. In the end, the only way to deal with the problem was to abolish Prohibition.

It was not only Prohibition which made America violent in the 1920s: there was widespread intolerance. The *Ku Klux Klan*, a Southern white supremacist society, was active in the 1920s in support of 'pure Americanism'. This theoretically secret organization had a membership of well over four million, who hunted down and terrorized those who seemed to threaten the purity of the USA. Those who were black attracted their vicious attention, and Jews and Roman Catholics were also attacked, as were those who tried to introduce un-American ideas. To members of the Klan, it was un-American to believe in international co-operation, the theories of Darwin, communism or racial equality. And the Klan was not without influence over the government.

Americans as a whole, however, were little interested in the ideas of the outside world. Many regarded socialism, the League of Nations and even trade unions as un-American and undesirable. The Ku Klux Klan and the frequently violent denunciation of suspected communists merely carried to more extreme lengths the views which many Americans held during the Republican domination of the 1920s.

The American bubble burst in 1929. Prosperity gave way to the Depression. The Republicans gave way, shortly afterwards, to the Democrats. Democracy survived but many other American attitudes had to be changed (see Unit Four).

(b) Great Britain in the 1920s

Before 1914 it had become a feature of democracy in Britain that the electors would choose to be ruled either by the *Conservatives* or by the *Liberals*. In 1906, they chose the Liberals and, at the same time, elected to the House of Commons twenty-nine members of the *Labour Party*. The Liberals continued to rule until the First World War brought about first a coalition government and then a change of Prime Minister. The new Prime Minister, at the end of 1916, was David Lloyd George. He was a Liberal but, when he became Prime Minister, he displaced Asquith, the leader of the party. Many Liberals considered that this was an act of disloyalty. Thus when Britain held a general election in December 1918, party politics were in a state of some confusion.

Lloyd George had gained a reputation as 'the man who won the war', through his energy and capacity for producing new ideas. He wanted to remain

Prime Minister. The act which extended the right to vote (see Section 3.1) prepared the way. An armistice ended the war on 11 November and three days later the date of the general election was announced. Some people thought that it was too soon to hold a general election and that Lloyd George was rushing things simply to make the most of his current popularity.

(*i*) **The election of 1918.** The Labour Party withdrew from the Coalition at once and prepared to offer itself as an alternative government. Britain had never had a Labour government and the party had only a few MPs in the House of Commons. In 1918 it provided itself with a new constitution, with some commitment to socialist policies ('a new social order' and 'planned co-operation in production and distribution'). But few considered that the Labour Party could win the election. The traditional choice between Liberals and Conservatives was of more immediate interest.

Lloyd George could not rely on wholehearted Liberal support. He was not willing to give way to the section of the party which thought he should now step down in favour of Asquith. The war had been won and Lloyd George was now full of enthusiasm to win the peace. The Liberal Party was thus divided between Lloyd George supporters and Asquith supporters (the Squiffites).

The Conservatives were led by Bonar Law. On 22 November, Lloyd George and Bonar Law issued a joint election manifesto. They argued that it would be sensible to continue the Coalition to tackle the formidable problems of postwar reconstruction. Lloyd George thus obtained substantial backing (from the Conservatives and some of the Liberals), the Conservatives could cash in on the magic of the Prime Minister's name, and, for the Conservatives, the arrangement would have the added advantage that it further embittered divisions among the Liberals. The election was thus a three-cornered contest between the Labour Party, the Squiffites and the Lloyd George-Bonar Law Coalition.

Coalition supporters received a letter from Lloyd George and Bonar Law recommending their election. Asquith called the letter a 'coupon', meaning the term to be disparaging, and the election came to be called 'the coupon election'. Lloyd George remained Prime Minister. But the election was a disaster for Asquith's Liberals: they won only 26 seats. The Labour Party won 59; the rest were Coalition supporters, the bulk of them Conservatives. It was a massive victory for Lloyd George but it was a dangerous victory which left him almost a prisoner of the Conservatives, who provided 338 of his 484 supporters in the new House of Commons. Lloyd George would now have to keep the Conservatives happy in spite of his strong anti-Tory inclinations. When it suited them, they could abandon him.

Lloyd George's difficulties over the Chanak Crisis have been mentioned (see Section 2.7). After 1922, Lloyd George never held office again.

(*ii*) **Lloyd George's government 1918–22.** Baldwin later referred to Lloyd George as 'a dynamic force'. The government was often vigorous but fewer major reforms were passed than might have been expected. The housing problem was an urgent one and, in 1919, Addison's Act laid down the new principle that the government would help local authorities to build 'council houses'. About 200 000 were built while Lloyd George was in power. The scheme was not perfect but it went some way towards the 'homes fit for heroes' which the Prime Minister had promised. The Unemployment Insurance Act of 1920 extended to many more of the working classes the scheme of insurance against unemployment which Lloyd George himself had introduced in 1911. In the following year, the 'dole' was introduced. This allowed those who had been unemployed for so long that they did not qualify for unemployment benefit to get 'extended' benefits, paid for by the government. The government might have done better service to tackle the causes of unemployment (see also Section 4.2.)

An immediate postwar boom gave way to a slump, and serious economic problems led to economies and the shelving of ambitious schemes. The government was plagued by industrial troubles. It avoided taking decisive action such as nationalizing the coal mines, which would have been of benefit in the years to come. But Lloyd George could not afford to annoy his Conservative supporters. Like American Republicans, they were unwilling to spend public money and, in 1922, government spending was actually cut when the business world became obsessed with the idea that it was leading to bankruptcy. (Economic problems are considered, together with industrial problems in Unit Four.)

Lloyd George's government was also swamped with problems in other parts of the world. The Peace Conference at Paris (see Unit Two) claimed attention almost as soon as the election results were published. The government was then never free from problems of foreign policy (see Unit Seven). The Empire demanded urgent attention, with problems particularly acute in Ireland, Egypt and India (see Section 6.2). Lloyd George bubbled with ideas and his government often tried to be constructive in domestic and foreign affairs, and in bringing the Empire up to date. But by 1922 postwar problems were already overwhelming.

(*iii*) **Baldwin's government 1922–3.** By 1922 the Prime Minister was no longer so popular. Prodded by Stanley Baldwin in a famous meeting at the Carlton Club, the Conservatives decided to withdraw their support. Lloyd George resigned, and a general election was held. The Conservatives had little difficulty in winning against a still-divided Liberal Party and a still-young Labour Party. The new Prime Minister was the Conservative leader, Bonar Law, whose almost immediate retirement, on the point of death, resulted in a scramble for the leadership.

The choice fell on Baldwin who was a loyal party man and who, unlike Austen Chamberlain and Lord Curzon, had not made personal enemies. He was also very different from Lloyd George, unlikely to get involved in crises like that at Chanak, a man who might be expected to usher in a quiet time. He was quickly able to create his own legend as 'Honest Stan'; with the coming of radio, indeed, he was able to present himself as the nation's uncle, calmly unfolding his policies to the people through their wirelesses and inspiring every confidence. In a man of such virtue, ability seemed to be of secondary importance.

At the start, however, Baldwin's behaviour was hardly predictable. His party had a substantial majority and seemed likely to hold office for another four years. But at the end of 1923, Baldwin decided to hold another election. Economic problems were grave: to solve them, Britain needed to abandon free trade and follow the example of the USA and other countries in putting tariffs on foreign goods. This had not been part of the Conservatives' policy at the 1922 election so it would be honest to hold another election and put the issue before the people. This was democracy at its finest. Of course, there were suggestions that Baldwin had other motives, perhaps to declare support for tariffs before Lloyd George could do so, lest Lloyd George work some miracle and once more become a popular hero.

The Liberals scrambled to re-unite their party and managed to win 158 seats. Labour did even better and raised their total to 191. The Conservatives lost substantially and secured only 261 seats. No party had an overall majority. Baldwin's gamble had failed. Since the Liberals would not support a Conservative government, George V invited Ramsay MacDonald to take office. For the first time, Britain had a Labour Prime Minister.

Fig. 3.3 Ramsay MacDonald (Margaret Bondfield and J. H. Thomas to his left), Britain's first Labour Prime Minister, 1924

(iv) **MacDonald's government 1924.** The minority Labour government lasted only from January to October 1924. It could only remain in office with Liberal support—so it could pursue only those policies of which the Liberals approved. It was impossible to bring about the 'new social order' which the Labour Party had been advocating since 1918, and the country's economic problems (see Section 4.2, page 68) were too deep-rooted to be dealt with quickly. The Labour government treated the trade union movement with near-indifference and industrial unrest remained acute. As Foreign Secretary as well as Prime Minister, however, MacDonald worked hard for international goodwill (see Section 7.2(*c*)).

MacDonald's government passed only one outstanding Act. The Wheatley Housing Act allocated £9 million a year to be paid by the government to help local authorities build more 'council houses' (which expanded the building industry). When the Act was scrapped in 1933, 500 000 houses had been built under its provisions.

MacDonald then doomed his government to commit suicide like Baldwin in 1923. He stubbornly refused to accept a Liberal demand for an inquiry into why the prosecution of the editor of the *Workers' Weekly* had been dropped. The editor, J. R. Campbell, had written an article which, some said, was an incitement to mutiny. The *Workers' Weekly* was a communist paper and the government was already suspected of being too friendly to communist Russia (see Section 5.1, page 87). The Campbell affair was no more than a storm in a teacup, but MacDonald's refusal to accept an inquiry was fatal. The government was defeated and resigned. Britain held yet another general election, the third in less than two years.

(v) **Baldwin's second government 1924–9.** What was needed was a clear electoral verdict and a period of stable government, preferably by a government which would tackle basic social and economic problems. Partly due to the *Zinoviev Letter*, the electoral result was clear and until 1929 Britain secured the stable government of Baldwin. The Letter was said to have come from Zinoviev, acting for the *Comintern* (a Russian-based organization for the spreading of communism). Its purpose was to encourage communist revolution in Britain but it may well have been a forgery. In any case, it said nothing new, though it said it at an inconvenient moment. Conservative newspapers did their best to promote a 'red scare', to daub MacDonald and the Labour Party with unsavoury connexions with the Bolsheviks.

When the votes were counted, Labour had actually collected over a million votes more than in the previous election, but such were the oddities of the British electoral system that they managed at the same time to lose 40 seats. The Conservatives won 419 seats, ensuring a stable Conservative government. The Liberals, on the other hand, lost both votes and seats and had only 40 MPs in the new House of Commons.

Opinion had apparently polarized and the majority of voters now looked on elections as involving a choice mainly between Conservatives and Labour.

Voters now put the Liberals as a sort of middle-of-the-road party, somewhere between Conservatives and Labour. On issues such as the Zinoviev Letter, they tended to choose one of the main parties, either to demonstrate their own loyalties or to try to keep those they disliked from power. It was often claimed that British democracy rested on a two-party system. The Liberals had now ceased to be one of the two major parties, apparently the real victims of the Red Letter scare.

Baldwin's government did almost nothing to solve basic economic problems (see Unit Four). Probably the most spectacular event in these five years was the General Strike of 1926 (see Section 4.2). The Strike passed with remarkably little violence. It was undoubtedly one of Baldwin's achievements that he gave the country 'tranquillity'. Even the class war, so active elsewhere after the Bolshevik revolution of 1917, was lulled almost to sleep. When the next election occurred, in 1929, the Conservatives put their faith in posters of Stanley Baldwin and the slogan 'Safety First'; they even produced a song in his honour for grateful and musical electors to sing. Unfortunately posters, slogans and songs were unavailing. Baldwin was defeated.

His government left on the statute book a variety of useful *Acts*. The most outstanding was the Local Government Act of 1929. The most unexpected was the Franchise Act of 1928. The Franchise Act gave the vote to women on the same terms as men and enfranchised the 'flappers', the young women aged from twenty-one to thirty. It was almost the first occasion on which the Conservatives had seized such an initiative in extending democracy in Britain.

Neville Chamberlain, a highly successful Minister of Health, put a great deal of thought and work into the Local Government Act. It was one of the outstanding Acts of the interwar years. The poor law unions, which dated from the previous century, were abolished. County and borough councils took over their responsibilities for the poor. Sweeping changes were made in local government, the powers of county councils enlarged and new arrangements introduced to assist local government with money from government funds. The Act was the government's and perhaps Neville Chamberlain's most impressive achievement.

Earlier Chamberlain, working with Winston Churchill, the Chancellor of the Exchequer, produced a Pensions Act in 1925. It further extended the insurance schemes of Lloyd George, now making provision for widows and orphans and for old age pensions for workers and their wives. The first old age pensions dated from 1908 but they had been little more than a form of meagre state charity. The new pensions were to be part of the insurance scheme. Workers contributed to the insurance fund and secured pensions as a right when they reached sixty-five.

The Conservatives also set up the Central Electricity Board to control the generation of power and to distribute it throughout the country on a national grid, a measure of considerable importance. In the same year, 1926, the BBC (British Broadcasting Corporation) was established, taking broadcasting out of the hands of private companies in favour of a national organization.

These were among the solid achievements of Baldwin's government. Some other accomplishments were more open to question. In 1925, Churchill returned Britain to the gold standard (see Section 4.2, page 69) with results that were damaging to Britain's exports. Unemployment did not fall below the million mark and the government seemed to have few ideas for dealing with the problem. The government had every intention of keeping down public spending and, although generally unsuccessful in this, it added to its unpopularity by holding down the payments of unemployment benefit.

Baldwin's government also showed hostility to trade unionism. The General Strike was followed by the Trades Disputes Act, in 1927. This Act made both general strikes and strikes in sympathy illegal, forbade civil servants' unions to link with the Trades Union Congress and the Labour Party, and struck a damaging blow at unions which used funds for political purposes. The working classes, especially the miners, had already suffered a major defeat in the General Strike. This Act could easily be made to look petty. Labour supporters continued to grieve about it and Attlee's government repealed it after the Second World War.

(*vi*) **MacDonald's second government 1929–31.** The *election of 1929* again produced an indecisive result, and once again MacDonald became Prime Minister without a majority in the House of Commons.

This second Labour government lasted only until 1931. Margaret Bondfield became the first woman to hold Cabinet rank when she was appointed Minister of Labour. Arthur Henderson became Foreign Secretary and showed the concern for international co-operation which had been a feature of MacDonald's first government (see Unit Seven, page 116). The government also showed an interest in the Empire and especially in trying to improve the situation in India by holding Round Table Conferences (see Section 6.2, page 106). But like all governments between the wars, this one had no convincing policies to deal with economic problems. It was also unfortunate in coming to power when the problems were worsening; only a few months after MacDonald took office, the world made a steep dive into the *Depression* (see Unit Four, page 73).

The need to rely on Liberal votes in the Commons was once again a severe handicap. The government made a study of the unemployment problem, which produced hardly any results at all. Public works were undertaken to provide a few jobs, but unemployment had risen sharply since 1929. Snowden was the Chancellor of the Exchequer and he had a deep dislike of spending public money. The crisis deepened and the government was reduced to a state of near-paralysis.

Its death blow was struck in August 1931. A deep division developed within the Cabinet. Unemployment was nearing three million. A variety of committees of 'experts' produced gloomy reports. All the 'respectable' organizations such as those of financiers, employers and newspaper-owners maintained that the only salvation lay in cutting public spending. There was now a financial crisis as well as the basic economic crisis with its high level of unemployment. Cutting public spending would restore confidence among financiers. But it would not help the unemployed; trade unions and most of the Labour Party recoiled in horror at the suggestion that rates of benefit to the unemployed should be cut, along with the salaries of public servants, in order to help the confidence of financiers. In fact, benefits to the unemployed were in 1931 a third higher than they had been ten years earlier and the cost of living had fallen, but the issue was an emotional one. To most Labour supporters, it seemed indecent to kick the unemployed to help the Bank of England. But MacDonald, Snowden and Jimmy Thomas, the Lord Privy Seal, all had great respect for authority and insisted on making the cuts. The rest of the Cabinet protested. MacDonald resigned. Thus the economic crisis and the financial crisis combined to produce a political crisis (see Unit Four, page 73 for economic and political crises).

(*vii*) **The Coalition government 1931–5.** MacDonald handed in his resignation as Prime Minister of the Labour Government but took on a new appointment as Prime Minister of a National (Coalition) government. For the next four years, like Lloyd George before him, he led a government which was mainly supported by the Conservatives. The electors favoured this arrangement, and in the election of October 1931 they returned 521 supporters of the National government, 52 Labour MPs and 37 Liberals. MacDonald remained Prime Minister while Baldwin looked over his shoulder as Lord President of the Council. The Labour Party licked its wounds as the Opposition and waited for better times.

It was a remarkable tribute to British democracy, that in its gravest economic crisis in history, when other states were turning desperately to imagined saviours such as Adolf Hitler, Britain sought salvation in a quietly unimaginative government which was a sort of double-act between MacDonald and Baldwin.

(British political history in the 1930s is continued in Section 4.4.)

(*c*) **France to 1939**

The Third Republic, established in France in 1870, lasted until 1940. The head of state was an elected president. Government was carried on by a prime minister supported in and responsible to parliament. It was a democratic, but not always an efficient system. Unlike Britain, France had no tradition of a choice between two major parties. There were so many parties that governments could only be formed by grouping several of them together in coalitions. With the first heated controversy, such coalitions then tended to fall apart. As a result, French democracy from 1917 to 1940 produced 44 different governments, and called on over 20 different prime ministers. But France did not abandon her democratic system until she was invaded by Germany in 1940.

After the Peace Conference of Paris Clemenceau was Prime Minister only until January 1920. At this time, the dominant groups in French politics were right wing. They were known as the *Bloc National* and their main aim was to ensure the weakness of Germany. Poincaré was Prime Minister from 1922 to

1924 and gave expression to the Bloc's anti-German feelings by occupying the Ruhr (see page 56 and Section 7.2).

A swing of opinion against the Bloc brought in a series of governments in which Aristide Briand was influential. He controlled French foreign policy from 1925 to 1932, and was Prime Minister in 1925–6 and again in 1929. In all, between 1909 and 1929, Briand was Prime Minister of eleven governments and yet his total time in the office was less than that of Baldwin from 1924 to 1929. French foreign policy under Briand's influence became more constructive with the making of international agreements, some of them involving Germany.

France, being less dependent on foreign trade than other major European nations, suffered fewer economic problems than Britain in the 1920s (see Unit Four). The war left tremendous problems of reconstruction but by 1924 much progress had been made. Agriculture regained a degree of prosperity. An influx of foreign workers helped to repair losses in manpower. Heavy industry developed rapidly: the need to replace devastated industrial plant enabled France to equip herself with the most up-to-date and efficient machines. Tariffs were used to protect both agriculture and industry. After the immediate period of postwar reconstruction, the main problems were the stability of the franc and the balancing of successive governments' budgets. France also faced industrial unrest.

Poincaré was again Prime Minister from 1926 to 1929 and while Briand pursued better relations with foreign governments, Poincaré took measures to stabilize the value of the franc and encouraged a measure of prosperity based partly on cheap money (loans, that is, at low rates of interest).

Major reforms were few in this period. In 1928 and 1930, social insurance schemes were introduced. In 1932, family allowances were added. But by this time, the world was in the grip of the Depression (see Section 4.3). Although the effects on France were less severe than elsewhere the Depression did coincide with another period of serious instability in French politics. Briand and Poincaré were elderly and with their retirement, a new generation of politicians took control. Few of them showed outstanding qualities.

French politics became so unstable in the 1930s that there even seemed to be a possibility that France would abandon democracy. Particularly serious were the riots in 1934 which resulted from the *Stavisky Affair*. When Stavisky, a shady financier, was found to have committed 'suicide', rumours circulated that he had been murdered to cover up corruption among politicians and the police. Political and financial scandals were not new in France, but the Depression was beginning to take effect; unemployment figures were rising; discontent was widespread and a succession of weak governments, under Daladier, Sarraut and Chautemps produced only despair. The Stavisky Affair led to street rioting. The extreme right demonstrated in favour of strong government. The extreme left demonstrated in favour of a communist system. A government led by Daladier lasted for only nine days. Paris rioters tried to break into parliament.

But democracy survived. A new government under Doumergue was appointed and given sweeping emergency powers. The government was a broad coalition, almost an all-party government. Its powers, in effect, temporarily suspended democracy in order to weather the storm; but in 1936 the elections brought a new experiment. The parties of the left drew together to present a Popular Front, with policies of reform and a determination to preserve France from Fascism. Blum became Prime Minister of the first Popular Front government, which passed a spate of reforms but fell apart in 1938. Blum had to dissolve revolutionary Fascist groups and Daladier, who took office with a Radical government in 1938, had to deal with a general strike. Economic problems and political instability weakened France throughout the 1930s, playing into the hands of Hitler and Mussolini (see Unit Eight). Daladier was still holding office precariously when the Second World War began.

3.3 Unsuccessful Democracies

Popular Front governments were unable to preserve democracy in Spain in the 1930s (see page 63). In many other parts of Europe it was already too late to save democracy by this time. A democratic experiment in Russia (see Section 5.1) lasted for less than a year. Similar experiments in Hungary, Poland and Austria quickly ran into difficulties. Mention has already been made of the collapse of democracy in Jugoslavia (see page 27). When Hitler came to power in Germany, the Weimar Republic was quickly destroyed although it had lasted longer and been more successful than many other democratic systems. In Italy the failure of democracy, which had not been new in 1918, occurred earlier than that in Germany. This seriously weakened the alliance of democratic powers which had made the Peace Settlement and set up the League of Nations. For supporters of democracy, such changes were disheartening and even bewildering.

(a) Italy to 1923

(i) **Instability after the war.** Italy had combined a monarchy with a system of parliamentary government since 1861. The right to vote was given only to a minority of the population and political life was handicapped by the opposition of the Pope who instructed Catholics not to take part in Italy's government. As in France, numerous political parties gave rise to weak coalition governments. Frequently, politicians seemed to be concerned more with manoeuvring for power (and bribery was not unknown) than with the solution of Italy's many serious problems.

When the First World War ended, the Pope withdrew his ban on political life and a Sicilian priest formed a Catholic Popular Party. This party (like the Socialists) gained considerable support in the postwar years. But parliament became even more fragmented than before, and it was even more difficult for stable coalitions to be formed. Ministries continued to be short-lived and unstable, just when Italy needed a period of lengthy and stable government.

The country was discontented and frustrated. The war had caused many casualties. The economy was disrupted and exports, mainly luxury goods, could not be sold. There were few tourists to boost Italy's income and it was

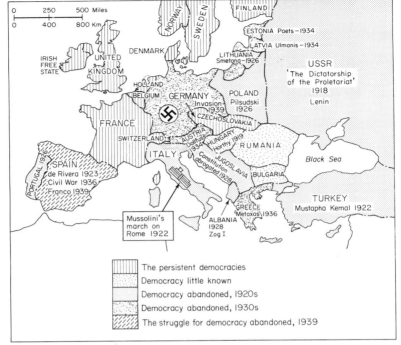

Fig. 3.4 The eclipse of democracy in Europe, 1918–39

difficult to pay for vital imports. Unemployment increased the industrial unrest which had already been serious before the war (with a general strike and a
near-revolutionary situation in 1914). There was a deep-rooted problem of
poverty, especially in the south of Italy and bandits plagued the country, their
numbers swelled by deserters from the war.

From 1917 to 1919, Orlando was Prime Minister but he lost favour during
the Paris Peace Conference, and after him nobody could establish effective
government. The parliamentary system and professional politicians were discredited. Italians began to look elsewhere for effective action to deal with unemployment, high prices, lawlessness and what appeared to be a weak foreign
policy.

The left wing took their inspiration from the Bolshevik Revolution in
Russia and conflict between right and left grew fiercer towards the end of 1920.
Strikes were common; factory-owners replied with lock-outs and some workers then seized control of factories, only surrendering when minor concessions
were made. A few soviets were also established, on the Russian pattern, and
early in 1921 the Communist Party separated from the Socialists, apparently
committed to the violent revolution being preached from Moscow.

Giolitti, the Prime Minister, wavered uncertainly and then decided to hold a
general election in April 1921. The Communists won only 13 seats (out of

535). A new, right-wing party, the Fascists, whom Giolitti had foolishly regarded as allies in the election, won 35 seats and at once turned against his government. Unable any longer to cope Giolitti resigned, but his successor, Bonomi, was equally helpless in a country becoming increasingly violent. When he resigned, the divisions in parliament were such that it took weeks to find a new Prime Minister. When one was found, Facta, he led an even weaker coalition, almost powerless to act at all. It was only a matter of time before the manoeuvres in parliament became altogether irrelevant. Such an unstable political situation was ready-made for a seizure of power by some unscrupulous and ruthless man of action.

(*ii*) **Mussolini and the Fascist Party.** Benito Mussolini led the 35 Fascists in the Italian parliament. He had been born in 1883, the son of a socialist blacksmith. At first his career was totally undistinguished. He narrowly avoided expulsion from school but qualified as a teacher. After a year's teaching, he left Italy for Switzerland, thus avoiding military service. Manual labourer and vagrant, he was expelled from Switzerland for his violent socialist opinions, spent some time in France and returned to Italy to do his military service. A breach of the peace brought a short spell in prison, in 1908, after which he went to Austria from where he was deported.

When the war began in 1914, Mussolini had made a certain mark as a violent socialist agitator and editor of *Avanti*, a left-wing journal. But his career was littered with quarrels to which he was soon to add another. Italy was at first neutral in the war but it was Mussolini's opinion that she should join it. He set up his own paper, *Il Popolo d'Italia*, and tried to combine socialist and nationalist views. The Socialists disapproved and he was expelled from the party.

Mussolini persisted. His paper preached violent nationalism and he set up action groups to demonstrate, mainly in Milan. They were known as *Fasci di Combattimento*. When Italy joined the war, in 1915, against the Central Powers, Mussolini was conscripted into the army but discharged in 1917, having been wounded in an accidental explosion. He returned to Milan and his paper.

At the end of the war, Mussolini was able to continue to express violently nationalist views, to spread them through his paper and through the *Fasci* which were now revived. He had a contempt for democracy and for pacifism and at this point he developed a new mission: to save Italy from communism and to bring her strong government. Industrialists and landowners provided funds—to destroy the 'Reds' and protect their own property—and the movement grew. Mussolini's supporters were dressed in black shirts. They adopted the Roman salute and carried daggers, taking as their symbol the *fasces* of Ancient Rome, a bundle of rods bound round an axe. They organized a national party, the Fascist Party—but, in 1919, they could not win a single parliamentary seat.

The Fasci, however, developed, with practice, into highly successful thugs. They broke up communist meetings and beat up their opponents. Early in

1921, they claimed to have a quarter of a million members although they could still win only 6 per cent of the seats in parliament and had little in the way of a coherent programme. They did much to break up the socialist organizations which Mussolini had previously supported and to smash trade unions, to the delight of many employers. All over Italy, walls were decorated with Mussolini's portrait and the new Fascist slogan, 'Believe. Obey. Fight.'

In July 1922, the left tried to fight back with a general strike. It was a disastrous failure but it was Mussolini's opportunity. While Mussolini pointed to the weakness and inadequacy of the government, his Fascists kept the public services running and launched new attacks on left-wing organizations. They burned the printing presses of *Avanti* and their lawlessness went unpunished.

(*iii*) **The March on Rome.** Mussolini thought it important to act quickly, to make the most use of the discontent and chaos. He intended that Fascists would at least share in the government, in spite of being so few in parliament. Showman that he was, however, he felt that this needed a grand gesture.

Already Mussolini had helped to make himself more respectable, declaring that he had no hostile intentions toward the monarchy or the Church, thus reversing previous declarations. Now the Fascists planned a march on Rome: 50 000 Fascists, armed and drilled like soldiers, would occupy the capital. Mussolini had powerful friends among the propertied classes but the loyalties of the army were uncertain—he could, however, slip into exile again if the plans misfired.

In the event, no march was needed. The King, Victor Emmanuel III, refused Facta's demand for emergency powers. He, too, lacked confidence in the government and was unsure of the army. It was simpler to give in to the Fascist leader. Facta resigned. A telegram was sent to Mussolini and he came to Rome to be Prime Minister, arriving in borrowed morning suit, top hat and spats. The Fascist Blackshirts followed, in time to hold a victory parade. Mussolini had succeeded with the mere threat of a march.

In spite of the bluster, Mussolini had come to power almost legally. His first government was yet another coalition, with only four Fascists in the cabinet. But within a month, parliament granted him full powers until the end of 1923. In 1923, it was agreed that the party with the most votes in an election would have two-thirds of the seats in parliament. In 1924, a general election, in any case, gave the Fascists two-thirds of the votes. A few months later the forceful Socialist parliamentarian, Matteotti, was found murdered, a victim of the Fascists who resented his outspoken book, *The Fascists Exposed*. Italy was clearly on the road to dictatorship, especially when Mussolini resorted to censorship and repression, as well as filling local appointments with Fascists. (The history of Italy under Mussolini continues in Section 5.2, page 92.)

(*b*) Germany to 1933

William II, the German Kaiser (Emperor) was forced to abdicate two days before the armistice in November 1918. In February 1919, a Constituent

Assembly met at Weimar to work out a new German constitution. The details were agreed within six months and the *Weimar Republic* created. The government moved from Weimar to the capital, Berlin, in 1920.

On paper at least, the new constitution provided Germany with an almost perfect democracy. There would be elections every four years, to elect (by universal suffrage, secret ballot and proportional representation) the Reichstag (lower house of parliament). Every seven years, the people would elect a President, as head of state. It would be one of the President's duties to appoint a Chancellor who, with his ministers, would be responsible to the Reichstag and would therefore need the support of the majority of that House. According to their size, the German states such as Prussia and Bavaria would send representatives to the Reichsrat, an upper house with a delaying power similar to that of the British House of Lords. The constitution contained guarantees of basic human rights. It even provided for plebiscites, to register the wishes of the people on matters of grave importance.

The Chancellor was more important than the President. The success of the system depended on whether a Chancellor could command a clear majority in the Reichstag. If not, Germany, like France and Italy, would be plagued by short-lived and weak coalition governments. Success also depended on the readiness of Germans to turn almost overnight from the authoritarian system of the former Kaiser to the liberal and democratic system of the Weimar constitution. From the beginning, some Germans showed a preference for different systems and a willingness to back their opinions with violence.

(*i*) **Opposition to the system.** Communists wanted a revolution similar to that of the Russian Bolsheviks. Nationalists and militarists hated the communists and despised republican democracy. They associated democracy with surrender and with the allegedly unfair treatment of Germany in the Treaty of Versailles (see Section 2.4). The new constitution was soon under attack from both left and right.

The left struck first. The German Spartacus League (*Spartacists*, who took their name from a rebel-gladiator and slave-leader of Ancient Rome) aimed to establish communism. Soviets were set up in Berlin and the Baltic ports. Revolutionary sailors briefly took prisoner Ebert, the first President of the Weimar Republic. Eisner proclaimed an independent socialist state in Bavaria. But Karl Liebknecht and Rosa Luxemburg, the leaders of the Spartacists, were murdered. Eisner met the same fate and, after a bitter struggle, the authorities regained control of Berlin. For the moment, victory lay with the moderates. In the first postwar elections, German communists won no seats whereas nearly 40 per cent of the Reichstag consisted of moderate socialists, the Social Democrats. On the right, however, nationalists won 10 per cent of the seats.

The nationalists wanted a Germany which was strong. They condemned those who had accepted Germany's surrender and forced the Kaiser to abdicate as 'November Criminals' (a term used at various times to denounce democrats, republicans, communists, socialists and Jews). Many who supported the nationalists volunteered for service in the *Frei Korps*, a sort of vigilante army with a passion for order and a hatred of communism. In 1920 there were further attempts to destroy the new republic. A communist-led rising in the Ruhr was put down by the army and the *Frei Korps*, but when, about the same time, other army units and members of the *Frei Korps* tried to seize Berlin they were defeated by the city's workers who paralysed the capital with a general strike after the government had fled to Dresden. This attempt came to be known as the *Kapp Putsch*. The government was too weak to punish many of the conspirators. Only the luckless Dr Kapp was singled out and imprisoned. He died in prison.

The courts showed a reluctance to punish right-wing law-breakers throughout the violent period of the early 1920s. There were further communist-led risings of workers. Munich and Bavaria became a breeding-ground for nationalist (often anti-Jewish) agitation, and a base from which to plot the overthrow of the republic. The nationalists showed open hostility to democracy in the Reichstag. Political assassinations were not uncommon. With a series of weak coalition governments from the outset and with a variety of chancellors, the Weimar Republic struggled for its life.

(*ii*) **The crises of 1923.** Matters came to a head in 1923. Coalition governments had been no more successful in managing the economy than in dealing with lawlessness. Germany's balance of payments position had been precarious since the war. Exports were difficult to sell. Reparations had to be paid. The mark was weak and its value fell steadily. In a short-sighted effort to solve immediate difficulties, governments simply issued more money and inflation resulted. Prices galloped ahead more quickly in Germany than elsewhere in Europe and in 1922 the situation was already grave.

In January 1923 French troops, assisted by the Belgians, occupied the Ruhr. Germany was unstable, economically weak, unable to keep up her payments of reparations, and the French decided to help themselves by seizing the rich Ruhr industrial area. On the advice of their government and Chancellor Cuno, the Ruhr workers refused to co-operate with the French: they were punished by mass arrests and France imposed an economic blockade of the whole area, including much of the Rhineland.

The occupation of the Ruhr created even more havoc in Germany. The French gained little but their invasion disrupted the German economy and dealt a death blow to the mark. In 1914, it took just over 4 marks to purchase an American dollar. At the end of 1922, it already took over 7 000. In July 1923, the figure was 160 000. The Germany currency was out of control and in November one needed 4 200 000 000 000 marks to equal a dollar. Printing-presses could not keep up with the changes. Bank notes and stamps were printed and overprinted with ever more crazy figures. It was easier to resort to barter than to try to keep up with the useless flood of paper money. Bank balances became valueless, wiping out savings. A suit-case became more useful than a purse for carrying one's money.

Not unnaturally, there was a wave of anger which agitators were quick to exploit. There was a communist rising in Hamburg which was routed by the police. Left-wing and right-wing plots multiplied. But the army remained loyal. Chancellor Cuno resigned and Ebert called on Stresemann to form a new government.

Stresemann took office in August 1923, with a widely-based coalition to save the republic. In November, the *Munich Putsch* occurred. It was already too late and was also badly-planned. Supported by the veteran soldier General

Fig. 3.5 Stresemann gave new hope to Germany and to Europe in the mid-1920s

Ludendorff, who had already backed the *Kapp Putsch*, it was organized by Adolf Hitler who intended to take control of Bavaria and then lead a nationalist attack on Berlin. The Bavarian police killed sixteen of Hitler's supporters but Hitler, sufficiently insignificant for the authorities to risk punishing him, was sent to prison for five years. Ludendorff was acquitted.

The Weimar Republic had at last produced an able politician in Stresemann. He quickly overcame the threat of civil war, ordered a return to work in the Ruhr, pacified the French with a resumption of reparations payments and set about restoring the currency. It was impossible to recover lost savings and it was not until well into 1924 that an entirely new currency was devised, based on the Reichsmark and an independent Reichsbank. But from the appointment of Stresemann, the outlook brightened. Although he remained Chancellor for only three months, he did much to restore confidence. He was in charge of German foreign policy from the end of 1923 to his death in 1929, and he provided an element of stability in the Weimar Republic. One of his first achievements in foreign policy was to persuade the French to leave the Ruhr.

(*iii*) **Prosperity and optimism.** The crises of 1923 which had threatened to destroy the Weimar Republic proved, in fact, to be the beginning of a more hopeful period. The Dawes Plan and the Young Plan (see Section 4.2) helped Germany to keep up with reparations payments. Foreign investment in the country provided capital for expansion. Unemployment was reduced, although as in Britain it obstinately refused to fall below a million. From 1925, Germans began to enjoy a degree of prosperity. There was more confidence in the republic. International relations were also improving, for the Locarno Treaties heralded a more co-operative period, to which Stresemann and Briand of France made considerable contributions (see Section 7.2), and Germany was admitted to the League of Nations in 1926.

Ebert's death made it necessary to elect a new President and in 1925 Field Marshal Hindenburg took office. He was already nearly eighty, but his aristocratic and military background pleased the nationalists: portly and nearly immobile, he seemed to personify stability.

Governments also seemed slightly more stable. Marx held office as Chancellor for much of the period from 1923 to 1928, with a coalition of moderate parties. Meanwhile, the Social Democrats played the part of a normal democratic opposition and although the nationalists did well in the 1924 elections they lost ground in 1928. The communists throughout kept about 10 per cent of the seats. The Reichstag was thus not free from extremist parties, but the moderates were making the system work satisfactorily. In addition, they passed useful reforms. In 1927, for instance, Marx introduced an extensive scheme for unemployment insurance and created machinery for the settlement of labour disputes.

Prosperity and optimism were short-lived, however. By the end of 1928, trading prospects were less hopeful. October 1929 brought a double disaster. The death of Stresemann in Germany and the Wall Street Crash in America again put the Weimar Republic in danger. Germany depended on foreign loans. When these suddenly ceased and when export sales rapidly dwindled, there was an almost immediate rise in unemployment. Memories of the inflation of 1923 were revived as Germany plunged into a period of deflation and the Depression (see Section 4.3).

Confidence in democracy was again shaken. As in MacDonald's British Cabinet, there were arguments among members of the government about what was to be done. Unemployment was the first problem but before long the Reichsbank was in trouble and the Reichsmark under pressure. As in Britain (see page 49), there was heated argument about whether to cut unemployment benefit. A general election in 1930 showed markedly increased support for both left- and right-wing extremist parties.

(*iv*) **Hitler and the Nazi Party.** At last, the climate was right for Adolf Hitler to emerge from insignificance. Hitler had been born in Austria in 1889 but he joined the German army in 1914, attracted by what seemed to him the greater efficiency of the Kaiser's Germany. In any case, he had been outstandingly unsuccessful in Austria, unsuccessful at school, denied admission to art college and for years a near down-and-out on the streets of Vienna. His military career earned him two Iron Crosses and Germany's defeat filled him with shame. When the war ended, he remained in Germany and, in 1919, joined the German Workers' Party in Munich. He was not attracted by the socialism of some members of the party, but by their extreme nationalist and anti-Jewish opinions.

Hitler became one of its most fanatical members and soon rose to the party's leadership. The name was changed to National Socialist German Workers' Party, then abbreviated to National Socialists, the first four letters in the German producing *Nazi*. They developed their organization further afield than Bavaria but did not win seats in the Reichstag until after the Munich Putsch of 1923.

The Putsch and the trial which followed helped Hitler to gain notoriety. In prison, he began work on *Mein Kampf* (*My Struggle*), much of it dictated to Rudolf Hess, a fellow-prisoner. By the mid-1920s, the party had (like Mussolini's Fascists) developed many of its theatrical trappings—the Swastika, uniform and salute—with an incoherent programme (see Section 5.2(*b*)) based mainly on hatred of 'November Criminals', France and Russia, the Treaty of Versailles and anything weak. In 1924, the Nazis won 7 per cent of the seats in the Reichstag but lost most of them almost at once. But when the crises of 1929 began, the Nazis were waiting.

(*v*) **The Nazi rise to power.** Hitler had already gathered his principal henchmen, among them Hess and Goering. His Brownshirts (the SA, *Sturmabteilung*) had some skill in thuggery. Hitler himself had skill in oratory, a master of abuse but also a master of promises. Others had 'betrayed' Germany, 'knifed her in the back'. Hitler and the Nazis would make Germany great again, purify the country from inferior races such as Jews and traitors such as communists, solve outstanding problems such as unemployment and end the nonsense of reparations. In the election of 1930, they won nearly a fifth of the seats in the Reichstag although the communists also achieved their best results so far. It was a turbulent election with open violence especially by Nazis and communists.

The economic situation also grew worse. In the summer of 1931, unemployment rose to about 4 million, early in 1932 to above 6 million. The presidential election was then due. The aged Hindenburg got over $18\frac{1}{2}$ million votes and kept his office but Adolf Hitler polled a remarkable 11 million, increasing this to nearly $13\frac{1}{2}$ million in a second ballot which was necessary for Hindenburg to establish an absolute majority according to the rules of the constitution. Hitler was at last a major national politician.

The President was now senile, befuddled by the intrigues of army officers, landowners and industrialists, dismayed by the economic problems but still possessing as President the deadly power to make and un-make governments in a Reichstag where no one had a clear mandate to rule. Hindenburg appointed the aristocratic von Papen who tried in vain to gain more substantial support in two elections in 1932. The only significant result of the elections was that the Nazi Party became the largest single group in the Reichstag with 37 per cent of the seats in July 1932, falling back to 33 per cent in November. The Social Democrats were the next largest party with the communists close on their heels. Von Papen represented none of these. For a time he kept office by using emergency powers but at the end of the year Hindenburg replaced him and called on von Schleicher.

The Weimar Republic was now in its death agony. Even the ending of reparations could not save it. The President floundered ineffectively. Only the Nazis, who despised the system, could rely on substantial support in the Reichstag. The Depression was acute and Hindenburg grabbed at what seemed to be the only workable compromise, appointing Hitler Chancellor on 30 January 1933. This was the result of the latest deal among the politicians. Von Papen had thrown in his lot with Hitler in return for the office of Vice-Chancellor.

Hitler promptly arranged another election for March 1933. The campaign was a vicious one: rival parties were handicapped, their meetings broken up, members battered and newspapers muzzled. The Reichstag went up in flames, evidence, Hitler claimed, of a communist plot. The result, for the Nazis, was hardly satisfactory. They won only 44 per cent of the seats and had to rely on the nationalists to secure a majority in the new parliament. That, however, was enough. The opposition was quickly weakened by arresting or expelling communist members and the *Enabling Law* was passed. This Act, 'For the Removal of the Distress of the People and Reich', destroyed the Weimar Republic. It gave the government full powers for four years, including the right to make new laws. Like Mussolini, Hitler achieved power by means which were almost legal; and having got power, he proceeded to destroy German democracy. (The history of Germany under Hitler continues in Section 5.2.)

(c) Elsewhere

Supporters of democracy found little comfort elsewhere in Europe. Among the new states only *Czechoslovakia* (see page 25) could make the system work well, and there it was destroyed by Hitler in 1939 (see Section 8.3(*d*)). In *Hungary*, it hardly worked at all. While still in the provisional stage, the new republic was overthrown by Bela Kun's communist revolution. With the defeat of Bela Kun in August 1919, the right wing took control. Admiral Horthy was appointed Regent for life, deputizing for a Habsburg king who was not allowed to return. The regime carefully safeguarded the privileges of the nobility. There were a few trappings of democracy but the system was nearer to dictatorship. In the 1930s, Gömbös was a Prime Minister who shared the fascist views of Mussolini and the anti-Jewish prejudices of Hitler. Hungary joined Nazi Germany in fighting Russia in the Second World War, and Horthy retained his grip on the country until its closing stages.

The *Austrian* democratic system, set up in 1918 (see Section 2.5), was not unsuccessful in the 1920s. Social Democrats and Christian Socialists worked together to establish a measure of prosperity; and international aid was given to the weak Austrian economy, which also helped to make the democracy more stable.

By the end of the 1920s, however, there was a growth of extremism. Tension had always existed between Vienna (Social Democrat in sympathy and intent on ambitious socialist reforms) and the rest of Austria, which was conservative and suspicious of socialism. Reactionaries organized the *Heimwehr* (like the German *Frei Korps*) and a political machine similar to Mussolini's Fascists. They had always resented the Peace Settlement forbidding Austria to unite with Germany. When Hitler came to power, they further stepped up their agitation.

The Depression also imposed new strains, with unemployment and a financial crisis in which Austria's leading bank went bankrupt. The republic began to totter. Dollfuss became Chancellor in 1932. He regarded the democratic system as a legacy of defeat in 1918 and, with the opposition of the Social Democrats, he suspended the constitution and gave himself emergency powers in 1934. Civil war followed in which the army and the Heimwehr defeated the Social Democrats and the workers. Dollfuss did not live long to enjoy his success, being murdered by the Nazis in July 1934, during a premature attempt to unite the republic with Germany. But an independent Austria was not to survive for long: in 1938 Hitler seized the country and incorporated it in Germany (see Section 8.3(*b*)).

Poland experimented with a parliamentary republic which was represented at the Paris Peace Conference by the pianist-Prime Minister, Paderewski. The constitution, however, worked badly. There were too many parties for stable government, partly owing to an elaborate system of proportional representation. In 1926 the veteran Polish nationalist, Pilsudski, returned from retirement to seize Warsaw with three regiments of soldiers. From that time until his death in 1935, Pulsudski was a dictator in all but name. His regime was not entirely illiberal and elections continued to be held. After his death, army officers continued to rule, but with a viciousness which nearly provoked civil war. They admired the other dictatorships in Europe which seemed to function with an efficiency they could not achieve. And they fell victim to the efficiency of the German army in 1939.

Bulgaria, alone among the Central Powers, retained a monarchy after 1918. Until 1923 King Boris combined his monarchy with a curious peasant dictatorship led by Stamboliisky. Stamboliisky, himself of peasant origin, so organized the state that peasants got the maximum benefit at the expense of the rest of the community. He was murdered. His successors were usually nominated by the King. The country continued to be turbulent, frequently torn by the violent activities of the IMRO (Internal Macedonian Revolutionary Organization) who had a passion for assassinations. Not surprisingly, in 1934, a dictatorship of military officers came to power, with strongly fascist sympathies. The regime was further modified before the Second World War but such parliaments as were allowed had little power. Only the throne of King Boris was stable.

Albania became a monarchy. An attempt was made to set up a democratic republic in the years immediately after 1918 but the country had only existed since 1913 and there were serious economic problems. The first President of the Republic proclaimed himself King Zog I in 1928. His regime was close to dictatorship and, in any case, Italian Fascists were already preparing to take over Albania, but it was not until 1939 that Mussolini felt confident enough to chase Zog into exile.

In *Rumania* democracy might have succeeded, but the monarchy offered poor leadership, politicians were corrupt and in the 1930s the governments were often right wing and anti-Jewish. King Carol II paid little regard to popular wishes in choosing his ministers, swung from one group to another and only in 1938 arrived at the decision to devise a new constitution and to exercise more effective control through a Party of National Rebirth. It was too late. The country was soon under the control of Hitler.

Western Europe and *Scandinavia* showed greater abilities in working democratic systems of government but Spain and Portugal were unable to hold out against the general drift to dictatorship. *Portugal* had driven out her King in 1910 in favour of a democratic republic but economic backwardness, corruption and inefficiency proved stronger than the will to democracy and in 1926 the country fell to a military dictatorship. In 1932, Salazar became Prime Minister and, a year later, was confirmed in power by a new fascist constitution. Under Salazar, Portugal managed to remain apart from the rest of Europe, avoiding association with other dictators and concentrating on the economic improvements the country desperately needed.

Spain, in 1918, retained her monarchy. King Alfonso XIII paid some attention to the wishes of the Cortes (a parliament which mainly represented the propertied classes), but governments were weak and unstable. To economic backwardness was added a revolt in Spanish Morocco. Like Pilsudski in Poland, a military leader, Primo de Rivera, despaired of democratic inefficiency. In 1923, with the support of Alfonso and the powerful Catholic Church, he seized power.

The Cortes was dismissed and freedom curtailed. De Rivera injected new life into the economy, developed industry, provided work and improved communications. The Moroccan rebels were put down. But when he retired because of ill health and declining popularity, an attempt was made to re-establish democracy. Republicans had not forgiven the King for supporting the dictatorship. He was driven into exile and a republic proclaimed under President Zamora, with Azaña as Prime Minister. They vigorously attacked Spain's old problems, the powerful Catholic Church, the wealth of the property-owners and the influence of the army. For a time Spain had something like real democracy with a vote for all adults and a thorough attack on privilege.

For the republicans, however, the results were disappointing. In 1934 the elections showed a swing to the right and the new government began to undo much of Azaña's work. The workers went on strike in protest but were routed by the army with heavy casualties.

Elections in 1936 showed some return of support to the left-wing parties which united in a Popular Front, much influenced by Azaña, now President. On the right wing, fascists, influenced by the successes of Mussolini and Hitler, prepared to resist by force. On the left wing, communists, hopeful of support from Russia, were prepared to defend the government. Thus, the stage was set for the Spanish Civil War (see Section 5.2, page 97).

3.4 Why Did Democracy Not Succeed?

Economic problems partly answer this question. A democratic system must rest upon agreement. Poverty, unemployment and insecurity produce little incentive to agree. In post-1918 Europe, poverty and unemployment afflicted almost every country (see Unit Four), providing a powerful stimulus to discontent in countries such as Italy, Germany and Austria.

Democracy is also a sophisticated form of government. In Britain and the USA, democratic systems developed over a long period of time. In many European countries after 1918, the system had no roots, the people little experience of such a system. Germans, for example, were used to an authoritarian regime. Democracies which appeared perfect on paper, such as that of the Weimar Republic, often produced so many parties in parliament that stable government was impossible, and it was necessary to form coalitions. To get agreement within a coalition government usually meant avoiding controversial questions altogether; yet controversial questions demanded solutions. It was all too easy to believe a Mussolini or a Hitler who promised the action which was obviously lacking.

For several powers, moreover, democracy was associated with defeat in the recent war. Dollfuss in Austria, like Hitler, thought of the system as part of an Allied plot to impose an ineffective system of government and thus prevent any radical reversal of the Peace Settlement. Nationalists, such as Mussolini, had no patience with democratic systems which were ineffective in foreign policy, which did not impose their will by force.

Force, indeed, had more appeal in the post-1918 world than the Allied statesmen at Paris thought possible. Unit Eight will show how force was often applied in foreign policy, to the dismay of the League of Nations. The violence of the First World War not only left horror behind it but even some admiration and it divided Europe's statesmen into two camps, those like MacDonald and Neville Chamberlain who had a horror of war, and those like Mustapha Kemal and Mussolini to whom war could be a means to an end. The difference was often that between democracy and dictatorship.

Unit Five will take a closer look at the dictatorships which sprang up after

1918. Meanwhile Unit Four will examine some of the economic problems which faced the world between the wars, the rocks on which democracy often foundered.

Further Reading

Morgan, R.: *Modern Germany*. Hamish Hamilton (London, 1966), Chapters 4 and 5.
Musman, R.: *Hitler and Mussolini*. Chatto and Windus (London, 1968), includes accounts of the dictators' early lives.
Seaman, L. C. B.: *Post-Victorian Britain*. Methuen (London, 1967), includes a detailed history of Britain in the 1920s.
Tint, H.: *Modern France*. Hamish Hamilton (London, 1966), Chapters 8 and 9.
Watson, J. B.: *The Member for Eccles* (Central Library, Eccles, 1963), contains a potted history of British elections.

Documentary

Phillips, D. M.: *Hitler and the Rise of the Nazis*. Arnold (London, 1968).

Exercises

1. 'In the 1920s, politics in the USA and Britain involved two main parties, but in France more were involved.' How does this Unit illustrate the truth of this statement?
2. What reasons are suggested in this Unit for the survival of democracy in the USA, Britain and France?
3. 'A decade of violence.' How does this description of the 1920s apply to: the USA; Italy; Germany? Was Britain a less violent country? How do you account for this?
4. Why did democracy not survive in (*a*) Italy and (*b*) Germany?
5. Make a list of European dictators in the 1920s and 1930s, using the text of this Unit and Fig. 3.4. Arrange them in the order in which they came to power. Find out more about Mussolini, Hitler and one other dictator.

Unit Four
Economic Rocks, 1919–39

4.1 General Problems

Before 1914, an enormous expansion of industry had taken place which made the USA and some European countries richer than any others in the world. Individuals and nations pursued profits, and technological advances in production processes and communications held out the hope of ever-increasing wealth. The prosperous nations expected to grow more prosperous. Others envied them and struggled to catch up. Vigorous competition was the basis of the system. Nations competed with each other to obtain more raw materials from which to make manufactured goods, and to find new markets in which to sell them.

Production continued to expand after 1918; the world's output of manufactured goods almost doubled between 1918 and 1939. In this period, however, economic problems which had seemed of limited importance before the war became acute.

(a) Trade

Nations such as America and Russia had the advantage of size. They were big enough to be almost self-sufficient (able to supply the food and raw materials their populations needed). Other countries had to buy such supplies, paying for them with exported goods. For Britain, this had not been difficult in the nineteenth century although, even before 1914, increasing competition had caused problems about finding markets. After 1918 competition was even fiercer. The situation was worsened because countries defeated in the war were struggling to pay their debts and repair the devastation, and could not afford to import many manufactured goods.

Protection worsened the position further. Developing nations were accustomed to protecting their own infant industries with *tariffs* (imposing duties on foreign goods to make them more expensive). Widespread tariffs made the sale of exports more difficult. Britain was heavily dependent on international trade; she rejected tariffs as a hindrance and steadfastly refused to agree with the Dominions who wanted her to impose tariffs on goods from outside the Empire. After 1918 most countries preferred to protect their own industries while resenting the tariffs which other countries imposed. Britain persevered with free trade almost alone.

It was disastrous for Europeans that the USA also adopted protection (see Section 3.2). The USA was a wealthy customer, desperately needed by the rest of the world. But Republican America in the 1920s was concerned more with the prosperity of the USA than with the prosperity of Europe.

Faced with serious obstacles in selling their goods, producers hesitated to manufacture more. As a result, unemployment became a problem in many countries. Unit Three has already shown that high unemployment persisted in Britain, Italy and Germany after the First World War.

(b) Rich and Poor

Industrialization produced wealth, but it did not share out that wealth evenly. The result was resentment. Even before 1914 the conflict between rich and poor, between capital and labour, was producing violence in many countries, among them Britain, Russia and France. Industrial relations grew increasingly bitter. The workers wanted a fairer share of the wealth their work produced. They pressed their employers and governments for concessions, through trade unions (where they were permitted), through strikes and sometimes through demonstrations and rebellion. Frequently the workers turned to socialism and communism which held out the promise of a more equal distribution of wealth. The propertied classes almost invariably resisted, not infrequently turning to fascism with its seemingly attractive belief in discipline, law and order.

Vast differences in wealth existed between nations as well. In Europe envy and jealousy often embittered international relations. Mussolini and Hitler developed aggressive ambitions, partly as a means to increase national wealth. France resented and feared a return of German prosperity. In Asia, Japan was determined to grow rich like the white nations. And communist Russia worked with back-breaking fury to catch up with the capitalist powers.

Commissions of the League of Nations did their best, but before the Second World War little thought was given to the development of the world's wealth by co-operation. Attitudes were determined by economic nationalism: national prosperity almost invariably came first. Debtors were expected to pay what they owed. The rich intended to become richer.

(c) Confidence

Confidence was essential for the stable growth of prosperity. Unfortunately the world between 1918 and 1939 was far from stable. There was ideological conflict between capitalism and communism. International relations, especially in Europe, were often stormy (see Units Seven and Eight). Governments were frequently unstable. Even currencies wobbled, undermining confidence in money. The German and Austrian inflations of 1922-3 created near-panic: in the financial crisis of 1931 Ramsay MacDonald carried an inflated German bank-note as a dreadful warning of what, so he argued, might happen in Britain. The uncertainty discouraged financiers and businessmen from investing in industry. Expansion did continue but it was at a slower rate than before 1914. Thus, in the interwar period, nations were trapped in a vicious circle: selfishness and economic nationalism, protective tariffs, unemployment and inequalities of wealth created tensions; tensions undermined confidence; and without confidence, the basic problems remained unsolved.

4.2   The Particular Problems of Individual Countries

(a) The United States of America

The USA's prosperity in the 1920s was the envy of the world (see Section 3.2(a)). But it was not based on solid foundations. Industry and agriculture produced more goods than could be sold. America had much money invested overseas in countries which found repayment difficult since they were handicapped by American tariffs. Even within America the prosperity was denied to millions. President Hoover looked forward to an America with 'a chicken in every pot and two cars in every garage', but Republican governments did almost nothing to spread purchasing power evenly. Chickens and cars were produced. Neither in America nor in the rest of the world could enough people afford to buy them.

Over-production led to a slowing down of trade in the late 1920s. As goods remained unsold, production was cut back and men became unemployed. Accustomed by the boom years of the 1920s and the complacent speeches of politicians to an ever-expanding economy, Americans suddenly became less confident. Many of them were deeply in debt. They owed for goods bought on hire-purchase, for houses bought on mortgage. Five per cent of the population earned one-third of personal incomes in the USA and the majority of people had only limited resources or none at all. They now became unwilling to spend. Even so, enthusiastic speculation on the stock exchange continued well into 1929.

Many Americans had discovered what seemed to be a key to untold wealth: buying shares, often on borrowed money, and reselling them at a profit. While industry boomed and share prices rose, quick profits could be made. In September 1929, share prices ceased to rise. Confidence wavered. Some of those who held shares began to suspect that the prices were artificially high. Instead of a rush to buy shares (which forced up their price), there was a desire to sell them (which forced their price down). Many shareholders, having gambled with their savings and even borrowed to get the shares, panicked. The rush to sell forced prices still lower until, on 24 October, 13 million shares were sold.

Prices continued to plunge for two years. Thousands of shareholders were ruined. This collapse of the New York Stock Exchange (the Wall Street Crash) was a disaster not only for America but for the world. Debt and bankruptcy spread in all directions but most damaging of all was loss of confidence. The value of the shares had little direct relation to the industries they represented. They were no more than a claim to a share in the profits of those industries. But those who were ruined in the Wall Street Crash could not repay their debts and mortgages. They had to withdraw their savings from the banks. Banks and financial houses then felt the effects. Even fewer goods were sold in the shops, leading to more closures of factories and more unemployment. By the end of 1931 the USA had almost eight million unemployed and the figure was still rising. The trade recession of the late 1920s, prodded by the Wall Street Crash, became the Great Depression.

(b) Great Britain

From 1920 until the Second World War the level of unemployment in Britain never fell below one million. Exports in 1920 were valued at nearly £1 350 million. After that, they dropped dramatically. From 1919 until 1927 there were frequent and bitter industrial disputes which culminated in the General Strike. While, in 1939, the USA produced a third of the world's manufactured goods, Britain in that year produced less than 10 per cent and trailed behind both Russia and Germany. The decline was, however, only comparative. Britain as a whole remained a wealthy nation, although the wealth was unequally shared out, and the smallness of Britain made it inevitable that she would fall behind America and Russia. The complacency of successive governments, which did little in the period 1919–39 to tackle basic economic and social problems, stored up trouble for the future rather than producing an immediate decline in Britain's economic status.

(i) **Basic industries.** Britain's nineteenth-century superiority was based mainly on textiles, coal, iron, steel and heavy industries such as shipbuilding. It was these industries which suffered most in the highly-competitive world after 1918. In the coalfields, in the Lancashire textile towns, in shipbuilding areas such as the Clyde and Jarrow, the workers felt the full force of the difficulties, and the interwar years were years of hardship.

Markets lost during the war were not won back in many cases. British production costs were often too high to compete successfully. Countries which industrialized later than Britain or re-equipped their war-damaged industries with new machines after 1918, had an advantage over Britain, with its old-fashioned machinery and out-of-date plant. In new industries such as chemicals and motor-car manufacturing, Britain did better and areas such as the Midlands and the South East escaped many of the problems of the basic industries.

Coal-mining suffered most from the changes. Production fell from 287 million tons in 1913 to 220 million tons in 1934. In the same period, exports fell from 94 million to 53 million tons. There was strong competition from Germany and Poland. Russia also began to supply her own needs. There was competition, too, from oil. The percentage of coal-burning ships gradually declined in favour of oil-burning vessels.

Many British mines were small and uneconomic. The owners usually thought of producing coal more cheaply by paying lower wages. During the war, the mines had been under government control. The miners wished this to continue, and called for the nationalization of the pits. By the chairman's casting-vote, the Sankey Commission of 1919 recommended this, but Lloyd George rejected the idea because he knew it would be unpopular with his Conservative supporters (see page 44). For the next twenty years the industry was in depression. Industrial relations were bitter. Modernization proceeded slowly and, by 1937, still only about half of Britain's coal was cut by machine. The whole industry was generally demoralized by the low wages, unemployment and inefficiency. Other basic industries were not much better off.

(*ii*) **Exports and the balance of payments.** Coal was one of the few raw materials Britain produced. It was essential to export to pay for other raw materials which were needed, like grain, cotton, iron, timber and rubber. Until 1932, however, Britain persisted with a policy of free trade. This made it easier for foreign countries to sell to Britain than for Britain to sell abroad.

Interwar governments hardly reacted to this unhealthy situation, except during the crisis of the Great Depression. In 1925, Baldwin's government even made the situation worse. Having lost the election of 1923 on the issue of protection (see Section 3.2(*b*)), Baldwin abandoned his idea of departing from free trade but joined other European countries in linking the nation's currency to the price of gold. Others devalued their currencies but Winston Churchill, Baldwin's Chancellor of the Exchequer, fixed the value of the pound in relation to gold at only a fraction below the 1914 level. Other countries considered the pound was too expensive and, consequently, British exports were too expensive. In terms of Britain's trade, it was a costly attempt to gain prestige. Exports slumped after 1925 and, during the Great Depression, it was necessary to allow the pound to depreciate (float downwards) to a lower, less ambitious level.

The weakness of Britain's position was partially disguised by her invisible exports. These earnings from investments, services such as insurance and banking and the carrying trade continued to augment the earnings from the sales of exports. In the 1920s, Britain continued to enjoy a surplus on her balance of payments and in the 1930s went only occasionally into the red. Both the First and Second World Wars badly damaged her 'invisible exports', however, and it was a sign of trouble to come that, in 1938, Britain's overall balance of payments showed a deficit of £70 million.

(*iii*) **Industrial relations and the General Strike.** The Triple Industrial Alliance (an alliance of unions representing miners, railwaymen and transport workers) had been set up shortly before the war at a time of much bitterness in industrial relations. It was thought that such an alliance was powerful enough to force the authorities to pay attention to the grievances of the working classes. Before 1914, its strength remained untested. After the war, the miners soon called upon it to help them in their troubles.

In March 1921, the government ended the wartime control of the mines. The private owners promptly cut the pitmen's wages. When the miners resisted they were locked out. Unemployment had already soared well over the million mark and there was general unrest throughout industry. The miners called for a general strike and the government prepared a middle-class Defence Force. On *Black Friday*, 15 April, the Triple Alliance backed down. By the end of June, the pitmen accepted defeat. A general strike had been avoided but nearly 90 million working days were lost that year in industrial disputes. This was even worse than the turbulent pre-1914 period.

The workers felt cheated. The savage war had brought them few benefits. Politicians' promises were unfulfilled. Unemployment topped the two million mark and wages were generally low. The Bolshevik Revolution in Russia inflamed the class war. But the crisis passed, for the moment, and in the years 1923–5 the unemployment figures dropped slightly.

The coal industry, however, ran into new difficulties with vigorous competition from the German Ruhr coalfield. As usual, the owners saw salvation in a wage cut, coupled this time with lengthening the working day. Baldwin appointed a Commission of Inquiry under Samuel, which found no case for longer hours since the owners could not sell existing coal supplies. It recommended modernization of the industry and, for the time being, a rather less severe cut in wages than the owners wanted.

The coal-owners instantly seized on the recommendation that wages be cut. They had little interest in costly modernization. But the pitmen were determined: 'Not a Penny off the Pay, not a Minute on the Day'. The Trades Union Congress felt unable to desert the miners on this occasion but had made few preparations, resting on the woolly hope that a showdown could be avoided. Coal-owners and miners reached deadlock. The miners would not work for lower wages and the owners locked them out at the end of April 1926.

Without much enthusiasm, the TUC called a General Strike on 3 May. A visit to the Prime Minister at the last moment failed to save them: Baldwin had gone to bed.

The General Strike lasted for nine days. The miners' stoppage lasted for seven months. Middle-class volunteers worked with enthusiasm but not much efficiency to operate essential services, such as buses and trains. The TUC helped them, being reluctant to cause too much suffering. Churchill edited the *British Gazette* which, in the absence of the usual newspapers, tried to frighten the workers with charges of treason or something near it. Baldwin branded the strike as a challenge to 'the existing Constitution of the country' and as an attempt to 'substitute the reign of force' for the existing authority. The TUC defended itself in the *British Worker*: 'The General Council does not challenge the Constitution' but 'is engaged in an Industrial Dispute'. The strike, it argued, was to defend 'the mine-workers against the mine-owners'.

But the TUC defended the mine workers poorly for on 12 May it deserted them. Much influenced by J. H. Thomas, a leader of the railwaymen who had a great respect for authority, the TUC leadership called off the strike without any concessions from Baldwin. The miners' leaders were not consulted but neither Herbert Smith, the President, nor Arthur Cook, the Secretary of the Miners' Federation, would have agreed to the surrender. The Federation continued the strike alone but had to accept defeat at the end of the year when the pitmen returned, on the owners' terms.

The General Strike was remarkably free of violence. No one was killed. When it was called off, there was bitterness against the TUC leaders and for a time some workers (in addition to the miners) refused to go back to work. Some were victimized, in spite of promises to the contrary, and forced to join the unemployed. Ringleaders among the miners were similarly singled out. The working classes had been defeated and, for a time, trade union membership fell dramatically, from 5½ million in 1925 to 4½ million in 1932. Some argued that Baldwin had won a great victory for quiet and peaceable leadership. Certainly the class war seemed to die down after the strike. Over 162 million working days were lost in 1926 but the figure did not rise again above 10 million in any year before the Second World War. Many left-wingers turned from industrial action to political action, working to strengthen the Labour Party in parliament. The strike had little effect on the country's economy as a whole. Equally, it failed to prod complacent governments into action. The ever-present fear of unemployment continued to demoralize the working classes and within a few years the Great Depression caused unemployment figures to soar.

(c) Germany

Germany's main economic problems after 1918 were the same as those of other European countries: the transition from war to peace, finding markets for exports and jobs for her workers. In addition, Germany was required by the Treaty of Versailles to pay reparations (see Section 2.4 and Fig. 4.1). The figure finally agreed (136 000 million marks) seemed enormous. In fact, it was only a fraction of Germany's wealth. Reparations payments produced heated arguments but they did not produce economic disaster.

Reparations contributed to the lack of confidence in the German mark and thus to the inflation of 1923 (see Section 3.3). After 1924, Germany became more entangled in debts to the USA since, from the Dawes Plan of that year, Germany made her reparations payments with borrowed money. But reparations were unjustly blamed for weaknesses which already existed, and were used unscrupulously by German politicians to whip up discontent.

They were also used by the French as an excuse to invade the Ruhr in 1923 (see Section 3.3), creating turmoil which delayed Germany's economic recovery and quickened the inflation. When a new start was made in Germany under Stresemann, it was with American help. The Dawes Plan provided for foreign loans and laid down a new scale of payments which were then made regularly. In 1929 the Young Plan worked out a scheme for payments up to 1988 but cut the amount to be paid quite savagely; but the Plan was stillborn. With the beginning of the Great Depression, the world faced a general financial collapse and reparations payments were suspended. A new, low token figure was fixed at Lausanne in 1932, a mere 3 000 million marks. Nothing more was ever paid, however, for Hitler simply refused to accept the continuation of reparations.

Between 1924 and the end of reparations, Germany borrowed 18 000 million marks and paid back 11 000 million. Not until 1952 did Germany even agree to repay this profit on her reparations dealings. Meanwhile the loans had helped Germany to recover a measure of economic stability. They also pumped dollars into Europe, which helped to stimulate trade.

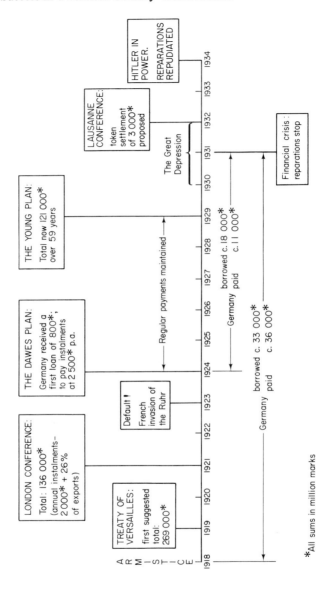

Fig. 4.1 German reparations

4.3   The Great Depression

The trade depression at the end of the 1920s shattered whatever confidence was beginning to grow in Europe. In 1929, there was a trade recession in America and it spread rapidly to the rest of the world. Unsold goods accumulated. Production slowed down and stopped. Producers of coffee in Brazil could find no better use for their beans than as fuel for railway engines. Tons of grain rotted in America and other farming areas. With factories falling silent, unemployment figures began to rise. There was even less money in the pockets of the unemployed, so even fewer goods were sold.

A financial crisis quickly developed from the trade depression. Just as individuals had to draw on their savings, so creditor nations looked for the repayment of outstanding debts. Feeding on the panic produced by the Wall Street Crash, Americans tried to recover money they had loaned to Europe. There was an all-round demand for money, often in the form of gold. Banks began to totter as their reserves drained away and in May 1931 Credit Anstalt, Austria's leading bank, had to close. Driven to further panic by their losses in Austria, financiers put pressure on other banks. There was a swift loss of confidence in Germany. The German Reichsbank was seriously weakened and within weeks the crisis spread to London, with a run on the reserves of the Bank of England. Stirred by almost irrelevant memories of the German inflation of 1922–3 (irrelevant since the problem was now one of deflation, not inflation: prices were very low, not high), Europeans had a general distrust of paper money. In this crisis of confidence, they wanted gold and few countries outside America had large gold reserves.

The close relationships of banks such as the Bank of England and the German Reichsbank to governments inevitably produced political crises. Would governments be strong enough to weather the storm? Democracy, where it still survived, was sorely tested. It seemed to be essential to governments, such as MacDonald's in Britain, to practise thrift. For one thing, American financiers insisted on it. With dwindling reserves, the Bank of England desperately needed help and, in the summer of 1931, only the USA was still strong enough to give it. First, however, the Americans insisted that the British government should reduce its spending. A series of committees drew a gloomy picture of Britain's economic position and, at the end of July, the May Report recommended increases in taxation and fierce cuts in expenditure. Otherwise, it was suggested, the British government would go bankrupt. The cuts were made, especially in unemployment benefits. American loans rescued the Bank of England and the financial crisis subsided, helped by the *Hoover Moratorium* of June 1931 (which imposed a standstill on the settlement of debts between governments). Nevertheless, the strain was too much for Britain's Labour government which resigned in August (see Section 3.2, page 49). The strains in Germany resulted in the destruction of the Weimar Republic (see Section 3.3).

The crises of 1929 onwards were, therefore, not merely concerned with unemployment. But the economies thought necessary to overcome the financial crisis made unemployment worse by reducing purchasing power still further.

Fig. 4.2 The search for work: men queue anxiously for jobs at a Birmingham labour exchange during the Depression in 1930

By 1932, unemployment figures were nearing 14 million in America, 6 million in Germany and 3 million in Britain. Although the position was less serious in Britain, production in the USA and Germany had been cut almost in half since 1929. Recovery would take many years.

4.4 The Effects of the Great Depression and Recovery

(a) The United States of America

Hoover's Presidency was disastrous for the Republicans. His name came to be associated with *Hoovervilles*, the squalid shelters built by unemployed ex-servicemen who flocked to Washington in 1932 to demand government aid. Demonstrators produced placards with the slogan, 'In Hoover we trusted. Now we are busted.' Hoover produced a feeble programme of public works and unemployment relief, but it was still a Republican belief that the government should not interfere with 'rugged individualism'. They paid a heavy price in the Presidential election of 1932 and won only six states.

Franklin Delano Roosevelt romped home as the new President, with the largest majority ever known. He was the first Democrat to become President since Woodrow Wilson. He remained in office until his death in 1945, being re-elected in 1936, 1940 and 1944. His immediate aim was to restore confidence in banks, in business and in spending. 'The only thing we have to fear is fear itself,' he said. He pledged his party, as he pledged himself, 'to a new deal for the American people'. 'Action, and action now' became his government's motto.

Roosevelt took office at the beginning of 1933. He began with a vigorous period of a *Hundred Days* to tackle immediate problems, programmed a *First New Deal* from 1933 to 1935 to set the country on the road to recovery and a *Second New Deal* from 1935 to 1939, mainly to expand the welfare services. This vigorous government was popular but not with some industrialists and Republicans, who were bitterly hostile to such governmental activity, accused Roosevelt of socialism and tried to use the Supreme Court to block some of the new laws by declaring them 'unconstitutional'.

(*i*) **The Hundred Days** did much to restore confidence in the banks, which were closed while experts examined their accounts. The Emergency Banking Act then forced weak banks out of business and gave government backing to sound ones so that when the banks reopened, they were again trusted. A Federal Emergency Relief Administration was set up to help the unemployed and the poor; it did not distribute charity but provided work. At the same time, Roosevelt aimed to win the confidence of businessmen by cutting some of the government's spending. The Economy Act reduced pensions and the salaries of state employees. Americans were impressed most of all by the new

Fig. 4.3 'FINIS'—Roosevelt bustles into office and Hoover departs, leaving his slogans to the trashcan. Philadelphia Daily News, *3 March 1933*

Fig. 4.4 The End of Prohibition: the queue outside the Board of Health offices in New York for licences to sell beer

bustle in government offices. Lights burned late. Prohibition was swept aside and an attack made on corruption.

(*ii*) **The First New Deal** kept up the pace. The Civilian Conservation Corps (CCC) found work for the young in reforestation projects, planting trees and strengthening river banks. The Civil Works Administration (CWA), later the Works Progress Administration (WPA), combined relief for the unemployed with work of public value. At first, money was often paid out for very little work, to increase purchasing power, but later the WPA built roads and schools, and even organized painters and actors into activities which enabled them to earn. The National Industrial Recovery Act regulated conditions of work, forbade child labour, encouraged trade unions and created the Public Works Administration for major projects. The WPA built the Hoover Dam on the Colorado River. Even more ambitious was the Tennessee Valley Authority (TVA) to tame the Tennessee River and use its waters for irrigation, shipping and hydro-electric power. The TVA cut into the authority of seven state governments and there was some resentment of this federal interference from Washington, but Roosevelt was concerned with national well-being, not sectional interests. Through the activities of all these various bodies, the 'alphabet agencies', the Depression began to lift. There was money to buy goods and factories returned to a higher level of production. But the USA did not regain its former prosperity until about 1940.

Meanwhile, the First New Deal gave special assistance to farmers. The Agricultural Adjustment Administration (AAA) set out to increase their earnings. With the help of government subsidies, farmers were encouraged to reduce their output. A smaller output of grain, cotton and other produce would make prices rise and farming would become profitable. The scheme was drastic, but it worked. Farmers were also encouraged to use more modern methods and machinery. The hungry found it hard to see the logic of destroying food but Roosevelt's work strengthened American agriculture.

Most of the new organizations dated from 1933 and in that year Roosevelt also introduced the Home Owners' Loan Corporation which helped the poor to overcome their difficulties in repaying mortgages.

(*iii*) **The Second New Deal** placed more emphasis on helping the poor. The government's efforts to provide work continued, especially through the WPA. The Social Security Act of 1935 was passed, introducing insurance against unemployment for millions of workers. It also provided pensions for the old, widowed and maimed. The USA still lagged behind the most advanced nations in welfare services but the Social Security Act was a major breakthrough.

In the election of 1936, Roosevelt won support in every state but two. Shortly afterwards, the President tackled the problem of the Supreme Court which had several times proved hostile to parts of the New Deal. Congress refused to agree to his proposal to create additional members of the Court to outvote his opponents there. Some things even Roosevelt could not do, but the Court learned its lesson and gave him little further trouble.

The Second New Deal therefore went on. At the same time, Roosevelt strengthened American democracy. 'People who are hungry and out of a job,' he said, 'are the stuff of which dictatorships are made.' He believed that trade unions should be strong enough to protect their members and the Wagner Act of 1935 gave them protection. Hours of work and wages were regulated by the Fair Labour Standards Act of 1938. The National Housing Act of 1937 set aside government money for homes and attacked rents which were too high. Monopolies were investigated to protect the consumer and small businesses which found it difficult to compete with the giants. In 1940, Roosevelt was re-elected as President, defeating Wendell Wilkie, although his victory was less decisive than in former years.

Roosevelt had not intended to seek further office, for it was a tradition that Presidents did not serve a third term. But in 1940 there was war in Europe and in Asia. America was not yet involved but at this moment the country needed Roosevelt's leadership. The Democrats had not done well in the Congressional elections of 1938 but the country still had faith in Roosevelt as President.

Roosevelt's foreign policy before 1940 differed little from that of the Republicans in the 1920s. He made some limited changes, recognizing the USSR and then launching a 'Good Neighbour Policy' with Latin America in 1935. He himself visited South America, spreading goodwill and promoting trade and defence agreements. But towards Europe, the USA remained cool. A series of Neutrality Laws in 1935 and 1937 aimed to sever connexions with countries which might go to war although Roosevelt himself was not indifferent to the aggression taking place in the Pacific and in Europe (see Unit Eight).

He was eventually to lead the USA into war against the dictators and the aggressors (see Unit Nine).

(b) Great Britain

Britain was ruled by National governments from August 1931. MacDonald's acceptance of office as Prime Minister of a National government (see Section 3.2, page 49) began a period of conservatism, for although governments were coalitions in theory, they were Conservative in practice. MacDonald remained Prime Minister until June 1935; Baldwin succeeded him until his retirement in 1937 and from then until 1940, Neville Chamberlain led the government. Britain had no New Deal so recovery was slow and painful. Unemployment did not fall below two million until 1936 and it remained obstinately high until the war. Exports were similarly slow to recover and were always lower than in the 1920s.

(i) **Economic policies.** Much that the National government did was accidental. It abandoned the gold standard in September 1931 to stop the drain on gold reserves, although MacDonald had intended to preserve it as an aid to confidence. Again almost accidentally, the government introduced a policy of cheap money. Interest rates on government stock were cut to $3\frac{1}{2}$ per cent to reduce the government's interest payments. This set a new low level of borrowing rates and did a little to stimulate business activity. At the same time, the government was intent on reducing spending. Almost nothing was done to follow Roosevelt's lead, his ambitious schemes to provide work. The National Government wished to please the financiers, balance its budget and avoid all accusations of recklessness and extravagance (see Fig. 4.5).

In 1932, Britain abandoned free trade. A 10 per cent duty was placed on most foreign goods. It was soon raised to 20 per cent, but it was not applied to food, raw materials and Commonwealth produce. An attempt was made to promote trade agreements within the Commonwealth (see Section 6.2(a)), but with limited success. Britain had at last come into line with the rest of the world but the tariffs were too low to be very effective, and the Depression still hung over her basic industries.

Government money to promote industrial activity was issued with the utmost caution. In 1936, there were subsidies to tramp-shipping and Cunard was helped to build the luxury liner, *Queen Mary*. Special Areas Acts, the first in 1934, made a feeble effort to encourage production in the depressed areas but provided very little money for the purpose. In 1938, mining royalties were nationalized to relieve some of the difficulties of the coal industry and the thousand mining companies were encouraged to join together in larger units. A year later, Chamberlain's government set up the British Overseas Airways Corporation (BOAC), showing a willingness to consider the sort of economic planning and control which Keynes and other economists considered essential. Their advice was welcomed by the Labour Party but, on the whole, it found little favour with the government.

| USA | | | | BRITAIN | | | |
UNEMPLOYED (Millions)	GOVERNMENT INCOME *	GOVERNMENT EXPENDITURE *	YEAR	YEAR	GOVERNMENT INCOME ⊖	GOVERNMENT EXPENDITURE ⊖	UNEMPLOYED (Millions)
	4·0	3·1	1928	1928–9	C 836	818	1·2
	4·0	3·3	1929	1929–30	N 734●	749	1·2
4·3	4·2	3·4	1930	1930–1	A 776●	799	1·9
8·0	3·1 ●	3·5	1931	1931–2	U 770	770	2·7
12·0	1·9 ●●	4·6	1932	1932–3	N 745●	777	2·7
12·8	2·0 ●●	4·6	1933	1933–4	A 699	697	2·5
11·3	3·0 ●●	6·7	1934	1934–5	T 716	689	2·2
10·6	3·7 ●●	6·5	1935	1935–6	I 753	750	2·0
9·0	4·0 ●●	8·2	1936	1936–7	O 797●	803	1·8
7·7	4·8 ●●	7·6	1937	1937–8	N 876	847	1·5
10·4	5·5 ●●	6·8	1938	1938–9	L 945	944	1·8
9·5	4·9 ●●	8·7	1939	1939–40		W A R	
8·1	5·1 ●●	8·8	1940	1940–1			
	W A R		1941	1941–2			

(USA government party shown vertically: REPUBLICAN / DEMOCRAT; Britain government shown vertically: CONSERVATIVE / NATIONAL)

*Thousand million dollars   ⊖ £s million

USA: Government spending in the New Deals   ● Budget deficit   ●● Major budget deficit   BRITAIN: The financial orthodoxy of balanced budgets

Fig. 4.5 The USA and Britain: unemployment and government spending, 1928–40. British governments remained reluctant to spend to cure the Depression

A revival in house-building did something to break the grip of the Depression but that owed almost nothing to the government. Wheatley's Housing Act (see Section 3.2, page 46) was scrapped in 1933 although new legislation in that year and in 1935 encouraged some slum clearance work. Fortunately builders found a market for private houses, which could be bought through building societies, and their activities helped to provide work for some of the unemployed.

(*ii*) **Social policies.** The most-detested measure introduced by the National government was the Means Test. On top of the cuts in unemployment benefit imposed in 1931 (but restored in 1934), the unemployed were required to reveal the income of the entire family. If the family's means were sufficient, the dole could be cut or stopped. This enabled the government to pursue its passion for saving money, but at the expense of the pride of those jobless who now found themselves supported by wives and children. The system of the dole and the means test became a little less harsh in the later 1930s but for the long-term unemployed these were bitter years.

The 1930s were not unprosperous for those with a steady income. Prices remained low. The new consumer industries, making such goods as wirelesses and gramophones, and exciting new entertainments such as the cinema, coupled with expanding home ownership, left many unaware of the hardships of distressed areas. From the latter, in the Jarrow Crusade of 1936 for example, the jobless marched to London to seek assistance. Such Hunger Marches brought charity from the middle classes, but the government was less responsive.

The years before the Second World War were remarkable mainly for governmental inactivity. Only occasionally did the National government rouse itself to significant action: in 1938 the Holidays with Pay Act made it legal to have a week's paid holiday each year. But the lengthy and unpaid holidays of a million-and-a-half unemployed continued.

(*iii*) **Retirements.** The Statute of Westminster (1931) went a long way to satisfying the Dominions (see Section 6.2). The India Act (1935) went a little way to satisfying India (see Section 6.2(*c*)). MacDonald had continued to show an interest in the outside world. He resigned in 1935 and, a year later, Baldwin considered it a triumph and a fitting seal on his years in politics that he managed a peaceful change of the monarchy. He too resigned when Edward VIII had abdicated (to go through with a marriage thought unsuitable by the Archbishop of Canterbury) and George VI was safely on the throne. MacDonald died in 1937. An outcast from the Labour Party since his political somersault of 1931, he had been abused and defeated in the election campaign of 1935. If his National government of 1931 had, as he believed, saved the country from complete disaster, it had also done much to wreck the Labour Party. In the election of 1935, the party won 158 seats and for it, too, recovery from the Depression was slow.

(*iv*) **Foreign policy.** Britain in the 1930s was deeply involved in European affairs (see Unit Eight). There were problems in the Commonwealth, especially in India and Ireland, and a heavy burden had to be carried in the League of Nations. It seemed to be the final failure of the National government that Britain became involved in the Second World War in 1939.

Britain was slow to react to the growing might of the continental dictators. Pacifism was strong in the Labour Party, and the National government was reluctant to spend money. Baldwin had accepted the need for rearmament in 1936 but began hesitantly. Chamberlain stepped up the programme although the results were still disappointing, both in terms of jobs and military strength.

(*v*) **Democracy and fascism.** Britain was reluctant to arm against continental fascists, but fascists in Britain showed little sign of overturning British democracy. From 1931 until 1939 there was a British Union, a fascist movement which condemned free speech, was anti-Jewish but showed an enthusiasm for the Commonwealth. Its leader was Oswald Mosley, who left the Labour Party in 1931, having previously left the Conservatives. He visited Italy in 1932 and returned with an admiration for Mussolini and a passion for black shirts. In a book *The Greater Britain*, he advocated the strong government which Britain did not apparently want.

But the violence and extremism of fascism did not appeal to the British. Like the communists, the British Union of Fascists attracted only a minority. There were clashes of extremists in Hyde Park; the fascists created disorder in East London, but by the late 1930s their support fell away. The British were fairly content with the tranquil administrations of MacDonald, Baldwin and Chamberlain, at least until they were shaken by the outbreak of war.

(c) The Totalitarian Powers

The Great Depression had little effect on Soviet Russia, already largely isolated. In Germany, it enabled Hitler to come to power (see Section 3.3, page 60). It had a similar effect in Austria (see page 61). In Italy, Mussolini countered its effects with a Battle for the Lira, a Battle for Grain and even a Battle for Births (see Section 5.2, page 93). Japan turned to aggression in Manchuria (see Section 8.1).

Democracy was weaker, totalitarianism stronger, as a result of the Depression. The history of the major totalitarian powers is treated in the next Unit.

Further Reading

Ayling, S. E.: *Portraits of Power*. Harrap (London, 1965)—Roosevelt.
Cootes, R. J.: *The General Strike, 1926*. Longman (Harlow, 1964).
Hill, C. P.: *Franklin Roosevelt*. Oxford University Press (London, 1966).
Hill, C. P.: *Franklin Roosevelt and the New Deal*. Arnold (London, 1975).
O'Callaghan, D. B.: *Roosevelt and the United States*. Longman (Harlow, 1966).
Seaman, L. C. B.: *Post-Victorian Britain*. Methuen (London, 1967).
Seaman, L. C. B.: *Life in Britain Between the Wars*. Batsford (London, 1970).

Documentary

Bettey, J. H.: *English Historical Documents 1906–1939*. Routledge & Kegan Paul (London, 1967) includes texts on the mining industry and the General Strike.
Lane, P.: *Documents on British Economic and Social History 1870–1939*. Macmillan (London, 1968).
Mowat, C. L.: *The General Strike*. Oxford University Press (London, 1966).
Yass, M.: *The Great Depression*. Wayland (London, 1970).

Exercises

1. What is the meaning of each of the following terms: Balance of Payments; Depression; Inflation; Deflation?
2. How did the following come to be combined in Britain in 1931: the trade depression, a financial crisis and a political crisis?
3. What points about government policies are illustrated by Fig. 4.5?
4. Explain how troubles in the mining industry led to a General Strike in Britain.
5. How did Roosevelt's policies for dealing with the Depression differ from those of the National government in Britain?
6. Using this Unit and Unit Five, show how Hitler and Mussolini tried to deal with the Depression.
7. Using Fig. 4.1 and the Index, outline the history of German reparations.
8. Why was Russia so little affected by the Depression?
9. Discover how the unemployed suffered in Britain in the 1930s. (See, for example, George Orwell, *The Road to Wigan Pier*. Penguin (Harmondsworth, 1970).)

Unit Five
The Totalitarian States: the Alternatives to Democracy

5.1 Communism

Two firmly-held beliefs gave strength to communists. They were convinced that communist systems would one day succeed everywhere; and they believed that a co-operative communist society offered the highest form of civilization. They drew inspiration from the writings of Karl Marx who, in the *Communist Manifesto* of 1848 wrote: 'What the bourgeoisie produces above all is its own gravediggers'. He argued that history was a series of conflicts out of which new societies developed. In Marx's time, industrial development was producing bourgeois (middle-class) capitalism which he saw as a greedy, competitive free-for-all in which the workers were exploited for the profit of the bourgeoisie. The workers (the proletariat) would eventually be the gravediggers of this system, overthrowing it in violent revolution and putting in its place a communist society. The new society would be based on co-operation and equality, free from exploitation, in such harmony that eventually government itself would wither away, being no longer needed. When all states became communist, there would be world harmony and no more wars.

The greater the advance of industrialism and capitalism, Marx believed, the greater the class strife and the nearer the proletarian revolution. When Marx died in 1883, he expected the revolution to come first in Britain or Germany, the two most industrialized nations. But the first successful communist revolution occurred in Russia, in 1917.

(a) Russia: the Revolutions

Russia under Tsar Nicholas II was corrupt, inefficient and lagging behind Western Europe in almost every form of development. During the First World War the country suffered heavy military defeats by the Germans. Russia was accustomed to hunger, poverty and savage repression, but in 1917 discontent reached a new peak.

Only the Tsar really mattered in the system of government. He had reigned since 1894, a period littered with disasters and stupidities. He had ignored all advice and refused any real partnership with the *Duma* (a toothless parliament which he had been forced to accept in 1906). When he left his capital in March 1917, vague as ever about whether to inject energy into the war effort or merely to rest and play dominoes, there was sudden agreement in St Petersburg (Petrograd) and other towns that his rule must end. Railway workers halted his train at Pskov. In Petrograd the army, diluted with discontented conscripts, sided with the rioters. Nicholas abdicated on 15 March.

The Revolution was unplanned. It was simply an explosion of deep anger with Tsarism. A scramble for power was now inevitable. First in line were the mainly middle-class members of the Duma. A Duma Committee was set up under Prince Lvov to act as a provisional government. They had hoped to set up a democratic monarchy like that in Britain but the Grand Duke Michael Alexandrovitch, Nicholas's brother, refused to be a puppet king. Russia then became a republic. The Provisional Government intended to hold a constituent assembly to draw up a new constitution but it was frequently postponed.

The Petrograd Soviet, a Council of Workers', Peasants' and Soldiers' Deputies, was another important body. There was an uneasy relationship between the Soviet and the Provisional Government, although a few men were members of both, Kerensky outstanding amongst them. His influence grew and, in July 1917, he became Prime Minister and Lvov retired.

Kerensky was a socialist but also a democrat. His aim was a democratic republic, an aim supported by the middle classes mainly through the party known as Kadets (KDs, constitutional democrats). Stronger in the Petrograd Soviet and in Soviets elsewhere were the Socialist Revolutionaries (SRs), a party long given to violence, close to the peasants, but often incoherent in their aims. Marxists were also numerous and influential in the Soviets. Although known as Socialist Democrats (SDs), they had little faith in western democracy. One group of SDs, the Bolsheviks, was dedicated to communist revolution. The other SDs, the Mensheviks, were less fanatical but Marxists nevertheless. SRs and SDs were critical of the Provisional Government but uncertain as to their own roles.

Vladimir Lenin, leader of the Bolsheviks, was not uncertain. He had been surprised by the suddenness of the March Revolution. He could not get back to Russia from exile in Switzerland until April 1917, but promptly produced his *April Theses*. At first they astounded even the Bolsheviks. The time had come, Lenin argued, for the proletariat to take control, to destroy bourgeois capitalism in Russia. (Compared with the West, Russia had so far seen little bourgeois capitalism: Tsarist Russia was mainly agricultural and peasant, a more primitive form of society.) But Lenin convinced the Bolsheviks and even some of the Mensheviks such as Leon Trotsky. While Lenin adapted Marxism to Russia (*Marxism–Leninism*), he also planned the Bolshevik strategy, seizing on two slogans: 'Peace, Bread and Land' and 'All Power to the Soviets'. The first had a wide appeal especially to poverty-stricken peasants.

The Provisional Government had continued the war, hoping vainly for a victory to restore Russian morale. They also postponed settlement of the land problem until the Constituent Assembly could meet. The Revolution therefore brought little immediate relief, and discontent continued. Lenin whipped up the hope that the Soviets could do better, although the Bolsheviks were not yet strong enough to dominate the Petrograd Soviet or the congresses of soviets which met from time to time. They must wait until their own strength grew.

For most of 1917 Russia remained unstable and sometimes violent. There were army mutinies, strikes and riots, especially in Petrograd. The Bolsheviks were blamed for an outbreak of violence in July (the July Days), their leaders arrested and Lenin forced to flee. Kerensky's government, however, was weak and unconvincing, taking too long to establish democracy and produce results. In August, forces on the right wing under General Kornilov made a bid for power, intent on bringing discipline to Russia, hanging Bolsheviks and troublemakers, stamping out strikes, strengthening the army and preserving the authority of landlords. They failed, but Kerensky had to rely on the left to help him and left-wing extremism began to flourish again.

Support for the Bolsheviks grew and, in November, Lenin felt they were ready. He returned secretly from exile. On the eve of a meeting of the All-Russian Congress of Soviets, Bolsheviks seized control of Petrograd. They had a tiny majority in the Congress and won support from some of the SRs. The Congress became a law-making body and the right to govern was conferred on a Council of People's Commissars (Sovnarcom) of which Lenin was Chairman. With very little bloodshed, power had passed to the Soviets and to the Bolsheviks. A week later their rule was accepted in Moscow.

(b) Lenin's Government 1917–24

(i) **1917–18.** The Bolsheviks at once produced a flood of decrees. The Decree on Land seized 540 million acres, without compensation, from private landlords and the church, to be shared out among poor peasants. A Supreme Council of National Economy was created to plan the economy. Banking and foreign trade were nationalized. Comprehensive social insurance was planned. Wages were fixed, an eight-hour day introduced, foreign debts repudiated. Such activity was in marked contrast to Kerensky's government.

Priority was also given to making peace with Germany and the Treaty of Brest-Litovsk was signed (see Section 2.8).

The Constituent Assembly met in January 1918, but Bolsheviks got less than a quarter of the votes. The majority of Russians had voted for democratic socialism or for the SRs. KDs had already been outlawed and the Assembly met with armed revolutionary sailors in the gallery and surrounded by troops. A Sovnarcom decree abolished it on its second day. To transform Russian society into a communist one, the Bolsheviks intended to rule with a dictatorship, 'the dictatorship of the proletariat', through Sovnarcom and the Congress.

But 1918 brought further chaos. The economy was already in ruins. There was inflation: like Kerensky the Bolsheviks paid their way by printing banknotes. There were food shortages: the peasants had bourgeois ambitions and wanted to make profits, not simply to feed the towns out of a duty to society. The Bolsheviks had to requisition grain and direct labour and, with workers seizing control, there was anarchy in many factories.

The Bolsheviks were too ambitious. With a flood of decrees, they hoped to make Russia communist. Private inheritance was abolished in April 1918, all major industries nationalized in June, mortgages cancelled in August. By that time, however, there was civil war. For a time, Lenin's government tried to impose War Communism. They nationalized smaller industries at the end of

1918, put the peasants under state control, seized their surplus crops and fixed official prices. They also created the *Cheka* (a committee for fighting counter-revolution) under Dzerzhinsky. It came to employ a staff of 30 000 and its own army. As a political police force, its main purpose was to keep the Bolsheviks in power. Some Bolshevik leaders were assassinated and Lenin himself was wounded in August 1918; the Cheka struck back with 'a mass red terror' to deal with 'the bourgeoisie and its agents'.

A new constitution in July 1918 consolidated the system the Bolsheviks had created. Russia became the Russian Soviet Federal Socialist Republic (RSFSR). The constitution made no mention of the Communist Party nor of the Cheka. But like the KDs, other parties were gradually eliminated, first the Mensheviks and finally even the left-wing SRs who had helped the Bolsheviks in November 1917. Thus Russia became a one-party state. Moscow was its new capital.

(*ii*) **Civil war: the wars of intervention, 1918–21.** Resistance to the Bolshevik Revolution began in Russia as early as December 1917, and by the summer, hostile *White* governments were proclaimed at Samara, Omsk and Archangel. Supporters of the Tsar, of landlords and of democracy and all anticommunists rallied to them, as did foreign powers who feared the spread of communism which Lenin so confidently expected. The Allies were angry that Russia had withdrawn from the war so troops arrived from Britain, the USA and Japan to help the Whites. Before long French and Germans joined in. Communist Red Guards were rapidly expanded to make a *Red Army*, brilliantly led by Trotsky, but it seemed unlikely that the Bolsheviks could survive. At one time, they held little but Petrograd, Moscow and the industrial areas west of the Urals.

The armies involved in the struggle were never large and major battles were few. The intervention of the capitalist powers was half-hearted and the Whites lacked unity. Their popularity with landlords made them unpopular with peasants, and their association with capitalist interventionists was regarded as treacherous, part of a plot perhaps to exploit Russia's resources during her troubles. There was great cruelty on both sides, with White atrocities at least as great as the ruthlessness of the Cheka. By the end of 1920, the civil war faded out leaving Russia in even greater economic ruin. Meanwhile Nicholas II and the royal family vanished, presumably murdered by Bolsheviks in Ekaterinburg.

The Bolsheviks were still denied peace, for Poland launched an attack and, in May 1920, advanced as far as Kiev. The Red Army rallied again, chased the Poles almost to Warsaw and were stopped only when the French sent General Weygand to assist Pilsudski. By the Treaty of Riga, Russia surrendered extensive parts of White Russia and the Ukraine to Poland, lands which Stalin recovered through a deal with Hitler in 1939.

(*iii*) **1921–4.** In March 1921, the Kronstadt sailors, previously loyal Bolsheviks, raised a new cry: 'Soviets without Communists'. They were routed in ten days

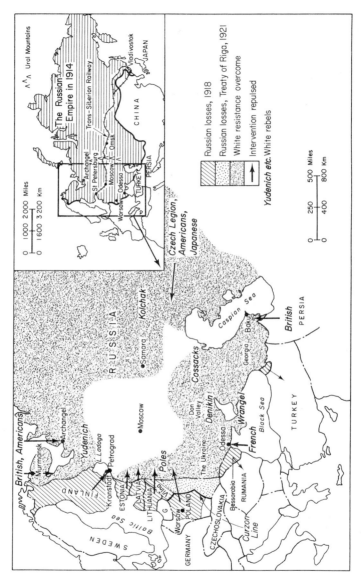

Fig. 5.1 Civil war and wars of intervention in Russia, 1918–21

of bloodshed but for Lenin it was 'the flash that lit up reality'. Faced with economic chaos, seething discontent and a cry for a Third Revolution even among those once loyal, Lenin had to compromise to save communism in Russia. He had to water down Russian Marxism and allow time for the Russian people to be educated to understand and accept true communism. At no time had the Bolsheviks had the mass support of Russians. Peasant support for 'Peace, Bread and Land' was support for peasant ownership, not the nationalization of land. By the New Economic Policy (NEP), Lenin accepted some return to private enterprise. Peasants were allowed, after tax, to sell surplus crops; some private trading was allowed; small factories were denationalized together with some banks. Incentives and bonuses were introduced. Individuals were able to prosper again, and some peasants built up large and profitable farms. These men were the *kulaks*, who were hostile to communism. NEP did a lot to restore stability to Russia but it was a marked retreat from the full-blooded War Communism of 1918–21.

Lenin also sought contacts with foreign powers. By the end of 1921 he had made trade pacts with fourteen countries including Britain, Finland and Turkey. In 1922, a treaty of friendship was made with Germany, the Treaty of Rapallo. In 1924, the Communist government was recognized by many European countries, including the Labour government in Britain (see Section 3.2, page 46).

Russia also had a new constitution in 1923 which owed much to Stalin. The state became known as the Union of Soviet Socialist Republics (USSR). All adults had the right to vote for a local soviet. Elections to higher levels were indirect and the system of 1918 remained basically unaltered. The Congress of Soviets remained the law-making body. The People's Commissars, invariably communist, continued to rule. Although the Cheka had in theory been wound up, there was still a political police force, known now as OGPU. It gave Russia effective government although, in western eyes, an undemocratic one.

Lenin died in 1924. He had been a professional revolutionary for most of his life and was in exile for almost all of the years from 1900 to 1917. He was remembered with near-devotion by millions: his body was embalmed and Petrograd was renamed Leningrad. With Marx, he shares a place of honour among communists everywhere. Above all, Lenin gave Russia hope in the stormy years of 1917–24. There would be no return to Tsarism but the task of establishing real communism still remained to be tackled. One communist historian has suggested that that could take two hundred years.

(c) Stalin's Government 1924–53

(*i*) **The struggle for power.** Unlike Lenin, Josef Stalin was of peasant birth. He returned from exile in Siberia in March 1917, to edit *Pravda*, the Bolshevik paper. He became Commissar for Nationalities in Lenin's Government, then Secretary-General of the Communist Party in 1922. As Commissar, he had much success in holding together the union of Russian states, using force in

Fig. 5.2 Lenin and Stalin: Lenin had grave misgivings about allowing Stalin to come to power

his native Georgia and elsewhere. As Secretary, he built up great personal power within the party, adding to the prestige he had won in the Civil War. Lenin, always modest and personally unambitious, had distrusted Stalin as 'the crafty Georgian', hoping to be succeeded as ruler of Russia by Leon Trotsky.

Trotsky shared many of Lenin's idea. He believed in world revolution to spread communism and had a similar dislike of personal advancement. Under Lenin, he served as Commissar for Foreign Affairs, then Commissar for War to organize the Red Army in the Civil War. Trotsky himself might have been Chairman of the People's Commissars in 1918 but he was Jewish and he preferred to accept the leadership of Lenin lest anti-Semitism should rise against the Bolsheviks. When Lenin died, a coalition of Stalin, Kamenev and Zinoviev made sure that Trotsky did not succeed him.

Stalin had no time for the intellectual arguments on which Trotsky thrived. It was his aim to rid the Communist Party of argument and to pursue the policy of 'Socialism in One Country' (to make Russia strong and self-sufficient, to avoid becoming entangled in international revolutions and to enforce obedience in Russia). Full communism could later grow out of that obedience. Stalin's first aim was to smash the influence of Trotsky and, in 1929, Trotsky was exiled to Turkey. (He later went to France and wrote a lengthy *History of the Revolution*, underwriting his own part in it; but his continued hostility to Stalin's policies was fatal. In 1940, in Mexico, he was killed by a Stalinist agent with an ice-pick.)

Meanwhile, Stalin overcame all opposition to his rule. Kamenev and Zinoviev were also expelled from the party in 1927 for urging rapid industrialization and an attack on the kulaks. Stalin found new allies such as Bukharin, but then turned on them. From about 1928, Stalin's position within the Communist Party was supreme. The Communist Party controlled Russia and Stalin was, in effect, a dictator.

(*ii*) **Further purges.** Stalin insisted on total obedience. Rivals were struck down. In 1933 and in the great purges of 1936–8, Stalin removed all opposition. After the Second World War, he carried out further purges and was planning yet more when he died in 1953. The purges which began in 1936 destroyed almost all that remained of the Bolshevik Party of Lenin's day. In a series of spectacular trials the accused often 'confessed' their guilt and even asked for death in order to purify the communist system. Kamenev and Zinoviev were among the victims.

After the purges of politicians, there were purges of the armed forces. Marshal Tukhachevsky and seven other army leaders were shot, as well as thousands of lesser men. No hostile peasant was too unimportant to escape Stalin's savagery. His terrorism was similar to Hitler's in the same period; at times, it was even anti-Jewish.

No freedom of expression remained in Russia. Stalin's verdict was final in everything. He dictated to writers, scientists and composers, pronounced official verdicts on works such as Shostakovich's Fourth Symphony and imposed his own version of Soviet Culture. A new constitution in 1936 gave an appearance of democracy which was no more than a hollow pretence.

(*iii*) **The Constitution of 1936.** This Constitution preserved much of the earlier communist constitutions. All adults over eighteen could vote, by secret ballot. There were written guarantees of human liberties. Candidates could be nominated by bodies such as trade unions but local soviets then pruned the list, offering only one to the voters. Russia's parliament, the Supreme Soviet, was divided into two houses: the Soviet of the Union represented the people in proportion to population, the Soviet of Nationalities represented the many states which made up the united states of Russia. Power remained with the Communist Party, for all the candidates were communists, and the Council of Ministers was much the same as the Party's Central Committee. Real power lay with an inner group of that Committee, the *Politburo*, and since Stalin controlled the whole party, with Stalin.

(*iv*) **Economic planning.** Stalin carried the control of the economy begun by Lenin much further. NEP was abandoned in 1928, and from then on Russia's economy was driven forward with ruthless fury. The Five-Year Plans, introduced in 1928, 1933, 1937, 1946 and 1951, laid down production targets and penalties for failure. Russians worked with tremendous energy and not only from fear. There were incentives and rewards, called 'socialist competition'. Outstanding workers were called Stakhanovites in honour of a miner who, in 1935, cut over a hundred tons of coal in a single shift. By the outbreak of war in 1939, nearly half the industrial work force were Stakhanovites.

Stalin based the First Plan on rapid industrialization and the collectivization of agriculture, adopting policies he had previously rejected. In industry, the emphasis was on development to produce the means for further expansion—machinery, tractors and power stations. Hydro-electric power was essential to fulfil Stalin's intention of doing in a decade what other countries had done in a century. The Second Plan continued with this emphasis. The Third envisaged a great production of consumer goods to reward the people for their efforts but it was interrupted by the war with Nazi Germany.

By the end of the 1930s, Russia was a major industrial power, second in production only to the USA. There were huge new power stations on rivers such as the Dnieper, vast steel plants such as that at Magnitogorsk and new railway links, such as the Turkestan-Siberian. The output of chemicals, steel and coal soared as workers were diverted from agriculture into industry. In spite of a heavy price paid in freedom and blood for Stalin's rule, there was a new pride in Russia. Russians continued to endure shortages of consumer goods but they thought it an honour to be classed as a 'Hero of Socialist Labour' and there were other rewards in the form of educational opportunities and welfare services.

The peasants, especially the kulaks, took less readily to the aims of the First Five-Year Plan in agriculture. Communists believed that the countryside had a duty to feed the towns and Russia needed grain to export, to buy machinery. There were two obstacles. Russian agriculture was often inefficient, many farms too small, and the more prosperous farmers, the kulaks, put personal profit before the public good. With collectivization, the farms would be grouped into larger units (*kolkhozee*), mechanized and directed in the interests of the state. When Stalin died, there were 100 000 large, collectivized units in place of the 25 million holdings which existed in 1928.

The transition was painful. In quick succession, Stalin tried cajolery, the ruthless extermination of kulaks which reached a peak in 1930, and then a mixture of incentives and penalties. By 1935 the future of collectivization was assured, but at heavy cost. Millions had died, either brutally murdered, perishing in forced labour camps, or dying of starvation, for Stalin's battle with the peasants resulted in famine. The agricultural system came near to total collapse with the mass killing of livestock by kulaks who would not yield their animals to the collective farms. In 1932 Russia had to import grain to survive and in the same year, sickened by the ruthlessness, Stalin's wife committed suicide.

Collectivization did, however, make Russian agriculture more efficient and transformed rural society. Each *kolkhoz* sold some 90 per cent of its output to the state at fixed prices and drew on a pool of machinery such as tractors from a tractor station. Members of the *kolkhoz* kept their own small patches of land and homes and got a share in the income of the collective, so that the principles of NEP were, in the end, not entirely dead. Nevertheless, there was no room for kulaks in the system. Some 25 million peasants were moved to the towns to work in industry in the 1930s. Those who remained trebled the output of grain by 1939, compared with 1914, and doubled that of meat and milk. Even so, Russian agriculture produced less than was expected of it for generations to come.

(*v*) **Welfare services.** The brutality of Stalin's rule must be set alongside improvements in the quality of life for Russians. Trade unions, with a membership of nearly 20 million in the 1930s, had important functions in supervising a Labour Code for the welfare of workers. State health services and social security schemes were expanded. The Constitution of 1936 laid down the right to pensions in old age and benefits during sickness, although there was not always sufficient money to pay them. There was emphasis, too, on education, especially in science and for workers' children. Illiteracy was cut from about 50 per cent in 1924 to 19 per cent in 1939. In 1934, four years' elementary education for all children was made a priority with seven years' secondary education to follow, although a new effort was needed in 1949 completely to implement the latter. Stalin had said that Russia was about a hundred years behind the advanced countries. In many ways, the gap had been closed when he died.

(*vi*) **Foreign policy.** Stalin's policies remained isolationist even when Russia joined the League of Nations in 1934. The *Comintern* (the Communist Third International, set up in 1919) was still pledged to international revolution but its voice was subdued and the policies of the Russian Foreign Office were less aggressive. In the 1920s, Russia had a limited alliance with Germany (the Treaty of Rapallo) and gave some limited assistance to the communists in China. For the rest, Russia was content simply to seek recognition. In the 1930s, Stalin attempted to co-operate with the West against Nazi Germany (see Unit Eight), but there was distrust on both sides. Stalin made his own pact with the Germans in 1939, claiming to see evidence of a capitalist plot to turn Hitler against Russia (see Section 8.3(*f*)). But two years later Hitler launched *Operation Barbarossa* and attacked the USSR. Russian victories enabled Stalin greatly to expand the power of Russia and the appeal of communism. After 1945, most of Eastern Europe became communist (see Unit Twelve). 'Socialism in One Country' thus kept the communists in power in Russia in the interwar years and provided a base for massive advances in the years to come.

5.2   Fascism

Fascism was a fiercely anti-communist, intensely nationalistic creed which began in Italy and was developed by Mussolini. Although the word 'Fascist' has since been widely applied to many regimes based on the admiration of force, national prestige, theories of racial superiority and hero-worship, Fascist systems were strictly a feature of the interwar years. Their aims were often woolly but they claimed to support neither capitalism nor communism and to oppose the class war. Sometimes, as in the Italian Corporate State, they sought to create a partnership between classes in the interests of national greatness. They had a belief in active government and in radical measures to deal with problems such as unemployment. Their policies could sometimes be vaguely socialist and Hitler called his movement National Socialism. It was more nationalist than socialist and, in the end, Fascists usually rested their confidence in slogans of obedience. The essence of Italian Fascism lay in the slogan, 'Mussolini is always right'. Germans expressed it more briefly: 'Heil Hitler'.

Fig. 5.3 'One People. One Nation. One Leader.' Fascism in Germany

(a) Fascist Italy

(*i*) **Fascist government.** It took Mussolini some time after the March on Rome (see Section 3.3, page 54) to establish all the trappings of Fascist dictatorship. By the time Matteotti was murdered there was a Fascist Grand Council to run the Party and the *Fasci* were reorganized as a sort of private army to keep Mussolini in power. As leader of the Party (*Il Duce*), Mussolini controlled the Fascists. In 1925, he began to make certain that the Fascists had complete control of Italy.

The Italian parliament weakly gave way to the Duce's every demand. Fascists took over all important appointments. Mussolini gained the right to rule, legislate and even direct the course of justice. At the end of 1926, all political opposition was outlawed. The monarchy remained but the King was powerless, and parliament was filled with Mussolini's stooges. After 1928, the Fascist Grand Council presented the electors with a list of approved candidates. Electors could accept or reject the whole list: they had no other choice. In 1939, parliament was abolished in favour of a Chamber of Fasces and Corporations representing the party and the Corporations.

Censorship, propaganda and the persecution of opponents helped to keep the Duce in power. Endless publicity proclaimed the brilliance of Mussolini, until he believed in it himself. In fact, Fascist Italy was corrupt and inefficient, and Mussolini himself was a windbag, who achieved little except to remain in power for some twenty years. An appearance of bustling efficiency was given by black shirts, the Fascist salute, politicians and even schoolteachers in uniform, speeches, posters and parades. Organization was the keynote. Even sport was mobilized and regimented for the glory of Fascism. Football had a chief referee in Rome, his symbol of office a gold whistle. Mussolini's Fascism was a theatrical and, for a time, successful confidence trick. On the other hand, the system was far less vicious than Hitler's, and far less brutal than Stalin's, although there was thuggery and some opponents were murdered. Italians lost not only freedom but their sense of reality and their dignity under Mussolini.

(*ii*) **The corporate state.** Fascists claimed that they made class warfare unnecessary. In its early days, Fascist Italy strongly supported private enterprise. Later, it turned to government economic controls but was seldom consistent. Corporations lay at the heart of the system in the 1930s. They were based on occupations and within them Fascists tried to unite employers, managers and workers so that, subject to a Minister of Corporations, each could organize co-operative effort. Trade unions were merged into the Corporations, strikes and lock-outs forbidden and disputes settled by officials of the Corporations. On paper, the system was a recipe for harmony and progress. In practice, there was gross inefficiency and much corruption, the Fascists using the Corporations to muzzle opposition.

(*iii*) **The economy.** Mussolini's aim was to make Italy self-sufficient, but the winning of prestige was frequently confused with projects of real value. When the currency was in difficulties in 1925, Volpi revalued the lira, but fixed the value too high.* It became even more difficult to sell Italy's exports and unemployment rose. The Great Depression made the situation even worse. Wages fell, the jobless increased and the government ceased to issue statistics. Mussolini resorted to propaganda.

There was a dramatic *Battle for Grain*. More was produced, often on land better suited to fruit-growing, but the Battle distorted the economy. Impressive public works were launched. Land was reclaimed and the Pontine Marshes successfully drained. Railways were electrified, impressive motorways (*autostrada*) built. Progress was made in developing hydro-electric power. Imposing new public buildings such as railway stations and sports stadiums as well as

* Compare Churchill, page 69.

blocks of flats were erected. But the effects on unemployment were small, although propaganda made the most of every Fascist achievement.

The Fascists made little impression on poverty in the south. Their record showed an improvement on the work of previous governments but welfare schemes were low on the list of Fascist priorities. There was economic assistance for large families but the motive was not humanitarian. Mussolini wished to increase Italy's population. He ordered a *Battle for Births*. Bachelors were taxed to encourage them to do their duty to the state—marry and father children; but the birth rate remained disappointing.

(*iv*) **The Church.** In 1929, however, Mussolini won success in healing the long quarrel between the Italian government and the Pope (see Section 3.3, page 51). By the Lateran Treaties, Pope Pius XI agreed to recognize the Italian government. In return, Mussolini paid compensation for lands which the Pope had lost to Italy in 1870, accepted Catholic authority over Italian morals and gave official recognition to the Catholic religion.

(*v*) **Foreign policy.** 'I adore war,' declared Mussolini, 'war is to men what childbirth is to women.' He had visions of a great Italian empire, dominating the Mediterranean and extending Italy's possessions in Africa. Usually, he selected his victims with care. The weak states in the Balkans attracted him, Jugoslavia (see Section 2.9(*a*)), Greece (see Section 7.1) and Albania (see Section 3.3(*c*) and 8.2). In Africa, he launched an attack on Ethiopia (see Section 8.2). In 1940, he felt confident enough to attack France, on the point of defeat by Germany. The results were disastrous (see Section 9.4).

Nothing was more typical of Fascism than its intense nationalism and aggressiveness. Yet Mussolini was, at times, a responsible statesman until he finally threw in his lot with Hitler in the late 1930s. Britain and France long continued to hope that Fascist Italy could be a force for international stability and for the effectiveness of the League of Nations. It was one of the illusions from which well-meaning politicians suffered between the wars. Mussolini was carried away by his own propaganda. 'The twentieth century will be the century of Fascism,' he once proclaimed. He became fascinated with the power of '8 million bayonets'. For the peace of Europe it was a tragedy that the weakness of democracy in Italy produced only Mussolini, weakening still further the Alliance on which the League of Nations was founded (see Units Seven and Eight).

(*b*) Nazi Germany

(*i*) **Nazi ideology.** The official policy of the National Socialist Party included socialist ideals about nationalization and welfare. It also demanded 'ruthless war' on all whose activities injured the common interest, and was rooted in a respect for force, strong central power, hatred of Germany's enemies, and anti-Semitism. ('No Jew,' it was stated, 'may be a member of the nation.')

The socialist part of the programme helped to win support for the Nazis.

But the socialists within the party were later purged: Hitler himself had too much contempt for his fellow-men to be a socialist. His philosophy rested on a belief in a master-race of Aryans, a *Herrenvolk*. Purged of those who polluted the race, for example Jews, this *Herrenvolk* would dominate Europe, destroy communism and restore Germany to her rightful superiority, expanding where necessary to gain *Lebensraum* (see Glossary, page 366) at the expense of lesser breeds, such as Slavs. Hitler carried the Fascist admiration for national glory and the Fascist readiness to obey a vigorous leader to extremes, demanding robot-like obedience to himself, the *Führer* (leader) of the *Herrenvolk*. Fanatical in his hatred of Jews, he also extended to horrifying lengths the Fascist ideas of racial superiority.

(*ii*) **Nazi government.** The Enabling Law which followed Hitler's appointment as Chancellor (see Section 3.3, page 60) suspended the Weimar constitution until 1937. Hitler completed its destruction long before that year. In 1934 he abolished the separate parliaments of the states (e.g. Prussia) and then all parties except the Nazi Party. In the 'Night of the Long Knives', 30 June 1934, he destroyed many former supporters including Strasser who deplored Hitler's ruthlessness, Röhm and others in the SA who had socialist ideals, and General von Schleicher, an ally no longer needed. The SA (Brownshirts) were less reliable than the Blackshirts (*Schutzstaffel*, SS), fanatically led by Heinrich Himmler, a sadistic ex-schoolteacher. Hitler intended to have no rivals, only devoted followers. When Hindenburg died in August 1934, Hitler combined the offices of President and Chancellor, called himself *Führer* and, in a plebiscite, won the approval of nearly 90 per cent of those who voted. Hitler also took charge of the army, and soldiers took oaths of personal loyalty to him.

The Reichstag was packed with Hitler's supporters, ready to agree on every issue. Trade unions were abolished. All free expression was muzzled. In the hands of Goebbels, the Ministry of Propaganda distorted all truth in the service of the Führer. The young were indoctrinated in schools and youth organizations. Himmler set up the *Gestapo*, a vicious political police force. From 1934, all power lay with the Nazis and above all with the Führer.

(*iii*) **Opposition.** A Concordat (agreement) with the Pope in 1933 gave Hitler some support from the Roman Catholic Church but his racialist theories and persecution of the Jews led to a quarrel. In 1937, Pius XI condemned Hitler's doctrines in the Encyclical, '*Mit Brennender Sorge*' (With Burning Anxiety). The German Lutheran Church was equally uneasy and a section led by Pastor Niemöller expressed opposition. Those who protested were sent to concentration camps (bestial prison camps which reinforced the activities of the Gestapo and the SS to stifle all opposition).

On the other hand, many Germans approved of Hitler's regime and the majority expressed no opposition. In 1935, the Nuremberg Law deprived Jews of their rights as citizens, required them to wear a distinguishing patch and imposed many humiliations; in 1938, vicious persecution followed humiliation. Germany only had about half a million Jews but when Poland was invaded in 1939 many more Jews fell into Hitler's hands and he eventually embarked on 'The Final Solution', a policy of genocide to destroy their race.

Hitler exercised hypnotic control over the young, turning many of them into state spies, ready to denounce even their own families. One could join the Little Fellows at six, the *Jungvolk* at ten and the Hitler Youth at fourteen. Boys swore to devote their lives to the Führer, 'the saviour of our country'. Girls were trained, in the League of German Maidens, to regard the mothering of Hitler's soldiers as their highest aim. Mussolini and communist Russia had dedicated youth organizations but nowhere was more attention paid to regimenting children than in Hitler's Germany. Not all of them took readily to Nazi training but the youth movements gave Hitler a deadly weapon both against opposition within Germany and later in war.

Fig. 5.4 Hitler addressing some of the Hitler Youth at Nuremberg, 1938

(*iv*) **The economy.** Hitler's promise to reduce unemployment was to some extent fulfilled; it fell from 6 million to 1 million by 1936. Public works such as the building of motorways (*Autobahnen*) provided some jobs, but many of the jobs which the Nazis provided were in unproductive organizations such as the Gestapo. Vacancies were also created by dismissing Jews and enemies of the state, and rearmament and the expansion of the armed forces helped to provide work. Like so much in Hitler's Germany, the solving of the unemployment problem was less successful than it seemed at first sight.

Nevertheless, many had grounds for satisfaction. Prices and rents were controlled. Slums were cleared. State health services were expanded. Attention was paid to the welfare of workers. The 'Strength Through Joy' movement

(*Kraft durch Freude*) made available to them cheap holidays and sports facilities. Nazi parades and torchlight processions brought colour to drab lives and even attracted tourists to help the economy. For those to whom politics and the right to think and speak were unimportant, Nazi Germany seemed, in the 1930s, to offer more than did democracy.

Hitler aimed at self-sufficiency. Frantic efforts were made to cut down imports by producing substitutes for materials such as rubber. But by 1939 Germany was faced with serious difficulties in paying for imports, and stealing vital supplies from other countries by an aggressive foreign policy became increasingly attractive to the Nazis. Hitler's Germany had a major balance of payments problem, and by 1939 the Nazi economy, geared to military might, was an unhealthy one.

(*v*) **Foreign policy.** Germany's power produced instability in international affairs. It is unlikely that Hitler had deliberate plans for European war, but his was the major responsibility for the Second World War (see Unit Eight).

(*c*) **Falangist Spain**

(*i*) **The Civil War.** In July 1936, a rising by the armed forces in Morocco and Spain began the Spanish Civil War (see Section 3.3, page 63). Their aim was to overthrow the government of the Popular Front and their leader was General Franco, the Chief of the Army General Staff. The rebels were soon supported by right-wing groups, among them the Falangists (a group of nationalists founded in 1933 by the son of the former dictator, de Rivera). By the end of the year, the rebellion had won control of much of the north and west of Spain and laid siege to Madrid. Mussolini and Hitler saw an opportunity to win an ally and gave support to Franco, who was declared Chief of the Spanish State in October 1936, and a year later *El Caudillo*, the leader. The official policies of Britain and France were not to interfere, and a non-intervention committee met in London in the autumn of 1936.

Spain, however, became a battleground for ideologies. The USSR sent advisers, food and military aid to fight the rebellion. Volunteers, eager to halt the spread of Fascism, formed International Brigades. Communists, socialists, liberals and democrats rallied to the Popular Front and for three years a vicious and costly struggle raged.* The aims of the supporters of the Popular Front were varied and imprecise. They quarrelled amongst themselves and in the end were no match for Franco, some 50 000 Italians and the German air force which perfected its new technique of dive-bombing, notably at Guernica.

In 1936, the rebels won about half of Spain. In 1937, their progress was checked although they were successful against the Basques in the far north. In

* Among the volunteers was George Orwell, the British journalist and novelist, who recorded his experiences in *Homage to Catalonia*, as he had previously recorded the sufferings of the English working-classes in *The Road to Wigan Pier*. But Orwell was disillusioned by the cruelty and intrigue.

1938, they cut through the middle of Spain and reached the Mediterranean coast. Madrid was besieged again and with the capture of Barcelona, at the beginning of 1939, the hopes of the Popular Front crumbled. Russia withdrew support.* The International Brigades broke up and in March 1939, Madrid surrendered. The Civil War had taken three-quarters of a million lives, given Germany and Italy a dress rehearsal for the Second World War and resulted in yet another defeat for democracy. Britain and France recognized the government of Franco but he failed to repay his debt to Hitler and Mussolini by joining them in the Second World War. He preferred 'benevolent neutrality' which enabled him to concentrate on Spain's problems.

(*ii*) **Franco's government.** Franco's regime was usually regarded as fascist because of his association with Hitler and Mussolini and because of the nature of the Civil War. It was fiercely anti-communist and had some trappings of fascism, including a violent, political police force. At the same time, it was peculiarly Spanish—a Catholic dictatorship based on a right-wing, nationalist coalition which included the Falangists. It ruled for the benefit of the privileged—the army, the Church, financiers and industrialists. The Cortes, Spain's parliament, was restored in 1942 but the system remained a dictatorship and, in 1947, Franco was declared Chief of State for life with the power to appoint his successor.

After 1945, when Hitler and Mussolini were dead, the survival of Franco was an unhappy reminder of pre-war Fascism. But no rebel body was strong enough to topple him. Like Salazar in neighbouring Portugal (see Section 3.3, page 62), he remained in power although many states preferred to ignore him. Portugal, after 1960, however, had an influence on African affairs which it was difficult to ignore, reviving memories of fascist theories of racial superiority (see Section 16.5 and Section 21.2(*c*)).

5.3 Nationalism

Parallel to European fascism between the wars there developed a variety of intensely nationalist regimes in other parts of the world.

(*a*) Turkey

(*i*) **The government of Mustapha Kemal.** The opposition of Turkish nationalists to the Treaty of Sèvres resulted in the new Treaty of Lausanne and the downfall of the Sultan at the hands of Mustapha Kemal (see Section 2.7). From then until he died in 1938, Kemal ruled the Turkish Republic. He was elected President of the Republic in October 1923, and he created and dominated the Republican People's Party. Rivals were purged in 1924 and, some years later, Turkey became a one-party state. Kemal was a dictator but he seldom resorted to the brutalities of the fascists and he kept alive the hope of

---

* Stalin had probably wished only to prolong the war. He did not wish to antagonize the West by achieving a communist victory.

a return to democracy; he was also progressive and determined to modernize his country. He earned the gratitude of the Turkish people and there was general agreement when, in 1934, he took the surname Atatürk ('Father of Turks').
One obstacle to modernization was the power of the Mohammedan Church and, in 1928, Islam ceased to be the state religion. Politics were divorced from religion and Turkey became a secular state.

(*ii*) **Reforms.** In the nineteenth century, Turkey was referred to as 'the sick man of Europe'. Kemal Atatürk was determined to use strong government to make Turkey well. Central to his policies was westernization. By reducing the influence of religion, he was able to introduce new codes of law, to raise women's status in society and to attack the traditions which held Turkey back. The western weekend, western dress and the western alphabet were introduced. Education was expanded and modernized. Women gained social and political rights. Polygamy was abolished, divorce and civil marriage legalized, and Turkey's health services and social insurance schemes were developed.

(*iii*) **The economy.** Kemal built up economic strength through state management. The state took control of railways and industries such as sugar, and the government set aside money for industrial development, protecting the Turkish economy with tariffs. Some farming co-operatives were set up and scientific farming methods encouraged.
Kemal's management did not make Turkey a wealthy, industrial state but he gave the nation stability in a critical period. By 1938, the Turks had come to terms with the twentieth century and regained their self-respect.

(*iv*) **Foreign policy.** After negotiating the Peace Treaty at Lausanne in 1923, Kemal was prepared to live in peace. He made trade pacts with his neighbours and favoured international stability. In 1926, he accepted League of Nations arbitration in a frontier dispute over Mosul, which Britain claimed as part of the mandate of Iraq. Turkey joined the League six years later. Kemal disliked Russian communism and Turks continued to dislike Greeks but relations with both remained amicable. Kemal also supported Britain and France in trying to ensure stability in Europe: his nationalism was concentrated on the internal development of Turkey. In foreign policy, he sought only Turkey's security.

(*b*) **Japan**

(*i*) **Imperial government.** Japan adopted the principle of a vote for all adult males in the mid 1920s, but the Prime Minister, Kato Takaaki could do little to alter the fundamental weakness of the Japanese constitution. The power of governments rested on placating vested interests not on elected members of parliament. The army had a traditional grip on Japanese politics; the emperor was surrounded by influential conservatives, and the influence of businessmen was growing. All these groups combined to resist the development of real democracy, and left-wing ideas were frequently suppressed by a powerful police force. The creation of a small Japanese Communist Party in 1922 led the police to be even more watchful, alert for 'dangerous thought'.

Hirohito, the emperor from 1926, had some progressive attitudes but any hopes that the Japanese system of government could grow into a truly democratic one were shattered by the Great Depression. There was already dissatisfaction with the weakness, corruption and inconsistencies of the parliamentary system. The administration of Kato, for example (1924–6), maintained close connexions with the Mitsubishi industrial empire. As a result governments were short-lived and charges of self-interest common.

In 1931, disregarding the civilian government, the Japanese army launched an attack on Manchuria (see Section 8.1). Army leaders were far from united, but for the rest of the 1930s the militarists were the dominant force in Japan. They tried to solve by aggression Japan's social and economic problems— overpopulation, a shortage of raw materials and of markets. Hirohito was little more than a figurehead, appointing a bewildering number of prime ministers, some civilian, some military. But, although elections were still held, the system was even less democratic than in the 1920s. Japan had turned to fierce nationalism and militarism, not to democracy.

(ii) **The economy.** Private enterprise, in which the big industrial combines (*zaibatsu*) played a leading part, was the basis of Japan's industrial expansion after 1918. At first, textiles dominated Japanese industry but there was expansion into other fields such as chemicals. Not until about 1937, however, was great emphasis placed upon engineering and heavy industry; by that time, the aggressive foreign policy required the country to be geared to war. The output of steel was expanded and new industries developed such as the production of motor vehicles. The government, which had previously interfered little beyond providing protective tariffs, began to exercise more control over industry for military reasons.

Agriculture was generally efficient. In the early twentieth century Japan became the world's greatest producer of silk and silk made up over a third of the country's exports. The Great Depression, therefore, hit Japan hard, for silk was a luxury which the world could do without. Japan's trade in other goods made new progress in the later 1930s, however. Her goods were often cheap, and she won extensive markets in Asia and Africa. But without the help of 'invisible exports' Japan would seldom have been able to pay for her imports.

Japan provided formidable competition to European producers, especially of textiles, but she was also a customer with many needs to be supplied. The militarists intended to improve Japan's trading position by getting a stranglehold on China. Later in the 1930s, they were attracted by fascist theories of self-sufficiency. Expansion became as essential to Japan as it was for Hitler. The Japanese consequently developed the idea of a 'Co-Prosperity Sphere' in East Asia (an area from Manchuria to Indonesia, self-supporting and dominated by Japan), a sort of Japanese *Lebensraum*.

(*iii*) **Foreign policy.** The nature of Japan's political system thus combined with greed to produce a foreign policy which became increasingly aggressive. It was based upon rampant nationalism and encouraged by the weakness of Japan's neighbours. China seemed likely to be an easy victim but aggression in the years after 1931 led eventually to conflict on a much larger scale. Japanese ambition resulted in the Second World War in the Pacific (see Unit Eight).

Further Reading

Ayling, S. E.: *Portraits of Power.* Harrap (London, 1965)—Lenin, Stalin, Mussolini, Hitler, Franco, Kemal.

Cash, A.: *The Russian Revolution.* Benn (London, 1967).

Elliott, B. J.: *Hitler and Germany.* Longman (Harlow, 1966).

Footman, D.: *The Russian Revolutions.* Faber (London, 1966).

Jackson, N. C.: *Russia in the Twentieth Century.* Pergamon (London, 1977).

Jamieson, A.: *Leaders of the Twentieth Century.* Bell (London, 1970)—Lenin, Stalin, Mussolini, Hitler, Franco, Kemal.

Jardine, C. Bayne: *Mussolini and Italy.* Longman (Harlow, 1966).

Pearson, R.: *Revolution in Russia.* Harrap (London, 1975).

Procktor, R.: *Nazi Germany.* Bodley Head (London, 1970).

Robottom, J.: *Modern Russia.* Longman (Harlow, 1969).

Snellgrove, L. E.: *Franco and the Spanish Civil War.* Longman (Harlow, 1965).

Williams, B.: *Modern Japan.* Longman (Harlow, 1969).

Documentary

Berwick, M.: *The Third Reich.* Wayland (London, 1971).

Gregory, D.: *Mussolini and the Fascist Era.* Arnold (London, 1968).

Stacey, F. W.: *Lenin and the Russian Revolution.* Arnold (London, 1968).

Exercises

1. How would you define and illustrate *Communist government* from the history of Russia under Lenin and Stalin?
2. How would you define and illustrate *Fascist government* from the history of Italy under Mussolini?
3. In what ways was Mustapha Kemal a *Nationalist*?
4. Draw columns for the following countries: Russia, Italy, Germany, Turkey, Japan. State briefly in these columns:
     (*a*) the basic system of government in each of these states in the period dealt with in this Unit;
     (*b*) how opposition parties were treated;
     (*c*) how the economy was organized;
     (*d*) what you consider were the basic aims of the state.
   In what ways were Italy and Germany similar? How did Russia, Turkey and Japan differ from Italy and Germany?
5. How were the lives of ordinary citizens affected by the government of either Hitler in Germany or Mussolini in Italy? (There are revealing accounts of the effects on young people in *No Retreat* by Anna Rauschning, extracts from which appear in C. B. Firth, *From Napoleon to Hitler.* (Ginn, London, 1947, Reference Book).)

Unit Six

Restless Empires

6.1 Nationalism

The huge overseas empires of the Europeans (see Fig. 1.4) survived almost intact until after the Second World War. Under the mandate system (see Section 1.3), the German and Turkish Empires had been broken up among the victorious powers. In the 1930s, Italy and Japan endeavoured to expand their empires. But, in the interwar years, the most significant developments were the growth of nationalism among subject peoples and the beginning of the British attempt to transform the British Empire into a Commonwealth.

Nationalism took the form of a demand for independence, a demand which was to grow to a clamour after 1945. The Versailles Settlement had encouraged the growth of nationalism; President Wilson had proclaimed the need for colonies to be ruled in the interests of the inhabitants. The Commonwealth grew in time to become a novel twentieth-century experiment, a multi-racial partnership of equals. Before 1939, however, few people had clear ideas about where these developments were leading.

6.2 The British Empire

(a) The British Commonwealth of Nations

The White Dominions (see Section 1.3) were a unique feature of the British Empire. By 1914 they had won rights of self-government in almost everything except foreign policy. Canada was the first to achieve this, in 1867. Australia, New Zealand and South Africa followed. A government 'like Canada's' gradually became the aim of many states within the British Empire, but after 1918 Canada and other White Dominions wanted independence in foreign policy too. They began to agitate for a definition of *Dominion Status*.

Britain placed few obstacles in their path. The Dominions were represented at the Peace Conference in Paris. They joined the League of Nations, and some took charge of mandates. In 1926, Balfour, a former Conservative Prime Minister, found words to define Dominion Status and, in 1931, MacDonald gave this definition the force of law in the Statute of Westminster. Britain confirmed that her laws no longer bound the Dominions. They were completely free. They 'freely associated' with Britain and each other as members of the British Commonwealth of Nations. The British King remained Head of State of each Dominion, but the Commonwealth was a partnership of equals. By 1931, the number of Dominions had already increased with the granting of Dominion Status to the Irish Free State and Newfoundland.

There was talk before 1939 of making India a Dominion as well but the deed itself was delayed. The Irish Free State was a reluctant Dominion, too anti-British to wish to remain in the Commonwealth and, in 1934, Newfoundland reacted to economic difficulties by returning to colonial status as a prelude to joining Canada in 1949. Nevertheless, the foundations of the Commonwealth had been laid. Eventually it became multi-racial, but until 1939 it was a white man's club.

The partnership of the Commonwealth helped to preserve democratic governments and human liberties. The members had a common language, English. Most of them played cricket and they established many ties for mutual assistance. All except Ireland freely chose to join Britain in the war against Germany in 1939, recognizing the value of what Britain sought to preserve against fascism. On the other hand, the results of the partnership were sometimes disappointing. The Commonwealth had almost no machinery for co-operation. Prime Ministers, and such people as defence experts, met fairly regularly, but co-operation was often haphazard.

Trade may serve as an example. In 1924, Britain staged the Empire Exhibition at Wembley to encourage the buying of 'Empire' goods. In 1926 the Empire Marketing Board was set up, only to be abandoned six years later. In the Dominions, it was argued that Commonwealth countries could help each other with a system of imperial preference such as that practised by Canada: tariffs were imposed on foreign goods but lower duties, or none at all, on Commonwealth goods. In the 1920s, Britain clung to free trade; the system of imperial preference did not appeal to her.

When Britain abandoned free trade in 1932, Baldwin, Neville Chamberlain and Thomas represented the country at the Ottawa Conference where members of the Commonwealth tried to work out a trading system to help each other in the Depression. There was no general plan but some partial agreements were reached. Britain gave preferences to the Commonwealth under the Import Duties Act (see Section 4.4(b)). Even within the Commonwealth, however, countries were reluctant to put the welfare of others above self-interest. All wanted to sell rather than to buy, and all now wanted to protect their own agriculture and industry against competition. Quarrels were not unusual. Australia put duties on British cloth and Lancashire cotton workers retaliated by trying to boycott Australian produce. Even so, members of the Commonwealth, in 1938, sold almost 50 per cent of their exports within the association.

(b) Irish Nationalism

In 1918, Irish nationalists wanted a complete break from Britain. Ireland had long been denied self-government and when, in 1916, Britain savagely repressed the Easter Rising of Irish republicans, opinion swung behind *Sinn Fein* (the Irish Republican party). Sinn Fein won most of the Irish seats in the general election of 1918. The party was in favour of a free Ireland and its MPs boycotted Westminster, setting up an illegal Irish parliament in Dublin.

In the Government of Ireland Act of 1920 Lloyd George offered only Home Rule. The Act offered Ireland less than Canada had gained in 1867—self-government in only a limited number of matters and the right to continue electing MPs to Westminster. Moreover, it divided Ireland, with Home Rule for the north at Belfast and for the south at Dublin. In a strongly Conservative House of Commons, Lloyd George felt obliged to satisfy the Protestants of Northern Ireland, and they refused to be ruled by the Catholics who made up 75 per cent of Ireland's total population. This problem of the Protestant minority had delayed the settlement of Ireland's future before 1914 and it has embittered the history of Ireland ever since.

Sinn Fein rejected the Act. They wanted more than Home Rule and they angrily rejected the division of Ireland. A fighting wing, the Irish Republican Army (IRA), was too strong for the Royal Irish Constabulary and Lloyd George had already recruited extra help for the police (whose emergency uniforms gave rise to their nickname, 'Black and Tans'). A bloody conflict developed. The Black and Tans and the IRA, led by Michael Collins, were both guilty of barbaric atrocities. When elections were held in the south, however, it was obvious that the Catholics were solid in their support for Sinn Fein and De Valera who led the party, so Lloyd George had to negotiate.

It was impossible for him to abandon the Protestants. They were numerous enough in the six counties of Northern Ireland to accept the act of 1920 for that part of the country. Southern Ireland, on the other hand, agreed to Dominion Status in 1921. Britain hastily passed the Irish Free State Agreement Act of 1922. Ireland was thus divided after all, but in the Irish Free State (the south) parliament accepted the settlement by only the narrowest of margins. De Valera rejected it as a betrayal. Michael Collins, who had been one of the Irishmen who signed the agreement, was murdered. The Irish Free State was a Dominion but it had still to accept the British monarchy.

For a time, during 'The Troubles', there was civil war in the Free State. The IRA fought a bloody campaign against the Irish government which had agreed to partition. Stability did not return until De Valera resumed his place in parliament in 1926 with a new party, *Fianna Fail.*

In 1932, De Valera became Prime Minister, an office he held until 1948 and to which he returned in the 1950s before becoming eventually the President of Ireland. He could not reunite Ireland but he won some successes against the British in the 1930s. The Irish language was revived, the name of the Free State changed to Eire and links with the British monarchy steadily undermined. Neville Chamberlain was persuaded to write off most of the debt the Irish still owed to Britain and to abandon certain ports which Britain had retained since 1922. In spite of these efforts to appease her, however, Eire played little part in Commonwealth affairs.

In 1939, De Valera chose neutrality and it was not much more than a formality when Eire was declared a republic, in 1949, and left the Commonwealth. The actual break was made by John Costello but it was De Valera who had prepared the way, building a successful democracy in the Free State after uncertain beginnings and making a start on economic development. The quarrel with Britain in the 1930s had involved a costly trade war but Irish nationalists thought this a price worth paying.

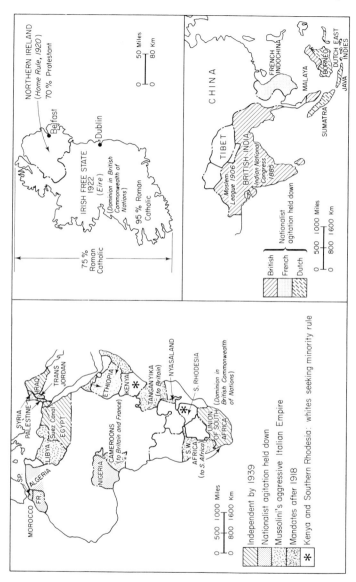

Fig. 6.1 Awakening nationalism in (a) The Middle East and Africa; (b) Ireland; (c) India and South-East Asia

Ireland was the first area, after 1918, in which Britain began to come to terms with nationalist demands for independence.

(c) Indian Nationalism

The concessions to Indian nationalism which Montagu promised in 1917 (see Section 1.3) first took shape in the Government of India Act of 1919. They did not go far enough. Indian nationalists in the Indian National Congress (a mainly Hindu party) and in the Moslem League were dissatisfied with the Act and enraged by the 'massacre' of Indian demonstrators at Amritsar in April, the same year. At Amritsar, General Dyer had ordered his troops to open fire on an unarmed mob. Unable quickly to scatter, 379 were killed and Dyer was recalled to Britain. The massacre was the culmination of a series of clashes. The British had taken special powers to imprison agitators without trial and even, locally, to require Indians to crawl in the presence of Europeans. Indians had attacked Europeans and their property. Dyer thought they needed a lesson. The massacre inflamed Indian nationalism, and from then until India gained independence in 1947, agitation seldom ceased. That much of it was non-violent was due largely to Mohandas Karamchand Gandhi.

Gandhi's main weapon was *satyagraha*, sometimes translated as 'soul force'. He believed in boycotts, strikes and non-co-operation. With passive resistance he fought against injustice wherever he found it. Before 1914, his energies had gone into a struggle against racial discrimination in South Africa. When he returned to India, he campaigned to help underpaid textile workers, poor peasants, the untouchables (see Glossary) and Indian nationalism. He never deviated from his insistence on non-violence, but India was often a violent country and it was frequently difficult for him to control the passions even of his supporters. They called him the Mahatma, Great Soul, but he denied that he was a saint. Others denied that he was a politician or an economist, arguing that his simple ideas were naïve. Not infrequently he went to prison, for the British responded during much of the first half of the twentieth century by imprisoning nationalist agitators in the Empire who plagued them. From 1922 Gandhi was troublesome enough to qualify for regular imprisonment.

One of the main problems in Anglo-Indian relationships was the part to be played by Indians in the government of their country. The British wanted to admit them to responsibility gradually. Indian nationalists were impatient to rule. The Act of 1919 left government in the hands of the British viceroy, but allowed Indians some control of minor areas of government in the provinces, such as Bengal. Gandhi led the chorus of protest. Indians boycotted the Prince of Wales's visit to India in 1921. When Baldwin sent the Simon Commission to investigate Indian problems, they boycotted that.

In 1931 Gandhi visited England, where MacDonald hoped to secure agreements on India's future in the Round Table Conferences. The scraggy frame of Gandhi, his eastern peasant dress and apparent sincerity won him many friends, among them the Lancashire mill-workers to whom he explained India's poverty and his boycott of British textiles. But his lack of formality disturbed King George V and infuriated Winston Churchill. Many Indian politicians boycotted the Conferences and little was achieved. Nevertheless, the Government of India Act of 1935 was passed.

This went a long way to giving Indians control of the provincial governments. The Indian National Congress, in 1937, gained power in eight of the provinces in which elections were held. India as a whole remained subject to the viceroy but, in certain matters, he shared power with the Indians. This was still not enough for them—Indians had no say in foreign policy, for example. When, in 1939, the Viceroy, then Lord Linlithgow, foolishly declared war on Germany

GANDHI AND THE VICEROY—By LOW

THE ELUSIVE Mr GANDHI.

Fig. 6.2 Cartoon in the Evening Standard, *28 July 1931. Gandhi was a constant source of exasperation to the British*

without consulting them at all, he showed an arrogance which could only anger the nationalists.

Meanwhile, Gandhi gave up the leadership of the Indian National Congress, leaving it in the hands of more professional politicians, among them Nehru and the more conservative Patel. Gandhi himself continued to advocate Indian independence. His message to Britain was simple: 'Quit India'. But he underestimated a basic difficulty which became more important the nearer India came to independence. As in Ireland, it was the problem of a minority. Mohammedans were unwilling to be ruled by Hindus. They feared that the Indian National Congress would rule India after independence and most of its leaders were Hindu. The Moslem League, led by Mohammad Ali Jinnah, favoured the division of India, with Pakistan as a separate state for Moslems. Congress and Gandhi wanted a united India and Gandhi worked tirelessly to encourage brotherhood and goodwill between the religions.

The Second World War gave Britain an excuse to delay the final settlement. India was encouraged by the promise that Dominion Status would follow the war. Those who disrupted the war effort were sent to prison. Gandhi was, of course, among them, and his wife, Kasturba, died in prison before the war ended. In 1942, the British Government sent the Cripps Mission to India and confirmed the promise of Dominion Status. When the war ended, in 1945, India was high on the list of problems that had to be settled quickly (see Section 16.6(*a*)).

(*d*) Nationalism in Other Parts of the British Empire

Nationalism in Ireland and India, between the wars, was more advanced than in other parts of the British Empire, but the *Arab states* did not trail far behind them. Lloyd George granted near-independence to Egypt in 1922 but Britain continued to meddle in her affairs and ceased only in 1936. Even then British troops remained in the Canal Zone to protect European interests in the Suez Canal.

Of Britain's mandates in the Middle East, two moved fairly smoothly to independence, Iraq in 1932 and Transjordan in 1946. The third was Palestine where Britain became involved in a struggle, partly of her own making, between Arabs and Jews. In the end, she could do no more than hand back the responsibility to the United Nations with the problem unsolved, in 1948 (see Section 19.1(*b*)). None of these Arab states chose to remain in the Commonwealth after independence. British government had no deep roots in them and they had few British inhabitants.

Africa before 1939 was comparatively quiet. In 1924 and 1926, the Ormsby-Gore Reports announced Britain's intention of ruling her African possessions for the welfare of their inhabitants. As in India, there seemed to be a rather vague policy of preparing Africans eventually to rule themselves. But African nationalism was not yet strong. Like the Indians, they organized Congress Parties and future leaders such as Jomo Kenyatta and Hastings Banda were waiting, but there was no serious threat to British rule in this period.

Some Africans welcomed British rule not only for the stability it provided but as a protection against white settlers. Since giving South Africa Dominion Status in 1909, Britain had begun to have second thoughts about white minority rule. Whites in Southern Rhodesia had a large measure of self-government, although they were a small minority in the country. The constitution of 1923 gave most of the power in Southern Rhodesia to those wealthy enough to qualify for the right to vote. They were nearly all white. But Dominion Status was withheld and Southern Rhodesia remained a British dependency. In Kenya, whites were an even smaller minority in the population but they, like the settlers in Southern Rhodesia, hoped to gain the same privileges as the whites in South Africa. Black Africans realized that Dominion Status, before 1939, could only mean the rule of white settlers and were, therefore, content to defer independence until African nationalism developed. But they were dissatisfied with the rate of economic progress. Britain passed a Colonial

Development Act in 1929 which expanded some of the benefits of European rule—schools, hospitals and meagre social services—but the pace was slow.

In the *West Indies*, dissatisfaction with British rule was mainly a protest against low wages and unemployment. Nationalists were also dissatisfied with the slow progress towards self-government but much of the rioting in the 1930s, in Trinidad, Guiana, Jamaica and elsewhere, sprang from poverty. A Commission of Inquiry revealed an alarming picture of squalor, illiteracy, sickness and juvenile delinquency. Britain passed a new Colonial Development Act in 1940. Up to that time, however, little thought had been given to the political future of the British West Indies.

The same was true of other parts of the Empire. Neither in tiny colonies such as *Mauritius* nor in larger areas such as *Malaya* did Dominion Status seem a matter of urgency. It was the Second World War which quickened the rate of nationalist development and made essential new thinking about the future of the British Empire and Commonwealth.

6.3   The French Empire

Unlike Britain, France allowed her colonial possessions to be represented in the French parliament. On the other hand, French rule of her dependencies was quite undemocratic. The Arabs who made up the bulk of the population of *Algeria* were denied political rights. Arab nationalism and nationalism elsewhere in the Empire was discouraged. In French *Indochina*, the economy was ruthlessly exploited for the benefit of the Europeans. Almost all power lay with the French, and nationalism inevitably took revolutionary forms, often influenced by communist ideas which thrived where there was poverty and unemployment. France resorted to repression, adding strength to the argument of Russian Bolsheviks that imperialism, the exploitation of empires, was 'the last stage of monopoly capitalism' which needed to be eliminated. French Indochina became the scene of one of the most long-drawn-out struggles between capitalism and communism after the Second World War (see Section 16.3). Before 1939, however, the French Empire continued and nationalism was held down.

Nationalism was also held down in *Syria* which France received as a mandate. The French were so vigorous that, after savage repression in 1925 and 1926, they were censured by the League of Nations Mandates Commission. Syria was broken into two states, Syria and the Lebanon. Republics were established but France refused to grant them independence, and discontent was never far below the surface. French control was not removed until the Lebanon was liberated by the British in 1941, when the French there declared support for fascism, and until Syria, in the same year, was occupied by the Allies and the Free French, who agreed to its independence. Even then, France made a half-hearted attempt to recover Syria in 1945.

By the end of the Second World War, the French Empire was doomed. By the end of the 1950s it had collapsed in an explosion of dammed-up nationalist feeling.

6.4   The Italian Empire

Italy had cherished the idea of a Mediterranean Empire from her early days as a united state. The foundations for such an empire were laid before 1914 when Italy secured Eritrea, Somaliland and Libya. It was Mussolini's ambition to expand it. Between the wars, Italy was almost alone among Europeans in producing grandiose schemes for imperial expansion overseas. Mussolini's most impressive success was the conquest of backward *Ethiopia* (see Section 8.2). As yet Africans were no match for Europeans, their spears hardly effective against aeroplanes, tanks and flamethrowers. With such instruments, Mussolini intended to 'civilize' them. His Empire was short-lived, however, overthrown not by nationalist organization but by Italy's defeat in war. When Mussolini committed himself to the support of Hitler in 1940, he doomed Italy's African Empire to premature collapse. It was quickly occupied by other powers and at the end of the Second World War remained to be disposed of like Germany's Empire in 1918.

Libya became independent in 1951 as the result of a decision in the United Nations General Assembly. Italian *Somaliland* was merged into Somalia which became an independent republic in 1960. *Eritrea* became part of Ethiopia which had been liberated from the Italians in 1941. Italy also lost islands in the Mediterranean to Greece and Jugoslavia and was expelled from the other areas at which Mussolini had nibbled, among them Albania.

6.5   Other Empires

The *Dutch* were already fighting a rearguard action against nationalism in Indonesia when the islands were invaded by Japan in 1941. They developed ideas about the welfare of their colonial subjects and their preparation for self-government in the interwar years, like the British. But for Indonesian nationalists, the pace was too slow. In 1926, there were serious revolts in Java. Indonesian nationalism was influenced by communism. The Dutch suppressed the risings and preserved their Empire, but by 1941 the National Indonesian Party had been well-established on the lines of the Indian National Congress and its leader, Sukarno, was waiting, like nationalist leaders elsewhere, for an opportune moment to proclaim independence (see Section 16.2).

Spain possessed little compared with other European empires. Her most important colony was Spanish Morocco and even that, in 1921, was in revolt. These first rebels, the Riffs led by Abd-el-Krim represented tribal interests but in the 1930s a more broadly-based Moroccan nationalism developed. Not until the 1950s, however, was it strong enough to win complete independence.

The once-large Spanish Empire in South America and the West Indies had already broken free—Cuba with the help of the USA at the end of the nineteenth century, for example. Only in Africa, still politically backward before 1939, could the small European states retain their grip. Much of the Portuguese Empire had already been lost, but *Portugal* retained Angola, Mozambique and Portuguese Guinea, an impressive share of the African continent.

Before 1939, the Empire gave Portugal little trouble. Later, it was to be remarkable for its survival at a time when other empires disintegrated. *Belgium* too had large interests in Africa: the Belgian Congo was eighty times the size of Belgium itself. It was ruled with an almost total disregard for African nationalism and for the future. Nowhere was the aftermath of European rule to be more tragic, for when Belgium withdrew in 1960, there had been hardly any preparations for independence and the country plunged into savage civil war (see Section 20.2).

Further Reading

Ayling, S. E.: *Portraits of Power*. Harrap (London, 1965)—Gandhi.

Pandey, B. N.: *The Rise of Modern India*. Hamish Hamilton (London, 1967)—Chapters 4 and 5.

Watson, F.: *Gandhi*. Oxford University Press (London, 1967).

Watson, J. B.: *Empire to Commonwealth 1919 to 1970*. Dent (London, 1971)—pages 34–74 cover Ireland, India, nationalism in other parts of the British Empire.

Documentary

Breach, R. W.: *Documents and Descriptions, the World Since 1914*. Oxford University Press (London, 1966), Sections 26 and 38.

Exercises

1. What do you understand by *Nationalism* in this Unit? How did nationalists try to achieve their aims?
2. What other forms have you seen nationalism take, in earlier Units of this book?
3. What facts make it possible to argue that Gandhi was 'the champion of the oppressed'?
4. What evidence can you find in this Unit to suggest that Mussolini's ideas were 'out-of-date'?
5. What similar minority and religious problems did Ireland and India face?
6. Refer to J. H. Bettey, *English Historical Documents 1906–39* (Routledge & Kegan Paul, London, 1967), pages 164–6 to see how Dominion Status was defined in 1926 and 1931; pages 151–6 for British legislation on Ireland in 1920 and 1922; and pages 130–5 for Montagu's ideas on the future of India.

International Relations to 1931

7.1 The Crises of Readjustment, Early 1920s

Almost as soon as the Settlement of Paris was made (see Unit Two), discontented states began to amend it. Alterations were made to the treaties throughout Europe and sometimes outside it. Many were made by force of arms and, although most of the changes were small ones, involving squabbles between minor powers, precedents were established. The use of force brought rewards.

(a) Major Crises

The most extensive upheavals concerned Turkey (see Section 2.7) and Russia (see Section 5.1). But there were other trouble spots.

(i) **Poland.** In 1918 Poland was reconstituted as an independent state after more than a century of foreign control. At once, the Poles looked for opportunities to make their new state as large as possible. Because of the confused condition of Russia, Poland's eastern frontier was ill-defined and, in 1920, Lloyd George suggested a boundary which came to be known as the Curzon Line. It was unsatisfactory to the Poles who wished to free their fellow-countrymen to the east of the line. War against Russia and the Treaty of Riga (see Section 5.1(b)) added over 50 000 square miles of land to Poland. At about the same time Polish troops occupied Vilna, a district claimed both by Lithuania and Poland. Vilna had formerly been a part of the empire of the Russian Tsar and during the Russo-Polish war it was, for a time, over-run by the Red Army. The Russians gave it to Lithuania but it was reoccupied by a Polish general. The League of Nations showed little interest. Vilna was eventually incorporated into Poland, in 1922, and the settlement was confirmed by the Conference of Ambassadors a year later.

The Polish army had already been in action in other areas. In 1919, they successfully put pressure on the Paris Conference to grant the whole of Eastern Galicia around Lvov to Poland. In a similar way, they gained an area rich in coal and steelworks in Silesia. At Teschen (see Section 2.9), in conflict with Czechoslovakia, they were rather less successful and over 100 000 Poles remained under Czech rule.

(ii) **Italy.** Italian discontent seized first on Fiume (see Section 2.9). Another crisis developed from Italian ambitions in Albania, which was the nearest of the Balkan states to Italy across the Adriatic Sea. In August 1923, an Italian general and four of his staff were ambushed and shot on Greek territory while mapping the Greek–Albanian frontier on behalf of the Conference of Ambassadors. Within days, Mussolini resorted to force to avenge this insult to

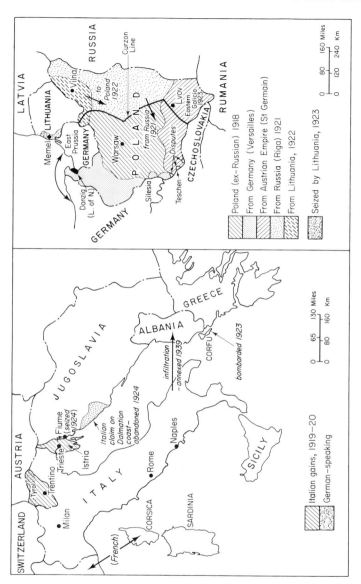

Fig. 7.1 Discontent in the early 1920s in (a) Italy; (b) Poland and Lithuania.

Italian honour. He demanded 50 million lire from the Greek government and demonstrated Italian power by bombarding and occupying the Greek island of Corfu. The League of Nations had no answer to irresponsibility such as this on the part of a major power, and left it to the Conference of Ambassadors to persuade the Greeks to apologize and pay. Within a month, Mussolini withdrew from Corfu, boasting of his triumph. The successful outcome of the dispute over Fiume with Jugoslavia in the following year was another triumph for Mussolini, and he was now prepared to behave less aggressively for a time.

(*iii*) **France.** The Italian occupation of Corfu lasted only a few weeks. The French occupation of the Ruhr lasted for over two years (see Section 3.3(*b*)). Unlike Mussolini, however, France gained little from her invasion. For a time, under the new provisions of the Dawes Plan, Germany kept up steady payments of reparations after the occupation (so France could claim some success) but the invasion was hardly a legal action. It demonstrated once again the readiness of even major powers to use force in pursuit of self-interest.

(*b*) **Minor Crises**
Smaller nations were involved in a bewildering number of disputes in the years after the Settlement of Versailles. At first, the League of Nations was unable to cope with the problems which mushroomed in the wake of the Settlement. It was even unable to defend its own property for Lithuania, robbed of Vilna by Poland, seized the port of Memel from the Allies. Detailed settlements at Vilna, Corfu and elsewhere were often left to the *Conference of Ambassadors*, which met in Paris under the chairmanship of Cambon and included the representatives of Britain, France, Italy and Japan. In 1924, MacDonald ruled that the Conference was concerned only with matters arising from the Peace Settlement but the Conference was not dissolved until 1931.

Meanwhile, the League of Nations began to win respect. In 1921, it successfully settled a dispute between Sweden and Finland about the Aaland Islands. Sweden's acceptance of the League's ruling was in contrast to the selfishness of other nations. Arbitration was also successful between Colombia and Venezuela in 1922, Chile and Peru in 1925 and Guatemala and Honduras in 1938. The League mediated over Mosul in 1926 (see Section 5.3(*a*)).

The attack by Greece on Bulgaria in 1925 may serve as an example of the League's intervention. The Greeks had learned from Mussolini and after a series of border incidents they sought satisfaction by force. They were unfortunate. The League intervened and forced them to withdraw and pay compensation to Bulgaria. For once, force did not bring rewards but it did seem that the League of Nations had one law for the large states and another for the small fry. Nevertheless, from 1925 there was now a new hopefulness for peace and goodwill among nations. In July of that year, the French left the Ruhr.

7.2   Pieces of Paper, International Treaties

At the same time, there was a tendency for the nations to conduct much of their diplomacy outside the League of Nations and to put their trust in paper

REMOVING THE TREASURES.

Exclusive picture from the "Valley of the Tomb of the Kings."

Fig. 7.2 French aggression in the Ruhr. Daily Mail, *19 January 1923*

treaties. The second half of the 1920s brought more stability and some prosperity. There was continuity in foreign policy in Britain, Germany and France in the hands of Austen Chamberlain, Stresemann and Briand. The USA assisted Europe financially and there seemed to be more goodwill, which the statesmen tried to capture in pacts and treaties. Many of them were, however, of little value. They represented no more than the hopes of decent men.

(a) The Washington Agreements

Towards the end of 1921, the USA held a conference in Washington to discuss the Far East and naval disarmament. A series of agreements was reached.

Japan agreed to withdraw from Kiao Chow. Guarantees of independence were given to China and there was general recognition of the rights and possessions of America, Britain, France and Japan in the Pacific. The declarations sounded impressive and a few years later Europeans tried to make similar agreements about Europe at Locarno.

The most substantial agreement at Washington, however, concerned the sizes of navies although they dealt only with capital ships (battleships and cruisers). None was to be built for ten years and others were scrapped to arrive at a fixed ratio of 5:5:3 for the USA, Britain and Japan. France and Italy would have just over half the ships of the Japanese. This was the most specific agreement on disarmament to be reached between the wars, but it was limited in scope and some alleged that the scrapped ships were obsolete anyway.

(b) The Treaty of Rapallo, 1922

At about the time that the Washington Conference met, Lloyd George, ever fertile in new ideas, proposed a world economic conference. He wanted discussion of economic problems and co-operation for reconstruction. He also wanted to include the defeated Central Powers and Soviet Russia. Briand was interested and the powers met in Genoa. Britain was prepared to offer more concrete promises of help to France in the event of any attack from Germany but required, in return, evidence of French goodwill to Germany and Russia. Briand could not obtain the necessary support in the French parliament and was forced to resign. The French doomed the meeting to failure and nothing was achieved.

An unexpected consequence was a treaty between Germany and Soviet Russia, signed at Rapallo in April 1922. Both were treated as outcasts, especially by France. They therefore drew together. In fact, the Treaty said little. They renounced financial claims, the one against the other, undertook to co-operate in economic matters and, most important, Germany recognized the Communist government. Secretly, Russia undertook to allow Germany to build and test weapons on Soviet soil, in defiance of the Treaty of Versailles. Russia was now able to enjoy normal diplomatic relations with a major power and other states followed suit in recognizing the Soviet government, especially after Britain did so in 1924. The USA dragged behind but Roosevelt recognized Russia in 1933.

(c) The Treaties of Locarno, 1925

During his brief period as Prime Minister in 1924 and with the co-operation of Herriot of France, MacDonald set in motion a series of events which were designed, first, to strengthen the League of Nations. The Geneva Protocol was drafted: members were required to recognize as compulsory the authority of the Permanent Court of International Justice and more thought was given to sanctions against aggressors. MacDonald's government fell before the Protocol was ratified. For Baldwin, Austen Chamberlain and the Conservatives, the Protocol went too far and so the project was abandoned.

Chamberlain was, however, prepared to undertake some further commitments in Europe and it seemed to be time to reconsider Germany's part in world affairs. France, now again influenced by Briand, was ready to co-operate. Stresemann was eager to obtain German admission to the League of Nations. The result was the signing of a series of complicated agreements at Locarno in December 1925.

One of the Treaties of Locarno was a Rhineland Pact. France, Germany and Belgium confirmed the sanctity of their boundaries as laid down in the Treaty of Versailles and of the Rhineland as a demilitarized zone. Britain and Italy joined in guaranteeing these frontiers and the demilitarization. Another Treaty, of Arbitration, bound Germany and France to accept mediation in disputes. Germany made similar agreements on arbitration with Belgium, Poland and Czechoslovakia. France, in separate treaties with Poland and Czechoslovakia, guaranteed to protect them in the event of German aggression.

A few months later, to satisfy Russian fears, Germany renewed the Treaty of Rapallo with the USSR. And later in 1926, the League of Nations admitted Germany to membership with a seat in the Council.

It was too readily assumed that all this treaty-making meant the end of Europe's problems. The Rhineland Pact was broken by Hitler in 1936 when he remilitarized the Rhineland, and no country moved to honour the Locarno obligations. Similarly, France deserted Czechoslovakia in 1938 and 1939 (see Unit Eight). The Treaties of Locarno, overlapping the Treaty of Versailles as they did, cast doubt on how far the earlier treaty was now valid. Britain had undertaken only very limited commitments, as had Italy. For the moment all seemed well, however, for Chamberlain, Briand and Stresemann were genuine in their hopes for international goodwill. Locarno was greeted with enthusiasm in Britain. There was general satisfaction in Germany. But France had reservations and Italy was almost indifferent. In Eastern Europe, Germany's failure to confirm her Polish and Czechoslovak frontiers was noted and, even after the renewal of the Treaty of Rapallo, the USSR continued to suspect that Locarno was part of some capitalist plot against the Soviet system.

(d) The Kellogg–Briand Pact, 1928

Two years after Locarno, Briand produced a new plan. He proposed that France and the USA should sign a pact to renounce war. Kellogg, the American Secretary of State, was enthusiastic. He suggested extending the declaration to more countries and, in 1928, 65 states signed the Pact. They included Soviet Russia as well as the USA and, at first sight, it seemed an important, world-wide agreement, helpful to future peace. In fact, nations retained the right to fight in defence of national interests, and the Pact said nothing about punishing aggressors. One of the signatories was Japan who only three years later resorted to war in Manchuria, carrying out naked aggression in alleged defence of national interests.

(e) **Ententes**

Meanwhile, the lesser powers tried to protect themselves in a confusion of alliances and treaties of friendship. One of the most significant was the 'Little Entente' between Czechoslovakia, Rumania and Jugoslavia. It developed from a series of separate treaties between these states which were consolidated into one alliance in 1929. Their first concern was to protect themselves against the possibility of a war of revenge by Hungary and their aim was to guarantee the frontiers laid down in the Treaties of St Germain and Trianon. In 1933, the Entente developed into an economic community with a common secretariat, but the community and the alliance collapsed at the end of the 1930s.

The pieces of paper multipled but it became apparent in the 1930s how little they were worth. The fate of Czechoslovakia in 1938 and 1939 revealed the emptiness of paper guarantees.

7.3   The League of Nations

The League of Nations had a respectable record in the 1920s. Its Commissions and Committees achieved a great deal and the League began to cope with international disputes (see Sections 2.9(b) and 7.1(b)). It overcame some of the Central Powers' hostility towards it though not yet that of Soviet Russia. It functioned smoothly as the international climate improved in the later 1920s.

There was, however, awareness that the League lacked teeth. The Locarno Treaties and other alliances also showed some lack of confidence in the League, for they represented a search for additional security. The League would not really be tested until it was confronted with a major international crisis. Such a crisis did not occur until 1931.

Germany was the only great power to be admitted to the League in the period from 1923 to 1931. At Locarno, she had been promised a permanent seat on the Council but this created difficulties. Poland was apprehensive about Germany's new friendships and demanded a similar concession. Quarrels between Poland and Germany became frequent at League meetings after 1926, for, after some hesitation, the League gave a permanent seat on the Council only to Germany. As a compromise, they increased the elected members from six to nine and made re-election possible. This did not satisfy Poland, and Brazil and Spain also resented the privileges Germany obtained. Brazil withdrew from the League in protest. To smaller powers and non-Europeans, the League now seemed to be too much dominated by the Locarno powers.

7.4   Disarmament

There was hope, however, that the Treaties of Locarno would at last make possible some real progress towards disarmament as envisaged in the Covenant of the League of Nations. In 1919, the reduction of German armed forces was held to be the first step towards 'a general limitation'. At Washington, in 1921, some progress was made in reducing navies (see Section 7.2(a)). Other steps added up to nothing but running on the spot.

There was general agreement that disarmament was desirable but no state wished to be the first to reduce its own security. The Disarmament Commission of the League therefore proposed, in 1923, a Treaty of Mutual Assistance, a system of collective security under which countries would help to protect each other. It was accepted by France, Czechoslovakia and others, criticized by Poland and some Balkan states as inadequate and rejected by Britain as too binding. The Disarmament Commission, therefore, prepared the ground for an international Disarmament Conference in 1926, but with little on which to build except a woolly hopefulness that the Locarno Treaties had somehow stiffened the will to disarm.

The Commission laboured for five years without results. Germany constantly reminded the powers that she had been disarmed and that it was time for others to follow suit. Litvinov, who became Russia's Foreign Minister in 1930, made a vigorous attack on capitalism and proposed immediate and total disarmament. Such a startling idea was rejected, after a decent interval in which to consider it. The Russian composer, Shostakovich, wrote a new ballet, *The Age of Gold*, bitingly satirical about capitalist society and scathing on the subject of disarmament diplomats. When, at the end of 1930, the Commission finally agreed on a draft convention, the USSR and Germany voted against it. The League decided to shift the action to a wider stage and, in February 1932, sixty nations met in the Disarmament Conference.

Meanwhile, in 1930, there was a Naval Conference in London to follow up the earlier agreements at Washington. This time, they considered ships other than capital ships and fixed a ratio, including submarines, for the USA, Britain and Japan of 10:10:7. Nothing was agreed for Italy and France.

The Disarmament Conference met under the chairmanship of Henderson, the British Foreign Secretary, who later devoted himself to working for the League of Nations. It largely ignored the previous work of the Disarmament Commission and it was handicapped by Russian opposition and the instability of German politics. France still wanted guarantees of mutual security before disarmament. Germany wanted equality, which appeared to mean rearmament. The delegates were also perplexed about how to enforce an agreement, assuming they reached one. In 1933, MacDonald produced a new plan for a reduction of armaments, partly designed to meet Germany's demand for equality, but by that time Hitler had become Chancellor. The French raised difficulties about the weapons to be allowed to Germany and, in October 1933, the Germans walked out. Hitler also withdrew from the League of Nations. With Germany now openly rearming there was no hope for disarmament and the Conference held its last session in 1934. In that year, France completed the building of the Maginot Line which fortified her eastern frontier.

7.5   Collective Insecurity

Progress towards disarmament was, therefore, almost non-existent. In spite of the creation of the League of Nations and the signing of treaties many states still felt insecure at the end of the 1920s, chiefly France and Poland. Europe's basic problem was collective insecurity. France would get no help from the USA in the event of an attack. America would not even join the League of Nations. The French also lacked confidence in Britain, for several times in the 1920s Britain showed an unwillingness to take on further obligations in Europe. The British withdrew most of their occupation forces from Germany in 1926, nine years earlier than had been laid down in the Treaty of Versailles. France hung on but, in 1930, under British pressure, all the occupying armies were withdrawn. The rise of Hitler only confirmed French fears, yet German rearmament was inevitable as long as other powers refused to disarm.

The distrust and fears among the European powers pleased the USSR. The Russians could attribute them, together with the failure of disarmament talks, to capitalism and competition. Like the USA, Russia took little part in European affairs in the 1920s. She valued the Treaty of Rapallo with Germany and often claimed to detect capitalist plots against the Soviet Union. Occasionally, with or without the approval of the Russian Foreign Ministry, the Comintern stirred up communist agitation in Europe but, especially when Stalin rose to power, internal problems claimed most of the Russian government's attention. Not until Hitler destroyed the Treaty of Rapallo was the USSR willing to play a more active part in Europe.

Stresemann died in 1929. In the same year, Briand resigned for the last time as Prime Minister* and Austen Chamberlain lost office in Britain in the general election. In that same year too, the Great Depression began. These events brought to a close the most hopeful period in international relations between the wars. Japanese aggression in 1931 opened a new and more disturbed period in which the initiative passed from the democracies which supported the League of Nations to the totalitarian regimes which held the League in contempt.

Further Reading

Bloncourt, P.: *The Embattled Peace, 1919–39*. Faber (London, 1968).

Bruce, M. G.: *From Peace to War, Europe 1918–1939*. Thames and Hudson (London, 1967).

Hastings, P.: *Between the Wars*. Benn (London, 1968).

Richards, I., Goodson, J. B. and Morris, J. A.: *A Sketch Map History of the Great Wars and After*. Harrap (London, 1965). This book is extremely useful on international relations from 1918 onwards.

Exercises

1. What made the 1920s a period of hopefulness in international affairs? Why did this hopefulness not lead to confidence?
2. 'The League of Nations had one law for the large states and another for the small fry.' How would you support this statement by referring to events mentioned in this Unit?
3. What attempts were made between the wars to bring about disarmament? Why did they have such limited success?

* He died in 1932.

4. Make a balance sheet of the successes and failures of the League of Nations from 1919 to 1931.
5. Find out more about the foreign policies of two of the following: Austen Chamberlain; MacDonald; Briand; Stresemann.
6. Using *Fifty Major Documents of the Twentieth Century* by L. L. Snyder (Anvil, London, 1955) find out what was agreed in
    (*a*) the Locarno Pact
    (*b*) the Kellogg–Briand Pact.
7. Compare the progress of disarmament in this Unit with that of disarmament after 1945 in Section 17.2 (*b*).

Unit Eight
International Relations, 1931–41

8.1 Japanese Aggression

Various factors made Japan an aggressive nation. One was the prestige and influence enjoyed by the armed forces, all the greater when set alongside the weakness of civilian governments (see Section 5.3(*b*)). Others were economic: Japan looked for space for her expanding population, food to feed the people and raw materials. She also sought racial equality and brooded on the refusal of the statesmen at Paris, in 1919, to insert a declaration of support for that principle into the Covenant of the League of Nations. The suspicion that white nations regarded Japan as inferior grew in the 1920s, feeding on the immigration laws of such countries as the USA and Australia. The 'White Australia' policy closed that country's doors to Asians and was resented by them. The suspicion also fed on the Washington and London Naval Agreements (see Sections 7.2 and 7.4) which denied Japan equality with the USA and Britain. After the Agreement of 1930, a Japanese naval officer made his protest by committing suicide although the minister who signed the treaty declined an invitation to do likewise.

Japan was also tempted to aggression by China's weakness, and hoped to exploit the split in China between the communists and nationalists (see Section 15.2(*c*)). One outcome of the Washington Conference of 1921–2 was the Nine-Power Treaty, binding Japan, with others, to claim no special rights in China. It did not prevent Japan from meddling intermittently in Chinese affairs in the later 1920s.

(*a*) Manchuria

Japan first leased the territory of Kwantung around Port Arthur in Manchuria as a result of the Russo-Japanese war of 1904–5. Manchuria was part of China but the Japanese made vast investments in the area and gained a stranglehold on the South Manchurian Railway and other economic enterprises. Power in Manchuria, however, was exercised by the Japanese army, which demonstrated its independence of the government by bombing the train of the warlord ruler of Manchuria in 1928. The Prime Minister, Tanaka, was not consulted. In 1931, the army took a more ambitious decision, to occupy the whole of Manchuria (Fig. 8.1).

To avenge alleged sabotage of the railway by the Chinese, the Japanese army seized the city of Mukden and went on to over-run all of Manchuria by early 1932, an area five times the size of Great Britain. China appealed to the League of Nations.

The League sent a commission under Lord Lytton, which eventually made a leisurely journey by sea, produced a report in October 1932 and stated the

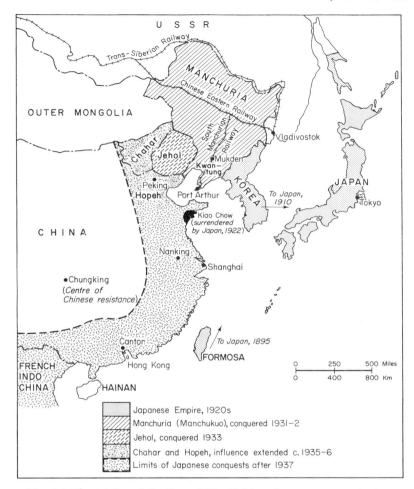

Fig. 8.1 The origins of the Second World War: Japanese expansionism in the 1930s

obvious. Japanese aggression was condemned. It was recognized that Man-churia belonged to China but that Japan had special interests there. A large measure of self-government was recommended for the state but the Japanese must give up their conquests and withdraw their troops. Instead, Japan gave notice of withdrawal from the League of Nations, in March 1933, and ex-tended her conquests into Jehol.

The Lytton Commission was much too late. Before it arrived in Manchuria, the Japanese had declared the state to be *Manchukuo*, nominally independent under Pu Yi, China's last Manchu Emperor who had been overthrown in

1912. Pu Yi was no more than a Japanese puppet and Manchukuo was developed as an economic appendage to Japan.

The League of Nations was powerless. Outside it, Stimson, the American Secretary of State, recommended a policy of moral force, designed in some way to shame Japan into more lawful actions. The policy was called the 'Doctrine of Non-Recognition' which meant a refusal to accept the fact that Japan had over-run Manchuria. The USA applied it with an equal lack of effect towards the government of Mao Tse-tung when China became communist in 1949. Only Italy and Germany recognized Manchukuo but Japan

THE DOORMAT.   (Copyright in all countries.)

Fig. 8.2 Sir John Simon, Britain's Foreign Secretary, repairs the face of the League of Nations while Japan tramples on the League in Manchuria. Evening Standard, *19 January 1933*

was unperturbed. The state was remote from Europe, Europeans were hampered by the Depression and Britain could expect no support for a policy of resistance to Japan. So Japan went on to penetrate further into northern China and by the mid-1930s had taken the provinces of Hopeh and Chahar. She also renounced her obligations under the Naval Agreements.

The League rescued only one shred of prestige. Inspired by the example of their army in Manchuria, the Japanese navy tried, at the end of 1931, to seize Shanghai in central China. With some prodding by Britain, the League persuaded Japan to withdraw in May 1932. Shanghai was thus saved for the moment.

(b) The 'China Incident'

In July 1937, the Japanese army claimed to have been provoked again, this time in an incident at the Marco Polo Bridge, near Peking. They alleged that the Chinese had fired on a Japanese night patrol. Japan struck back with a full-scale war against China which went on until 1945 and which in the first year alone uprooted sixty million Chinese from their homes. The Japanese absurdly referred to this war as the 'China Incident'.

Shanghai was taken after months of fierce struggle. The Japanese then drove quickly southwards, capturing Nanking and then Canton. The Chinese government retreated inland and set up headquarters at Chungking. It was forced to leave almost the whole of the Chinese coast in Japanese hands and, when it refused to surrender, the Japanese set up another puppet ruler in Nanking in 1940. But stubborn Chinese resistance and the sheer size of the country prevented the Japanese from winning total victory. Half their forces were still tied down in China when the more widespread war in the Pacific began in 1941.

Again China appealed to the League of Nations but the Council merely recommended individual members to apply sanctions against Japan, a recommendation they ignored. Europeans were now preoccupied with the aggressions of Hitler and Mussolini. Before embarking on the 'China Incident', Japan had signed an Anti-Comintern Pact with Hitler to which Mussolini attached himself a year later. Britain wanted the USA to take the lead in defending China but even when the Japanese sank an American gunboat on the Yangtse River at the end of 1937, the USA accepted their apology.

The USSR took more positive action. Russia and China signed a non-aggression pact in 1937. The Red Army moved troops to the Manchurian border and, when Japanese anti-communists challenged them, they were quick to inflict heavy casualties on the Japanese. In 1939 Russo-Japanese fighting began again, and for the first time Japan suffered a major defeat. By that time, however, war had broken out in Europe and Japan signed an armistice with Russia, ready to turn her attention elsewhere.

(c) Expansion Southwards

The outbreak of the Second World War in Europe quickened Japanese interest in extending the 'Co-Prosperity Sphere' southwards (see Section 5.3(b)). The rapid defeat of France and Holland left Indochina and Indonesia exposed to a Japanese invasion but, at first, Japan proceeded cautiously. Britain's weakness in the summer of 1940 was exploited by persuading the British to close the Burma Road and cut off supplies to the Chinese. Britain was anxious to avoid involvement with another enemy. But within months Japan signed a new treaty with Germany and Italy, turning the Anti-Comintern Pacts into the Tripartite Axis Pact for joint defence against any power 'not already engaged in war'. Japanese troops moved into the north of Indochina and Britain re-opened the Burma Road. A year later, Hitler's puppets in the Vichy government in France agreed to a joint protectorate with Japan over the whole of Indochina and Japanese troops landed in the south.

Compromised by his pact with Germany in August 1939 (see Section 8.4), Stalin accepted a non-aggression pact between Russia and Japan in April 1941. The USA, on the other hand, viewed Japanese activities with increasing displeasure. When Japanese troops landed in the south of Indochina, the USA stopped the sale of oil to Japan, having already cancelled trading agreements between the two nations. Britain and Holland took similar steps. Japan was still dependent on the West for oil and certain metals such as copper. But America's terms were too high for the Japanese militarists: the USA had insisted that Japan must evacuate both Indochina and China. The Prime Minister was replaced by General Tojo whose policy was to take what Japan needed by force, particularly Indonesian oil. The USA would not tolerate this and so Tojo decided to strike first.

Japanese negotiators continued to discuss a settlement with the Americans while preparations were made. Japanese aircraft carriers put to sea towards the end of November 1941. On 7 December they launched their attack on Pearl Harbor, Hawaii, where they crippled the American Pacific fleet. At the same time, they attacked American airfields in the Philippines and British bases in Malaya, Singapore and Hong Kong. Japan had achieved surprise and success. The USA and Britain instantly declared war; and Germany and Italy honoured their obligations to Japan under the Axis Pact and declared war on America.

Thus the wars of the late 1930s truly became the Second World War, exploding from Japan's war against China, which began in 1937 (or, it may be argued, in Manchuria in 1931), the war in Europe which began in 1939 and the war between Germany and Russia which began in June 1941.

8.2   Italian Aggression

In the late 1920s, Mussolini was in a mood for signing pieces of paper. He arrived at Locarno by speedboat, on the last lap of an appropriately dramatic journey which also included a special train and a racing car. He signed the Kellogg–Briand Pact in 1928 and, in the same year, a pact of friendship with Ethiopia. In 1933, he wanted to sign a pact to preserve peace between Italy, Germany, Britain and France but that ended with only the signatures of Mussolini and Hitler. Mussolini's foreign policy seemed to be a peaceful one and his aggression in Corfu was long past.

Mussolini, however, was easily impressed—impressed by Japanese vigour in Manchuria and by German rearmament, by the weakness with which other states responded, and above all, by the apparent defencelessness of Ethiopia which lay between the Italian colonies of Eritrea and Somaliland. He was also impressed by his own show of strength, when he sent four Italian divisions to the Brenner Pass in 1934.

The occasion was a disturbance in Austria in the course of which Austrian Nazis murdered Dollfuss, the Chancellor (see Section 3.3(c)). Hitler hoped to use the occasion to incorporate Austria into Germany, but there was a general outcry which deterred him. At the time, Mussolini had no wish to see Germany expand to his frontiers and the movement of Italian troops contributed to preserving the peace. In 1935 Mussolini met the Prime Ministers of Britain and France at Stresa to declare solemn disapproval of Hitler's intrigues and re-armament. They undertook 'close and cordial collaboration' to maintain treaties. Britain and France hoped that the *Stresa Front* would guarantee peace in Europe; but Mussolini was turning to aggressive policies again, looking for victories abroad to compensate for economic disappointments and repression at home.

(a) Ethiopia

At the time of the Stresa Conference, Italy and Ethiopia were already in dispute about the obscure oasis of Walwal on the border of Italian Somaliland. Following a skirmish there in December 1934, Mussolini demanded both the oasis and compensation for the deaths of thirty Italian soldiers. Haile Selassie, Emperor of Ethiopia, appealed to the League of Nations, who recommended him to negotiate with Italy. Mussolini was massing troops but it seemed more tactful at Stresa not to raise the matter, lest the Duce should be less firm against Hitler. Throughout the summer Italian troops streamed through the British-controlled Suez Canal on their way to East Africa.

A quarter of a million Italians launched their attack on Ethiopia in October 1935. The League of Nations reacted swiftly. Within a week, first the Council and then the Assembly declared Italy an aggressor and *economic sanctions* (prohibitions on trade) were applied to deprive her of supplies. It took a month for them to take effect and Austria and Hungary, as well as Germany, refused to apply them. In any case, the League excluded oil, coal and steel from the sanctions, the very commodities Mussolini needed most desperately. The USSR, Rumania and the oil-producing countries, were willing to impose oil sanctions but Britain and France objected, out of self-interest. They even kept open the Suez Canal, preserving Italy's supply-lines.

In December, Hoare, the British Foreign Secretary and Laval, Prime Minister of France jointly produced the *Hoare–Laval Plan*. Italy would be given about two-thirds of Ethiopia, some parts on the borders of Eritrea and Somaliland to enlarge those colonies and a large area in the south of Ethiopia for 'economic expansion and settlement'. In return, Ethiopia would gain a tiny strip of land to secure access to the sea. The Plan was rejected by everybody.

In Britain, Hoare was replaced by Anthony Eden, who had more enthusiasm for sanctions but not to the extent of making them work by including oil. The conquest of Ethiopia went on unchecked and in May 1936, Marshal Badoglio made a triumphant entry into the capital, Addis Ababa. Haile Selassie went into exile and Victor Emmanuel III of Italy was proclaimed the new Emperor of Ethiopia. Mussolini reconstructed all his possessions in the area into one huge colony, *Italian East Africa* (see Fig. 8.3(*b*)). Shortly afterwards the League abandoned sanctions.

The Ethiopian war was a disaster for collective security through the League of Nations. The League had failed miserably, undermined by the feebleness of Britain and France, although the absence from the League of important states such as Germany and the USA was a contributory factor. Sanctions were discredited and force had once again succeeded. Worst of all, for Britain and France, the Stresa Front collapsed: by tolerating Mussolini's aggression they had still failed to retain his support against Germany.

For Mussolini, too, the Ethiopian War was a disaster in spite of his apparent triumph, because it brought him closer to Hitler. Hitler had taken the opportunity of the Ethiopian crisis to remilitarize the Rhineland (see Section 8.3(*a*)) and he and Mussolini now found themselves in partnership in intervening in the Spanish Civil War (see Section 5.2(*c*)). Mussolini's fancy was captured by a line from Rome to Berlin which he called an *Axis*. In 1937, he joined Germany and Japan in the Anti-Comintern Pacts and left the League of Nations. In May 1939, he strengthened his understanding with Hitler in an alliance, dubbed 'The Pact of Steel', which was extended, in 1940, to the Tripartite Axis Pact with Japan. Misled by the glory of his soldiers in Ethiopia, Mussolini thus sank ever more deeply into the fatal alliances which were to destroy Fascist Italy in the Second World War. Italian East Africa was a short-lived empire.

(*b*) Albania

From 1936 to 1939 the centre of European attention shifted steadily from Rome to Berlin; Mussolini was increasingly overshadowed by Hitler. He won some minor victories, however. The activities of Italian submarines which preyed on supplies to the Popular Front in the Spanish Civil War caused anger in Britain and France. They made an agreement at Nyon to patrol the Mediterranean and to take action against such submarines, although they stopped short of identifying them as Italian vessels. Mussolini demanded an equal share in the patrol duties and was given a zone of the Mediterranean to police, a curious arrangement which made his meddling in Spain all the easier. The Duce was also a leading figure at the Munich Conference in 1938 (see Section 8.3(*c*)) and he basked in the glory of visits exchanged with Hitler, martial displays and the photographs which recorded their friendship.

Above all, he was inspired to demonstrate yet again the strength of a fascist army. He turned to Albania. There seemed little chance of effective resistance since that country was already economically dependent on Italy, its army Italian-trained. Mussolini struck in April 1939: King Zog fled and Victor Emmanuel was given a new crown. Mussolini celebrated by signing the Pact of Steel with Hitler. But when Hitler became involved in war over Poland in September (see Section 8.3(*f*)), Mussolini at last showed wisdom in remaining neutral.

By June 1940, however, Mussolini was convinced that Germany would win. He hoped for new gains, especially at the expense of France. He even dreamed of an Italian Mediterranean Empire stretching from Gibraltar to the Suez Canal. So on 10 June 1940, Italy declared war on Britain and France.

8.3   German Aggression

In the years before 1936, Hitler watched the progress of the Japanese and Italians with interest. He made no secret of his hostility to the Treaty of Versailles and to communism. After leaving the League of Nations (see Section

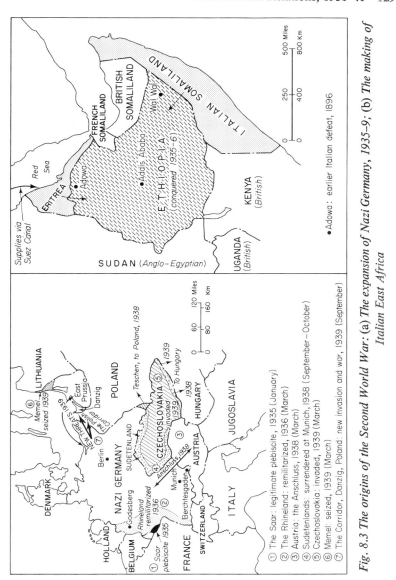

Fig. 8.3 The origins of the Second World War: (a) The expansion of Nazi Germany, 1935–9; (b) The making of Italian East Africa

7.4), he went ahead with rearmament, especially of the navy, and missed no opportunity to remind Europe of Germany's grievances over such matters as the Saar and the Polish Corridor.

The Nazi accession to power produced a flurry of diplomatic activity among Germany's neighbours. Stalin felt there would be advantages in seeking better relations with Russia's neighbours and had signed a non-aggression pact with Poland in 1932. In September 1934, the USSR was admitted to the League of Nations, with a permanent seat on the Council. In 1935, Litvinov, Russia's Foreign Minister, secured mutual assistance treaties with France and Czechoslovakia. The French Foreign Minister, Barthou, worked tirelessly to bring about for Eastern Europe the sort of guarantees given to Western Europe at Locarno. European countries continued to sign a bewildering collection of pieces of paper in their search for collective security. When the leaders of Britain, France and Italy met and reached agreement at Stresa in April 1935 (see Section 8.2) security seemed to have been reached. It was almost instantly destroyed by Mussolini's invasion of Ethiopia.

(a) Hitler's First Moves

At the beginning of 1935, the plebiscite provided for in the Treaty of Versailles was held in the Saar. Nine votes in every ten were cast in favour of reunion with Germany, which was quickly arranged. The Saar was added to Hitler's state quite legally but Hitler hailed it as a victory for the Nazis. He followed up this alleged triumph by announcing conscription in Germany and a massive new programme of rearmament, in public defiance of the Versailles settlement. The programme was instantly condemned at Stresa. Checked in Austria in 1934 (see Section 8.2) and apparently surrounded by hostile powers, Hitler's scope for more assertive action was limited.

But in June 1935 Hoare, the British Foreign Secretary, still anxious to pacify potential enemies, agreed to sign a Naval Agreement with Germany. It was a triumph for von Ribbentrop who served Hitler as a roving ambassador. The *Anglo-German Naval Agreement* allowed Germany to build a navy up to 35 per cent of the tonnage of that of Britain. This could include as many submarines as there were in the Commonwealth, although both powers looked forward to the abolition of submarine warfare, at some suitably vague time. Hitler was jubilant. The Agreement accepted a revision of the Treaty of Versailles and it antagonized the French, who regarded the Agreement as an act of betrayal. Within two months of the Stresa Conference, Britain was beginning to appease Hitler.

In March 1936, Hitler had another success. While Italian troops were overrunning Ethiopia, German troops marched into the Rhineland, a demilitarized zone in the Treaty of Versailles to which Germany had given additional agreement in the Rhineland Pact at Locarno (see Section 7.2(c)). The League of Nations condemned the German action, but France hesitated and Britain gave her no encouragement to act. For months, the Locarno powers negotiated with Hitler about the matter and in the end they did nothing.

(b) **Austria, the Anschluss**

By the end of 1937, Hitler had made the Anti-Comintern Pacts and further advanced the cause of fascism in the Spanish Civil War. Purges in Russia, the disarray of the League of Nations and the shift of Mussolini's allegiance from Britain and France to Germany combined to increase Hitler's confidence. German military power was growing and, like the Japanese militarists, Hitler looked for further conquests. An interview with Lord Halifax in November 1937 convinced him that Britain would not oppose expansion in Austria, and perhaps not in the Sudetenland.

In February 1938, therefore, Hitler summoned the Austrian Chancellor Schuschnigg to pour on him a torrent of abuse for the alleged ill-treatment of Austrian Nazis. An ultimatum was issued which Schuschnigg accepted, agreeing among other things to appoint Seyss-Inquart, an Austrian Nazi, as Minister of the Interior. Schuschnigg then tried to seize the initiative by ordering a plebiscite in Austria to test opinion for an *Anschluss* (a total union with Germany). Hitler demanded that Seyss-Inquart should be appointed Chancellor and Schuschnigg reluctantly resigned. Seyss-Inquart at once claimed the discovery of a communist plot, and requested German assistance. It arrived promptly and in two days Austria ceased to be independent, with Seyss-Inquart ruling the state as a province of Germany. Over 99 per cent of those who voted in a plebiscite approved the *Anschluss*. All possible resistance to the Nazis was eliminated by arrests, which filled the concentration camps, and by murder.

Neither Britain nor France had the will to resist the *Anschluss*, although it was forbidden in the Peace Settlement of 1919. Austria appeared to want it. Austrians and Germans were racially similar and so the matter rested. It remained to be seen whether Britain and France would defend Czechoslovakia, for Hitler now pressed on that country from three sides and he had a grievance about the Sudetenland.

(c) **The Sudetenland**

Since 1933, Germans in the Sudetenland (see page 26) had been creating disturbances under the leadership of Henlein. They claimed they were ill-treated and demanded self-government. By the summer of 1938 Henlein was little more than Hitler's puppet, but his antics persuaded Britain and France that the question of the Sudetenland was now an urgent one. Hitler ordered the German army to make ready but expressed no specific objectives. On the other hand, Neville Chamberlain, who came to power as Prime Minister in Britain in 1937, took it upon himself to try to settle the problem.

Lord Runciman was sent to Prague in August 1938. He seemed anxious to persuade the Czechs to grant whatever Henlein wanted and President Beneš went a long way to meet his wishes. Henlein could have had self-government but Hitler was unwilling to let the crisis stop there. Further disturbances were whipped up and Hitler abused Czechoslovakia as an 'artificial state', all the more objectionable for its treaty with the USSR.

On 15 September, Chamberlain personally went to see Hitler at Berchtesgaden and a week later to see him again at Godesberg. Between the two meetings, with the help of the French Prime Minister Daladier, he produced a plan to transfer those areas of Czechoslovakia where the population was more than 50 per cent German to the German Reich. Beneš was not consulted but merely required to agree, which he did under protest. At Godesberg, however, Hitler raised the stakes. He now wanted the immediate evacuation of the Sudeten areas which would be occupied by the German army. Chamberlain was taken aback. He passed Hitler's new demands to the Czechs who promptly rejected them.

War seemed imminent. Czechoslovakia was prepared to fight. The French mobilized reservists and sadly accepted the need to honour their treaty to defend Czechoslovakia. The USSR was also bound to help the Czechs, but only if the French did so first. On the other hand, Poland and Hungary, encouraged by Hitler, were also making claims on Czechoslovakia. In a radio broadcast, Chamberlain solemnly observed, 'How horrible, fantastic, incredible it is that we should be digging trenches and trying on gas masks here because of a quarrel in a faraway country between people of whom we know nothing.' Britain had no treaty obligations to Czechoslovakia but felt obliged to assist France.

Chamberlain made a final effort and proposed a third meeting with Hitler. He sent a telegram to Mussolini too and the Duce was partly instrumental in persuading Hitler to meet Chamberlain at Munich, together with Daladier and himself. They met on 29 September. No invitation was sent to Russia and Czech delegates were left in a hotel while the Big Four decided the fate of their country. The Big Four simply agreed to Hitler's terms: the Sudetenland was to be handed over to Germany; an international commission would later hold plebiscites where necessary and draw up final boundaries. On the following day, Hitler signed another piece of paper expressing with Chamberlain his confidence in 'consultation' as a means of avoiding war. Chamberlain returned home to a warm welcome. He waved Hitler's paper. 'I believe it is peace for our time,' he said.

In the House of Commons Churchill summed up Chamberlain's achievements at Munich: '£1 was demanded at the pistol's point. When it was given, £2 were demanded at the pistol's point. Finally the Dictator consented to take £1.17.6 and the rest in promises of goodwill for the future.'

(d) The Rest of Czechoslovakia

After Munich, Czechoslovakia could now fight alone or submit. Beneš resigned and the country submitted. The loss of the Sudetenland robbed her of vital industries and the only defendable frontiers. Poland claimed and took the town of Teschen. Hungary made claims, on which Germany and Italy sat in arbitration. She too got her way. As Churchill put it, 'Czechoslovakia recedes into the darkness'.

The state began to break up. Slovakia and Ruthenia questioned the authority of government from Prague and the new President, Hacha, had to accept a

Fig. 8.4 Neville Chamberlain and Mussolini, two of the men of Munich, pictured later in Rome, 1939

federal constitution. This was of little importance for, in March 1939, Hitler demanded special rights for any Germans still left under Czech rule. The demand was followed by invasion and Czechoslovakia came under German rule, except for Ruthenia which Hungary made haste to occupy.

(e) Memel

A week later, Hitler persuaded Lithuania to surrender Memel (see Section 7.1(b)). Before the month was out, Britain, now obviously worried by the rapid succession of German gains, made an alliance with Poland, a pledge to defend Polish independence. France took steps to strengthen her existing alliance with Poland. The following month, they both gave guarantees to Rumania and Greece who were alarmed by Mussolini's invasion of Albania. It no longer seemed possible to contain the dictators by appeasement.

(f) Poland

Geography made improbable the defence of Poland by Britain and France. But Chamberlain's pride had been injured and Halifax wanted a strong statement to deter Hitler from further aggression. Hitler was already discussing the future of Danzig and the question of a route across the Polish Corridor (see Fig. 8.3) to East Prussia. At first, he expressed no intention of breaking the non-aggression pact which he had made with Poland in 1934 but Poland could not be sure. At the end of 1938, the Poles signed a new treaty of friendship with the USSR.

The role of the USSR was now a vital one for, clearly, Hitler would hesitate to commit further aggression if this were to result in a war on two fronts. Britain and France began to explore the possibility of some joint agreement with Russia to deter Hitler but neither side showed a great sense of urgency. The Soviet Union felt anger at having been excluded from the Munich Conference and Stalin had suspicions that the capitalist powers would have no regrets if Hitler were to launch an anti-communist war against Russia. Litvinov was replaced as Soviet Foreign Minister by Molotov in May 1939. Molotov was less anxious to make agreement with the West and he had not the hatred for Hitler of his Jewish predecessor. By July he was negotiating with both the West and Germany but only with Hitler did he make progress. On 23 August a non-aggression pact was signed between Russia and Germany—by Ribbentrop and Molotov in the presence of Stalin. Secret clauses made provision for the division of Poland and the Baltic states, if any changes were made there. The Pact was a triumph for Hitler. The threat from Britain and France seemed irrelevant. They were remote from Poland, even if they were to honour their treaties with that country. For Stalin, the Pact held out the prospect of recovering much that Russia had lost in the years after 1917 and of neutrality in any European war which Germany might fight with the West. He could thus preserve communism while the capitalists fought among themselves. Nevertheless, it was a bizarre agreement, a marriage of convenience between fascism and communism.

Hitler attacked Poland on 1 September 1939. On 3 September Britain and France declared war on Germany. 'Everything that I have worked for,' Chamberlain lamented, 'has crashed into ruins.' The long struggle for peace in Europe had failed. The League of Nations had become almost irrelevant as a peace-keeping body although it lived on until 1946. Negotiations outside the League and Britain's policy of appeasement had also become irrelevant. From 1939 until the defeat of the Axis powers, war spread relentlessly to almost every corner of Europe and across the whole world.

8.4   Russian Aggression

The Red Army entered Poland from the east two weeks after Hitler attacked in the west. Russians and Germans met in the middle of the country and consolidated their conquests. The Russians also moved troops into the Baltic states, but only in Finland, did the Soviet Union meet significant resistance.

The Russian demands were not extravagant. They required bases as a future safeguard against German expansion into Finland. The Finns protested and Russia attacked at the end of November 1939. The difficulties of the terrain and Russia's casual preparations for the campaign resulted in setbacks to the

Red Army and the war lasted for over three months. Newsreel pictures of this strange conflict in the snow, where soldiers often moved on skis, produced a considerable effect in Britain and France. Plans were made to send assistance to the gallant Finns but nothing came of them. In a last expression of vigour, the League of Nations expelled Russia from membership. But in March 1940 Finland had to submit, and Russia demanded additional territories as the price of defeat.

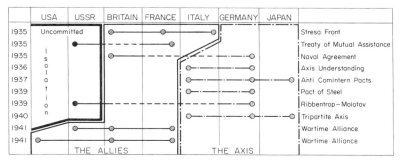

	USA	USSR	BRITAIN	FRANCE	ITALY	GERMANY	JAPAN	
1935	Uncommitted							Stresa Front
1935								Treaty of Mutual Assistance
1935	I s o l a t i o n							Naval Agreement
1936								Axis Understanding
1937								Anti Comintern Pacts
1939								Pact of Steel
1939								Ribbentrop–Molotov
1940								Tripartite Axis
1941								Wartime Alliance
1941								Wartime Alliance
			THE ALLIES			THE AXIS		

Fig. 8.5 The origins of the Second World War: some treaties and alliances, 1935–41

8.5   Why Did the Second World War Come About?

'War sets the seal of nobility on those peoples who have courage to face it.' Such was the opinion of Mussolini. The Second World War had its roots in the willingness of Japanese militarists, German Nazis and Italian Fascists to go to war to get their own way. Their countries had grievances, which militarists, Nazis and Fascists strenuously encouraged. There were flaws to be found in the Peace Settlement after the end of the First World War. But the flaws were exploited to serve the purposes of unscrupulous leaders bent on power. By 1931, the faults were widely acknowledged. In Britain and France, there were even feelings of guilt which led to a willingness to admit, for example, that the union of Germany and Austria was legitimate. In the end, the Second World War occurred because Japan and Germany were prepared to use force for illegitimate purposes. Their reasons were partly economic, the quest for supplies which could only be obtained by plundering.

To place the blame for the Second World War on others is to do no more than criticize a man for defending his property. It can, of course, be argued that the weakness of their neighbours tempted the aggressors to strike. The League of Nations showed many weaknesses and from its birth was severely handicapped by the non-membership of the USA. It lacked an effective weapon with which to resist aggression and when attempts were made to strengthen it, they failed. Baldwin would not accept the Geneva Protocol. Instead, the search for collective security (joint defence against aggression) led to the signing of almost endless pieces of paper which undermined the authority of the League (see Unit Seven). Even worse, the pieces of paper were not honoured in times of crisis, for example when Hitler remilitarized the Rhineland and raped Czechoslovakia. But the only way to honour them was to go to war or at least to be prepared to go to war.

There were occasions when the aggressors might have been deterred by a firmer show of resistance. The sanctions imposed on Italy after Mussolini's attack on Ethiopia might have been effective if extended to oil and passage through the Suez Canal. Hitler might have been persuaded to retreat from the Rhineland. It is legitimate to blame both Britain and France on these occasions. On the other hand, Britain and France bore an unfair burden. They were not free from pressing internal problems; they were unassisted by the USA, they were bewildered by the rise of fanatical totalitarian regimes and they had a naïve belief that the dictators could be appeased. Hitler constantly declared that each claim was his last and that the settlement of a legitimate demand would be a guarantee of peace. In their eagerness to preserve peace, the democracies were hoodwinked.

At the same time, Britain and France were guilty of sluggishness. Throughout the 1930s, the National governments in Britain showed a talent for ignoring problems rather than solving them, while France staggered from one political crisis to another (see Unit Three). At times they blundered. Too often, there was a lack of trust between Britain and France and both failed utterly to tackle the problem of involving the USSR in a policy of collective security.

Under Stalin's ruthless rule (see Section 5.1(c)), Russia seemed as unattractive to the democratic powers as Hitler's Germany. But Stalin's foreign policy was not aggressive until 1939. The USSR often expressed a willingness to play a part in defending the weak and demonstrated against Japan, in 1938 and 1939, a capacity to act effectively. How far Russia's expressed willingness was genuine remained untested. In 1939, Britain and France went to war with Hitler in defence of Poland, a cause already lost. Stalin made a sordid deal with Hitler and remained neutral. Anti-communists would argue that such lack of scruple was only to be expected. Russians argued that, in excluding the USSR from the Munich Conference, the West showed its contempt and perhaps something more sinister, a readiness to gang up with Hitler against communism. It was the final tragedy which made war in Europe inevitable in 1939 that Britain and France reached no agreement with Russia but Germany did—and that removed the fear of a war on two fronts for Hitler. He was able to attack Poland, safe in the knowledge that the USSR would not interfere. Britain and France alone no longer alarmed him. 'Our enemies are little worms,' he had said, 'I saw them at Munich.'

But Poland was only one among many victims. The Second World War really began when Japan attacked China. China was the first victim. Ethiopia, Austria, Czechoslovakia and Albania followed. General war was only avoided until 1939 because no country went to the rescue of these victims. In attempting to rescue Poland, albeit in vain, Britain and France only enlarged a conflict which had already begun. The blame for starting it can lie nowhere but with

Japan and Germany, supported by Italy. It was in the nature of fascism to be aggressive and expansionist. 'I want to make Italy great, respected and feared,' Mussolini said. Japan and Germany shared his ambitions and, in the end, all three chose war as their instrument.

Further Reading

See **Further Reading** for Units Five and Seven.

Documentary

Bettey, J. H.: *English Historical Documents 1906–39*. Routledge & Kegan Paul (London, 1967), pages 167–98.

Breach, R. W.: *Documents and Descriptions, the World Since 1914*. Oxford University Press (London, 1966), Section 6.

Parkinson, R.: *The Origins of World War Two*. Wayland (London, 1970).

Stacey, F. W.: *Anglo-Russian Relations 1854–1939*. Arnold (London, 1969).

Gramophone Record

Taylor, A. J. P.: *Chamberlain and Munich* (Discourses, DCL 1207).

Exercises

1. What do you understand by *aggression*?
2. Why did *collective security* fail?
3. Identify Hitler's grievances in international affairs, by referring to Units Two and Eight.
4. Why were (*a*) Italy and (*b*) Japan aggressive in the 1930s?
5. 'All three (Italy, Japan and Germany) chose war as their instrument' (above). List the states which were victims of these powers in the years up to 1939.
6. Explain how the Second World War could be said to have begun in the Far East.
7. Why did Mussolini (*a*) come to admire Hitler and (*b*) become Germany's ally in 1940?
8. Show how Britain pursued a policy of appeasement from the end of the First World War to 1938 but then suddenly abandoned it. How do you account for the change in Britain's policy?
9. Write an explanatory account of Fig. 8.5.
10. Find out more about how the Japanese conducted their campaigns in China, the Italians treated Ethiopia and the Germans treated Czechoslovakia.

The Second World War: an Outline of Events

9.1 The Nazi Conquest of Europe

(a) Poland

The declaration of war on Germany by Britain and France could do nothing to save Poland. German *blitzkrieg* (lightning war) tactics proved too successful; and Poland faced overwhelming odds. By 1939, six German *Panzer* divisions (heavily-armed, mobile forces) had torn into Poland while the *Luftwaffe* pounded the country from the air. Polish soldiers and civilians made a heroic effort to hold Warsaw but the city was battered into submission on 27 September. Poland capitulated a week later, and the Nazis began to herd Polish Jews into ghettos.

No country experienced the savagery of Nazi rule more than Poland. Two-and-a-half million Poles were taken to Germany for forced labour. Two hundred thousand young children were taken to be 'Germanized'. From 1941, Polish Jews were shipped steadily to concentration camps and a final attempt to resist in the Warsaw Ghetto, in 1943, brought terrible retribution. The Nazis killed over 3 million Polish Jews before the war ended. Russia also deported thousands of politically suspect Poles from the areas of Poland she occupied.

(b) The 'Phoney War'

The war subsided with the conquest of Poland. German generals were reluctant to launch an immediate attack on France, and Britain and France wanted more time to gear their countries to war. There was even hope that the war would be called off or that Germany could be blockaded and starved into submission without fighting. The *Maginot Line* defended the French frontier from Luxemburg to Switzerland. Hitler had built the *Siegfried Line* facing it, but extending further north to cover the Belgian frontier. With absurd optimism, a British popular song declared the intention of hanging out 'the washing on the Siegfried Line'. But few hostilities occurred in the winter of 1939–40. Rearmament and training went on but the terrible events the democracies had feared were confined to Poland. In the west, the war was dubbed 'phoney'.

(c) Scandinavia and Britain's Change of Government

Many plans were made on paper during the 'Phoney War' to achieve some dramatic master-stroke. The attention of all three belligerents, Britain, France and Germany, came, curiously, to centre on Norway. During the winter, Britain and France thought of sending help to Finland against Russia (see

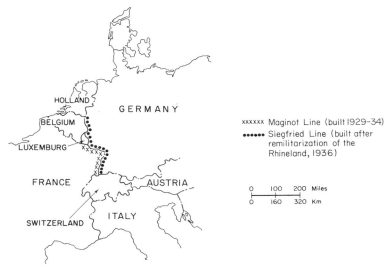

Fig. 9.1 The Maginot and Siegfried Lines

Section 8.4). Norway lay along the route. The idea of a British landing there appealed first to Churchill, then to Chamberlain. Quisling, a Norwegian fascist, went to warn Hitler. In February 1940, a German ship, the *Altmark*, was chased into a Norwegian fjord and boarded by the British. Both sides were now interested in control of the Norwegian coast but Germany struck first. On 9 April both Denmark and Norway were attacked by the Nazis. Denmark was in no position to resist. Norwegian resistance was handicapped by Quisling and his supporters. A British landing near Trondheim did nothing to save southern and central Norway, and Germany soon completed the conquest of the rest of the country. Norway's neighbour, Sweden, managed to remain neutral throughout the war.

In Britain, Chamberlain was made a scapegoat for the failure to keep Norway out of German hands. The failure of appeasement before the war, the inactivity of the 'Phoney War', and Chamberlain's rash prophecy that Hitler had 'missed the bus' combined with the Norwegian setback to convince even many Conservatives that there must be a change of Prime Minister. Chamberlain was replaced by a Coalition government under Churchill, an outspoken critic of British foreign policy in the later 1930s. Churchill made no optimistic promises, offering only 'blood and toil and tears and sweat' to put the country on the road to victory. He took office on 10 May 1940. It was too late to save Norway. Within a few months, Britain was being fully tested to save herself.

(d) The Low Countries and Dunkirk

On the day that Churchill became Prime Minister, Germany attacked Holland, Belgium and Luxemburg. Holland surrendered almost at once. Belgium resisted for less than three weeks. This was a grave situation for France, for the Maginot Line did not extend along the Belgian border. Even worse, German *Panzer* troops driving through Luxemburg struck across the northern edge of France to reach the Channel coast south of Calais, cutting off British and French troops in Belgium. Total disaster seemed inevitable.

As the Germans closed in, nearly 200 000 British and 140 000 Allied troops were rescued from beaches pulverized by shells and bombs. The evacuation went on until 4 June and was remembered as the 'Miracle of Dunkirk'. It was a magnificent achievement even though almost all the military equipment had to be left behind. Hundreds of vessels, many of them small craft able to get close inshore, and almost anything capable of floating, were organized by the British navy. The RAF provided the best air cover possible. A gallant holding action at Calais helped to delay the Germans and the operation was aided by a calm sea and soft sand which lessened the blast of bombs. But the main factor which made it possible was that Hitler meddled with the plans of his generals and slowed down the German advance. This provided time for the miracle to be performed.

(e) The Fall of France

The collapse of Belgium made the Maginot Line irrelevant. A week after the evacuation from Dunkirk ended, General Weygand informed the French Prime Minister, Reynaud, that the Germans could not be stopped. The Germans entered Paris on 14 June. Reynaud resigned; his place was taken by Marshal Pétain, a veteran of the First World War, who signed an armistice on 22 June. Hitler insisted that the armistice should be signed in the same railway coach and at the same place as the armistice in 1918 at which Germany had surrendered.

Meanwhile, on 10 June Mussolini felt sufficiently confident of a German victory to declare war on France and Britain. He was just in time to make a separate armistice with France, taking a small strip of French territory.

Pétain's government felt that there was no alternative but to collaborate with the Nazis. By the terms of the armistice, Germany occupied the western coast and northern France, including Paris, and France agreed to bear the costs of this occupation. Pétain took the title 'Head of the French State' and his government made its headquarters at Vichy. The Vichy government agreed to return German refugees to the Nazis and to leave French prisoners of war in German hands. They were allowed to keep control of the French fleet but much of it was destroyed by the British navy to keep it from use by the Nazis. Pétain then broke off relations with Britain. The Vichy government shared with the fascists a belief in authority, law and order but it was not until its final year, 1944, that it became wholly fascist. It collaborated with the Germans but Hitler felt sufficient distrust to order the German occupation of the whole of France in 1942. The Vichy politicians were, in fact, distrusted by both sides, and were regarded as traitors after the war.

The *Free French* set up an alternative to Vichy collaboration in 1940.

General Charles de Gaulle escaped to London and called on Frenchmen to continue the struggle. In exile and in the *maquis* (an underground resistance movement), the Free French rejected both Nazi domination and Vichy peace-making.

(*f*) The Battle of Britain

Hitler's next objective was Britain. Churchill refused to abandon the struggle and so the Germans prepared Operation Sealion, the launching of a new invasion. In July 1940, the *Luftwaffe* began a preliminary bombardment of Britain's shipping and airfields. Goering was confident that the RAF could be destroyed, and then the invasion could take place. His confidence was misplaced, for the Luftwaffe suffered heavy losses at the hands of Fighter Command. British *Spitfires* and *Hurricanes* piloted by the 'few' airmen to whom Churchill paid tribute,* destroyed over half of Goering's aircraft. By mid-September, the Luftwaffe had lost the Battle of Britain. Operation Sealion was postponed indefinitely and German bombers changed their tactics. British cities became their main targets. The Nazis intended to punish and terrorize British civilians for stubbornly continuing to resist.

This was Hitler's first major setback. His armies were supreme on the continent but they could not reach Britain because of the strength of the British navy and the apparent strength of the RAF. But in September 1940 Britain was equally powerless to invade Europe.

(*g*) The Balkans

London provided a rallying-point for exiles from the lands Hitler had conquered; but his complete mastery of continental Europe was demonstrated again before the middle of 1941. His attention turned to the Balkans where an Italian attempt to invade Greece met disaster in the autumn of 1940. The Greeks replied by invading Albania and Mussolini needed German assistance. Hitler needed supplies: agreements with Hungary and Rumania, in November 1940, provided food, oil and stepping-stones to the south. In March 1941, Bulgaria also decided to collaborate with Germany and, in April, Hitler attacked Jugoslavia and Greece. Sixty thousand British troops went to Greece's defence but they were quickly driven from the mainland and then from the island of Crete. By the end of May, the whole of the Balkans was under Axis control although the independence of Turkey was guaranteed by the USSR.

9.2   The Extension of the Conflicts

(*a*) The Position in June 1941

Spain, Portugal, Switzerland, Eire and Sweden still clung to neutrality. The Soviet Union followed her own policy and only Britain and the Commonwealth continued to resist Axis aggression in Europe. In the Far East, Japan

* 'Never in the field of human conflict was so much owed by so many to so few.'

continued her own war against China and expanded into Indochina (see Section 8.1(c)). Of the Axis powers, only Italy suffered defeats. By June 1941, the Italians had been driven from their Empire in East Africa and Haile Selassie had returned to his throne in Ethiopia. The Italians had also failed in an attack on Egypt, and now relied upon German troops to hold on to Libya. It was at this point that Hitler made a decision which was ultimately to prove disastrous. On 22 June, a hundred German divisions marched against Russia, setting into motion Operation Barbarossa.

(b) Operation Barbarossa

At last Hitler felt confident that he could destroy communism. He also coveted Russia's resources and looked forward, perhaps, to creating a massive link between Nazi Europe and the militarists of Japan. At first, Germany's advance was rapid but Hitler had badly underestimated the strength, size and determination of the Soviet Union. Stalin rallied the Russian people not to the defence of communist ideology but to the 'Great Patriotic War'. Hitler had also disastrously delayed the invasion of Russia for six weeks while his troops went to the aid of Mussolini in the Balkans. The Duce was now proving to be an albatross around the neck of the Führer. Casualties in the conflict with Russia were enormous. By 1945, the USSR had something like 20 million dead. It was a savage struggle from the outset. The Germans, who were supported by Hungary, Rumania and Finland, reached the outskirts of Leningrad and Moscow by the end of 1941 but they advanced over 'scorched earth'. (The Russians devastated the countryside rather than leave food, shelter and supplies to the enemy.) The German supply-lines grew longer, a constant target for guerilla fighters (see Glossary). The Russian winter took a heavy toll of both sides. Russia also received assistance from Britain and the USA and at last the German army found that it had embarked on a campaign which could not be won in a few weeks or even a few months.

(c) South-East Asia

In December 1941, the Japanese attack on Pearl Harbor (see Section 8.1(c)) extended the conflict still further and directly involved the USA in war against the Axis powers. Like the Nazis in Europe, Japan was at first highly successful. In only three months, Japanese armies seized Hong Kong, over-ran Thailand, Malaya and Singapore, wrested Indonesia from the Dutch and the Philippine Islands from the USA and made inroads into Burma and New Guinea. They cut the Burma Road, the main road for supplies to China, and so threatened India and Australia that the latter recalled troops from North Africa.

The advance was stemmed in May 1942, when the USA won a naval action in the Coral Sea to the south of New Guinea. American and Australian troops prevented the total conquest of New Guinea itself. East of Japan, aggression was halted when the Japanese were defeated at Midway Island. Burma proved the limit of their advance towards India. The position stabilized in the second half of 1942. For a time, Japan was able to reap immense profits from her new

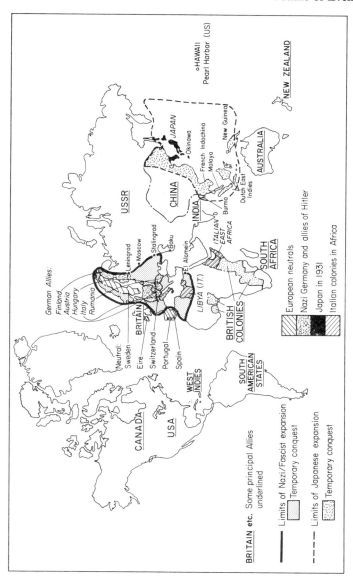

Fig. 9.2 The Second World War

conquests but her Empire was surrounded by enemies against whom further advances were now impossible.

9.3   The Turning of the Tide

(a) Russia

In the summer of 1942, the Germans were unable to break the Russian resistance at either Leningrad or Moscow. They desperately needed to defeat the Red Army. So far the Russians had resisted, destroyed the countryside (including many hard-won achievements of the 1930s, such as the Dnieper Dam), and retreated. Now the Russian forces fell back to Stalingrad and once again the winter closed in on the fighting. A terrible battle developed for possession of the city, and 21 German divisions were committed to the struggle. On 31 January 1943, 90 000 Germans were forced to surrender; thousands more were already dead. Leningrad was also under relentless siege until 1944, with the Russians suffering casualties on a vast scale: over three-quarters of a million died, most of them from starvation. (Shostakovich later commemorated their sufferings in his 'Leningrad' Symphony (No. 7).) But the German advance had been halted.

(b) North Africa

In 1942 General Rommel and the German Afrika Korps succeeded in driving the Allies from their last foothold in Libya. They were pushed back into Egypt as far as El Alamein. In October, British and Commonwealth forces took the offensive. They were led by General Montgomery and after another struggle at El Alamein, the Germans began to retreat. In little more than two months, they were driven right across Libya and into Tunisia. Meanwhile, British and American forces landed in Algeria and drove eastwards to squeeze the Axis forces from two sides. On 7 May 1943, Tunis was entered and a week later the Axis troops in North Africa admitted defeat.

(c) The Pacific

For Japan, too, 1943 was an ominous year. The USA, 'leap-frogging' over strongly-held Japanese positions, began to retake islands in the Pacific and to turn them into bases for future air-strikes. The war output of American industry steadily increased. For the moment, the Japanese Empire remained almost intact but Japan was rapidly losing the initiative that had been seized at Pearl Harbor.

9.4   The Defeat of Italy

The American General, Dwight Eisenhower, launched the invasion of Sicily only two months after defeating the Axis powers in North Africa. The island was captured by the end of August 1943, and the following month Allied

Fig. 9.3 Allied reinforcements land in Normandy, 1944

forces landed in the 'toe' of Italy and at Salerno, south of Naples. This blow into 'the soft under-belly of the Axis' by the forces of the USA, Britain, members of the Commonwealth and countries such as Poland, created consternation among Italians. The landings in Sicily produced the instant downfall of Mussolini who was overthrown, arrested and imprisoned by the Fascist Grand Council. Badoglio took over the leadership, intending at first to continue the war, but when Allied troops crossed to the mainland of Italy, he promptly agreed to unconditional surrender. Any Italian hopes that their country would not become a battlefield were, however, destined to disappointment. Germans instantly prepared to defend Italy from a line slightly north of Naples.

The struggle for Italy lasted until the spring of 1945. The Germans were gradually forced back but they resisted stubbornly. Rome was not taken until June 1944. Further north, the Germans constructed new defences, where the Allies were delayed until 1945. By that time, Germany was also under severe pressure from both the west and east.

Mussolini was rescued from his imprisonment by German parachutists in September 1943. Hitler established him as a puppet-ruler of a new Fascist Italy, behind the German lines, but his *Fascist Republic of Salò* shrank steadily. At last, German resistance in Italy was broken. Mussolini tried to join them in a retreat into Austria but he was captured by guerillas and shot. At almost the same time, the end of April 1945, Hitler also died, cornered among the ruins in Berlin.

9.5   The Defeat of Germany

(a) Western Europe

On 6 June 1944 the Allies made landings on the Normandy beaches, with Eisenhower as the Supreme Commander. Stalin had long demanded the opening of a 'Second Front', always ready to argue that the Russians were bearing the brunt of the war. But the landings were not made until thorough preparations had been undertaken. Apart from special landing craft, the Allies had PLUTO (a fuel pipeline under the ocean) and prefabricated harbours ready to tow into position. Highly-trained troops stood ready. A hundred and thirty thousand men were landed on the first day, a million by the end of the first month. There was fierce resistance but the bridgehead was held. The Germans had thought their defences in the Atlantic Wall were strong enough to make invasion impossible. But Hitler had expected the invasion to be attempted near Calais and, once the foothold was secured in Normandy, the Germans were driven back. Paris was liberated and on 25 August, de Gaulle and the Free French were able to enter the city. In September, the whole of France was free.

Germany took much longer to be defeated. The river Rhine was still a formidable obstacle and a premature attempt to use parachute troops to establish a bridgehead at Arnhem in Holland proved costly. In the winter of 1944, the Germans launched a vigorous counter-attack in the Ardennes mountains which further delayed the Allied advance. The Rhine was crossed in March 1945 and at last Germany was opened up to attack from the west. At about the same time, the Allies finally broke German resistance in Italy.

(b) Eastern Europe

The Russians began their advance in the summer of 1943, driving the Germans back in the Ukraine. At about the time of the opening of the Second Front in Normandy, the Germans were driven from Russian soil. Before the end of 1944, Rumania and Finland surrendered. Hungary surrendered in January 1945. Guerillas under Marshal Tito produced an uprising against the Germans in Jugoslavia. The Russians pressed on through Poland and entered Germany from the east in February 1945. In late April, Berlin was besieged and Hitler was trapped. On 30 April he chose to commit suicide rather than face capture and it was his successor Admiral Doenitz, who agreed to *unconditional surrender* on 7 May. On 8 May VE Day was celebrated: Victory in Europe was achieved.

It was a Europe in ruins, pounded and trampled by armies. Most of Germany's cities and towns were devastated, shattered by the massive bombing which accompanied the final defeat of Nazism. Dresden, hardly a significant military target, was reduced to ruins in February 1945, with the loss of over 100 000 lives. Almost every nation emerged from the war with dreadful scars, although none suffered more than Poland, Germany and Russia. On both sides, the wounds would take many years to heal.

9.6   The Defeat of Japan

(a) The Japanese Retreat

In 1944, American forces were 'island-hopping' northwards. A decisive naval victory at Leyte made possible the reconquest of the Philippines by General MacArthur. At the same time, British and Commonwealth troops pushed into Burma.

Fig. 9.4 'Island-hopping.' The Americans were forced to pay a heavy price for the liberation of Iwo Jima

Early in 1945 with the fall of Rangoon, Burma was liberated. Supplies to China could again be sent along the Burma Road. In June 1945, MacArthur took Okinawa: he was now within 400 miles of the southern tip of Japan. But the campaigns were costly in lives and the Allies still faced daunting problems. The Japanese continued to hold most of South-East Asia and large areas of China; to invade Japan itself could be even more costly. As in Europe, the Allies insisted on unconditional surrender and the Japanese showed no signs of yielding.

(b) Atomic Bombs

Scientists in all countries had experimented with new and more terrible weapons throughout the war. In 1944 Germany produced the V1 flying-bomb, pilotless and jet-propelled, refining it in the V2, a higher-flying rocket bomb. For a time they caused extensive damage but they came too late and the Allied troops, advancing in Western Europe, over-ran their launching sites. A far more deadly weapon was developed in the USA, the first nuclear weapon, the atomic bomb. The bomb became available in July 1945. The decision whether it should be used fell to Harry Truman, who had become President of the USA three months earlier on the death of Roosevelt.

The first atomic bomb was dropped on the Japanese industrial town of Hiroshima early on the morning of 6 August. A third of the population of nearly a quarter of a million were killed instantly and the whole town was devastated. Another 100 000 were injured, many of them condemned to intense suffering and lingering death from the effects of radiation. The USSR declared war on Japan two days later. Still the Japanese hesitated and a second atomic bomb was dropped on Nagasaki on 9 August. Again the results were devastating. Hastily, Japan agreed to unconditional surrender although the final capitulation was not signed until 2 September. By that time, American troops had already landed in Japan.

The atomic bombs undoubtedly shortened the war in the Pacific and thus saved the lives of many Allied soldiers but arguments soon raged about the morality of their use. Nuclear weapons heralded a new era in human destructiveness and the effects of the radiation they created are still incalculable. American possession of such weapons created fear in the USSR and a determination to match them. Russia developed an atomic bomb in 1949 but, by then, even more destructive nuclear weapons were being invented in the USA. The Soviet Union rushed on to match America with a hydrogen bomb which both had perfected by 1953. A new, more terrible arms race was under way in which America and Russia were soon joined by Britain, France and China.

Meanwhile, peace was restored in the Pacific and Japanese armies were withdrawn from China and South-East Asia.

9.7 Why Did the Axis Powers Lose the War?

The early successes of Japan and Germany were the result of ruthlessly efficient war machines. Of the Axis powers, only Italy proved incompetent in war. But the aggressors over-reached themselves and by their greed built up such a hostile coalition of powers that disaster became inevitable. Hitler's failure to defeat Britain seemed unimportant at the end of 1940, as did Japan's failure totally to defeat China. But by keeping the struggle alive, Britain and China denied complete success to the aggressors and with the involvement of the USSR and the USA in 1941, Allied strength grew steadily.

All the Axis powers underestimated their enemies. Hitler failed to understand that war against Britain involved war against almost the whole of the Commonwealth. He expected communist Russia to collapse and Japan imagined that victory at Pearl Harbor would paralyse the USA indefinitely. They underestimated not only the strength of their enemies but also their will to resist.

The British navy played havoc with German shipping. Casualties on both sides were heavy and German submarines took a dreadful toll of Allied shipping but Germany never won control of the seas. By the summer of 1943, German submarines had also been tamed and Hitler was penned in his European fortress. The Allies drew on supplies from almost the whole of the world but the Axis powers were increasingly forced to exploit and rely on the lands they conquered.

Similarly, in spite of early successes, the Japanese navy was battered in the Pacific, mainly by the USA. Thus Allied operations were supported from the sea with a power that even Japanese suicide pilots could not break. In the air, the Allies also achieved superiority. At first, it was a massive achievement for the RAF to prevent a German invasion in the Battle of Britain. London, Liverpool, Coventry, Plymouth and many other British cities and towns had to endure ferocious bombing by the Germans but the pendulum swung in the opposite direction. Agents and supplies were dropped behind the Axis lines to encourage sabotage, Axis ships were tracked and often destroyed and, from about 1942, Nazi Germany was steadily pounded with bombs. The Americans could not reach Japan with land-based aircraft until Iwo Jima fell, but air superiority also came to play an important part in the Allied victory in the Pacific. Accurate bombing, however, was only perfected in the later stages of the war. In 1943, precision bombing was demonstrated by the Dambusters on Germany's Möhne Dam and, in the invasion of Western Europe in 1944, it played an important part in disorganizing German communications. Moreover, the sheer weight of bombs also increased until thousand-bomber raids on German cities produced almost unimaginable destruction.

Germany and Japan fought desperately to the end. They were required to surrender unconditionally: there would be no argument about the terms of an armistice such as there was in 1918. Devastation throughout Germany, Italy and the Pacific, in Hiroshima and Nagasaki, bore witness to the total

Table 9.1   What governments spent on the Second World War*

Allies	£m	Axis Powers	£m
USA	84 500	Germany	68 000
USSR	48 000	Italy	23 500
Britain	28 000	Japan	14 000
Canada	4 000		
France	3 750		
Total	171 250	Total	105 500

* Adapted from Purnell's *History of the Twentieth Century*, Vol. 5, pages 2 048–9.
Compare spending in the First World War, Table 1.1, page 9.

Table 9.2   The dead in the Second World War

Allies	millions	Axis Powers	millions
USSR	20·0	Germany	4·2
Poland	4·3	Japan	1·2
China	2·2	Rumania	0·5
Jugoslavia	1·7	Hungary	0·4
France	0·6	Italy	0·4
USA	0·4	Austria	0·3
Britain	0·4		

Compare total dead in First World War, Section 2.1.

collapse of the Axis powers. Devastation elsewhere showed something of the price which had been paid to secure that collapse.

Further Reading

Ayling, S. E.: *Portraits of Power*. Harrap (London, 1965)—Churchill.

Jardine, C. Bayne: *World War Two*. Longman (Harlow, 1968).

Savage, K.: *The Story of the Second World War*. Oxford University Press (London, 1957).

Sellman, R. R.: *The Second World War*. Methuen (London, 1964).

Documentary

Breach, R. W.: *Documents and Descriptions, the World Since 1914*. Oxford University Press (London, 1966), Sections 14 and 23.

Ray, J.: *The Second World War*. Heinemann (London, 1977).

Yass, M.: *Hiroshima*. Wayland (London, 1971).

Yass, M.: *The Home Front*. Wayland (London, 1971).

Exercises

1. What evidence can you find in this Unit (including Fig. 9.2 and the Tables) to suggest that the odds against the Axis Powers were *overwhelming*?
2. Trace the rise and fall of German armed might under Hitler.
3. Show what parts were played by each of the following in the defeat of the Axis Powers: Britain and the Commonwealth; the USSR; the USA.
4. In what ways and for what reasons did Mussolini's Italy prove to be an unsatisfactory ally to Hitler's Germany?
5. Study in greater depth two of the following: the survival of Britain in 1940; Hitler's failure in Russia; the war in North Africa; the war in Western Europe, 1944–5; the defeat of Japan.
6. What were the main weapons used in the Second World War?
7. Account for the high number of dead in Poland and the USSR, listed in Tables 9.2 and 10.2.

Unit Ten

Aspects of the Second World War

10.1 The Atlantic Alliance

(a) The Arsenal of Democracy

Towards the end of the 1930s, President Roosevelt began to show increasing sympathy for the victims of the aggressors. At the same time, the USA was anxious to remain uninvolved, although she did try to deter Japan with words and then with an embargo on trade (see Section 8.1). Her first response to the outbreak of war in Europe was to supply Britain and France on the 'Cash and Carry Plan': they could buy the goods they needed for cash but must carry them from America in their own ships. But that, for the moment, was as far as Roosevelt could go, restricted as he was by Neutrality Laws and isolationist opinion in the American Congress (see Section 4.4(a)).

The ruthless expansion of German power in 1940 caused alarm in the USA. But Roosevelt had only contempt for Mussolini's attack on France. 'The hand that held the dagger,' he said, 'has struck it into the back of its neighbour.' Defence spending was stepped up and Congress agreed to give Britain fifty destroyers which were left from the First World War in exchange for the use of bases on certain British-owned islands. Roosevelt's success in the Presidential election at the end of 1940 strengthened his hand and on 29 December he told the American people, 'We must be the great arsenal of democracy.'

(b) The Atlantic Charter

More supplies were soon made available to fight the Nazis. In March 1941, the Lend–Lease Act was passed, to lend war supplies which, if they still existed, could be returned to the USA at an indefinite future date. At first the supplies were intended mainly for Britain and the Commonwealth, but they were extended to Russia after the launching of Operation Barbarossa (see page 142) and, by the end of 1941, to nearly forty other countries including China. Meanwhile, in August 1941, Roosevelt and Churchill drew up the Atlantic Charter, looking forward to the destruction of Nazi tyranny and to some form of future international co-operation for peace and the spread of prosperity.

The USA had now clearly declared her interests in the war. The Atlantic Charter also encouraged the hope that, when it ended, America would not return to isolationism. Her troops took over the defence of Greenland and Iceland (which Britain had occupied to try to prevent a possible German attack). The USA was still waging economic war against Japan, but America only formally entered the struggle against the Axis when the Japanese attacked Pearl Harbor.

10.2   International Co-operation

(a) Summit Conferences

The signing of the Atlantic Charter marked the beginning of a close personal relationship between Roosevelt and Churchill. They met again in December 1941, when Churchill went to Washington. They agreed to give priority to the defeat of Germany and set up machinery for united action. But America and Britain were not always in complete agreement: the USA wanted an early attempt to invade Europe but Churchill persuaded Roosevelt to accept Operation Torch instead (the invasion of North Africa from the west, see Section 9.3(b)). Churchill also went to Moscow to explain the strategy to Stalin and then met Roosevelt again at Casablanca, Morocco, in January 1943. This time they agreed on the invasion of Italy and that the Axis powers must make an unconditional surrender.

Stalin was impatient for them to begin a Second Front in Western Europe. Others fretted because they felt they were not always fully consulted, including Commonwealth leaders and leaders in exile, such as de Gaulle and the Free French. It was not practicable, however, to bring them all into the decision-making and most of them continued to be consulted, separately, mainly in London. Sometimes they reached particular agreements with the USA, like the Australians, with their special interests in the Pacific. But the USSR was powerful enough to demand more equal consultation and, in November 1943, Stalin, Roosevelt and Churchill met together for the first time in Teheran,

Fig. 10.1 The new 'Big Three' at the Potsdam Conference, July 1945—Attlee, Truman and Stalin

Persia. They agreed to co-ordinate Russian attacks in the east with the Second Front in Western Europe, to a postwar organization to preserve peace, and to a Russian declaration of war against Japan at some suitable moment. The war had produced a strange alliance between the leaders of world capitalism and world communism.

The Big Three met again in February 1945, at Yalta in the Crimea. They agreed to the temporary division of Germany into four zones (one of them French) after Germany's surrender, to the punishment of war criminals, reparations for war damage and the paralysing of German military power. They also agreed to a conference at San Francisco to launch a United Nations Organization. They reaffirmed the principles of the Atlantic Charter, to liberate conquered nations and Axis satellite states and to prepare the way for free and democratic elections. But they often disagreed on matters of detail. The boundaries of Poland, the size of reparations and the precise moment for Russia to join the war against Japan could not be settled, although Stalin undertook to declare war on the Japanese within a few months of the defeat of Germany.

Roosevelt died in April 1945. Churchill lost the general election in Britain in July and when the Big Three next met, at Potsdam, Berlin, in July 1945, Stalin faced new Western leaders, President Truman and Clement Attlee (see Section 11.1).

(b) The United Nations

Agreement on a new international organization had been reached at all the summit conferences since 1941. In November 1943, the principle was accepted by a meeting of Russian, American, British and Chinese representatives in Moscow. In August 1944 the same powers agreed on many details of the new organization's structure, although the right of the great powers to have a veto was not decided until the summit meeting at Yalta. In April 1945, fifty nations attended a conference at San Francisco to draft the Charter of the United Nations and the Statute of the International Court of Justice. The United Nations Organization came into formal existence in October 1945 and permanent headquarters were established in New York at the end of 1946 (see Unit Eleven).

(c) The Super Powers

Nothing did more to determine the outcome of the Second World War than the might of the USA. Americans built nearly 300 000 aircraft, 12 000 ships and 86 000 tanks before the war ended. Every Allied country relied on America for supplies, so it was inevitable that America would dominate much of the postwar world.

Estimates of the total dead in the war are sometimes put as high as 60 million (see Table 9.2). Of these only 400 000 were American (compared with 390 000 British, 100 000 in the rest of the Commonwealth and over half a million French). The USSR had some 20 million dead, almost half of them civilians. Poland too suffered enormous casualties, many of them Jewish victims of the

Table 10.1   Some important conferences during the Second World War

Date of Opening	Place	Those Taking Part	Purpose/Business	Page Reference
August 1941	Off Newfoundland	Roosevelt, Churchill	Atlantic Charter drafted	151
December 1941	Washington	Roosevelt, Churchill	Planning joint strategy	152
August 1942	Moscow	Churchill, Stalin, Harriman (USA)	Planning joint strategy	152
January 1943	Casablanca	Roosevelt, Churchill	Planning joint strategy—invasion of Italy	152
August 1943	Quebec	Roosevelt, Churchill, Mackenzie King (Canada)	Planning joint strategy—Far East	—
November 1943	Moscow	Representatives of USA, USSR, Britain, China	A new international organization	153
November 1943	Teheran	Roosevelt, Churchill, Stalin	Co-ordination of strategy	152
May 1944	London	Imperial Conference: Churchill, Prime Ministers of Dominions*	Commonwealth strategy	157
July 1944	Bretton Woods	44 nations represented	Trade and reconstruction	159
August 1944	Dumbarton Oaks, Washington	Representatives of USA, USSR, Britain, China	A new international organization	—
September 1944	Quebec	Roosevelt, Churchill	Co-ordination of strategy	—
February 1945	Yalta	Roosevelt, Churchill, Stalin	Co-ordination; final objectives	153
April 1945	San Francisco	50 nations represented	United Nations Charter drafted	153
August 1945	Potsdam	Stalin, Truman, Attlee	German problems; peace settlement	153 and 162

* Representatives of the Dominions also paid individual visits to London at various times.

Nazis. Even Jugoslavia had over a million-and-a-half dead. The war had thus taken a tremendous toll in Eastern Europe which was over-run by the USSR in the final stages of the conflict. The war had resulted in a tremendous shift in the balance of power. The League of Nations and world affairs before 1939 had been dominated by Britain, France and the rising Axis powers. After 1945, no country could match the USA. The only country which could even begin to challenge her was the Soviet Union. The postwar world was thus one in which two so-called 'super-powers' had emerged, neither of whom was concerned solely with Europe.

10.3   The Effects of the War in Europe

(a) The Nazi Tyranny

During the period of Nazi domination some parts of Europe were incorporated directly into the great German Reich, for example Alsace-Lorraine. Others, such as the Netherlands, had separate Nazi regimes. Yet others such as Vichy France and Quisling's Norway were under the puppet regimes of men considered traitors by many of their own countrymen. Hitler's Allies, such as Hungary and Rumania, managed to preserve only a small degree of independence.

Throughout Europe, Himmler and the SS had searched out the Nazis' enemies. Europe's economic activities were controlled for the benefit of Germany and the German war effort. Over seven million foreign workers were conscripted for German armaments production. The Nazis were ruthless and, in the end, even Mussolini had to obey their orders.

The most savage Nazi policies were directed against Jews and the peoples of Eastern Europe whom Hitler considered inferior. The 'Final Solution' of the Jewish problem began in 1941. In death camps such as those at Auschwitz and Treblinka, the Nazis attempted the total annihilation of the Jews. The Vichy government tried to protect French Jews. Italy and Hungary refused to yield to German pressures to deport their Jewish populations but, in 1944, both Italy and Hungary were occupied by the Germans and protection was no longer possible. In all, about six million Jews died.

Table 10.2   The Nazi slaughter of the Jews

	Poland	2 900 000
	USSR	1 000 000
	Rumania	400 000
	Czechoslovakia	300 000
	Germany	200 000
	Others	1 100 000
	Total almost	6 000 000

Hitler had almost equally vicious plans for the peoples of Eastern Europe, Czechs, Poles and Russians among them. Many were to be enslaved for the benefit of the Aryan *Herrenvolk*, and the rest were to be banished to Siberia, beyond the Urals.

Everywhere, resistance was suppressed with savage cruelty. Countless victims were hunted down by the SS and the Gestapo. Protest and sabotage brought brutal reprisals. In 1942, for example, the Nazis took revenge for the shooting of a close associate of Himmler's: they shot the entire male population of the mining community of Lidice in what had been Czechoslovakia, and burned the whole village.

(b) The Resistance

Resistance movements existed throughout Europe in spite of such reprisals. None was more active than the *maquis* in France and there too the Nazis struck back. In 1944 the male population of Oradour-sur-Glane was killed, the women and children herded into the village church and burned to death. But resistance movements constantly harassed the conquerors by sabotage and espionage, by massive strikes in the Netherlands and by guerilla warfare carried out wherever possible by partisans. The Allies and free governments in exile encouraged them by radio, by operations from the air and sometimes by commando raids on occupied Europe.

(c) Capitalism or Communism?

Resistance fighters agreed on the urgent need to harass the Nazis. But they were far from united about the future government of their countries. Some, like Tito's partisans in Jugoslavia, were communists. Communism won converts during the war, both in Europe and elsewhere. In China, Malaya and Indonesia, communists resisted the Japanese. In Europe and especially Eastern Europe they resisted the Germans. When Germany and Japan collapsed, there were often struggles to determine the new systems of government. The Western powers resisted concessions to communism. The countries they liberated were encouraged to set up systems based on Western democracy and capitalism. Where the Red Army advanced, however, communist systems developed. Where neither gained much of a foothold there was sometimes civil war to determine the outcome, as in China.

10.4   The Commonwealth at War

(a) Co-operation

Commonwealth troops fought with distinction in the war, even though in its early stages it threatened none of the Dominions. There was some hesitation in South Africa about joining the conflict. Australia and New Zealand did not hesitate and Canada waited only a week in order to make it clear that her declaration of war was a voluntary one. India could make no voluntary choice and like the rest of the British Empire became involved in the war when Britain did.

In its own way, the Commonwealth was an arsenal of democracy. West Indian colonies provided sugar; Malaya stepped up the production of rubber and each area provided what it could. In spite of disputes about Indian independence, India provided soldiers to fight in North Africa, Europe and the Far East. Dominion forces were active on all fronts, although South Africa restricted her forces to the African continent. The Commonwealth's contribution to victory was an important one and when, in 1940, Britain stood alone against Germany in Europe, the Commonwealth provided valuable support.

The Commonwealth dead in the war included nearly 40 000 Indians, about 30 000 from Canada and a similar number from Australia. Parts of the British Empire were over-run by the Japanese, so that Australia, India and Malta eventually found themselves in the front line. All made sacrifices in the cause of resisting fascism but at the same time the war inevitably caused changes in the Commonwealth's view of itself and the world.

(b) The Effects of the War

Many Dominion Prime Ministers visited London during the war, and an Imperial Conference was held in 1944. The increasing importance of American power, especially in the Pacific, persuaded Australia and New Zealand that they should look beyond the Commonwealth for future allies. Eventually the ANZUS Pact of 1951, an agreement for the joint defence of their interests, was drawn up by the two Dominions and the USA.

The shifting balance of power inevitably weakened some of the ties which bound Britain to the Dominions and her colonies, in spite of their close co-operation in the war. The authority of Europe in general was weakened by the war. Japan had conquered many of Britain's possessions in Asia: when these areas were restored, there were some who did not welcome the return of the British. Communists in Malaya claimed independence and resorted to civil war in an effort to obtain it. In fact there was a quickening of interest in independence everywhere. Dominion Status had already been promised to India, partly to secure wartime co-operation (see Section 6.2). Even in Africa and the West Indies there was greater awareness that British rule was unlikely to last for ever and that Europeans were not invincible. During the war small and poor states like Nyasaland had built up credit balances in London by supplying Britain's needs. This gave them new confidence in themselves. The Empire and Commonwealth could not revert to their pre-war positions: new relationships would have to be worked out.

10.5 The Effects of the War on Other Empires

During the war, Italy's Empire crashed in ruins. The Asiatic possessions of France and Holland were over-run by Japan. Reconstruction and reorganization were needed in South-East Asia and in Africa. It was unlikely that, with the myth of European superiority now exploded, either continent would meekly return to a situation similar to that of 1939. Nor were European countries in any condition to embark on vigorous attempts to reimpose their authority on reluctant overseas colonies. It was soon clear that overseas colonial empires had become time bombs. Explosions were inevitable. The first occurred only two days after the surrender of the Japanese when Dr Sukarno declared the Dutch East Indies the independent republic of Indonesia. The end of the great colonial empires was at hand (see Unit Sixteen).

10.6   Social and Economic Consequences of the War

(a) Refugees

In Europe alone, there were an estimated 21 million people who had been 'displaced' from their homes or were simply refugees from the conflict. Some were survivors of the Nazi concentration camps. There were over five million Russians, a million-and-a-half Poles and almost as many French. A vast resettlement operation was required. Some preparations had been made with the founding, in 1943, of UNRRA (the United Nations Relief and Rehabilitation Administration), to which the USA, Britain and Canada contributed funds for relief work. When the war ended, the Allies made an enormous co-operative effort to bring relief and repatriation to those in need. But it was impossible to do more than make a start on solving the problem. When UNRRA was wound up in 1947 new international agencies had been established by the United Nations, but huge problems still remained both in Europe and China.

(b) Devastation

Wreckage and devastation on a scale previously unknown also bore witness to the colossal disruption brought about by the war. In continental Europe and China, the destruction of homes, farms, factories, schools, hospitals and transport systems was on an immense scale. In Poland, a third of all buildings had been destroyed and in those parts of Russia invaded by the Germans the devastation was even greater. France, Belgium and the Netherlands suffered devastation equivalent to about three years' total production, reckoned in pre-war terms; and the damage to factories and communications meant that it would take many years to return to pre-war levels of production. Even in Britain, which had escaped invasion, a third of the houses had been destroyed or damaged by bombing and both industrial plant and people were worn out with the strains of total war.

(c) Disrupted Economies

Without massive aid to repair their economies, most countries faced a grim future. Apart from the devastation, many were deep in debt. Countries like Britain had used up many of their overseas assets to help to pay for the war. This reduced their income from 'invisible exports' and left them in difficulties over the balance of payments; it would be vital to sell exports in order to pay for imports.

Fig. 10.2 Wartime devastation: Allied tanks move through the ruins of Munster, Germany, in 1945

Again, there had been some preparations to meet these problems. At the Bretton Woods Conference in 1944, an International Monetary Fund (IMF) was set up to make gold and currency available to facilitate trading and a Development Bank was to provide loans for reconstruction. Efforts were made to reduce tariffs which had handicapped trade between the wars and 1947 saw the General Agreement on Tariffs and Trade (GATT). Inevitably, such attempts at international co-operation had to lean heavily on the wealth of the USA. This led to fear and resentment among the communist states and contributed to the development of the Cold War soon after 1945 (see Section 17.1). In spite of the fact that the war had wiped out much of the progress Russia had made in the 1930s, the Soviet Union preferred to recover by her own efforts. Stalin called upon the Russian people to make new sacrifices in the years after 1945.

(d) The Will for Change

Sacrifices were necessary almost everywhere. The end of the war brought a new struggle to re-establish at least the old standards of life. The old standards in themselves, however, were not good enough. The war accelerated the demand for social change. The Beveridge Report of 1942 had already provided a massive plan for the development of welfare services in Britain. The (Butler) Education Act of 1944 provided free secondary education for all and looked forward to raising the school leaving age to fifteen, and sixteen when possible.

The Family Allowances Act of 1945 provided state payments to assist larger families. In the general election of 1945, the British people showed a clear intention to move away from the pre-war complacency which accepted squalor and a high level of unemployment as inevitable. For the first time the Labour Party was returned with an absolute majority: the party programme contained a commitment to economic planning (the active intervention of the government in economic affairs to achieve certain fundamental objectives such as the reduction of unemployment). British electors seemed to show ingratitude in rejecting Churchill after his inspired wartime leadership, but Churchill and the Conservatives offered few ideas for the future. In 1945, Britain wanted real social improvements.

Some thought, wrongly in the case of Britain, that this shift in attitudes meant that there was now a desire for complete social equality and the end of class divisions. In some countries, such as China, there was certainly increased support for communism. But what was more widespread was the unwillingness of the underprivileged to endure further hardships. A new militancy developed after 1945 among the under-dogs. Colonies clamoured for independence and small nations for equal rights. Workers and trade unions, Jews, other minority groups and the underprivileged non-whites became keenly aware of injustices. In the 1950s and 1960s the world seemed to grow increasingly turbulent. At the same time, the war which ended in 1945 left violence in its wake, as did the First World War. The barbaric savagery of allegedly-civilized governments had made violence a way of life for millions.

10.7   War Crimes

In 1945, however, shock and horror were the main feelings about the war. Hitler and Mussolini were dead and Himmler also committed suicide. Other Nazi leaders were tried at Nuremberg, by representatives from the USA, the USSR, Britain and France. The offences with which they were charged were various but many fell within the category of 'crimes against humanity'. Twelve were sentenced to be hanged, among them Ribbentrop, Seyss-Inquart, Goering and Bormann. Bormann was tried in his absence and remained unfound. Goering committed suicide. Seven others received sentences of imprisonment, including Rudolf Hess, once Hitler's deputy, who was still in custody in 1973. Three were acquitted in spite of Russian protests.

In 1946 similar trials were held in the Far East. Seven Japanese leaders were sentenced to death by a tribunal representing eleven nations.

Trials in national and local courts continued for several years after the war. Thousands were charged for their parts in atrocities committed by the aggressors and about 2 000 were put to death. There were legal and moral arguments about whether the trials should have taken place at all. Controversy also raged about whether one could successfully argue that crimes were committed on the orders of a superior. The courts ruled that one could not, and many paid dearly for their obedience to the Nazis and the Japanese militarists.

Further Reading

Ayling, S. E.: *Portraits of Power*. Harrap (London, 1965)—Churchill, Roosevelt, Stalin and de Gaulle.

Gilbert, M.: *Winston Churchill*. Oxford University Press (London, 1966).

Smith, N. D.: *Winston Churchill*. Methuen (London, 1960).

Watson, J. B.: *Empire to Commonwealth 1919 to 1970*. Dent (London, 1971), Chapter 5.

Documentary

Snyder, L. L.: *Fifty Major Documents of the Twentieth Century*. Anvil (London, 1955).

Exercises

1. How did the Second World War influence attitudes? Note the changes in American policies towards the outside world; in colonies towards European mother countries; among the underprivileged towards injustice.
2. Why did it seem likely that a struggle would occur after 1945 between capitalism and communism?
3. Using Table 10.1 and documentary sources, show how, in international conferences, Allied war strategy was planned and preparations were made to deal with postwar problems.
4. Identify and explain *four* major international problems which existed in 1945 as a result of the Second World War.
5. Roosevelt called Stalin 'Uncle Joe'. How did each of Roosevelt, Churchill and Stalin regard his allies?
6. Find out more about the resistance movements in France and one other part of Europe.
7. What part did de Gaulle play in the war?

Unit Eleven
Peace After the Second World War

11.1 Peace-making

(a) The Conferences

There was no attempt to make an instant and comprehensive peace settlement. In August 1945, the Big Three (the USA, the USSR and Britain) followed up their Conference at Yalta with one at Potsdam (see Section 10.2). They agreed that the Oder-Neisse line would mark the new boundary between Germany and Poland. The division of Germany into zones of occupation was confirmed and, while it was agreed that for the time being there would be no central government for all Germany, the powers accepted that the country should be treated as a single economic unit. They also decided to send those Germans who were living in Poland, Hungary and Czechoslovakia to Germany, in the hope of avoiding another minority problem such as that in the Sudetenland. But already it seemed difficult for the USSR and the Western powers to reach agreement on the future of Germany, although they did agree to work out some details of the peace treaties in a Council of Foreign Ministers on which France and China would also be represented.

The Foreign Ministers held their first meeting in London a few weeks later. Agreements were not reached easily but on 29 July 1946, a Peace Conference of 21 nations assembled in Paris to consider their proposals. By February 1947, it was possible to sign treaties with the European allies of Nazi Germany, leaving the problems of Germany and Austria unsettled. The Council of Foreign Ministers paid further attention to these but it soon became clear that they could not bridge the fundamental differences which existed between Russia and the West.

A peace settlement with Japan was also delayed. After Japan's surrender, General MacArthur kept that country tightly under American control. The USA decided that the Council of Foreign Ministers was unsuitable for working out a Far Eastern settlement and the treaty was eventually drawn up by the Americans in separate consultations with interested governments. Like the other defeated powers, Japan was not consulted in the making of the treaty. In 1951, a Conference of 49 nations met in San Francisco to approve it.

(b) The Treaties

The decisions of the Council of Foreign Ministers were mainly those of the representatives of the USA, the USSR and Britain. There had been many differences of opinions and disputes were often lengthy and bitter but compromises were eventually reached and treaties were therefore signed at Paris.

(*i*) **The Treaties of Paris (1947)** were imposed on Italy, Hungary, Bulgaria, Rumania and Finland. They were all required to disband their fascist organizations and to limit their armed forces. All had to make reparations payments, mainly to Russia, Jugoslavia and Greece although Italy had to make repayment to Ethiopia.

Territorial changes were comparatively modest but the defeated powers had to give up their ambitions. Thus Italy had to abandon her claims to Albania and Ethiopia, and she also lost her overseas empire. Libya became an independent state; Eritrea was in due course merged into Ethiopia; Italian Somaliland eventually became part of the independent republic of Somalia in 1960. Fig. 11.1 shows the most important territorial changes made in Europe by the treaties.

(*ii*) **Separate treaties (1945)** were made by the Soviet Union with several of her neighbours. Poland agreed to an eastern boundary with Russia roughly along the old Curzon Line. Czechoslovakia transferred what had formerly been the eastern tip of the Czech state to Russia. The Soviet Union also pronounced a verdict in a long-standing dispute between Czechoslovakia and Poland over Teschen, deciding in favour of the former. A treaty with China went some

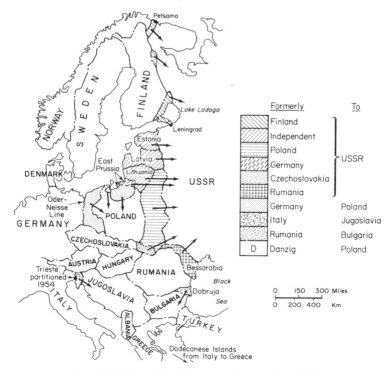

Fig. 11.1 Central and Eastern Europe after 1945

way to establishing a joint Chinese–Russian influence in Manchuria to replace that of Japan.

(*iii*) **The Treaty of San Francisco (1951)** removed Japan from the Chinese mainland and from the island of Formosa. Japan also surrendered the Pacific islands she had held as mandates since the First World War and gave certain other islands to the USA to hold as *trusteeship territories* of the United Nations. Reparations were not fixed but Japan undertook to negotiate with the states she had injured. On the other hand, by 1951, the USA was disturbed by the successes of the communists in China: the Treaty, therefore, gave Japan the right to make defensive alliances, a provision which the Soviet Union found objectionable.

(*iv*) **The Austrian State Treaty (1955)** completed the peace-making, except for the settlement of the German problem. Hitler had incorporated Austria into the German Reich. It was agreed at Potsdam that, like Germany, the state would be divided into four occupation zones. But unlike Germany, Austria was allowed to elect her own civilian government in 1945. The occupation continued and a treaty was delayed until 1955, partly because the Western powers (the USA, Britain and France) could not reach agreement with the USSR on Austria's boundaries or on the scale of reparations.

The Treaty pledged Austria to neutrality in the disputes between Western and Eastern Europe. She was restored to her 1937 frontiers and forbidden to unite with Germany. Her military strength was restricted and the USSR secured rights to Austrian oil and to reparations. Austria thus became a neutralized state with some similarities to Switzerland, her western neighbour.

Austria also agreed to hold free and democratic elections and, in spite of the frequent need for coalitions in government, she succeeded in establishing a stable democracy. Industrial development brought a measure of prosperity and, in foreign policy, Austria's only major anxiety concerned the South Tyrol. This area had been transferred to Italy in 1919 and the Italians were confirmed in possession by the Treaty of Paris of 1947. It included German-speaking peoples whose loss Austria resented (see Fig. 7.1). It was an international problem which added spice to Austro-Italian football matches but posed no threat to world peace.

11.2   The German Problem

Even in 1955 the powers could not agree on a solution to the German problem. Far from being settled, the problem merely produced a great deal of friction between the West and the Soviet Union in the years after 1945.

(*a*) The Division

The Allies began by dividing Germany into four zones of occupation in accordance with their agreements at Yalta and Potsdam. All former German

Fig. 11.2 The divisions of Germany and Austria in 1945

lands east of the Oder-Neisse Line were incorporated into either Poland or the USSR. Fig. 11.2 shows how the zones were proportioned and also that Berlin lay deep inside the Russian zone. Special arrangements were, therefore, made for the city which was divided into four sectors, reproducing in miniature the divisions of Germany as a whole.

These divisions were meant to destroy militarism and Nazism in Germany, to persuade Germans of the enormities of the Nazi regime and to prepare the way for democracy and reconstruction. It was expected that a peace settlement would follow and Germany would then be left to herself as Austria was in 1955. Meanwhile, an Allied Control Council representing the four occupying powers directed German affairs. Early co-operation between them to bring relief to suffering people and to deal with refugees quickly turned into recriminations and distrust.

The Russians felt fully justified in seeking recompense for the huge losses they had suffered in the recent war. They proceeded to take what they could from their zone, to press Germans to forced labour and to demand a share in the spoils of other zones. It was an attitude with which France had some sympathy but of which the USA and Britain disapproved. Each side accused the other of breaking faith over the Potsdam agreement to treat Germany as a single economic unit (see Section 11.1).

(b) Suspicion

Ideological differences inevitably became involved in the disputes. The USSR fostered communism in the Russian zone. The others discouraged it in their areas, the USA in particular arguing that communism would be less likely to make an appeal if economic recovery was rapid. The Council of Foreign Ministers reached deadlock on the question of Germany's future. Both sides paid lip service to the idea of reuniting the country but they could not agree on reparations and on the future political structure of Germany.

As early as March 1946 Churchill declared, 'From Stettin* in the Baltic to Trieste in the Adriatic, an Iron Curtain has descended upon the Continent.' To the east of this Iron Curtain lay the Russian zone of Germany and states such as Poland where communism took root. To the west lay the other zones of Germany and states which remained capitalist. Suspicion between the two sides hardened into a Cold War with an almost total lack of co-operation between them. Germany was trapped in the conflict and by 1947, it became clear that the German problem would not be solved for many years to come.

(c) Economic Conflict

Towards the end of 1946, the USA and Britain decided to merge their zones, forming one economic unit, known as the BiZone. In this area, Germans were encouraged to participate in local and regional government and to assume economic responsibilities, although recovery rested firmly on American assistance. The USSR protested, but in June 1948, the western zones adopted a new currency, to re-establish stability. Since the end of the war, Germany had suffered from inflation. Shortages and demoralization had produced a flourishing Black Market and extensive corruption. A new start with a new currency was essential, but no agreement could be reached on a single currency for the whole of Germany. When the West German mark was introduced, the Russians replied with an East German mark for their zone.

By this time, the Cold War was no longer confined to Germany. The Truman Doctrine (see Sections 14.5 and 17.1) and the Marshall Plan hardened, in 1947, the political and economic divisions between the West and the com-

* Churchill was not accurate. He should have said Lübeck, not Stettin.

munist states. The USA was clearly taking the lead in trying to prevent the further spread of communism. The USSR was equally determined not to yield the areas to which communism and Russian authority had already spread.

PEEP UNDER THE IRON CURTAIN

Fig. 11.3 The Daily Mail *cartoonist was quick to comment on Churchill's 'Iron Curtain' speech, 6 March 1946*

(d) Confrontation over Berlin

The new currency for the western zones produced an immediate confrontation over Berlin. In March 1948, the Russians began harassing the communications of the Western powers with their sectors of Berlin. They insisted on inspecting trains and, when an American troop-train refused to accept inspection, it was shunted into a siding, left for several days and forced to make an undignified withdrawal. On 24 June all land communications with Berlin were cut. Two million citizens in the western sectors of Berlin seemed likely to starve unless the city was handed over to the Russians.

France refused to use force. The West considered withdrawal, but that had the smell of appeasement. It was decided to ferry supplies by air, and for almost a year this was West Berlin's only source of supply. A procession of aircraft, sometimes at intervals of only twenty seconds, carried over two million tons of food, coal and all kinds of essentials into Berlin. Lives and aircraft were lost in accidents, but day and night the air-lift went on and, in May 1949, Stalin agreed to raise the blockade.

The Berlin Air-Lift was a considerable achievement but neither side gained anything from the confrontation. The USSR had not gained control of Berlin. The West had no guarantees that land communications with Berlin would not be cut again. Above all, the confrontation made both sides even more stubborn.

(e) Consolidation

One way that their stubbornness was shown was in the establishment of separate and independent states in Germany. In the West, a constituent assembly began work in 1948 on a new constitution for a state of Western Germany, and the Federal Republic of Germany came into existence in May 1949. It was not given complete independence until 1955 but from the beginning its independence was almost complete. Preparations in the Russian zone ran parallel to those in the West. The Democratic Republic of Germany came into existence in October 1949; that, too, gained independence in 1955 in a treaty with the Soviet Union. The Federal Republic (West Germany) had a democratic system on the Western pattern and an economy based on capitalism. The Democratic Republic (East Germany) had a system of government based on the Russian interpretation of democracy and an economy based on Marxism. Although discussions between West and East about a peace treaty for Germany continued to take place from time to time, neither side would abandon its own German state in order to bring about one, united German nation. (The history of East Germany is continued in Unit Twelve and the history of West Germany in Unit Fourteen.)

(f) Berlin

West Berlin continued to be occupied by the Western powers after 1949. It was given a new constitution in 1950 and in effect was self-governing. At the same time, the Federal Republic regarded it as a part of West Germany, although it was impossible to make it the capital city. With assistance from both West Germany and the Western Allies, reconstruction went on rapidly after 1949. The West was eager to make West Berlin a shop window in which to display capitalist prosperity to unsettle the communists, but it was also well-governed by a succession of mayors, among them Reuter who died in 1953 and Willy Brandt, both of them Social Democrats. Brandt later became Chancellor of West Germany.

Fig. 11.4 The division of Berlin: 'Checkpoint Charlie' from the US Sector in West Berlin

East Berlin, in the 1950s, was under a Social Unity administration, backed by the communists. In 1953, Russian tanks were needed to suppress disorders but in the 1960s extensive reconstruction was carried out and life improved for East Berlin's citizens. The area was incorporated into the German Democratic Republic in 1966.

West Berlin, in the meantime, was often used as an escape route to the West by those eager to flee from the East. After 1952, the German Democratic Republic made it almost impossible simply to cross the border which divided Germany. At the end of the 1950s, escapes by way of West Berlin were at the rate of about 200 000 a year. The numbers going in the opposite direction were a great deal smaller. In August 1961, therefore, an Iron Curtain in the shape of a concrete wall was built across Berlin. The Berlin Wall did not stop the movement but it did much to reduce it, for communist guards seldom hesitated to fire on those who attempted an illegal crossing. Thus the division of Berlin became as rigid as the division of Germany.

For thousands of individuals, such divisions were tragic but as the world moved into the second half of the twentieth century, the divisions brought a strange stability to international relations in Europe. Many, like President Kennedy of the USA, went to Berlin to peer over the Wall but ideas of using force became increasingly unpopular. For at least a generation the 'temporary' division of Germany brought a sort of peace by steering away from actually making a peace.

11.3   The United Nations Organization

(a) Foundations

A succession of wartime conferences agreed that a new organization was needed to maintain international peace (see Section 10.2 and Table 10.1). In 1945, fifty nations signed the Charter of the United Nations Organization at San Francisco. With 111 articles it was a more substantial document than the Covenant of the League of Nations. Unlike the Covenant, it was independent of the peace treaties, so that UNO was not regarded by the defeated as an instrument for their punishment, although the great powers took care to preserve their own interests and influence.

The original membership of 50 states grew to double that number by 1960 and to 127 by 1970. In the General Assembly, every state had a vote, regardless of wealth and size. Membership of UNO offered security and the chance to gain respect. The Republic of Ireland was able to play a significant part in UN peace-keeping operations and, although Indonesia resigned in 1965, she found it useful to resume membership in 1966. New states emerging from old colonial empires almost invariably hastened to seek admission to the United Nations and almost regarded membership as a badge of independence.

From quite early in its history, UNO became accustomed to a regular conflict of opinions between the Western bloc and the Eastern, communist, bloc. Many of the small nations, taking a lead from Nehru, Prime Minister of India from 1947, tried to stand aloof from these power blocs and with a flood of new admissions an Afro-Asian viewpoint began to be heard. This was in many ways a healthy development in international affairs but one which often exasperated the great powers, obsessed with their own interests and their efforts to outwit one another. The great powers sometimes blocked the admission of new members, particularly in the early years. Of 31 applications submitted between 1945 and 1950, only 9 were accepted. The most spectacular obstruction was that organized by the USA to prevent the admission of communist China to the Organization. The obstruction lasted until 1971 so that communist China was not accepted into UNO until the communists had been in power for more than twenty years.

The Charter began with a statement of UNO's ideals and it was over these that arguments raged as to whether applicants were fit to be accepted. The Organization aimed 'to save succeeding generations from the scourge of war', 'to reaffirm faith in fundamental human rights', to establish respect for international law and to promote 'better standards of life in larger freedom'. These aims were similar to those of the League of Nations and the two organizations had much in common. But in framing the Charter, the founder-members of UNO hoped to avoid some of the faults of the League and to learn from past mistakes.

(b) UNO at Work

Fig. 2.6 and the summary of the Charter on page 175 show at first sight many similarities between UNO and the League of Nations. The General Assembly, Security Council, Secretariat and International Court of Justice gave UNO the same basic framework as the League. The UN Trusteeship Council performed a similar function to that of the earlier Mandates Commission. The work of other League committees was drawn together under a UN Economic and Social Council, although in this field the work of the United Nations was more comprehensive. Those who framed the Charter, however, made important changes in the rules under which many of these bodies worked, mainly to try to secure more effective action in times of crisis.

The *General Assembly* still operates on the basis of equality, with one vote allowed to each member. It meets annually, in September, and additional sessions can be called in times of need. The UN's budget, admissions and all matters within the scope of the Charter, indeed almost all the work of the United Nations, come under the scrutiny of the General Assembly. Much of its work is done through committees and is carried on in the five official languages of the Organization—English, Russian, French, Chinese and Spanish. The League's requirement that all decisions must be unanimous has been dropped. In some matters, a simple majority is sufficient but major decisions require a two-thirds majority.

The *Security Council* follows in the footsteps of the Council of the League of Nations. In moments of crisis, it can meet almost immediately. Apart from carrying out decisions made by the General Assembly, the Security Council's principal role is to deal with all threats to peace. Beginning with eleven members, it now has fifteen. Since its foundation, five of these have been the victorious powers of 1945—the USA, the USSR, Britain, France and China. (China, in 1945, was the China ruled by Chiang Kai-shek. He preserved his seat in the Security Council even when he was driven from the Chinese mainland by the communists in 1949, and kept it until 1971.) Preserving the principle of the League of Nations Council that there should be permanent seats and elected seats, the five great powers were careful to make their places in the Security Council permanent ones. The other members, now ten, are elected for two-year terms by the General Assembly.

Two problems were fundamental in setting up the Security Council. The first concerned the rights of the great powers. At first, a decision required seven votes. It now requires nine. But, in all matters of importance, the great powers must be among those giving approval. This means that the USA, the USSR, Britain, France and China keep, in effect, the right of veto. This right they have used not infrequently, particularly the Soviet Union.

The second problem concerned the powers of the Security Council to act effectively. It has been given the right to call on members to apply *sanctions* (usually economic) against offending states and also, when necessary, to request them to provide armed forces. These operate as the forces of the United Nations. Until the Security Council takes action, states retain the right to act singly or together in their own self-defence. The Security Council's authority has not been greatly extended compared with the powers of the Council of the League of Nations. Forces have been assembled by the United Nations to deal with a number of crises, in the Middle East (see Section 19.1), Korea (see Section 17.1(c)), the Congo (see Section 20.2) and Cyprus (see Section 20.4) for example. But there is still no standing army; and it is often difficult to collect a United Nations force. The Big Five may also use their right of veto to prevent any attempt to raise a force if they so wish.

But it is sometimes suggested this right of veto may no longer exist. In 1950, the General Assembly passed a 'Uniting for Peace' resolution, which claimed that if the Security Council, through lack of agreement among its permanent members, failed to act effectively to maintain peace, the General Assembly could do so even to the extent of recommending the use of armed forces. The Charter was not amended and it remains open to dispute whether a two-thirds majority in the General Assembly could over-rule a veto in the Security Council.

The *Secretariat* operates in a similar way to that of the League. The Secretary-General is recommended by the Security Council and appointed by the General Assembly for a term of five years, during which time he controls the Secretariat and may bring before the Security Council matters which threaten peace. Differences among the great powers have sometimes led to difficulties in choosing a Secretary-General. But all the Secretaries-General have been chosen from the lesser powers. They have been men of ability, dedicated to the Organization. Trygve Lie, a Norwegian, served from 1946 until his resignation in 1952. His successor, Dag Hammarskjöld, who served until killed in an aeroplane crash in 1961 while seeking a solution to the crisis in the Congo, came from Sweden. U Thant of Burma then gave ten years of dedicated service but refused to continue in the office after 1971 and was replaced by Kurt Waldheim of Austria.

The International Court of Justice sits at the Hague and not at the UN headquarters in New York. Its fifteen judges are chosen jointly by the Security Council and the General Assembly, a third of them retiring every three years. Its functions are similar to those of the Permanent Court which it replaced and nations agree in advance to accept its findings, although some have expressed reservations about this. Britain, for example, excludes disputes with members of the Commonwealth from its jurisdiction.

The *Trusteeship Council* continues the work of the Mandates Commission in preparing colonial states for independence. By 1970, the work had been successfully completed in all but a very few cases, among them the New Guinea Territory under the control of Australia. The Trusteeship Council, when it began its work, made new trusteeship agreements with those states which still had charge of mandates and in these mandated/trust territories the work went on smoothly.

South Africa, however, refused to enter into a trusteeship agreement for her mandate in what had once been German South-West Africa and equally refused to concede independence to that territory. In 1950, the International

Court of Justice ruled that South Africa was still accountable to the United Nations but she was unrepentant. Even in 1973, no solution had been found to the problem which by that time was part of the greater problem of race relations in southern Africa (see Unit Twenty-One). African resentment in South-West Africa, particularly among the Ovambo tribe, led to strikes and extensive disorders but South Africa retained her grip and was protected in the Security Council by major powers such as Britain who were unwilling to permit any UN intervention. The United Nations did give its blessing to a change of name for the territory* but this was a poor substitute for action to wrest the mandate from the policies of apartheid applied there by South Africa.

The *Economic and Social Council* whose twenty-seven members are elected by the General Assembly, a third of them retiring each year, supervises the Organization's work in economic, social, educational and similar fields. The Council has established Commissions to deal with matters as varied as trade, drugs, population and the status of women. It has set up regional Economic Commissions in areas such as Africa and Latin America. It also co-ordinates the work of the *Specialized Agencies* of the United Nations whose activities and names, frequently reduced to initials, combine into a bewildering but vitally important pattern of effort to improve the lot of mankind. The International Labour Organization continues to be one of these Specialized Agencies, operating along the same lines as at the time of the League of Nations (see page 31). Its headquarters remain in Geneva. Other Specialized Agencies were also inherited by UNO from the League but many more were newly created after 1945. Among the new bodies was WHO (the World Health Organization), set up in 1948, to combat disease and to promote co-operation and knowledge in matters of health. WHO spends some 40 million dollars a year in this work.

There are Specialized Agencies for various types of communication. These include the Universal Postal Union, the International Telecommunication Union and the International Civil Aviation Organization (UPU, ITU and ICAO). Economic co-operation is encouraged by the International Trade Organization (ITO) and the Food and Agricultural Organization (FAO). Financial matters may be dealt with by the International Bank and the International Monetary Fund (IMF) (see page 159) and, since 1956, by the International Finance Corporation (IFC) which was established by the Bank in Washington to encourage investment and development. The United Nations Educational, Scientific and Cultural Organization (UNESCO) came into existence in 1946 to wage war against illiteracy and to further the projects which are associated with its name. In the same year, the United Nations International Children's Emergency Fund (UNICEF) began. It is now concerned mainly with the welfare of children in underdeveloped countries although its first duties were to assist children in countries torn by war. In 1965, UNICEF won the Nobel Peace Prize. But even this catalogue by no means completes the list of UN Specialized Agencies, to which thousands devote their services and which draw support from scores of nations.

* Namibia, the African name.

(c) Keeping the Peace

The United Nations Organization has undoubtedly accomplished much in its non-political work. Look at the Index of this book to trace the history of UNO since 1945. Like the League of Nations, it has made only disappointing progress with the problem of disarmament. Like the League, it has been caught up in the rivalries of the great powers and often prevented from taking effective action. It has frequently proved unable to solve even comparatively minor problems such as the Indo-Pakistani dispute over Kashmir, although it has achieved some success in areas such as the Congo.

What must be remembered, however, is that the success or failure of UNO is the success or failure of its members. The Organization represents the collective will of the nations of the world. It can have no existence in isolation. When

Fig. 11.5

it may be said to 'fail', therefore, the 'failure' is that of the nations as a whole, who have lacked the determination, the unity and perhaps the strength to achieve 'success'. All powers, great and small, resent interference in what they consider to be domestic affairs. Britain, for example, has argued that the affairs of Northern Ireland and even those of Rhodesia do not concern the United Nations at all. The Soviet Union expressed similar opinions about the uprising in Hungary in 1956 and that in Czechoslovakia in 1968. Nigeria maintained that the struggle over Biafra was a civil war and a domestic matter. The USA takes a similar stance on race conflicts within America.

As long as self-interest continues to govern the policies of the nations, the struggle for world peace and for the authority of UNO must be long and arduous, wearing down those who, like U Thant, become exhausted in the service of international co-operation. UNO has, however, already survived longer than the League of Nations, and although it may often achieve less than optimists expect, it is by no means totally ineffective. Its headquarters in New York provides a permanent forum in which to exchange ideas among almost all the nations in the world.

11.4   No Peace After the Second World War

Bitter new struggles began in some countries at the end of the Second World War, struggles which were of no direct concern to the discussions which led to the peace treaties. They would have to be solved separately. Upheavals had not been uncommon after the First World War and upheavals were to be expected after the Second. The world of the twentieth century was a world of rapid and often startling change. Units Fifteen, Sixteen, Seventeen and Nineteen show how turbulent conditions were in China, India and South-East Asia, the Middle East and even Greece after 1945.

11.5 Appendix

Summary of the Charter of the United Nations Organization, 26 June 1945

Chapter 1 (Articles 1–2): A statement of purposes and principles

Chapter 2 (Articles 3–6): Membership and expulsion

Chapters 3–5 (Articles 7–32): The machinery of UNO. The composition and duties of the General Assembly and Security Council

Chapters 6–7 (Articles 33–51): Procedure for the peaceful settlement of disputes by arbitration or for action against aggression. Articles 43 to 49 concern the procedure for raising armed forces when the Security Council considers it necessary, acting with the advice of a Military Staff Committee

Chapter 8 (Articles 52–4): Regional arrangements permitted if consistent with the aims of UNO

Chapters 9–10 (Articles 55–72): The organization of UNO's work in economic and social co-operation: the Economic and Social Council

Chapters 11–13 (Articles 73–91): Members undertaking the administration of territories not yet self-governing agree to regard as paramount 'the interests of the inhabitants of these territories' and to recognize the well-being of these peoples as 'a sacred trust'. In certain cases, 'trust territories' may be set up under the supervision of the Trusteeship Council

Chapter 14 (Articles 92–6): The International Court of Justice as 'the principal judicial organ of the United Nations'

Chapter 15 (Articles 97–101): The Secretariat in which the aim is to secure 'the highest standards of efficiency, competence and integrity'

Chapter 16 (Articles 102–5): Miscellaneous Provisions, amongst them an undertaking to make all agreements public

Chapters 17–19 (Articles 106–11): Transitional Arrangements until the Charter came into force and procedure for amending the Charter.

Further Reading

Cowie, L. W.: *The Super Powers*. Nelson (London, 1971).

Gibbons, S. R. and Morican, P.: *The League of Nations and UNO*. Longman (Harlow, 1970).

Midgley, J.: *Germany*. Oxford University Press (London, 1968).

Morgan, R.: *Modern Germany*. Hamish Hamilton (London, 1966).

Documentary

Breach, R. W.: *Documents and Descriptions, the World Since 1914*. Oxford University Press (London, 1966), Sections 8a, 15c and 46.

Exercises

1. How did the United Nations Organization (*a*) resemble and (*b*) differ from the League of Nations. Refer to this Unit and Fig. 2.6.
2. What was the *German Problem* after 1945? Why had it not been solved by 1955?
3. Using Figs 11.1 and 11.2, explain the territorial changes in Europe which resulted from the Second World War.
4. How did the aims and methods of the peace-makers after the Second World War differ from those of the peace-makers after the First World War?
5. What did Stalin, Truman and Attlee agree at Potsdam in 1945? Study the text of the Potsdam Declaration (L. L. Snyder, *Fifty Major Documents of the Twentieth Century*, Anvil, London, 1955, pages 111–18).
6. How did four-power occupation affect the lives of the citizens of Berlin?

(See also **Appendix: Into the 1980s,** page 365.)

Unit Twelve
Soviet Russia and the European Communist Bloc

12.1 The Communist Bloc

The Russian Red Army advanced over 1 500 miles from Stalingrad to the centre of Germany in the closing years of the war. It also penetrated deep into the Balkans. Stalin intended to establish regimes sympathetic to the Soviet Union in the countries of defeated enemies (Rumania, Bulgaria, Hungary and East Germany) and of liberated Allies (Poland, Czechoslovakia, Jugoslavia and Albania). Communists were already strong in many of these countries, where they were respected for their resistance to Nazism and popular among those accustomed to poverty. Stalin set out to create communist governments obedient to the wishes of Moscow from left-wing coalitions and Popular Fronts. The West called these countries 'Russian satellites', and Churchill called the division between them and the West an 'Iron Curtain' (see Fig. 11.2).

In return for political obedience, the satellites got Russian aid (although in the early stages the USSR was intent on collecting reparations from her former enemies). Some states, such as *Albania* turned readily to communism because they had little to gain by a return to the old form of government. In *Bulgaria*, a left-wing coalition of the Fatherland Front deposed the monarchy and won a general election. The communists then turned on their allies within the Front, hanged the Agrarian leader and, a year later, purged the Social Democrats. The Fatherland Front thus followed in the footsteps of Lenin, allowing almost no opposition.

A similar left-wing coalition abolished the monarchy in *Rumania* in 1947. Within the Popular Democratic Front, the communists took longer to establish total supremacy than in Bulgaria but they were always dominant in the country after 1945 when their leader became Prime Minister.

Hungary, too, put up some opposition to total communist domination. The communists became the largest single party in the elections of 1947 although they ruled in a coalition People's Independence Front. This had followed the Russian example of 1918 in giving land to the peasants and nationalizing major industries. Gradually, opposition was eliminated. Agriculture was collectivized and an attack launched against the powerful Roman Catholic Church.

In *Poland*, the communists were handicapped at first because rival governments had developed during the war. There was a communist one and one in exile in the West under Mikolajczyk. A provisional arrangement merged the two together in 1945 but, in 1947, Mikolajczyk fled, fearing arrest. Poland was then ruled by a coalition of Workers' and Peasants' parties, effectively under communist control and led by Gomulka.

In *East Germany* where the German Democratic Republic was created in 1949 (see Section 11.2(*e*)), there was a similar communist-controlled coalition under Grotewohl. Postwar hardships, shortages, the division of Germany and the suppression of opposition led to rioting in 1953. This affected both the Democratic Republic and East Berlin, but was put down by Russian troops. The regime then remained loyal to the Soviet Union under the influence of Grotewohl and Ulbricht, Secretary of the Socialist Unity Party and Deputy Prime Minister. Many citizens still tried to escape to the West, however, and in near desperation it was thought necessary to build the Berlin Wall in 1961 (see Section 11.2(*f*)).

Although the USSR abandoned eastern Austria in 1955 and made no attempt to impose communism on Finland, similar concessions were not made to *Czechoslovakia*. President Beneš returned from exile in 1945 hoping for a democratic system of government. The first postwar government was a coalition of left-wing parties and, in 1946, the communists won the largest number of parliamentary seats with 38 per cent of the votes. They set up a National Front government under Gottwald. But 1947 was a year of shortages and there were protests when Gottwald rejected Marshall Aid (see Section 14.5), as the Soviet Union instructed. A constitutional crisis resulted but the communists found sufficient allies to remain in power and to create a new communist-dominated National Front. Opposition candidates were not allowed to stand in the election of 1948 and President Beneš resigned. Jan Masaryk, the Czech Foreign Minister and son of Tómaš Masaryk, President before Beneš, was found dead in strange circumstances, having apparently fallen from an open window.

At the end of the war, Russia had incorporated the Baltic provinces of Estonia, Latvia and Lithuania into the Soviet Union. Except in Scandinavia, Austria and Greece, the communists were in control in every state in Eastern Europe by about 1950. But one communist state refused to accept dictation from Moscow. In *Jugoslavia*, Marshal Tito was elected President of the new republic by a large majority in 1945. Tito had won prestige as Jugoslavia's wartime resistance leader. He was a convinced communist but he was also determined to apply Marxist principles in Jugoslavia in his own way. He was unwilling to collectivize agriculture, preferring peasant smallholdings, and would not tolerate Russians agents within the Jugoslav Communist Party although he did make economic and military agreements with the Soviet Union. Such independence was not encouraged in Moscow and, in 1948, Jugoslavia was expelled from the *Cominform* (the Communist Information Bureau through which Stalin exercised Russian influence over communists in many countries). Tito was not intimidated. He stuck to his independent path and, while not deviating from his communist principles, made contacts with non-communist powers which would be beneficial to Jugoslavia. He received loans from the International Monetary Fund and later showed considerable interest in associating Jugoslavia with the Afro-Asian bloc in the United Nations. After Stalin's death the Soviet Union became reconciled to Tito's independent attitude.

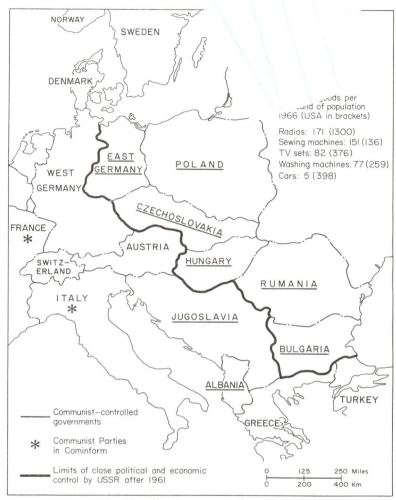

Fig. 12.1 The European communist bloc

12.2   The Soviet Union

(a) Stalinism

Josef Stalin died in the Kremlin on 5 March 1953. He had ruled Russia with an iron grip for almost thirty years (see Section 5.1), transforming it from a land of wooden ploughs to one of thriving industry. The victory over Nazi Germany brought him new prestige although the war left the USSR in need of massive reconstruction. Changed circumstances after 1945 made it easier to spread communism; but although Stalin extended Russian influence, he personally created few of the communist regimes in Eastern Europe and had even less to do with the rise of communism in China. He nevertheless believed that all communists should look to Moscow for leadership and he thought of Tito as a heretic. Opposition to Stalin's will both inside and outside the Soviet Union was ruthlessly repressed wherever possible and, when he died, many heard the news of his passing with relief. His supporters could argue that his ruthlessness was necessary to develop the USSR into an industrial power and to give it security in a world still dominated by capitalism. And certainly, by 1953, Stalinism had achieved both. But Stalin's opponents were uneasy about the cost in lives and about the personality cult which surrounded him. Although few dared to do so openly, they questioned whether Stalin had lost sight of communism's final objective—social revolution in the name of equality—and whether Stalinism was consistent with Marxism–Leninism. Lenin had been ruthless when he thought it was necessary, but he never sought personal glory nor lost sight of the ultimate goal. Stalin, it seemed, found glory and power sufficient in themselves.

(b) The emergence of Khrushchev

Stalin's death was followed by an attempt to distribute his power more widely. Beria, the police chief, was tried and executed and many other Stalinists were removed from their posts. Malenkov became Chairman of the Council of Ministers* (in effect Prime Minister), and Nikita Khrushchev became Secretary-General of the Communist Party. Molotov returned as Foreign Minister. Slowly tensions began to dissolve. There was a slight thaw in Russia's relations with foreign powers, a little more freedom within the Soviet Union and some attention to the production of consumer goods to improve living standards.

But intrigue within the party was already tilting the system towards Khrushchev. In 1955, Malenkov was replaced by Bulganin, who was perhaps more agreeable to Khrushchev. Russia's leaders continued to show a greater interest than Stalin in the non-communist world but, internally, the emphasis shifted back to heavy industry and conformity. Russia's basic policies did not change much even though Bulganin and Khrushchev visited Britain in 1956 and received both the French and Tito in Moscow.

Yet one event in 1956 was remarkable. At the Twentieth Russian Communist Party Congress, Khrushchev felt sufficient confidence in his own position to make a spirited attack on Stalin's reputation. The attack had three effects. First, it blackened Stalin's name and caused confusion over what to teach Russian children about the Stalinist period. Stalin now stood accused of abusing his powers, persecuting loyal communists, failing to prepare for the war and making strategical blunders. Second, it created confusion in the satellite states and helped to produce risings in Poland and Hungary. Third, it contributed to Khrushchev's growing influence within the Soviet system.

Khrushchev was criticized by Malenkov and Molotov but Zhukov and the army leaders rallied to the Secretary-General's defence. Malenkov and Molo-

* Council of People's Commissars until 1946.

tov were expelled from the party leadership. Zhukov, however, was discredited shortly afterwards and replaced as Minister of Defence by Marshal Malinovsky. Although disgrace now served as a substitute for execution, Khrushchev was nevertheless steadily pursuing Stalinist tactics by removing rivals from power. He pushed aside Bulganin, relegating him to the office of Chairman of the State Bank and, in 1958, added to his own appointment of Secretary-General of the party that of Prime Minister. Stalin's body had meanwhile been reburied in a less honoured spot, outside the Kremlin. Even the risings in Poland and Hungary did little, in the short term, to check the progress of the man who threatened to become Russia's new Stalin having, at the Twentieth Party Congress, so dramatically denounced the old.

(c) The Khrushchev Era

Tubby Nikita Khrushchev seemed almost jovial in comparison with other Russian leaders. He was the son of a mine-worker and had a long record of service to the party. He was 64 when he became Prime Minister. He had fought in the Red Army during the Civil War, worked for the party organization in the Moscow area, won the Order of Lenin for his services to the building of Moscow's underground railway and advanced slowly throughout the Stalinist period. He did not secure a major appointment until 1949, when he took charge of Russian agriculture. When he denounced Stalin, seven years later, he carefully exonerated himself and others like him from responsibility for the purges and the blunders. He won a certain admiration in the West, although he was unpredictable and once startled the United Nations by banging the table with his shoe. He kept a firm grip on the Soviet Union until deprived of his offices in 1964.

In 1956, Khrushchev could inform the Russian people that the Soviet Union was at last 'in a position to promote rapidly the production of both the means of production and of consumer goods'. This was the base which Stalin had achieved while paying attention at the same time to progress in such fundamentals as education and health services. After all their sacrifices, it now seemed possible that the Russian people could begin to enjoy the luxuries of shorter hours, more consumer goods and improved housing, although output was still carefully regulated by Plans. In 1961, longer-term objectives were laid down, declaring that socialism had now been achieved in Russia and that economic progress by 1980 would mean the country was closer to the full achievement of communism.

Russian achievements continued to be impressive: in 1957, the Soviet Union launched Sputnik 1, the first man-made satellite to orbit the earth in space. Two years later, a Russian space vehicle took photographs of the far side of the moon and, in 1961, Yuri Gagarin was the first man to travel round the earth in space in Vostok 1. Such space ventures were expensive but Khrushchev could rightly boast that they put Russia's technological mastery beyond dispute.

Khrushchev tried to achieve greater efficiency in industrial organization by dismantling much of the centralized management of Stalin's days in favour of regional authorities, the People's Economic Councils. But difficulties still remained.

Khrushchev also wished to achieve better returns from Soviet agriculture which still lagged behind the most advanced farming in the world. Again, he favoured regional control rather than centralized direction from Moscow. Stalin had achieved total collectivization and Khrushchev continued the process of reducing the number of collective farms by merging them into large units. He also reduced taxation and relaxed the restrictions on the private plots of land which peasants were allowed to keep within each *kolkhoz*. In 1958, tractor stations were abolished since each *kolkhoz* now possessed adequate supplies of its own machinery. Alongside the collectives, the Soviet Union also developed state farms (*sovkhosy*), owned entirely by the country. Khrushchev encouraged the further expansion of these. The produce belonged to the state and the workers were state employees.

Khrushchev's most ambitious agricultural exercise was the *Virgin Lands Project*. In 1954 he started the ploughing of many of the infertile lands of central Russia, particularly areas of Siberia. By 1962, 145 million acres had been reclaimed and hundreds of thousands of Russians were recruited to work on them, mainly in *sovkhosy*, encouraged by tax concessions. But increased production could do no more than keep pace with the expansion of Russia's population. Results were disappointing, for the climate and the nature of the soil made progress difficult, and agriculture in general continued to be handicapped by peasant hostility to the communist system. Khrushchev's successors tried to place the blame for the disappointing results on him but his principal fault was no more than over-optimism.

Russian society during Khrushchev's years in power began to change. Writers like Pasternak and Solzhenitsyn and composers like Shostakovich became increasingly fretful about censorship and restrictions. Western influences were more difficult to keep out. Modern art began to find a place alongside the People's Art, which glorified the people's struggle for socialism. Russians began to show an interest in Western fashion and pop music. There was more lawlessness and even hooliganism. Khrushchev travelled extensively and Russians inevitably became more interested in the outside world. Tourists were now cautiously admitted to Russia. The Government continued to practise censorship and to defend the system with propaganda and a rigorous code of law, supported by capital punishment which was extended in 1962 to cover bribery, but it was evident that the tyranny of Stalinism was now dead in Russia.

In foreign affairs (see Section 17.2), Khrushchev cautiously encouraged a lessening of the Cold War, although he would accept no interference in the affairs of the European communist bloc. He favoured a policy of coexistence with the West and warmed to them sufficiently to excite the mistrust of communists in China and elsewhere. In 1962 he came near to military confrontation with the USA over Cuba (see Section 17.1(*d*)) but showed the good sense to back down. The years after Stalin's death were difficult ones and Khrushchev inevitably attracted a considerable volume of criticism.

(d) The Fall of Khrushchev

In 1964 the Conservatives lost the British general election and Alec Douglas-Home ceased to be Prime Minister. At almost the same instant, Khrushchev ceased to be Prime Minister in the Soviet Union. Khrushchev fell not as the result of a general election but through the censure of the Communist Party's Central Committee. Age and ill health were at first put forward to explain his sudden dismissal. Later, the charges were stated more precisely and Khrushchev was accused of reviving the Stalinist personality cult and making blunders. His quarrels with China (see Section 15.3) and humiliation over Cuba, his mistakes in economic management and over-concentration on consumer goods were held to be sufficient for his forced retirement, both from the office of Prime Minister and from that of Secretary-General of the party. His retirement was quietly obscure and he died in 1971.

Fig. 12.2 Khrushchev with Mao Tse-tung, the leader of Chinese communism, 1959

(e) The Triumvirate

As in 1953, an attempt was then made to distribute power more widely. Kosygin became Prime Minister, Brezhnev Secretary-General and, from 1965, Podgorny Chairman of the Presidium of the Supreme Soviet. All had given long service to the Communist Party. This Triumvirate was still in power in 1973.

Few major changes were actually made in Khrushchev's policies. The People's Economic Councils were wound up in 1965 in favour of a return to centralized management in the search for the most efficient methods of planning. Adjustments were made in matters of emphasis, for example between consumer goods and other forms of production. But the central features of the post-Stalinist policies remained. Like Khrushchev, the Triumvirate would tolerate no dissent in the European communist bloc. Rebellion was put down in Czechoslovakia in 1968 as it had been in Hungary in 1956. The Soviet Union continued to apply the policies of coexistence towards the outside world. Kosygin visited Britain and the USA in 1967 and, in 1972, President Nixon of the USA visited Moscow, but alongside coexistence went a readiness to encourage communism elsewhere and competition with China for communist loyalties.

(f) Is the Soviet Union a Communist Country?

The West had long since grown accustomed to the phrase 'communist Russia'; but it has been seen that, in 1961, the Russian Communist Party only declared that *socialism* had been achieved (see Section 12.2(c)). The communist historian, Isaac Deutscher, frequently argued that the Bolshevik Revolution of 1917 was only the beginning of the journey to communism. In 1973, the Soviet Union is still trying to apply the principles of Marxism (see Section 5.1) and to achieve communism. This is one of the reasons why many people consider Russia to be a communist country.

The Soviet Union is also a one-party state. Political activity only takes place within the Communist Party: long service brings rewards, as it did for Khrushchev and Kosygin. Russians argue that under the constitution of 1936 this is a democratic system: there is room for discussion within the party. But the party also has a long tradition of obedience to decisions once made and, of course, argument can only be about the interpretation of Marxism–Leninism, not about alternatives to it.

A central feature of the system is the devotion to economic planning. Nothing important is left to private enterprise. All economic activities, through state-owned agencies and agricultural collectives, are carried on for the benefit of the nation. This requires a considerable bureaucracy (civil service) and decisions on priorities inevitably curtail the individual's freedom of choice. But this system also eliminates unemployment and it is possible to give priority to welfare services, especially the health service, to public transport, power stations and education. Differential payments, privileges and incentives remain—part of the difference, it is argued, between socialism and communism.

Outside the communist states, it is sometimes thought that communism means only repression, censorship, propaganda and the state control of work in schools. Communists think these devices are necessary to complete the transformation of their society. The Communist Party has brought enormous improvements to the Russian people but it also brought them much grief, especially in the days of Stalin. Cynics may argue that it can never bring the free and equal society at which Marxism–Leninism aims. The Russians have themselves named the 1980s as their goal for this achievement.

Meanwhile, priorities are often different from those in the West. In Volgo-grad (formerly Stalingrad), in 1972, state apartments were being built at the rate of 10 000 a year to be let at a very low rent. Few private houses existed, private building being forbidden. As in other towns the citizens of Volgograd received free medical services almost without parallel in other countries. Through their trade unions, the workers received benefits ranging from cheap holidays and day-nurseries for their children to pensions at the ages of 50, 55 or 60 according to the rigours of their work. Minimum wages were laid down by law and as early as 1922 workers had been protected and their rights guaranteed by a comprehensive Labour Code. Education was free, all fees having been abolished in the flood of reforms introduced by Khrushchev. There was education for all to the age of 15 and a wide range of opportunities for further education beyond that point. In addition to television, Russians enjoyed and supported a wide range of cultural entertainments. In the shops, the number of consumer goods increased steadily and the ownership of wash-ing machines, refrigerators, television sets and even cars was growing slowly. There were, however, still formidable waiting lists, especially for cars.

These were the state's priorities with which the majority of Russians seemed content. The aim was to raise the living standards of the *whole* population. Russians were free to grumble about poor workmanship, shortages and queues but they were not free to try to undermine the basic system. Only with-in the Communist Party was it possible to work for change and even there many decisions could not be questioned. The Committee of State Security (the KGB), the last of a long line of special police forces which began with the Cheka, kept open a watchful eye for sedition. But the days of Stalinist terror had passed. Many restrictions remained and seemed likely to remain for some time longer but the Marxist experiment, begun in 1917, was continuing.

The outcome of the experiment still remained in doubt. In some, it roused hatred and fear. Among communists, there was controversy about the best means by which to arrive at their goal. By 1972, other nations had followed the example of Tito in arguing that there could be different paths to communism. While the Soviet Union travelled along one road, other states like China, Jugoslavia, Cuba and Chile developed their own routes and even in the communist bloc in Europe where uniformity seemed most apparent, there were variations on the Russian pattern.

12.3   Co-operation in the European Communist Bloc

The Communist Information Bureau (Cominform) was established in 1947. Its purpose was to co-ordinate communist activities, which was interpreted by Stalin to mean that it would be the instrument for imposing Russia's will on all the communist parties in Eastern Europe and on those in France and Italy which were also represented. Its first headquarters were in Belgrade but, after Jugoslavia's expulsion in 1948, they were moved to Bucharest in Rumania. Rumania at this time toed the Russian line with enthusiasm. The Cominform played a major part in establishing a considerable degree of uniformity in the communist bloc. It was wound up by Khrushchev, in 1956.

The Council for Mutual Economic Assistance (Comecon) was set up in 1949 to organize economic co-operation in Eastern Europe. By 1950 Comecon included all the communist states in Europe except Jugoslavia. In 1962, it also admitted the Mongolian People's Republic (Outer Mongolia) and about the same time associate membership was allowed to other communist states including China and Cuba. Ten years later, Cuba was admitted to full membership. In 1964, it set up a Bank for Socialist Countries. The basic aim of the Council was economic development and co-operation along lines similar to those being pursued in Western Europe through organizations such as OEEC (see Section 14.5). Some conflict developed about whether members should specialize in production for the benefit of all or whether each member should aim at self-sufficiency. Other conflicts were ideological. In 1961 Albania withdrew in protest against the Soviet Union's quarrels with China. But, leaning on credits supplied by the USSR (as Western Europe often leaned on the USA), Comecon did much to bring recovery and some growth of prosperity among members of the communist bloc.

A military alliance was not signed until 1955 when the Eastern European Mutual Assistance Treaty (the *Warsaw Pact*) made provision for joint defence for twenty years. It was signed by all the communist states in Europe except Jugoslavia. Albania was excluded in 1961. The Warsaw Pact was a response to similar movements in the West, especially the creation of NATO in 1949 (see Section 14.5) and the granting of full independence to the German Federal Republic (West Germany) in 1955. Like NATO, it set up united military forces. These were under the command of Marshal Konev of the Soviet Union. The Pact also allowed Russia to continue to keep troops in the satellite states. The Treaty spoke only of peaceful intentions and defence.

In 1955 the USSR put forward a proposal for the abolition of both the Warsaw Pact and NATO, in return for an all-European security system. But the West feared the size of the Warsaw Pact armies and both alliances remained. Neither would West Germany agree to the Rapacki Plan, put forward by Russia in 1957, of a nuclear-free zone in central Europe to include the two Germanies, Poland and Czechoslovakia, because she feared such an arrangement would expose her to the danger of communism.

12.4   Dissent Among the Satellites

In 1949 Gomulka of Poland was removed from power and disgraced for giving support to Tito. While Stalin lived, no form of dissent among the communist powers was permitted beyond the successful defiance of Jugoslavia. But with Stalin's death in 1953 some reassessment was necessary of the relations between the communist bloc and Moscow.

(a) 1953
The first signs of protest against the tight grip of the USSR occurred in East Berlin and East Germany (see Sections 11.2 and 12.1) in the summer of 1953.

COUNTRY	COMINFORM (dissolved 1956)	COMECON	WARSAW PACT	POPULATION est. 1972 (millions)	MAIN EXPORT (% of whole) (1969)	EXPORTS MAINLY TO (% of whole) (1969)	IMPORTS MAINLY FROM (% of whole) (1969)
USSR	✓	✓	✓	241·7	Machinery 23%	East Germany 15% (Communist States, 66%)	East Germany 16% (Communist States, 65%)
POLAND	✓	✓	✓	32·6	Machinery 36%	USSR 35%	USSR 38%
EAST GERMANY		✓	✓	17·1	Machinery 38%	USSR 38%	USSR 40%
CZECHOSLOVAKIA	✓	✓	✓	14·5	Machinery 51%	USSR 34%	USSR 34%
HUNGARY	✓	✓	✓	10·3	Machinery 26%	USSR 35%	USSR 37%
RUMANIA	✓	✓	✓	20·3	Machinery 22%	USSR 28%	USSR 27%
JUGOSLAVIA	Expelled 1948	Associate		20·5	Machinery 11% Metals 11%	Italy 15% USSR 14%	West Germany 20% Italy 13% USSR 13%
BULGARIA	✓	✓	✓	8·5	Machinery 27%	USSR 55%	USSR 56%
ALBANIA		Left 1961	Excluded 1961	2·2	Fuel and minerals 54%	China 40%	China 63%

EXPORTS OF MEMBERS OF COMECON:

1970: 31·2 billion dollars (about 10% of world total)

about $\frac{1}{3}$ sold to USSR

about $\frac{1}{3}$ sold to other COMECON members

about $\frac{1}{3}$ sold elsewhere

Fig. 12.3 The European communist bloc

Russian troops put down the disturbances without difficulty, but a less harsh attitude followed and a start was made on winding up the collection of reparations.

(b) 1956

The changes within Russia led to a hope of further concessions, and in the summer of 1956 there were strikes and rebellions in *Poland*. Gomulka had returned to power in that year and the Poles were eager to reduce the level of Russian interference in their affairs. Gomulka was a loyal communist. Russian troops withdrew to the frontiers and left him to restore order. Some reduction of Russian interference in Polish affairs was sufficient to quell the dissent.

Hungary was encouraged to rebel by the success of the Poles and by dissatisfaction with the economy. By 1956 Hungary's political situation was unstable. Hard-liners blamed the Prime Minister, Nagy, and Nagy blamed Russian interference. In the summer there was a short-lived Stalinist government under Hegedüs but it only sparked off an anti-Russian rebellion and Nagy became Prime Minister again in October. He denounced the Warsaw Pact as well as Russian meddling and at first the Russians seemed willing to bargain as they had in Poland. Russian troops retired but Nagy could not control the disorders in Budapest and elsewhere. He took an increasingly anti-Russian line. Early in November, the Russians struck. Budapest was occupied and the rebellion put down. Hungary returned to a more obedient path under the reliable communist, Kádár. The Western world loudly lamented the fate of

Fig. 12.4 Russian tanks in Budapest, Hungary, November 1956

Hungary, but did nothing to interfere. International opinion was in any case simultaneously diverted in 1956 by the Suez invasion (see Section 19.1).

(c) 1968

There was no further major disturbance in the communist bloc until 1968. In *Czechoslovakia*, after the resignation of Beneš, Novotný emerged as communism's strong man, Secretary of the Party and President of the Republic from 1957 to 1968. Czechoslovakia took an increasingly independent line in economic development, being already more highly industrialized than most of the satellites. Competition was encouraged and planning even more localized than under Khrushchev. Expectations exceeded achievements and there was also tension between Czechs and Slovaks about the equality of their shares in the wealth produced. Novotný was discredited and an attempt made, as in Russia in 1953 and 1964, to distribute his powers more widely. General Svoboda became President, in 1968; Dubček was Secretary of the Party and Černík was the Prime Minister.

This Triumvirate inclined to the pursuit of 'Socialism with a Human Face'. They wished to adopt a more liberal organization of society with fewer restrictions. They sought more contacts with the West and less centralized economic planning. There was no question of abandoning socialism but this was not the path being travelled by the other Warsaw Pact countries. Černík even wished completely to abandon censorship.

In August 1968, most of the Warsaw Pact states except Rumania, now more independently-minded in foreign policy, sent troops into Czechoslovakia, and the Czech government was forced to come to heel. The Soviet Union vetoed a motion of censure in the United Nations but, in any case, the West had no intention of interfering. By an agreement signed in Moscow, the Czech leaders were required to abandon any movement towards neutrality in foreign affairs and to return to censorship, centralized planning and their obligations to Comecon. Husák took over the Party Secretaryship from Dubček, and a new federal constitution was adopted for Czechoslovakia, to try to resolve the rivalries between Czechs and Slovaks.

Further reconstruction followed when, in March 1969, a Czech ice-hockey victory over the Soviet Union led to riotous jubilation in Prague. Dubček was steadily down-graded, sent as ambassador to Turkey and finally expelled from the Communist Party. It was not a total victory for the hard-liners, for Husák and Svoboda continued to pursue some policies of moderation. But the Soviet Union, by a show of military strength, had returned the country to a path sufficiently close to that of the USSR to secure approval. In 1972, a series of political trials of so-called 'right-wing opportunists' confirmed Czechoslovakia's return to obedience. The communist bloc was again intact.

12.5 Communist Variations

Although *Jugoslavia* undertook no military alliances with the Soviet Union, diplomatic relations between the two countries improved after 1955. Inside

Jugoslavia, Tito became President for life although prime ministers and other members of the government were limited to four years in power under the constitution of 1963. At that time, about half of the population were still engaged in agriculture but industrialization was proceeding steadily and the encouragement of tourism brought Jugoslavia further links with the outside world. Tito found it possible to rule the country by less repressive measures than were often needed elsewhere among the communist states. He provided stable government which was also progressive in many ways.

(a) Industry and Trade

Tito clearly established the point that there could be differences among communist states in Europe. Geography, and the individual problems which the satellites faced, reinforced it. Czechoslovakia was nearer to the West and more industrialized than the others. Bulgaria was more remote and, with Albania, the most underdeveloped. Rumania had important oil fields. Thus the communist states pursued economic development within Comecon but by varying methods. East Germany introduced Five-Year Plans, beginning in 1958, and concentrated on engineering, chemicals and optical equipment, devising new methods for the production of iron and steel using brown coal as fuel. Hungary concentrated on engineering and electrical equipment and Rumania began to promote tourism. Most of the enterprises were under state control (although East Germany was much slower than the others in completing the programme of nationalization), and much of their trade was within Comecon but they varied in the degree to which, especially in the 1960s, they developed trading links outside the communist bloc. Poland built up a considerable proportion of her trade outside Comecon and Bulgaria strove to increase similar commercial exchanges. They differed, too, in their organization of agriculture. While almost 90 per cent of agricultural land in Poland remained in private hands, hardly any in Bulgaria was not collectivized and Rumania completed collectivization in 1962.

(b) The Church

Some states faced special problems such as the opposition of the Roman Catholic Church in Hungary and Poland. In Hungary, Cardinal Mindszenty took up residence in the American Legation in Budapest in 1956 and continued to symbolize a religious resistance to communism. In Poland, Cardinal Wyszinski similarly kept up a stubborn resistance to Gomulka's regime.

(c) Constitutions

Nor were the constitutions of the satellite states identical. All of them were dominated by communist parties but there were many variations in constitutional details. Some had frequent changes in personnel, others remained subject to long personal influence such as that Tito exercised. Gomulka dominated Poland until overthrown by demonstrations which led to Gierek's more conciliatory policies towards the workers. Grotewohl dominated the

German Democratic Republic (East Germany) as Prime Minister until his death in 1964, while the influence of Ulbricht in a variety of offices went on much longer. In Albania, Hoxha established a Stalinist supremacy as leader of the communists from 1945. In Bulgaria, Dimitrov died in 1949 and there was a succession of communist leaders until Zhivkov established his authority in the mid-1950s. In Hungary, Kádár resigned as Prime Minister in 1958 in order to concentrate on work within the party but returned to the office from 1961 to 1965 after which Fock became Prime Minister in 1967. His policy was to modify the rigidity of the regime, though more cautiously than the Triumvirate in Czechoslovakia.

Only in *Albania*, geographically isolated from other Warsaw Pact countries and economically backward, did communist rule continue as inflexibly as under Stalin in Russia. Hoxha maintained a rigorous police regime. Some industrial development took place on the basis of oil supplies and textiles, and at first Russian economic aid was extensive, for Albania gave the USSR a footing on the Adriatic Sea. But Hoxha disliked the changes which occurred in Russia after Stalin's death and, in 1961, he seized on the Soviet Union's quarrels with China to break off diplomatic relations with Moscow. Albania developed a strange new alliance with communist China and in 1968 resigned from the Warsaw Pact in which she had long since ceased to be active. At loggerheads with her neighbour, Jugoslavia, as well as with the communist bloc in Eastern Europe, Albania's isolation was almost complete.

Almost all the states of Eastern Europe which had turned towards communism after 1945 remained members of the communist bloc in 1973, allegedly satellites of the Soviet Union. Only Albania and Jugoslavia had withdrawn, each for a different reason. At first, poverty and firm police action had held the bloc together. By 1973, however, there was growing prosperity and less rigid control. Even communist ideology was questioned from time to time although it seemed unlikely that the Soviet Union would permit any extensive departure from it. What the Soviet Union had to permit was a growing number of national variations. Rumania adopted an increasingly independent line in foreign policy, joining the World Bank and the IMF. Poland relaxed restrictions on the Roman Catholic Church and Gierek encouraged trade unions to be more responsive to the wishes of their members. Hungary imported foreign books and everywhere there was an increasing interest in the outside world. It seemed impossible that the tight uniformity of Stalin's days could ever return to the European communist bloc.

Further Reading

Ayling, S. E.: *Portraits of Power*. Harrap (London, 1965)—Tito, Khrushchev.
Franchere, R.: *Tito of Yugoslavia*. Macmillan (London, 1971).
Fry, D. G.: *Russia, Lenin and Stalin*. Hamish Hamilton (London, 1966)—later chapters.
Gunther, J.: *Inside Russia Today*. Hamish Hamilton (London, 1958).
Miller, W.: *The USSR*. Oxford University Press (London, 1965).
Pryce-Jones, D.: *The Hungarian Revolution*. Benn (London, 1969).

Documentary

Breach, R. W.: *Documents and Descriptions, the World Since 1914.* Oxford University Press (London, 1966), Sections 24–5.

Exercises

1. Consider the appropriateness of each of the following terms to describe the Soviet Union in the 1970s: communist; socialist; authoritarian; democratic; wealthy.
2. How, at the present time, do the states of Eastern Europe (*a*) resemble one another and (*b*) differ?
3. Using the Index to this book, construct outline histories of the following states from 1919 to 1973: Czechoslovakia; Jugoslavia; Poland.
4. How did the USSR establish influence over the states of Eastern Europe after the Second World War? In what ways and to what extent has this influence been (*a*) maintained and (*b*) weakened?
5. What changes have occurred in the USSR since the death of Stalin?
6. How does life in the Soviet Union differ from life in your own country at the present time?
7. What is the importance of Marshal Tito?

(See also **Appendix: Into the 1980s,** page 365.)

The USA and the European Capitalist Bloc— 1 The USA and Britain

13.1 Democracy and Capitalism

It could be argued—indeed, many Americans argued it noisily—that the West held liberty to be the first essential and, in general, preferred liberty to equality. The democracies rejected the restrictions which were common in the communist bloc. Freedom of speech and of the press, free elections in the sense that voters had a choice of parties and a completely secret vote, and freedom from political police forces such as Hitler's Gestapo and the KGB were regarded as fundamental. Similarly private enterprise continued to play the major part in the economies of the democracies, with an emphasis on private ownership, private profit, competition and such consumer goods as the public, prodded by advertising, could be persuaded to buy.

But, after 1945, it was difficult to maintain that there should be no economic planning by governments and no interference in the management of the economy and in the making of social improvements. Governments in general were expected to interfere sufficiently to steer developments in desired directions, away from unemployment, poverty and squalor and towards greater efficiency, at least in public services such as the supply of electricity. Most governments in the democracies leaned a little towards socialism although less so in the USA than in Europe. They all faced the problem of finding a balance between private enterprise and state control.

The Labour Party in Britain and its counterparts in Europe, the Social Democrats, usually preferred a greater emphasis on state ownership (nationalization) than did private enterprise parties such as Conservatives and Liberals. But when, during the British election of 1945, Churchill suggested that the Labour Party would 'have to fall back on some form of Gestapo', his remarks were received with derision. The Labour Party and Social Democrats had little in common with communists except a general willingness to pay more attention to economic planning, put some limitations on the worst features of capitalism, and to move vaguely in the direction of equality. They were not ruthless and they were not prepared to sacrifice liberty. They had no rigid long-term plan for the complete transformation of society.

In the USA, however, Social Democrats had little appeal. The traditional American parties, Democrats and Republicans, maintained their grip and their devotion to private enterprise. In Presidential elections from 1948 to 1972, winning candidates got popular votes ranging from about 24 to 43 million votes but the highest vote for a socialist candidate was only 140 000, registered in 1948.

13.2 The United States of America

(a) Attitude to Communism

Many Americans regarded socialism and communism as a sort of treason and their hysteria reached fever pitch in the *McCarthyism* of the early 1950s. While a Commission on Employee Loyalty combed carefully through the records of state employees, and known communists were restricted under the Internal Security Act of 1950, Senator Joseph McCarthy began a more bizarre witch hunt for communist sympathisers. He made an exuberant claim to have detected 57 (quoted as 205 by some of his audience) in the State Department. A Senate committee failed to find any, but from 1950 to 1954 McCarthy conducted much-publicized inquiries into the communist sympathies of prominent citizens with all the enthusiasm of a medieval witchfinder. He imported into the USA something of the definition of communism current in South Africa, where the Suppression of Communism Act tried to outlaw almost anything which threatened the existing order. In 1954, McCarthy himself was censured in the Senate for conduct 'contrary to Senate traditions'. Nevertheless, a thorough determination to hold down communism in the USA survived McCarthy.

Less flamboyant methods did uncover Russian spies, though not as often as suggested in television serials. In 1953, Julius and Ethel Rosenberg were executed for passing atomic secrets to the Russians. But long before then, anti-communism had become a central policy of American politicians, both at home and in foreign relations. One way in which it found expression was in the remorseless pursuit of communists by J. Edgar Hoover, Director of the FBI (Federal Bureau of Investigation) from 1924 until his death in 1972. Before the Second World War, his G-Men hunted America's Public Enemies (mainly gangsters) and waged war against the Ku Klux Klan. After 1945, their energies were devoted to seeking out communists and everyone suspected of 'UnAmerican' activities.

(b) Social and Economic Problems

Every President from Truman to Nixon was also aware of the need to do something about America's two most serious internal problems. These problems were often inter-related: there was a great gulf in the USA between white and non-white citizens and between the rich and the poor. In 1960, nearly 12 per cent of the population were non-white and many of these were desperately poor. There were also a good many poor whites. Non-whites grew increasingly resentful of poverty, of the slums in which millions lived in the decaying city centres and of the continued discrimination against them by an arrogant section of the white population.

In the South, this arrogance was often rooted in the past, when plantation owners had kept slaves. It found some expression in the politics of George Wallace who became Governor of Alabama in 1963. He set himself up as the champion of property-owners, and the defender of the rights of individual states against federal interference. Above all, he took upon himself the defence of America against all 'UnAmerican' activities, whether negro, liberal, socialist or communist. As such he was the scourge of the Civil Rights Movement. In the presidential election of 1968, he got nearly 10 million popular votes, almost a third of the total given to Nixon who was elected. There could be no doubt that he represented a strong current of opinion which was not entirely confined to the South.

Presidential policies usually brought changes at a slower pace than in Europe. A 'war on poverty' was launched in the 1960s, further expanding welfare provisions in the USA, but about 20 per cent of America's families continued to be officially classified as 'poor'. The Civil Rights Movement campaigned to help them to get a more equal share in America's great wealth and also to free the non-whites and other under-privileged people from discrimination and squalor. In the North, non-whites often lived in ghettos in the large towns, such as Harlem in New York, too poor to follow the whites who moved out to the suburbs, away from the decaying slum property. Low wages, unemployment and atrocious housing conditions combined to turn such ghettos into breeding-grounds of angry discontent and, in the later 1960s, many American cities were rocked by violent riots in which racial antagonisms played a considerable part.

The USA had traditions of violence from the days of the sordid if not necessarily 'Wild' West, through the Civil War to gangsterism and the activities of the Ku Klux Klan before the Second World War. Americans cherished their right to possess guns and it seemed to some that the American population was armed to the teeth. Combined with the deep social divisions, festering slums and general turbulence of the twentieth century, this tradition encouraged new crime waves in the USA after 1945, which were complicated by the rapid expansion of drug-taking. In spite of this, however, the USA followed the example of more liberal countries in moving away from capital punishment.

Great wealth did not, however, bring great tranquillity to the USA. There were explosive labour disputes, bitter social conflicts and violent confrontations which frequently involved students in the 1960s. Even the stars of the American film industry became involved in the arguments. John Wayne stood forth for law and order like a latter-day Western Marshal. Ronald Reagan became an authoritarian Governor of California, in 1966. Marlon Brando inclined to the side of the under-dog and Charlie Chaplin left the USA, under suspicion of left-wing leanings. There seemed to be no real danger to the American Constitution but there was plenty of furious argument about the nature of society.

Involvement in the struggle over Vietnam (see Section 17.1) deepened the divisions within the USA and became an explosive issue in American politics, especially in the 1968 presidential election. This war also imposed heavy burdens on the American economy until, from 1971, even the dollar was involved in international currency crises (see Table 13.2).

(c) Truman's Presidency, 1945–53

Truman steered the USA through the last months of the Second World War, took the decision to use atomic weapons against Japan and then set America on her postwar course in foreign policy. He gave his name to the *Truman Doctrine* (see Section 14.5) for the containment of communism and deeply involved the USA in the defence of Western Europe. He committed America to the active support of UNO. He presided over the rehabilitation of Japan and the framing of the Treaty of San Francisco and, in 1950, he took a leading part in the Korean War (to preserve South Korea from communism). Probably no previous President of the USA had taken such an active and far-reaching part in world affairs.

At the same time, Truman was charting America's course in domestic affairs. There were problems to be faced in the transition from war to peace, in extending the reforms begun by Roosevelt and in dealing with new issues such as the peaceful application of atomic power. There was also the question of internal security, from which arose McCarthyism (see page 194). In 1946, Truman created an Atomic Energy Commission and, in 1949, a new Department of Defence. Atomic power was to remain under government control but the USA was willing to share its knowledge with other countries for peaceful purposes. Where security was concerned, however, Truman kept a tight grip. He avoided the hysteria of McCarthy but diligently searched out potential traitors, and preserved American military might. The army was run down and servicemen returned to civilian life smoothly and quickly, aided by training schemes and financial help. But the USA placed reliance on air power and nuclear weapons and, in due course, the Department of Defence in the Pentagon became strongly influential in American affairs.

Like Attlee in Britain, Truman gave the appearance of being modest and unassuming, but his policies were often firm and decisive. He was prepared to take control although he ran into difficulties in social and economic affairs, clashing with those forces in the USA which were quick to resent government interference.

In September 1945, Truman outlined his plans for continuing Roosevelt's domestic work with *Twenty-One Points*, hopeful of expanding social security and house-building and of improving working conditions. But labour unrest, linked with soaring prices, helped to swing American opinion to the Republicans in the mid-term elections of 1946 and for two years after that Truman was handicapped by a Republican majority in Congress. Although he had secured the passage of an Employment Act in 1946, economic planning and controls soon became unpopular. Truman abandoned most of them and was further embarrassed when the Republican Congress insisted on a new Labour Management Relations Act (Taft–Hartley Act) in 1947, to free employers from certain legal restrictions but to impose others on trade unions. Congress also insisted on cuts in taxation which undermined the extension of welfare schemes.

Rather unexpectedly, Truman won a narrow victory in the presidential election of 1948 and the Democrats regained control of Congress. He now put forward his programme for a *Fair Deal*, expanding the Twenty-One Points of 1945. It stopped short of any thorough economic planning but aimed to make improvements to assist the poor, for example, with a building programme, to secure more social justice (extending old age pensions) and to move towards more civil rights. Like Roosevelt, Truman pushed ahead with public works schemes and assistance to small farmers, always trying to raise the levels of those with small incomes. Much of the Fair Deal programme could not be made law, however, in the face of the combined opposition of Republicans and Southern Democrats.

(*d*) **Eisenhower's Presidency, 1953–61**

Fig. 13.1

In 1952, Eisenhower retired from the army and the command of the forces of NATO to stand for the Presidency as a Republican candidate. He served two terms in office. In foreign affairs, Eisenhower's first task was to wind up the Korean War in 1953 but the Cold War continued. Until his resignation and death in 1959, Dulles was mainly responsible for the foreign policy of the Eisenhower administration. These years saw few fundamental changes in international relations (see Unit Seventeen). A new alliance, SEATO, was set up in 1954 to contain communism in Asia. The *Eisenhower Doctrine* of 1957 announced America's willingness to contain it in the Middle East, and when it grew in Cuba under Castro, the USA broke off diplomatic relations in 1961. It was in this period too that America first undertook commitments in Vietnam (see Section 17.1) but, essentially, the foreign policy of the Republicans was not much different from that of the Democrats. After 1959, Eisenhower expressed a belief in personal diplomacy, but his summit meeting with Khrushchev in 1960 collapsed in recriminations over the U-2 affair (see Section 17.2). In domestic matters, Eisenhower himself was a moderate. He had few ambitious plans and envisaged no Deals, New or Fair. He was usually content to leave matters to experts, especially businessmen, and for most of his years in power the economy prospered. After 1956 he vetoed Democrat attempts to push him into greater spending on housing and welfare measures, but he made no attempt to dismantle what had already been achieved by Roosevelt and Truman. Most Americans enjoyed a rising standard of living but the problem of unemployment persisted and there were brief recessions in 1953 and 1957. There were also labour disputes including a serious steel strike in 1959. Congress hit back with a measure to attack the union bosses and to make America's trade unions more democratic.

Even more controversial than the status of trade unions was the question of *desegregation*. In 1954, the Supreme Court ruled that white and non-white children should be educated together and not in separate schools. Eisenhower supported the ruling but it was resisted in the South. Southern states claimed that it was an interference with state rights and Eisenhower had to send federal troops to Little Rock, Arkansas, to enforce the law. The troops had to protect non-white students at Little Rock's Central High School against the bigotry and prejudice of the whites. Even then, other states such as Alabama refused to accept desegregation.

In 1955, negroes in Montgomery, Alabama, began to protest against racial segregation on buses and, by 1960, such protests were challenging 'whites-only' drug-stores, hotels and libraries. This Civil Rights Movement found a dedicated and moderate leader in Martin Luther King and, by 1960, most Democrats and Republicans had accepted the principle of equality. Eisenhower meanwhile, accepted a Civil Rights Act in 1957, to protect the rights of minorities and especially the negro's right to vote.

(e) Kennedy's Presidency, 1961–3

John Kennedy was the youngest of all American Presidents. His father had been an American ambassador in Britain and Kennedy was a Roman Catholic, of Irish descent. The fact that he was the first Roman Catholic president seemed to many at the time to indicate a growing spirit of tolerance in the USA. He brought to the presidency a certain youthful vigour and a more outward-looking attitude than was usually associated with the office. This found expression in the *Peace Corps*, which was founded in 1961 to enable skilled volunteers to give active and constructive assistance to the under-developed nations. By 1966, the Corps had 12 000 Americans at work in over fifty countries, mainly in Africa, Asia and Latin America.

In the same spirit, Kennedy signed the Alliance for Progress with Latin America, for economic co-operation and to raise the standard of living. A year later, in 1962, he persuaded Congress to make sweeping tariff cuts in the

Trade Expansion Act, giving encouragement to international trade. From the Act developed the Kennedy Round, whereby GATT made progressive reductions in the tariffs of many countries. All this was in keeping with Kennedy's stated aims of moving towards a *New Frontier* with a world-wide attack on poverty, war and tyranny. In the Nuclear Test Ban Treaty of 1963, he was able to reach a constructive agreement with the USSR but he relaxed none of America's vigilance against communism. It was during Kennedy's Presidency that the USA became more deeply involved in Vietnam and confronted the communist world over Cuba (see Section 17.1).

Within the USA, Kennedy's plans for the New Frontier included progress in Civil Rights and Medicare (a health and welfare service for the aged). Federal troops were used, as at Little Rock, to protect the rights of negro students in the universities of Mississippi and Alabama. But Republicans and Southern Democrats in Congress blocked further legislation on the subject. Before the deadlock could be resolved, the President was assassinated in the streets of Dallas, Texas, in November 1963. Kennedy had brought a certain liberalism to the American Presidency but he was able to do little more than point the way before his violent death.

Violence continued to grow in the USA in the 1960s. Kennedy's younger brother, Robert, Attorney-General in 1961, was killed while seeking the Presidency in 1968, only two months after the assassination of Luther King in Memphis, Tennessee. Rioting, violent protest and violent retribution became increasingly common until many questioned the healthiness of American society. During the election campaign of 1972, Governor Wallace was shot and left paralysed.

Fig. 13.2

(f) Johnson's Presidency, 1963–9

Kennedy died in Texas. The Vice-President, Lyndon Johnson, his successor, was, by chance, a Texan. The Johnson administration became deeply enmeshed in the struggle in Vietnam (see Section 17.1(c)), which came to overshadow almost everything. In other American-communist relationships, the USA seemed to have settled for coexistence. No attempt was made to interfere in Czechoslovakia in 1968 (see Section 12.4) nor to change the balance of power which had developed between West and East.

But within America Johnson's administration was an active one. In 1964 he succeeded in manoeuvring Kennedy's Civil Rights Act through Congress, further extending Eisenhower's legislation. In the same year, he was able to extend vocational training for underprivileged youths in the Economic Opportunity Act, which also gave further help to small farmers. His community action schemes attacked poverty. When re-elected at the end of the year, Johnson put forward a new programme for the *Great Society*. The Democrats had more power in Congress after 1964 and a substantial amount of legislation was passed.

Johnson wished to spend freely in a 'war on poverty' and particularly in a campaign against slums. Aid for rebuilding decaying city areas was made available in the Development Act of 1966. Legislation allocated federal money for sewage disposal and educational expansion. A Social Security Act introduced medicare for those over 65. Administrative reorganization was undertaken to deal more effectively with problems of slums and transport. Minimum wages were raised and extended to cover more workers and some attempt was made to deal with unemployment. But a more liberal trade union law was blocked in Congress. Congress also passed a new Immigration Act to make the admission of immigrants more selective.

Republicans and Southern Democrats, who were stronger again after 1966, were reluctant to move too quickly in the matter of Civil Rights. Progress was made in this field, in 1965, with an act to give the vote to all, regardless of literacy and other tests which had often been used to disqualify negroes. An inquiry into the extensive rioting in negro ghettos, especially in 1967, placed the blame to a large extent on 'white racism'. The murder of the non-violent Luther King prodded Congress into action again and, in 1968, Civil Rights legislation was accepted to outlaw discrimination in the letting of accommodation and the sale of properties.

There was now little more Johnson could do. His involvement in Vietnam had lost him the support of many liberals but in any case the campaign for the complete equality of all America's citizens, white and non-white, could not be won quickly in the teeth of prejudice. Johnson himself was not a candidate in the election of 1968, faced, he admitted in his memoirs, by 'divisions' he 'felt powerless to correct'. The country moved to the right in electing the Republican Richard Nixon and even further to the right in giving a substantial vote to George Wallace. The Democrats, however, retained a majority in Congress.

(g) Nixon's Presidency, 1969–74

Nixon had been Eisenhower's Vice-President after 1956 but had failed to defeat Kennedy for the Presidency in 1960. Many people felt his chances of political power had vanished for ever. But over the next few years Nixon steadily built up support in the grass roots of the Republican Party.

Opinion in the USA was now deeply divided about the conflict in Vietnam and Nixon worked towards the withdrawal of American troops through a policy of Vietnamization. He hoped that South Vietnam would be able to resist communism without the American army, if not without the American air force. The *Nixon Doctrine* of 1969 continued to oppose communist expansion but expressed the hope that Asian nations would be able to defend themselves against it. The collapse of the South Vietnamese before a communist offensive in 1972, when America's withdrawal was well advanced, put Nixon in a dilemma, but he persevered to negotiate a peace-treaty in 1973 (see Section 17.1(*c*)).

He made other important changes in American foreign policy, agreeing at last to the admission of communist China to UNO and making a personal visit to Mao Tse-tung (see Section 15.3), followed by another to Moscow. He was prepared to travel extensively both in the communist and non-communist worlds and to follow the example of Kennedy in seeking agreements on armaments with the USSR. In 1969, he and Podgorny signed the Nuclear Non-Proliferation Treaty to try to limit the spread of nuclear weapons, and entered into the Strategic Arms Limitation Talks (SALT).

Nixon also worked to settle problems within America. On taking office, he appointed a Council for Urban Affairs to tackle the problems of the cities and for much of his first term as President, the USA was generally quieter than in the late 1960s. On the other hand, there were economic difficulties in the early 1970s. Unemployment rose to more than 4 million but, at the same time (quite differently from the Depression of the 1930s), it was accompanied by rapidly-rising prices. Nixon tackled the problems with further administrative reorganization and attempts to freeze wages and prices. The USA then ran into balance of payments difficulties which resulted in a 10 per cent surcharge on imports, to secure time in which to reconsider the levels of the world's currencies. After a prolonged currency crisis, adjustments were made and the surcharge removed but, at the end of 1971, the dollar had been devalued, particularly in relation to the West German mark and the Japanese yen. In 1973 the dollar was in trouble again. The strain of financing so many operations throughout the world was beginning to affect even the richest of all nations.

Nixon also encountered another crisis in 1973, for after a substantial re-election victory he faced a series of political scandals which came near to paralysing his government, the Watergate scandals (see Glossary).

(See also **Appendix: Into the 1980s,** page 365.)

13.3 Britain

(*a*) Party Politics

The general election of 1945 (see Section 10.6(*d*)) signalled Britain's return to party politics after the wartime coalition government. The Labour Party was in power from 1945 to 1951 and from 1964 to 1970, the Conservative Party from 1951 to 1964. By the end of this period, it was the Conservatives' view that Labour was the party of big spending and heavy taxation, and Labour's view that the Conservatives were the party of big business and missed opportunity. Conservatives taunted Labour over devaluation and low growth rates. Labour taunted Conservatives over 'thirteen wasted years' from

Table 13.1 Elections in the USA 1916–72

| Year of Presidential Election | President | State Votes | | House of Representatives |
		For	Against	
1916	Wilson (D)	277	254	D (Mid-term: R)
1920	Harding (R)	404	127	R
1924	Coolidge (R)	382	136	R
1928	Hoover (R)	444	87	R (Mid-term: D)
1932	Roosevelt (D)	472	59	D
1936	Roosevelt (D)	523	8	D
1940	Roosevelt (D)	449	82	D
1944	Roosevelt (D)*	432	99	D (Mid-term: R)
1948	Truman (D)	303	189	D
1952	Eisenhower (R)	442	89	R (Mid-term: D)
1956	Eisenhower (R)	457	73	D
1960	Kennedy (D)*	303	219	D
1964	Johnson (D)	486	52	D
1968	Nixon (R)	301	191†	D
1972	Nixon (R)	521	17	D

D: Democrat
R: Republican

* Died while in office
† Wallace (Ind.) 46

Note on American Elections

Presidents are elected by the votes of states' representatives in an electoral college. These representatives (usually) mandated to the support of a particular presidential candidate, are elected by the voters who are thus voting for presidential candidates indirectly. Each state elects as many members of the electoral college as it has representatives in Congress. For example, in 1964, there were 538 members in the electoral college and, of these, 43 represented New York, 29 Pennsylvania, 3 Nevada. The presidential candidate who obtains a majority in the electoral college takes office as president in the January following the election.

Congress is made up of two Houses: the House of Representatives (in proportion to population); the Senate (two senators from each state). Mid-term elections to Congress (in 1918, 1922 and so on) may alter party representation there and thus handicap or help the President in carrying out his programme. For example, in 1946, the Republicans won a majority in the House of Representatives and thus handicapped the President who was a Democrat. N.B. Eisenhower (in 1956) and Nixon (in 1968 and 1972) were elected without a Republican majority in the House of Representatives.

1951, and over the balance of payments deficit. Some who adhered to neither party alleged that there was little to choose between them anyway, an opinion to some extent encouraged by *Butskellism*.

This piece of jargon to describe the common ground between the parties took its name from the Conservative R. A. (Rab) Butler and Labour's Hugh Gaitskell. The common ground on which it was assumed they were in some agreement was that governments should be moderate and liberal, accepting great responsibilities for economic management and public welfare, but avoiding the extremes of doctrinaire policies. Yet 'Butskellism' was always misleading, for there were still many differences between the parties and although each leaned towards the centre, Labour remained a party of the left, the Conservatives a party of the right. They were often deeply divided in areas as varied as education, race relations, taxation and labour problems.

When in power, however, both parties found it necessary to seek practicable solutions to a multitude of problems for which theory alone was seldom sufficient. All governments had their own ideas on priorities and Conservative priorities were not those of Labour. But, above all, governments after 1945 were condemned to an everlasting struggle with the British economy and they were often judged, at least by electors, not so much for their principles as for their skills in management.

(b) The British Economy

In 1945, Britain stood £3 000 million in debt. Many overseas assets no longer existed. Britain's ability to pay her way and to retain a favourable trading balance of payments depended now, more than ever, on selling her exports (see Section 10.6(c)). Inevitably this problem was linked with the value of the pound in terms of other currencies, so that exports and the strength of the pound soon became almost an obsession in Britain (see Fig. 13.3). There was no easy solution to the problem, for after 1945 there was even fiercer competition for markets. Britain, moreover, faced the urgent need to modernize machinery, management, marketing and labour relations, matters which had been seriously neglected before the war.

Governments were also expected after 1945 to avoid a high level of unemployment and to secure rising living standards. There were expectations of affluence, particularly after 1950. The fundamental balancing act which was required of governments was to provide increased wealth together with a healthy balance of payments. But increased wealth often led to increased imports which had to be paid for in exports. Britain had constantly to try to produce goods which could be exported and these were no longer the earlier basic exports such as textiles, coal and ships.

The revolution in technology also created rapid change. In old industries such as textiles, coal and shipbuilding the number of jobs steadily declined. Heavy investment was needed to finance new industries, such as aircraft-construction, in which the costs were enormous, and to modernize old ones. The competition was so fierce that it was essential to keep down costs and everywhere the emphasis was on productivity (the maximum and most efficient production for the lowest cost). Machinery, although initially expensive, often provided the key to productivity. But this raised old fears of machines putting men out of work.

Governments thus became trapped in a new dilemma. Expectations of wealth drove up prices and wages. Expensive exports were difficult to sell. This led to balance of payments problems. At the same time, efforts to reduce costs and increase productivity placed great strains on workers or even made them

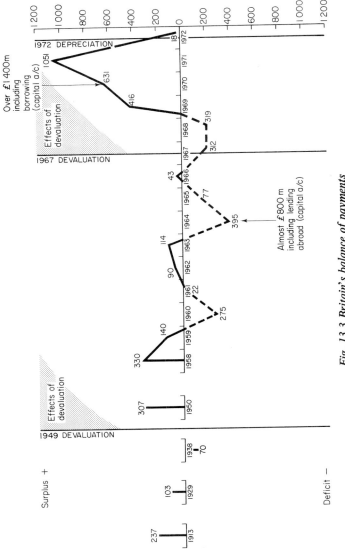

Fig. 13.3 Britain's balance of payments

unemployed, angering trade unions. And the costliness of new machinery and of wage increases helped to drive prices still higher.

Governments, not infrequently, solved part of this jigsaw puzzle. In the late 1960s, Harold Wilson's Labour government produced a healthy balance of payments position but when it fell from power, in 1970, both prices and unemployment were beginning to rise sharply. Early in 1972, under Heath, unemployment had again topped the million mark yet the inflationary price rise went on, particularly in the prices of houses. In many respects, the problem was similar to that in the USA, but Britain had an even more desperate need than America to sell exports and, inevitably, there were fears that high prices would undermine Britain's balance of payments again.

Technological improvements and productivity had, by this time, made Britain as a whole richer than ever before, but the wealth was still distributed most unevenly. There was much anxiety by 1972 about the plight of the poor, pensioners whose incomes could not keep pace with soaring prices, the unemployed and those whose wages remained stubbornly low. Unlike the USA, Britain had no fixed minimum wage. The system was still something of a free-for-all struggle of vested interests. The right wing blamed trade unions and the workers. The left wing blamed financiers, speculators and management. A new word, *gazumpers*, was coined to describe those who in 1971 were forcing up house-prices in their search for more profit. It seemed clear that greed was often the basic trouble but, as in the years before 1939 when the arguments were less about curing unemployment than about the level of unemployment benefit, so, by the late 1960s, the arguments were more about who was the most greedy than about fundamental solutions to the problem.

(c) Labour Government, 1945-51

Attlee's government, elected in 1945, was the first Labour administration to have an overall majority. It threw its energies into postwar reconstruction and social advances. It was already committed to implementing the Beveridge Report (see Section 10.6(*d*)) and measures for social welfare were given a high priority. The National Insurance Act of 1946 extended existing schemes for insurance against sickness, retirement and unemployment. The principle was the same as that in the first such act in 1911, that all workers would contribute to the insurance fund, together with contributions from employers and from the government out of taxes, and in return have the right to benefit in times of need. The National Assistance Act of 1948 provided additional help, from the central government and out of taxation, for all those in desperate need. The National Health Service Act of 1946, promoted enthusiastically by Aneurin Bevan as Minister of Health, placed hospitals under national control and made medical, dental and optical treatment free of charge, financed mainly out of taxation. No subsequent government has wished or been able to dismantle the framework of this welfare state to any great extent.

Attlee's government undertook extensive nationalization partly for more effective economic control and partly to provide better conditions for the workers. The major coal-mines were transferred to the National Coal Board in 1946, with compensation to their former owners. In 1947, railways, inland waterways and long-distance road-haulage were placed under the British Transport Commission. The British Electricity Authority and Gas Council* took over the supply of electricity and gas. The Bank of England was nationalized, in 1946. Public corporations, BEA and BOAC† were set up to run the principal airlines, and cable and wireless companies were also taken under national control. In the teeth of fierce opposition, the Iron and Steel Industry was nationalized towards the end of the government's period in office. It was returned to private ownership by the Conservatives after 1951 but was later nationalized again by Wilson.

Attlee's government also passed a variety of other reforms, among which were the granting of independence to India and the settlement of other problems in the Commonwealth (see Unit Sixteen). Free legal aid was made available to the poor in 1949. The Local Government Act of 1948 gave assistance to the poorer local authorities. The delaying power of the House of Lords was reduced to one year, the right of electors to vote in more than one constituency was abolished with the ending of the separate representation in parliament of universities, and a Town Planning Act was passed. As the Labour Party had long wished to do, the government also repealed Baldwin's Trade Disputes Act of 1927.

This legislation was passed against a background of international readjustment and economic struggle. The government wished to move carefully from war to peace and to establish a firm economic base for the future. Priority was given to exports. Wartime controls and rationing were retained. Loans from America and Canada, however, were not enough to stave off a crisis. In 1947, a bitter winter with an acute shortage of fuel held up production and handicapped exports. Confidence in the pound fell and Cripps, the Chancellor of the Exchequer, had to place severe restrictions on spending, cut imports and try to freeze wages, hoping to divert Britain's energies into exports. Large food subsidies were used to hold down the price of food and thus demands for higher wages. But there was new uncertainty about the pound in 1949 and the devaluation of Britain's currency became inevitable. In September, the value of the pound was reduced from 4.03 to 2.8 American dollars. This made British exports cheaper and relieved the pressure on the balance of payments. But Attlee's government continued to be cautious. Many restrictions remained, especially on wages, and the government itself made cuts in its spending, even trying to reduce its spending on the Health Service by making charges for certain prescriptions.

These cuts infuriated Bevan, especially when the government embarked on heavy expenditure on arms in connexion with the Korean War. Attlee made Gaitskell Chancellor of the Exchequer in 1950, clearly refusing to follow the more left-wing path of Bevan and Wilson, both of whom resigned in protest against health charges. This move was significant, for when Attlee retired in 1955, Gaitskell succeeded him as leader of the party. But, in the meantime, Attlee called another general election in 1951, considering his majority too

* In 1972, the Gas Corporation.   † In 1972, British Airways.

small to govern.* This time, the Conservatives under Churchill were returned with a small majority.

(d) Conservative Government, 1951–64

The Conservatives further increased their majority in elections in 1955 and 1959. Churchill retired in 1955 and Eden became Prime Minister. In 1957, Eden gave way to Macmillan and he, in turn, retired in 1963 to leave Douglas-Home to lead the party in the 1964 election.

The Conservatives believed in some movement away from controls in the direction of freedom. They had promised to return the iron and steel industry to private enterprise and, in the Steel Act of 1953, plants were restored to private owners but the Iron and Steel Board remained as a supervisory body. Long-distance road-haulage was also returned to private hands, making the planning of a national transport system almost impossible. Commercial television, financed by advertising rather than licence fees, was set up in 1954, to compete with the BBC. By that year too, Churchill was able to announce the end of food rationing. The government's most constructive work was probably in the drive for more home-building, led by Macmillan as Minister of Housing.

Churchill retired shortly before the election of 1955. Eden was successful in that election but his short administration was overshadowed by the Suez Crisis (see Section 19.1). The Clean Air Act of 1956, which did much to reduce smoke and fog in Britain's towns, was one of the most important measures passed by this government. A private member's bill to abolish capital punishment was rejected by the House of Lords, but Eden put through a Homicide Act, in 1957, to abolish the death penalty for all but a few types of murder.

Macmillan continued to build on earlier developments in town planning and hospital expansion. He introduced the system of life peerages in the House of Lords in 1958 and, in 1963, it became possible for peers such as Lord Hailsham (Quintin Hogg), to surrender inherited peerages in order to stay in the House of Commons. The Rent Act of 1957 removed rents from official control, leading to the charge that the Conservatives favoured landlords rather than tenants. Conservatives argued that profits were necessary if property was to be repaired. When Douglas-Home became Prime Minister, in 1963, he too had to surrender his peerage in order to secure election to the Commons. His Government was not long in office but Heath got through the Resale Prices Act, preventing manufacturers from denying supplies to those who wished to cut prices. In effect, 'recommended' prices replaced 'fixed' prices.

Much of the activity of governments in the years 1951–64 lay less in legislation than in economic management. It was also an age of inquiries and reports. The Robbins and Newsom Reports were voluminous studies of higher and secondary education. The Buchanan Report studied traffic in towns, the Beeching Report the problems of the railways. These were controversial subjects, as was the question of Britain's continued production of nuclear weapons,

---

* Labour had won only a small majority in the election of 1950.

first begun by Attlee's government, and the question of whether Britain should join the European Community (EEC) (see Section 14.5). There were also extensive changes taking place in the Commonwealth (see Unit Sixteen) and new towns and motorways were beginning to change the face of Britain.

1951 to 1964 has been called the *Age of Affluence*. Macmillan told the British public, 'You've never had it so good'. In fact, governments faced a continuous struggle with the economy, resorting in Macmillan's last years to a National Incomes Commission and a National Economic Development Council (Neddy). Even for the Conservatives, planning and at least some control now seemed to be essential.

Butler was Chancellor of the Exchequer under Churchill. Building on the foundations of Cripps and Gaitskell, he was able to reduce income tax and to encourage spending. But by 1956, labour disputes and a worsening balance of payments led to a reversal. Macmillan was now Chancellor and he raised taxes and tried to divert money from spending into savings with the introduction of Premium Bonds, a sort of state lottery. Thorneycroft, Chancellor in 1957–8, tried to reduce taxes while collecting money from increased charges for welfare services. Spending again threatened the balance of payments and now prices were rising quickly, leading to wage demands and further industrial troubles. Heathcote Amory, Chancellor from 1958 to 1960, stamped on wage increases but at the expense of a halt in the growth of output, an increase in unemployment and a squeeze on credit in 1960, to reduce spending. His successor, Selwyn Lloyd, found it necessary to fight a worsening balance of payments position. He introduced higher interest rates, new taxes, and a pay-pause to hold down increases in income. But he was replaced by Maudling, who again reversed the direction, perhaps with an eye on the coming general election. His aim was to stimulate the economy and let the people demonstrate their affluence by spending. The result was a record deficit on the balance of payments, approximately £800 million in one year and new worries about the strength of the pound.

In this 'Age of Affluence', the progress of Britain's economy was obviously erratic, moving on a stop-go pattern. The 'stops' cut back the rate of growth and led to jealous comparisons with other nations who seemed to grow richer, faster. Credit squeezes and efforts to hold down wages caused frustration and worsened industrial relations. On the other hand, 'go' periods led to problems with the balance of payments and some movement towards inflation. Moreover, unemployment still continued to fluctuate. In 1964, the electors were not sufficiently convinced that 'Life is Better under the Conservatives' to return them to power again. The Labour Party, led since Gaitskell's death by Harold Wilson, put forward a policy of 'getting things done' and won a tiny overall majority of four. In another election, in 1966, Wilson got a larger majority.

(e) Labour Government, 1964–70

Although there were differences in detail, Labour policies were in broad agreement with those of the Conservatives on a number of issues, among which were the control of immigration (see Section 21.4), Commonwealth affairs (see Unit Sixteen) and particularly Rhodesia (see Section 21.3), the EEC (see Section 14.5) and the general need to raise benefits such as old age pensions.

In other respects, they sought changes. The Rent Act was repealed in 1965 and tribunals set up to decide fair rents. Health charges were dropped, although Wilson found it necessary to reimpose them in 1968. After a lengthy struggle, the iron and steel industry was renationalized. In education, the Government tried to step up the movement towards comprehensive schools and finally fixed a date (the early 1970s) for raising the school leaving age to 16.

Wilson's government also placed emphasis on the development of policies for those regions of Britain which lagged behind the general affluence, and on schemes for compensating and retraining those who became redundant. The Plowden Report of 1967 produced a study of primary schools, emphasizing the needs of the under-privileged. The Open University, in 1969, provided more opportunities in higher education. Concern for the less-privileged led to rate rebates in 1966, to allow the poor to escape the payment of local rates, and to option mortgages in 1968 to allow them to borrow money to buy houses at lower rates of interest. National Assistance benefits were replaced by Social Security supplements and the Health Service was extended to include family planning.

Many other changes were made. The Road Safety Act of 1967 tried to discourage driving under the influence of drink. The Transport Act in the following year amalgamated local transport authorities in certain congested areas. The age of majority was lowered from 21 to 18. The Post Office ceased to be a government department and became instead a public corporation, similar to the National Coal Board. An Ombudsman was introduced, to investigate bad administration. A start was made on the development, with France of *Concorde*, a supersonic airliner. The government also began to tackle some of Britain's developing social problems, planning for the environment, investigating the role of trade unions and introducing a Race Relations Act to overcome some of the problems faced by coloured people. In 1965, the death penalty was completely abolished for a trial period which was later renewed.

The government also faced grave new problems in Northern Ireland (see Section 20.6) but it was the management of the economy which still provided its chief anxiety. The Labour Party confirmed its belief in planning by setting up a Department of Economic Affairs under George Brown. A National Board on Prices and Incomes was established and other bodies like Neddy continued. But the immediate problem which confronted Callaghan as Chancellor of the Exchequer was the balance of payments. To deal with the immediate crisis in 1964, the government borrowed heavily from IMF, imposed a surcharge on imports, cuts in spending and heavier taxation. Incentives were given to exporters and an attempt made first to freeze wages and then to restrain them and link them to productivity. In 1965, new taxes were imposed on corporations and capital gains. Even so, 1966 brought further troubles and a serious loss of confidence in the pound. As in 1931, a Labour government found it difficult to win the confidence and support of financiers. In 1967, the government decided that the pound had to be devalued, from 2.8 to 2.4 dollars. Further borrowing and another fierce attack on spending, which was continued by Jenkins who replaced Callaghan as Chancellor, finally brought improvement in 1969. The balance of payments began to appear more healthy, but there was an unpleasant upsurge in prices and unemployment.

It was at this point that Wilson called for a general election. It was won by the Conservatives under Heath, who had taken over leadership from Douglas-Home in 1965.

(f) Conservative Government, 1970–4

Heath became Prime Minister with some intention of moving away from 'Butskellism' towards a greater emphasis on private enterprise, competition, profits and efficiency. Comprehensive legislation was planned to deal with industrial relations, housing and rents and other outstanding problems. There were vigorous plans to restructure the tax system and many aspects of the welfare state, with lower taxes to encourage enterprise and more charges for services which had been subsidized out of taxation for many years. But results were not encouraging. Unemployment rose to its highest level since 1940, industrial relations were embittered, prices soared as never before and there was a considerable outcry on behalf of the poor who were increasingly required to submit to means tests in order to obtain help. It seemed that there were now fundamental differences between the Conservative and Labour parties in matters of principles and priorities.

Heath's government appeared to change direction with remarkable speed, however. Economic problems led to extensive government intervention. Some efforts were made to protect the poor with a Family Income Supplement and a variety of rebate schemes. In 1972, the pound was allowed to float downwards on the foreign exchanges, a form of devaluation. In 1973, the government was trying to control wages and profits. Right-wing Conservatives accused the government of leaning towards socialism. Once again, many voters considered that the major political parties in Britain were very similar, not least in the way they changed direction when elected to power. A series of by-election results showed dissatisfaction with both the Conservative and Labour parties in the early 1970s. Meanwhile, Britain faced serious inflation, high unemployment and new anxiety about the worsening balance of payments.

(See also **Appendix: Into the 1980s,** page 365.)

(g) British Foreign Policy, 1945–73

Attlee's selection of Ernest Bevin to be Foreign Secretary in 1945 was somewhat unexpected. Bevin had been a Chairman of the TUC and wartime Minister of Labour; but the appointment was in many ways a successful one. Bevin wore himself out in this gruelling office and retired in 1951 only a few weeks before his death. During this period, he committed Britain to the side of the USA in the Cold War and readily joined in both the defence of Western

Table 13.2   The pound and the US dollar

Some of the principal adjustments reflecting the trading difficulties of the democracies

Year	Dollars to the £
1914	4·86
1925	4·80 (Britain returned to the Gold Standard)
1931	c. 3·30 (pound allowed to depreciate; off Gold Standard)
1933	c. 5·00 (dollar allowed to depreciate)
post-1945	4·03
1949	2·80 (pound devalued)
1967	2·40 (pound devalued)
1971	2·60 (dollar devalued)
1972	2·35 (pound allowed to depreciate)
1973	c. 2·40 (dollar allowed to depreciate)

Europe and in the war in Korea against communist expansion. He also disentangled Britain from the developing crisis in Palestine (see Section 19.1). He took little part in the moves which produced the European Coal and Steel Community in 1951 and prepared the way for the EEC, for his health was failing and, in any case, Britain's ties with the Commonwealth seemed to exclude closer economic involvement in Europe. When Bevin retired, therefore, Britain had a major role in NATO but was already being left behind in the movement towards European unity (see Section 14.5).

Churchill's Foreign Secretary, Eden, made no substantial changes in Bevin's policies. Britain joined SEATO but refused to adopt the USA's hard line towards communist China. Eden negotiated the Geneva agreement of 1954 over Indochina but the summit meeting with Khrushchev and Eisenhower in 1955 achieved little. Eden was now Prime Minister and, in 1956, he became disastrously involved in the Suez Crisis and a short-lived war with Egypt (see Section 19.1). British forces were withdrawn amid a storm of criticism and in January 1957 Eden resigned.

Although Selwyn Lloyd was Macmillan's first Foreign Secretary and Douglas-Home took the office in 1960, Macmillan had ideas of playing an important part in world peace-making himself, but nothing could disguise the fact that Britain now had only limited influence on the USA and the Soviet Union. The 1960 summit meeting proved unproductive. Britain avoided involvement in America's growing commitments in Vietnam, and remained on the side-lines when the Berlin Wall was built in 1961 and a crisis developed over Russian missiles in Cuba in 1962. Ian Macleod as Colonial Secretary, however, managed to give a liberal appearance to his government's handling of Commonwealth problems. Macmillan also brought a new approach to Europe when, in 1961, he decided to explore the question of entry into the EEC, although long negotiations proved unproductive in the face of French opposition. Meanwhile Britain was a founder-member of the European Free Trade Association (EFTA) in 1959. Support was also given to the Test Ban Treaty of 1963.

Wilson ran into similar difficulties to those which defeated Macmillan. The

French blocked Britain's entry into the EEC though Wilson and Brown toured the members of the Community in 1967. Nor was it possible to make a dramatic breakthrough in improving relations with the Soviet Union although Wilson and Kosygin exchanged friendly visits. Britain signed the Nuclear Non-Proliferation Treaty in 1968 and joined in the discussions of SALT, but her principal problem in the late 1960s was Rhodesia, which Wilson was quite unable to bring to a successful conclusion. Wilson, however, showed a more sensitive regard for the feelings of the non-white world over the problems of southern Africa than did Heath who, upon taking office, promptly reversed a Labour decision not to sell arms to South Africa and aroused the anger of the Afro-Asian bloc in the United Nations.

In the opening years of his administration, however, Heath's principal objective in foreign affairs was to secure admission to the EEC, taking advantage of the changes in French policy which followed the retirement of de Gaulle.

(For international affairs, see Unit Seventeen; for Commonwealth developments, see Unit Sixteen; for the development of the EEC, see Unit Fourteen.)

Further Reading

Buchan, A.: *The USA*. Oxford University Press (London, 1971).
Chambers, W. N.: *The Democrats 1789–1964*. Anvil (London, 1964), Chapters 8–9.
Cootes, R. J.: *The Making of the Welfare State*. Longman (Harlow, 1966).
Druitt, B.: *The Growth of the Welfare State*. Hamish Hamilton (London, 1966).
Hill, C. P.: *History of the United States*. Arnold (London, 1966)—final chapters and appendices.
James, R.: *Towards the Welfare State*. Nelson (London, 1971).
Jamieson, A.: *Leaders of the Twentieth Century*. Bell (London, 1970)—Kennedy.
Lane, P.: *A History of Post-war Britain*. Macdonald (London, 1971).
Seaman, L. C. B.: *Post-Victorian Britain*. Methuen (London, 1967).

Documentary

Breach, R. W.: *Documents and Descriptions, the World Since 1914*. Oxford University Press (London, 1966), Section 16.
Lane, P.: *Documents on British Economic and Social History, 1945–67*. Macmillan (London, 1968).
Wroughton, J.: *Documents on British Political History 1914–70*. Macmillan (London, 1972).

Exercises

1. What does Table 13.1 reveal of the problems which arise from the constitution of the USA?
2. What do you understand by a *welfare state*?
3. In what ways have Britain's economic problems since 1945 been (*a*) similar to and (*b*) different from the problems faced before 1939?
4. Using the cross-references in this Unit, write an assessment of the achievements of *two* American presidents since 1945.

5. For what major developments were the Labour governments of 1945 to 1951 responsible? How do you account for the Labour Party's defeat in the general election of 1951?
6. Which, in your opinion, better deserves the description of 'wasted years'—the period of Conservative government from 1951 to 1964, or the period of Labour government from 1964 to 1970?
7. How should the line of Britain's balance of payments in Fig. 13.3 be continued to the present day?
8. Why has dissatisfaction been so widespread in the USA since the end of the 1950s?
9. With what justification did Macmillan tell the British people 'You've never had it so good'?

(See also **Appendix: Into the 1980s,** page 365.)

Unit Fourteen

The USA and the European Capitalist Bloc— 2 Western Europe

14.1 France

(a) The Mixture as Before

With the liberation of France in 1944, General de Gaulle became head of a French provisional government, assuming the office of President a year later. There was general agreement that the Third Republic, which had collapsed in 1940 after years of instability, should be replaced by a Fourth Republic with a new constitution. The latter was drafted by a constituent assembly and formally adopted in October 1946. Before then, however, de Gaulle had resigned his office, angered by the demands for reduced military spending but, above all, infuriated by what he suspected would be a return to instability and government by coalition. Under the new constitution, the powers of the president were less than de Gaulle thought essential. For some years, he campaigned, but with little success, for a stronger system of government, organizing right-wing opinion in the Rally of the People of France (RPF). In 1951, he retired from politics in frustration.

The constitution of the Fourth Republic gave women the right to vote and adopted proportional representation. The Senate was replaced by a Council of the Republic, with reduced powers, but the lower house of the French parliament, the National Assembly, continued to be the heart of the system. Unfortunately, divisions in this Assembly continued to produce only a procession of unstable coalition governments.

The early governments were dominated by Socialists, Radicals and the Mouvement Républicain Populaire (MRP), especially after the exclusion from office of the strong postwar Communist Party in 1947. Governments were too weak to deal effectively with France's basic problems of inflation and industrial unrest, although the French economy was propped up with American aid. In its first five years, the Fourth Republic produced twelve governments under seven prime ministers. Only one government, Blum's in 1946, was not a coalition: it lasted for six weeks. A government under Queuille, in 1950, lasted for only four days. The politicians pursued moderate policies and, for a time, resisted both the left-wing challenge of the communists and the right-wing challenge of the RPF. French democracy survived, though unconvincingly, as it had before 1939.

The 1950s brought little improvement. From 1952 to 1958, there were ten more governments, almost all of them conservative in their policies. There were now new frustrations. Defeat in Indochina in 1954 (see Section 16.3(a)) was accompanied by a fresh rebellion in Algeria (see Section 16.3(*b*)); intervention in the Suez Crisis in 1956 brought only humiliation (see Section 19.1 (*d*)). Pressing economic problems combined with the political instability to bring new waves of protest. Opinion generally tended to shift towards the right in a search for stable government. In 1953, the RPF was disbanded as a political force, freeing Gaullists in the National Assembly to exert pressure within the governments (although they could do little to strengthen the parliamentary system). Outside parliament, the RPF continued its campaign for a more effective constitution. A more violent attack on the system was made by the Poujadists, the followers of Henri Poujade who appealed in particular to the prejudices of the lower middle classes and aroused some echoes of Mussolini.

Only in its contribution to European unity (see below), did the Fourth Republic before 1950 seem capable of much effective action.

(*b*) The End of the Fourth Republic

A crisis which had long been in the making came to a head in 1958. French settlers and right-wing forces in Algeria rejected the authority of the French government. France seemed to face a situation not dissimilar to that in Spain in 1936, when Franco, launching his campaign from North Africa, challenged the republican government and produced civil war. President Coty and Pflimlin, the Prime Minister, now surrendered power rather than risk a French civil war. There was only one sufficiently heroic Frenchman to whom it was possible to turn and, in June 1958, de Gaulle came out of retirement. He was given full powers to rule and the authority to produce a new constitution. France would have a *Fifth Republic*, in which the president's powers would be greatly strengthened (although not to the extent of adopting the USA's presidential system). France continued to have prime ministers who relied on support in the Assembly but the president was no longer merely a figurehead. De Gaulle himself was President until 1969.

(*c*) The Years of de Gaulle

From 1958 to 1969, de Gaulle was largely able to impose his own will on France. He appointed sympathetic prime ministers, first Michel Debré and from 1962 Georges Pompidou, and there was strong Gaullist support in the Assembly. De Gaulle himself was elected to the Presidency in 1958 and re-elected in 1965 and he also made use of referenda (to obtain popular votes of confidence over specific issues). During this period, there was a steep decline in support for communism and, at least for a time, considerable satisfaction with a system of government which could produce results.

(*i*) **Foreign policy.** De Gaulle was a man of strong opinions, with a belief in French greatness. He supported the development of the EEC, although denying admission to Britain with whom he had strained relations as exiled leader of the Free French during the war. At the same time, he intended to restore

France's individual importance in the world. France developed her own nuclear weapons and refused to sign the Test Ban Treaty of 1963. In 1964, she recognized communist China and began to cultivate direct and friendly relations with the USSR. In 1966, de Gaulle withdrew from military commitments to NATO and forced the Alliance to move its headquarters from Paris to Brussels. His aim was to be independent politically and economically of the USA and, in general, he was a realist. He would not support any West German ambitions to recover lands to the east and he refused to prop up the selfish interests of white settlers in Algeria, although they had once seen him as a saviour. Nor did he wish to become involved in trying to preserve a French overseas empire, although the *French Community* came into existence with the constitution of the Fifth Republic (see Section 16.3(*d*)). He did, however, meddle unrealistically in Canadian affairs, even to the point of encouraging the breakaway movement of Canadian extremists of French descent.

Fig. 14.1 General de Gaulle touring Algeria after his successful referendum on the new constitution, October 1958

(*ii*) **Domestic affairs.** Within France, his main achievement was political stability but he also pursued efficiency and reform. He aimed to build up substantial gold reserves, and vigorous economic policies brought an impressive rate of growth in the early 1960s. Progress was made in education, the social services and town-planning and France had a minimum wage, related to the cost of living. But de Gaulle's regime was authoritarian. It tended to antagonize students and the trade unions and, by 1968, it was being criticized for currency troubles and a high level of unemployment. In May 1968, there were violent strikes, student demonstrations and bloody clashes. De Gaulle made concessions to the working classes by promising better wages, shorter hours and some consultation of their representatives by management. But in the autumn, the franc was under pressure and confidence in de Gaulle fell. It seemed to him an intolerable blow to French prestige to allow the franc to be devalued. He decided to make another grand appeal to the French people to confirm him in authority, linking a vote of confidence in himself to a referendum on a minor constitutional reform. The vote in April 1969 showed 10½ million in support of de Gaulle but almost 12 million against him. He promptly resigned and retired for the last time, to die in 1970 at the age of 79.

Yet in some ways de Gaulle lived on. The Fifth Republic continued and the new President was Pompidou, the Gaullist candidate. He had been a faithful supporter of de Gaulle since 1944 and his prime minister for six years. He agreed to devalue the franc and imposed restrictionist measures to meet France's economic difficulties. He also adopted a more open-minded attitude than de Gaulle to new admissions into the EEC, but, in other respects, Gaullism continued to be the most influential force in French politics. De Gaulle had designed the constitution of the Fifth Republic with care, making it very difficult for left-wing parties to come to power. The effects were still being felt in 1973 when the Gaullists again won the election in spite of increased support for a left-wing coalition.

14.2 Italy

By a narrow margin, in a referendum in 1946, Italy agreed to abolish the monarchy and thus set up a republic. From the outset, the Christian Democrats, a moderate conservative party, were the dominant political force. Their strength was matched, however, by the Socialist and Communist parties. Communism was more firmly established in Italy than in other western capitalist states but, under the leadership of Togliatti, Italian communists reserved a Tito-like right to follow a different path from that of Moscow. Italian communists, therefore, took an active part in trying to advance the welfare of Italians by working within the republican constitution.

Italian politics were fairly stable until 1953. De Gasperi was unable to win outright majorities for the Christian Democrats, but he proved an able prime minister as the leader of coalitions, with a talent for survival which might have been envied in France. From 1953 onwards the strength of the moderates began to decline and, after de Gasperi's death in 1954, the Christian Democrats themselves showed a tendency to split into factions. Christian Democrat-dominated coalitions continued to govern but they were based on constantly-shifting alliances and frequent changes of prime minister. At times the government came near to total paralysis but, although support for extremist parties inevitably grew, the Christian Democrats were able to hold on to enough votes to prolong the muddled series of coalitions into the 1970s.

International aid, especially that provided under the Marshall Plan, assisted Italy towards postwar recovery. From the outset, Italy also took part in creating the EEC. The Italian economy began to prosper but from the mid-1950s governments were usually too weak to tackle many basic problems. Southern Italy remained poor, backward in industrial development, plagued by the criminal activities of the *Mafia* (see Glossary) and constantly undermined by the migration northwards of those anxious for a higher standard of living. The north, too, had problems, not the least of them bad housing and periods of unemployment. Some areas were fortunate in having vigorous regional governments such as communist-dominated Tuscany, but many problems, such as that of inflation in the early 1970s, could not be tackled locally. Impatience with weak central government brought increasing violence and turbulence in industrial relations. The general election of 1972 was a violent one, although Italians still went through the motions, shuffling the pack of politicians once again. It was, however, ominous that the toyshops of Rome were now doing a brisk trade in plastic figures to recall Mussolini's March on Rome in 1922. The Neo-Fascists, led by Almirante, made significant gains.

Internationally, Italy remained firmly committed to the West, a founder-member of NATO and, unlike de Gaulle's France, firm in her alliance with the USA. Admission to UNO was delayed until 1955 by Russian opposition, but Italy was no longer equipped to play a dominant part in world affairs.

14.3   The German Federal Republic (West Germany)

(a) The Adenauer Years

The birth of the German Federal Republic in 1949 was the beginning of a success story (see Section 11.2). The Federal Republic had a similar constitution to that of the Weimar Republic, but it was stable and it was also soon prosperous. Konrad Adenauer, the first Chancellor, ruled from 1949 until 1963 when he retired at the ripe age of 87. He was a former mayor of Cologne who had been dismissed by Goering for opposition to the Nazis. After the war, he founded the Christian Democrat Party (CDU) which in coalition with the Christian Socials (CSU), a similar party based in Bavaria, and smaller groups with a similarly conservative outlook, formed the first government of the new republic. The CDU–CSU alliance provided stable government for many years, with the Social Democrats developing as the principal Opposition.

Adenauer's governments took vigorous action to avoid many of the difficulties of the Weimar Republic. Extremist parties, such as the Socialist Reich Party, with similarities to the Nazis, were banned and leaders like Werner Naumann, who sought to rally ex-soldiers into new versions of the Freikorps, were arrested. In 1956, the Communist Party was also banned. Adenauer's methods were sometimes autocratic but they helped to establish the political system of the new republic.

Adenauer also built up the republic's strength with the help of Erhard as Minister of Economic Affairs. The Federal Republic smoothly resettled a flood of refugees into the country, overcame the problem of unemployment and embarked on an *Economic Miracle*. Recovery and expansion in the early 1950s was remarkably rapid although Adenauer's commitment to rearmament and the introduction of conscription in 1957 antagonized the trade union movement, which had been moderate and co-operative. West Germany was fortunate in possessing vital raw materials but economic growth was also due to a vigorous national effort and enterprising leadership. The Federal Republic played a full part in the creation of the EEC. It undertook to pay compensation to the Jews of Israel as some reparation for the cruelties of the Nazis. At home the government pioneered an extension of welfare pensions, linking them not only to the cost of living but also to the growth of national wealth.

In the 1961 election, only three parties were elected to the Bundestag (the lower house of the republic's parliament). These were the CDU–CSU coalition, the Social Democrats and the Free Democrats. Adenauer had to make an alliance with the Free Democrats to retain power but the republic was able to continue with stable government; and when Adenauer retired two years later, Erhard smoothly took over the Chancellorship.

(b) Erhard and Kiesinger

Erhard governed from 1963 to 1966. At last the republic's economic progress began to slow down. Unemployment rose and a neo-Nazi Party, the National Democratic Party (NDP), was set up. Erhard was forced to resign when the Free Democrats withdrew their support from his government.

The new Chancellor was Kiesinger who managed to make a coalition between the CDU and the Social Democrats. The Social Democrats' abandonment of a commitment to Marxism in 1959 and adoption of a policy based on 'as much freedom as possible and as much planning as necessary' made the coalition possible. Kiesinger overcame the unemployment problem, but the NDP continued to cause alarm and, like France, the republic encountered student protests against crowded universities and the nature of western society. In the general election of 1969 the Social Democrats took office for the first time under Chancellor Willy Brandt.

(c) Brandt's Government

With only a tiny majority in the Bundestag, Brandt courageously committed himself to his *Ostpolitik* (a policy of seeking a new friendly relationship between West Germany and Eastern Europe). He also took advantage of de Gaulle's retirement to encourage new admissions to the EEC, and recognized the great strength of the mark in relation to other currencies by revaluing it upwards. This encouraged people who wished to sell to the Federal Republic, and made German exports more expensive. These were promising beginnings which helped to build up Brandt's reputation as a statesman, but his position in the Bundestag was insecure, a handicap in readjusting West Germany's relations with Eastern Europe. A more decisive victory in the general election of November 1972 strengthened Brandt's authority.

(d) West Germany and the German Problem

The division of Germany which produced the German Problem (see Section 11.2) had already begun to seem permanent rather than temporary when Adenauer came to power. The Federal Republic was allowed to establish a foreign office in 1951 and from then until 1955, Adenauer had personal charge of West Germany's foreign policy. This period culminated in his visit to Moscow which left the German Problem as far from solution as ever.

Adenauer has been criticized for being inflexible on the subject. He believed that Germany should be reunited as one nation but he also believed in western democracy and close links with the USA and, through the EEC and other organizations, with the capitalist states of Western Europe. Before he went to Moscow in 1955, Adenauer committed the Federal Republic to full membership of NATO. It seemed unlikely that such ties would help the German Chancellor to win concessions from the communists. On the other hand, it is also unlikely that it was ever within Adenauer's power to alter the division which had taken place.

Thus West Germany settled ever more firmly into the western capitalist bloc. The West agreed that the Federal Republic should rearm soon after the outbreak of the Korean War. On joining NATO, West Germany undertook to provide fourteen military divisions for the Organization. In Moscow, Adenauer agreed to normal diplomatic relations with the USSR in return for the release of 10 000 German prisoners-of-war (only a small proportion of those Germans who disappeared in Russia after 1945). But at the same time, the so-called *Hallstein Doctrine* declared that not only would the Federal Republic not recognize East Germany but that it would regard it as an 'unfriendly act' for other nations to do so. Thus the two Germanies kept their differing allegiances: the West refusing to recognize East Germany, and the East, apart from Russia, refusing to recognize West Germany. Both Germanies were therefore shut out from the United Nations—until 1973.

After a plebiscite in 1957, the Saar was returned to West Germany, having been in French hands since 1945. Although relations between Adenauer and de Gaulle were sometimes strained in the next few years, the German Chancellor pursued his plans for greater unity in Western Europe. He also made a trade agreement with the Soviet Union in 1958, but he would not accept the Rapacki Plan for a nuclear-free zone in Central Europe (see Section 12.3), fearing that such an arrangement would expose West Germany to danger and to communism. 'No concessions without concessions in return' remained Adenauer's basic principle in his dealings with the Soviet Union. No major concessions were made by either side during his Chancellorship or in those of Erhard and Kiesinger. NATO forces in the West and Warsaw Pact forces in the East preserved the balance and the division of Europe.

Brandt, on the other hand, took up an approach by Edward Gierek of Poland, Gomulka's successor, to try to reach more constructive agreements between East and West. He was prepared to accept the Nuclear Non-Proliferation Treaty and to recognize as final Poland's possession of lands east of the

Oder-Neisse Line. From Brandt's negotiations with Poland, there began to develop hopeful prospects for the whole of Europe. In the Soviet Union, Brezhnev also seemed anxious for a general improvement in relations. Brandt reached agreements in Warsaw and Moscow for easier relations between West Germany and the communist bloc, and a four-power agreement relaxed the tension surrounding Berlin. All these new understandings became foundations for the future exploration of a comprehensive European Security Pact (see Section 17.2).

14.4 The Lesser Powers

The European capitalist bloc was supported by a number of lesser powers.

The *Benelux countries* (Belgium, the Netherlands and Luxemburg) were overshadowed by their larger neighbours but they contributed to the defence and prosperity of the West. So too did the *Scandinavian countries*, with the exception of Sweden who preferred a more neutral position between West and East and channelled her enthusiasm for international activities into UNO.

Spain and *Portugal* were enabled by geography largely to stand aside. Franco continued to rule in Spain, a possible ally whom the West preferred, in general, to ignore. Salazar continued to rule in Portugal until his retirement in 1968. Although Portugal joined NATO and EFTA, the country was of little importance in European affairs.

Turkey joined NATO but in 1967 also accepted financial assistance from Russia, content with modest international commitments to obtain a degree of security.

14.5 Co-operation in Western Europe

Early co-operation in Western Europe was mainly economic and military. The USA was closely involved in both, at least in the early years after 1945. Inevitably, co-operation in Western Europe became intertwined with the German Problem and the Cold War between capitalism and communism (see Unit Seventeen).

(a) Economic Recovery

Although there was co-operative action to deal with refugees and reconstruction in Europe when the war ended in 1945 (see Section 10.6), it was not until 1947 that George Marshall, American Secretary of State, put forward his Plan 'against hunger, poverty, desperation and chaos'. He called on Europeans to produce a joint programme for recovery, and on the USA to give her assistance. Bevin, the British Foreign Secretary, was quick to welcome this initiative and, within a few months, sixteen European nations drew up the *European Recovery Programme* for action in the period 1948–51. The ERP was accepted in the USA and when the Programme was completed, 12 500 million dollars had been advanced to assist it. To administer and co-ordinate the Programme,

THE USA AND THE EUROPEAN CAPITALIST BLOC

COUNTRY	ECONOMIC CO-OPERATION: OEEC◆ 1948	ECONOMIC CO-OPERATION: EFTA 1960	MOVEMENT TOWARDS UNITY: COUNCIL OF EUROPE 1949	MOVEMENT TOWARDS UNITY: ECSC 1952 / EEC 1958	DEFENCE: WEU 1955	DEFENCE: NATO	POPULATION est. 1972 (millions)	MAIN EXPORT (% OF WHOLE) (1970)	EXPORTS MAINLY TO (% OF WHOLE) (1970)	IMPORTS MAINLY FROM (% OF WHOLE) (1970)
USA	□					√	208	Machinery 27%	Canada 21%: Japan 11%	Canada 28%: Japan 15%
CANADA	□					√	22	Vehicles 20%	USA 65%: Britain 9%	USA 71%: EEC 6%
BRITAIN	√	√	√	*	√ (Brussels Treaty Powers)	√	56	Machinery 28%	EEC 22%: USA 12%	EEC 20%: USA 13%
FRANCE	√		√	√	√	√ ⊙	51	Machinery 19%	EEC 48%: USA 5%	EEC 48%: USA 10%
BELGIUM	√		√	√	√	√	10	Iron/Steel 17%	EEC 69%: USA 6%	EEC 59%: USA 9%
HOLLAND	√		√	√	√	√	13	Chemicals 14%	EEC 62%: Britain 7%	EEC 56%: USA 10%
LUXEMBURG	√		√	√	√	√	0·4	(see Belgium – Economic Union, 1970)		
ITALY	√		√	√	√	√	57	Machinery 25%	EEC 43%: USA 10%	EEC 41%: USA 10%
WEST GERMANY	*		*	√	√	*	64	Machinery 29%	EEC 40%: USA 9%	EEC 44%: USA 11%
DENMARK	√	√	√	*		√	5	Machinery 21%	EEC 23%: Britain 19%	EEC 30%: Sweden 16%
ICELAND	√		*			√	0·2	Fish 78%	USA 30%: Britain 13%	W. Germany 15%: Britain 14%
SWEDEN	√	√	√				8	Machinery 25%	Britain 12%: W. Germany 12%	W. Germany 19%: Britain 14%
NORWAY	√	√	√			√	4	Ships 12%	Britain 18%: W. Germany 18%	Sweden 20%: W. Germany 14%
IRISH REPUBLIC	√		√	*			3	Meat/Livestock 30%	Britain 66%: USA 10%	Britain 53%: W. Germany 7%, USA 7%
SWITZERLAND	√	√	*				6	Machinery 30%	EEC 37%: USA 9%	EEC 58%: USA 9%
AUSTRIA	√	√	*				8	Machinery 20%	EEC 39%: Switzerland 10%	EEC 56%: Switzerland 7%, Britain 7%
PORTUGAL	√	√				√	9	Textiles 24%	Britain 20%: Angola 15%	W. Germany 15%: Britain 14%
SPAIN	*						35	Machinery 20%	EEC 36%: USA 14%	EEC 33%: USA 19%
GREECE	√		*			*	9	Tobacco 14%	EEC 46%: USA 8%	EEC 40%: Japan 13%
TURKEY	√		*			*	37	Nuts 21%, Cotton 21%	W. Germany 20%: USA 10%	USA 19%: W. Germany 19%

◆ Became OECD 1961 + USA, CANADA, FINLAND, JAPAN

√ – Founder Members
* – Later Members
□ – Associate Members

⊙ Withdrew from military side 1966

Fig. 14.2

the *Organization for European Economic Co-operation* was set up (OEEC), and so successful was this Organization that it continued after the original Programme was completed and, in 1961, was given yet a further lease of life in the *Organization for Economic Co-operation and Development* (OECD). The broad aims of both OEEC and OECD were economic development, co-operation and co-ordination and the promotion of trade. The latter was further assisted by the creation of a *General Agreement on Tariffs and Trade* (GATT) in 1947, to prevent further increases in tariffs and to secure agreed reductions.

The Marshall Plan was at first designed to assist all of Europe but it was boycotted by the communist bloc and OEEC was founded by the countries of Western Europe which later joined NATO plus certain neutral countries such as Austria and Sweden. West Germany also gained benefits and was admitted to membership in 1955. Spain joined a few years later. The USA and Canada were associate members of OEEC and both continued to assist the Organization after 1951, becoming full members of OECD in 1961. Japan joined OECD in 1963.

In 1950 OEEC set up the *European Payments Union* to encourage trade by making possible payments in any of the members' currencies. This in turn gave way to rather more sophisticated machinery in the *European Monetary Agreement* which replaced the Union in 1958. But in spite of all the USA's efforts and immense American spending in Europe in connexion with defence and NATO, Europe was still often handicapped by a shortage of dollars. Nevertheless, American aid was remarkably generous and recovery in Europe was much swifter as a result of it.

(*b*) **The Defence of Western Europe**

Three months before Marshall put forward his Plan, President Truman asked Congress for 400 million dollars to give emergency aid to Greece and Turkey. The President's main aim was to preserve these countries from communism. Thus the Truman Doctrine (of resisting communism) and Marshall Aid (to assist recovery) became linked, at least in the minds of communists. Economics and politics became inescapably mixed and, in 1949, the *North Atlantic Treaty Organization* (NATO) was set up for 'military and other aid and assistance' (see Fig. 14.3).

West Europeans were, however, already organizing their joint defence before the USA joined them in NATO. Bevin drew them together in the *Brussels Treaty Organization* of March 1948. Britain, France and the Benelux countries undertook mutual aid in the case of an armed attack, and agreed on co-ordinated foreign policies and economic co-operation. This Organization was expanded in 1955 to include West Germany and Italy, its name being changed then to the *Western European Union* (WEU).

The Brussels Treaty Organization states readily joined NATO which originally included twelve nations (see Fig. 14.2). Its membership later grew to include Greece, Turkey and West Germany. The Organization was administered by the North Atlantic Council and it established military headquarters,

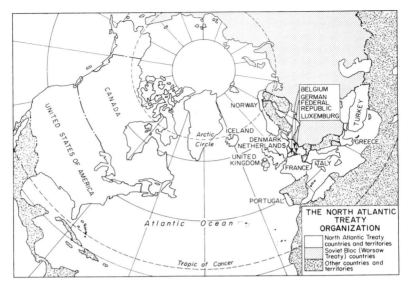

Fig. 14.3 How NATO sees the defence of freedom against the USSR

SHAPE (Supreme Headquarters Allied Powers Europe), first in Paris and later, under pressure from de Gaulle, in Brussels.

The Brussels Treaty Organization and NATO clearly existed to preserve their members against communist expansion. Yet the Brussels Treaty grew out of an earlier agreement between Britain and France mainly for mutual aid against future German aggression (signed at Dunkirk in 1947). Events moved swiftly and, in 1952, France, West Germany, Italy and the Benelux countries felt sufficient confidence in each other and sufficient fear of communism to draft a treaty to set up a *European Defence Community* (EDC) with a common army. In fact, the common army did not come into being, for France had second thoughts and refused to ratify the treaty. Thus the defence of Western Europe came to rest solely in NATO and the Brussels Treaty Organization (later the WEU).

(c) The Movement Towards the Unity of Western Europe

Both the USA and the USSR are unions of states in large and powerful units. Even before the Second World War ended there was feeling that the states of Europe should be similarly united. The first step in 1944 was only a tiny one: the exiled governments of Belgium, the Netherlands and Luxemburg agreed on a customs union, *Benelux*, which came into existence in 1947. From an agreement on tariffs, the Benelux states moved towards closer economic integration so that in 1960 they set up an Economic Union with free movement of people, capital and goods between the three states. By that time, however, a larger unit was in the making, the European Economic Community (EEC), often referred to in Britain as the Common Market.

In August 1949, the first meeting took place of the *Council of Europe*, representing foreign ministers and the parliaments of many of the states of Western Europe. It served mainly as a forum for discussion, although it eventually established a Commission for Human Rights and a Court to protect individuals against unjust treatment.

Robert Schuman, the French Foreign Minister, wished to go further than the Council of Europe. He proposed a common market in coal and steel, anticipating that close collaboration in these areas could then be broadened into a movement towards economic and even political unity. France, Italy, West Germany and the Benelux countries agreed to create the *European Coal and Steel Community* (ECSC), which came into being in 1952. ECSC was controlled by a High Authority to which all members had to surrender some of their independence and it was this kind of authority, reducing the individual sovereignty of member-states, which Britain and other nations were unwilling to accept. They therefore remained outside. But ECSC was very successful in boosting European steel production and, in 1957, its six members signed the Rome Treaties to set up the *European Atomic Energy Community* (Euratom) and the *European Economic Community* a year later. This step towards economic unity was also a step in the direction of a political federation, a united states of the six countries.

Sceptics argued that such integration would not work. Indeed de Gaulle's attempts to dominate the Communities caused strains which seemed likely to prove the sceptics right. Certainly, little progress was made in the 1960s towards political unity. On the other hand, the Communities were of great economic advantage to their members, so much so that Britain came round to applying for membership, first under Macmillan and then under Wilson. They made no progress in the face of resistance from de Gaulle, who regarded Britain as a rival to his own authority; he also claimed that Britain had too many economic problems in the 1960s to be a useful member. It took the retirement and death of de Gaulle and the dogged determination of Heath, apparently bent on admission at almost any price, to get Britain into the EEC. Britain joined the Community on 1 January 1973 along with Denmark and the Irish Republic. They joined amidst controversy. The people of Norway had rejected membership in a referendum and many in Britain had misgivings about the loss of a certain amount of national sovereignty and the acceptance of an enormous quantity of economic regulations whose effects upon prices, jobs, overall prosperity and regional development were not really calculable.

The Six had had a European Parliament since 1958 and, in 1967, the machinery of the Communities had been streamlined with a single Commission to exercise executive power and a Council of Ministers to assist in reaching decisions. Parliament, the Commission and the Council of Ministers were interlinked to ensure that all members were consulted in the affairs of the Communities. But national governments continued to exist in each member-state, only surrendering their powers in limited areas. There were no signs that a United States of Europe was imminent and real political unity seemed remote. In any case, all these movements towards unity took place only in Western Europe. Eastern Europe had its own organizations (see Unit Twelve). Until the new admissions to the EEC occurred in 1973, those outside the Six grouped themselves in the *European Free Trade Association* (EFTA). Seven countries (see Fig. 14.2), agreed to reduce tariffs and develop their trade without, in the way of the EEC, surrendering sovereignty and aiming at economic integration. There was some rivalry between the two trading blocs, and it was eventually fear that they would be at a grave disadvantage in selling goods to the EEC, which kept common tariffs against outsiders, that drove some members of EFTA to wish to change partners. A new mini-EFTA now came into existence, consisting of Austria, Finland, Iceland, Norway, Portugal, Sweden and Switzerland.

Fig. 14.4 UK stamp with the flags of the seven members of EFTA, 1967

Further Reading

All-in-one Guide to European–Atlantic Organizations (European–Atlantic Movement, Exeter, 1961).
Ayling, S. E.: *Portraits of Power*. Harrap (London, 1965)—de Gaulle.
Elliott, B. J.: *Western Europe After Hitler*. Longman (Harlow, 1968).
Farr, W.: *Daily Telegraph Guide to the Common Market*. Collins (London, 1972).
Jamieson, A.: *Leaders of the Twentieth Century*. Bell (London, 1970)—de Gaulle.
Pickles, D.: *France*. Oxford University Press (London, 1971).
Salvadori, M.: *NATO*. Anvil (London, 1957).

Documentary

Absalom, R.: *France, the May Events 1968*. Longman Flashpoint (Harlow, 1971).
Breach, R. W.: *Documents and Descriptions, the World Since 1914*. Oxford University Press (London, 1966), Sections 8–9, 15a.

Exercises

1. What can you learn about co-operation in Western Europe from Fig. 14.2?
2. Why did Western Europe and Eastern Europe create similar but opposing organizations in the years after 1945? (Use Units Twelve and Fourteen, including Figs 12.3 and 14.2)
3. 'Democracies based upon a two-party system were more stable than democracies based upon more numerous parties.' Illustrate the truth of this statement with

reference to the following states since 1945: the USA; Britain; France; Italy. In what ways did West Germany show that this statement was not invariably true?
4. Show how, after 1945, Western Europe moved towards (a) economic, (b) military and (c) political co-operation.
5. Investigate the career of General de Gaulle to explain:
   (a) why he was popular in France in 1945
   (b) why he retired from politics in 1951
   (c) why he became President in 1958
   (d) why he resigned in 1969.

What were his main achievements within France and in international affairs?

(See also **Appendix: Into the 1980s**, page 365.)

Unit Fifteen

The Expansion of Communism Outside Europe

As early as 1924 the *Mongolian People's Republic* came into existence in what had been Outer Mongolia. From that time onwards, this new communist-inclined state was much dependent on Russian support although it remained nominally subject to Chinese authority until 1945. With the ending of the Second World War, communism spread further but only in North Korea was it closely connected, as in Eastern Europe, with occupation by the forces of the Soviet Union. In North Vietnam, communism grew with the Viet Minh, an organization which, like Tito's partisans in Jugoslavia, first developed in resisting foreign invasion. China adopted a communist system in 1949, the outcome of a civil war in which the followers of Mao Tse-tung overthrew the corrupt and inefficient regime of the nationalists.* In Cuba, successful rebellion against corruption and exploitation hardened into communism partly in self-defence against the inept policies of Eisenhower and Kennedy, who put the weight of the USA behind the system the Cubans had rejected and drove the new government into dependence on the USSR. In Chile, there was a strong movement towards some sort of Marxism simply by way of free elections.

Other states went less far in establishing communist regimes although few indeed, after 1945, were entirely uninfluenced by socialist ideals. France and Italy had strong communist parties even in the European capitalist bloc and, among the emergent nations, many states produced leaders such as Nkrumah of Ghana, who saw merits in communism and wished to borrow at least some ideas from the communist world.

15.1 North Korea

Korea was seized by Japan in 1910 and remained in Japanese hands until their defeat in 1945. The USSR declared war on Japan just in time to put Soviet forces into North Korea before the Second World War ended. Like Germany, the country as a whole was then temporarily partitioned with the Russians occupying the area north of the 38th parallel and the USA the area south of it. North Korea adopted a constitution similar to that of the USSR and the

* Students are at some disadvantage in dealing with many of the communist states, especially China, North Korea and North Vietnam. Facts are often difficult to disentangle from propaganda, both communist and capitalist. In contemporary history in general, judgments must be made with caution. Nowhere is this more true than in relation to communism in Asia.

Democratic People's Republic of Korea came into existence in 1948. Power in this North Korean state lay with the leadership of the Workers' Party and particularly with Kim Il-sung, a communist.

Kim remained in power for decades and built up a personal control which many called Stalinist. With Russian help, much economic development took place. Agriculture was collectivized into co-operatives. Industry expanded on the basis of North Korean mineral resources and plant already built by the Japanese. Among the social improvements, it was claimed in 1970 that illiteracy had been eliminated. In trade, the republic relied heavily on other communist states and Kim tried to avoid involvement in the ideological disputes between China and the USSR. Russian troops had been withdrawn in 1948 and Kim did not intend to be a Russian puppet. His first aim was to continue his own regime. His second was to extend communism to the whole of Korea. But South Korea also developed rapidly, nurtured by the USA, and in the Korean War of 1950–3 (see Section 17.1(c)) it became clear that Korea could not be reunited by force. Both sides had to accept a stalemate and the 38th parallel hardened into another Iron Curtain.

15.2 China—the Years of Conflict

(a) The Revolution of 1911

The 'Save China League' which Sun Yat-sen set up in 1894 was just one of a variety of revolutionary movements which looked for the salvation of China in the end of the Manchu Empire. A few years later, Sun proclaimed his 'Three Principles'—Nationalism to rid China of interference and exploitation by foreigners, Democracy to create a more modern system of government and Socialism to bring about reforms and a better life, especially for the millions of Chinese peasants. The Manchu Empire, like Tsarism in Russia, was unfitted to make these advances, although a flood of reforms in the first decade of the twentieth century, including the abolition of slavery and the calling of a parliament, indicated a belated willingness to try. The effort came too late. China faced problems of backwardness, under-development, poverty and feebleness as vast as its size. Its size and the diversity of its peoples rendered it almost impossible for the Emperor to create one nation. When Pu Yi inherited the throne in 1908 at the age of two, the moment seemed ripe for the revolution which had long been brewing.

In fact, there were two revolutions, both towards the end of 1911. At Peking, as hostility to the Manchu Empire came to the surface throughout China, Yuan Shih-kai took the office of Prime Minister, intent on strong personal rule with or without the imperial dynasty. At Nanking, Sun Yat-sen was proclaimed President by revolutionaries intent on a republic. In February 1912, Pu Yi, now aged six, was persuaded to abdicate, while Sun stood down to allow Yuan to become President of the new Chinese republic. Civil war was avoided; and the Manchu Empire had fallen as easily as Tsarism was to fall in Russia in 1917.

(*b*) **Yuan, War Lords and the Kuomintang**

Yuan soon found himself in conflict with the followers of Sun in the *Kuomintang* (a nationalist party which dated from 1891). The Kuomintang wanted a democracy based on a majority in parliament. They themselves won a majority when the first parliament met under the new constitution in 1913. They argued that the President should be only a figure-head but Yuan meant to rule. He outlawed the Kuomintang, chased Sun into exile and dismissed what was left of the parliament. The Kuomintang regrouped in Canton where they set up a rival government. Yuan toyed with the idea of declaring himself Emperor but his authority was disputed in many areas and China seemed to be on the verge of anarchy.

Yuan's death in 1916 led to even greater confusion. Although an attempt was made to restore some sort of democratic government in Peking and the Kuomintang kept a precarious hold on Canton, China as a whole fell prey to the war lords (quarrelsome militarists who fought against one another like medieval barons, conscripting the peasants and ravaging the countryside in pursuit of personal power). The official government in Peking was unstable and weak, unable to gain much profit or prestige even from joining the First World War on the side of the victorious Allies.

In their disillusionment, a handful of Chinese turned to Marxism and Russia for guidance. In 1921, they formed the Chinese Communist Party. In 1922, they persuaded Sun Yat-sen to accept Russian help and within a year the Kuomintang and the Communists made an entente: Borodin came to Canton to advise Sun on transforming his party into an effective organization. They created a nationalist army which began to consolidate the authority of the Kuomintang in the area around Canton. Borodin brought from Russia advisers, money and equipment and, when Sun died in 1925, the Kuomintang had a new popular appeal, based on a programme of helping the poor and resisting foreign exploitation of the Chinese.

Chiang Kai-shek emerged as the successor to Sun. In 1926, he led the Kuomintang forces northwards and the following year occupied Nanking. The nationalist troops seized the properties of foreigners as they advanced, especially those of the British and the Americans, as well as routing the war lords, whose power had already begun to decline.

(*c*) **Chiang and Mao**

Chiang Kai-shek was a nationalist, a military man, trained in Japan before 1911. He had studied Russian military organization in Moscow in 1923 but he had no liking for communism and was disturbed by the activities of Chinese communists against businessmen and landlords. In 1927, when the nationalist army took Shanghai, Chiang turned against the communists and their supporters in the Kuomintang. In a bloody purge, many were killed and others fled; Chiang's example was followed by other military leaders in the Kuomintang. The communists were forced to retire to the south while Chiang pushed northwards, finally entering Peking in June 1928.

Insofar as China now had a single government, it was that of Chiang and the Kuomintang. They chose to make their new capital in Nanking but their authority was still confined largely to the east of China. The communists were steadily reorganizing in the rice-growing south, in the provinces of Hunan and Kiangsi. The Japanese were entrenched in Manchuria, which they were soon to turn into a puppet-state, and the vast areas of central and west China acknowledged no common authority. China seemed about to dissolve into fragments as had always seemed possible.

Fig. 15.1 Mao Tse-tung (standing, third from the left) *with other Chinese communists in 1927*

Chiang decided that his first priority must be to eliminate the communists completely. By the end of the 1920s, the latter had made steady progress in winning peasant support and in setting up soviets in Hupeh, Hunan, Kiangsi and Fukien. This gave them control of an area almost as large as that won by Chiang, in which their authority was based on a peasant rebellion against their landlords. Among the communists were Chu Teh, a trained soldier, and Mao Tse-tung, once a librarian. Together they created the Kiangsi Red Army and Mao initiated extensive land reforms in the province. He was deeply aware of the importance of the peasants in China. He likened them to the sea in which the communists would swim as fish. On another occasion he wrote, 'We communists are like seeds and the people are like the soil. Wherever we go, we must unite with the people, take root and blossom among them.' But in 1930 Chiang determined to uproot the communists and in a series of campaigns they were forced to abandon the soviets and finally to quit their last base in Kiangsi.

(d) The Long March

In October 1934, Mao led the retreat out of Kiangsi and across the River Yangtse. About 100 000 began the Long March. Their trek covered over 2 000 miles and took them a year before they arrived in Shensi. During the migration, Mao's wife died and their numbers dwindled, but they set up new headquarters at Yenan, in Shensi province, under the now undisputed leadership of Mao Tse-tung. The Long March was an ordeal but it demonstrated Chiang's inability to exterminate the communists and it brought them contact with more of China's peasants, among whom seeds could be planted. It also brought them nearer to the Japanese, whose conquest of Manchuria in 1931 (see Section 8.1) Chiang seemed content to ignore. When Chiang sent the northern militarist, Chang Hsueh-liang, to try to drive Mao's forces from Shensi, many of his troops responded to communist appeals that they should unite against the Japanese, rather than persist in civil war. Chang himself took Chiang Kaishek prisoner late in 1936, to force him to alter his priorities. Chiang gave way and an uneasy alliance was made between nationalists and communists to resist the invader. The alliance was soon to be needed for in 1937 Japan embarked on all-out war (see Section 8.1).

(e) World War and Civil War

The *Chinese–Japanese War*, one theatre in the Second World War, went on until 1945 and both nationalists and communists fought the invader. But rivalry between them was never far below the surface and long before the war ended their alliance had broken down. Chiang was forced by the Japanese to withdraw to Chungking where his rule became increasingly authoritarian. The strength of the Kuomintang had always been in the towns but many of them had fallen to the Japanese and Chiang made few new friends. Mao used guerilla tactics against the Japanese and continued to spread communist propaganda in the villages. Neither he nor Chiang could dislodge the Japanese from most of eastern China and each accused the other of making too little effort. Chiang was anxious to prevent supplies reaching the communists and Mao was anxious to preserve the strength of the Red Army. Any pretence of co-operation broke down and a renewal of the civil war seemed inevitable.

In the late stages of the Second World War, supplies from the USA began to reach China. Chiang, whose government was still recognized as the official one, began to hope for American support against the communists, but when the Japanese began to withdraw troops to fight elsewhere the communists were first into the areas they left. Chiang seemed to be obsessed with the hunting down of rivals and he stubbornly resisted the efforts of the USA to bring about a coalition of Chinese moderates based on the Democratic League of middle-of-the-road politicians. General Marshall, later the author of the Marshall Plan, could obtain no ccmpromise and, in 1946, the civil war broke out again.

At first, it was the nationalists who were successful. The Soviet Union had advanced into Manchuria in the closing stages of the war against Japan, but the Russians showed little interest in the civil war and actually returned Manchuria to the nationalists. Chiang had half-hearted American support, but the Kuomintang was torn with internal quarrels and American arms often found their way to the communists. From 1947, the latter also received supplies from the USSR. The peasants were strongly pro-communist and, in 1948, the nationalists suffered a major defeat in Manchuria. Other defeats quickly followed. At the beginning of 1949, Peking fell to the communists and in April they took Nanking. Chiang could hold neither Chungking nor Canton and, in December 1949, he set up his last headquarters on the island of Formosa (Taiwan). Formosa had been in Japanese hands from 1895 to 1945 but was confidently expected to be returned to China when the Japanese peace treaty was signed. Before that treaty was signed, at San Francisco in 1951, Chiang was in possession and, spurred on by the Korean War, the USA had undertaken his defence. The Treaty of San Francisco, therefore, ignored Formosa, which was to remain the final stronghold of Nationalist China for decades. In 1954, the USA signed a Mutual Security Pact with Chiang and until 1971 continued to maintain him as one of the Big Five with the right of the veto in the UN Security Council. Chiang's empire also included the tiny islands of Quemoy and Matsu.

Meanwhile, in October 1949, the communists set up the People's Republic of China at Peking, under Mao Tse-tung, Chairman of the Communist Party.

(f) Why did Chiang Kai-shek Fail?

The rout of the nationalists was due primarily to two factors. One was the arrogance, corruption and incompetence of the nationalists themselves. The other was the determination and widespread popularity of the communists. In the final stages of the civil war, the nationalists were totally demoralized. Inflation was rampant and in spite of some reforms in the 1930s, the Kuomintang had little to show for its long period as the official government of China. Of course, it had been constantly handicapped by the struggles against the warlords, the communists and the Japanese. But even as a patriotic force, its record was unconvincing, too often marred by a concern to keep itself in power and by the self-interest of its supporters. Chiang's methods were often brutal and authoritarian. Nationalist China was a one-party state and, when Chiang showed a readiness in 1947 to accept an elected parliament and go some way towards a return to Sun Yat-sen's 'Three Principles', it was already too late. His government had done far too little for the Chinese people. It was the regime of businessmen, landlords and vested interests and, above all, of Chiang Kai-shek himself, now quite discredited.

The success of the Chinese communists owed very little to the USSR. From about 1927 to the very last stages of the civil war, they had received little assistance from Moscow though deserters from Chiang brought them a steady supply of American weapons. 'Political power,' declared Mao Tse-tung, 'grows out of the barrel of a gun' and the Red Army became an efficient fighting unit. But, more important, the communists won the support of the masses. In their soviets, land was redistributed among the peasants, social reforms were made and the poor looked forward to a better life. The peasants were mobilized in a class struggle against landlordism. In 1957, Mao expressed the aims of the communists as being 'to ensure a better life for the several hundred million people of China and to build our economically and culturally backward country into a prosperous and powerful one with a high level of culture'. In 1949, it had seemed far more likely that this could be done by Mao's communists than by Chiang's nationalists.

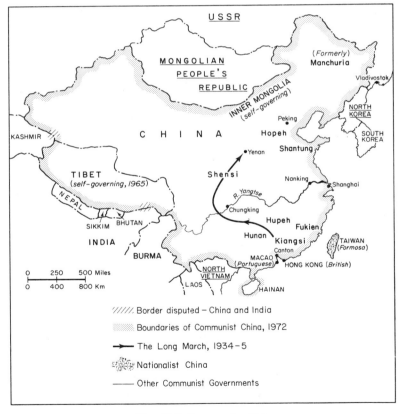

Fig. 15.2 Communist China

15.3 China Under Communism

(a) The Political System

Like Lenin, Mao believed that a period of dictatorship was necessary in order to lead the people to communism. After 1949, real power in China lay within the Communist Party, with Mao as its Chairman. In theory, he led a coalition government but it was subject to rigid communist control. Within this framework, the Chinese people had far more opportunity to take part in government and administration than ever before, but the system left little room for dissent from Marxism. Propaganda was intensive and censorship strict but China rapidly achieved a new degree of unity. There was little victimization of those willing to conform, even former members of the Kuomintang, but landlords and implacable opponents were ruthlessly rooted out.

Not until 1954 was a permanent constitution worked out. Like the Russian system it is based entirely on the Communist Party. All candidates for office belong to the party. A system of elected congresses corresponds to Russian soviets, with a central parliament known as the National People's Congress. In practice, most of the work of this Congress is carried on by a Standing Committee. A State Council exists as the governing body. After 1954, this government was led by Chou En-lai, in effect as Prime Minister. His deputy was Lin Piao, a survivor of the Long March, who did much to edit and circulate the *Thoughts of Chairman Mao* (see page 237). Lin, however, was disgraced and, in 1971, his aircraft was shot down over Mongolia, the prelude to the almost total removal of his memory from Chinese politics. Disgrace also came to Liu Shao-chi who, from 1954 to 1969, was Chairman of the Republic, the head of state. But all appointments in China are determined by the Communist Party and it was as Chairman of the party that Mao Tse-tung exercised the controlling influence. In spite of party upheavals, Chinese leaders have been long-lived and thus the system has, since 1949, provided the country with remarkably stable government, shaken only from time to time by fierce disputes about the interpretation of Marxist teachings.

(b) The Economy

Mao's first priority was the redistribution of land. The Agrarian Law of 1950 struck a mortal blow at landlords who were rooted out, often violently, in 'speak-bitterness' meetings, at which they were put on public trial and their former tenants were encouraged to testify to the cruelty and greed of the landlords. Their property was shared among the poor peasants. The tiny peasant holdings were then grouped into collective farms, although not without some resistance from those peasants who preferred private ownership. By the end of the 1950s, almost all the land had been collectivized, most of it in communes which originated in 1958 and which grouped the collective farms into larger units for more thoroughgoing economic organization, linking agriculture and industry and, at the same time, providing units for local government, education and Marxist indoctrination. The communes were part of the *Great Leap Forward*, a new ambitious plan for the second five-year period of development.

From the outset, communist control was extended to all aspects of the economy. One of Mao's first actions was to bring banking and trade under communist control and to halt the inflation which had set in under Chiang. Capitalists were no longer tolerated and, in 1953, the First Five-Year Plan set out to develop industry with extensive nationalization. Mineral deposits were developed and a considerable emphasis was placed on heavy industry and the production of capital goods, such as tractors and ships. Like Russia in the 1930s, China paid little attention to the production of consumer goods but attacked basic problems of hunger and illiteracy in an effort to build for the future.

The Second Plan of 1958, the Great Leap Forward, aimed to double the output of industry and increase that of agriculture by 35 per cent. It included ambitious schemes for power stations and irrigation but also the Campaign for Little Steel in village furnaces. The Campaign produced very little steel indeed; but it boosted national pride and enthusiasm for development. The Leap, in fact, fell short of its targets. The communes were often modified, even to the extent of allowing the reappearance of some cultivation in private plots. Other changes were also made in the Plan which was handicapped by bad harvests and by China's quarrel with Russia. Russian advisers and technicians were withdrawn in 1960.

Nevertheless, development went on. In 1964 China successfully exploded a nuclear weapon and by 1967 she had developed a hydrogen bomb, some evidence of industrial sophistication. Power supplies developed rapidly and industrial complexes grew in the 1960s in several parts of the country. The emphasis was still on capital goods rather than consumer goods and in many ways China remained underdeveloped. In the UNCTAD Conference of 1972 she was, therefore, able to appear in a strangely double role, identifying on the one hand with the world's poor nations (agricultural like herself) but on the other hand sufficiently advanced to be able to offer aid and technical assistance to many of them. Chinese help to Zambia and Tanzania in Africa seemed to be offered more in the spirit of co-operation among the poor than in the form of a charity poured out by the rich, who perhaps expected economic profit in return.

But China seemed less concerned than Stalin in Russia had been to pursue economic development and industrial wealth with ruthless single-mindedness. Progress was not measured only in factory output and railway mileages. A great expansion of cultural activity was encouraged. Much thought was given to how the individual could make his contribution in such a huge state. Communist goals remained but experiments were common. The communes, for example, were reduced in size and made less comprehensive in their functions so that by 1964 there were 74 000 compared with 26 000 in 1958 and, instead of about 5 000 families in each, there were now only about 2 000.

(c) Society and Ideology

There were similar experiments in other areas. Mao wished to revolutionize society, to create a 'new socialist man'. Certain changes were essential. One was mass literacy. Another was equality for women with equal rights to share in such provisions as health insurance, in political affairs and in ownership. Child marriages were made illegal and women could choose their partners in marriage as freely as men. But it was not Mao's intention simply to adopt the values of other states, not even those of the USSR.

In 1956, he encouraged a movement to *free expression*. He called for a 'hundred flowers' to bloom, with criticism and opinions of the regime. The 'flowers' bloomed only slowly but amongst them Mao found some 'weeds' and, in 1957, the experiment was called off and censorship restored. A number of those who had responded to Mao's invitation were banished and intellectuals in general were subjected to tighter control.

About this time too, China began to part company with the USSR. Since 1949, the Russians had given their poorer neighbour extensive aid but Mao began to question whether theirs was the right path to communism and by 1960 he was accusing them of 'revisionism' (revising the true teachings of Marxism–Leninism). In fact, China suspected that the USSR was paying more attention to Russia's interests as a great power than to the fundamental objectives of Marxism. The Russian leaders, especially Khrushchev, were suspicious of the soundness of Chinese economic planning, and Chinese revolutionary enthusiasm seemed likely to unsettle the balance of power, slowly developing between East and West. Moreover, China had a border dispute with India whom the USSR did not wish to antagonize. Even the Chinese–Russian border was not beyond dispute and as the population of China grew rapidly to well over 600 million in the 1950s, the Soviet Union became anxious about the sparsely-populated expanses of eastern Russia. Clashes occurred on the Russian–Chinese borders and, with the development of Chinese nuclear weapons, relations became particularly tense in the late 1960s, revealing the hollowness of the arguments of those who had once alleged that the quarrel was mainly a personal feud between Khrushchev and Mao.

From their beginnings, there had been differences between the communism of Russia and that of China. The Bolshevik Revolution in Russia had, to a large extent, been a revolution of industrial workers. That in China sprang from the peasants and the villages. But their rivalry was also that of two very large countries, both potentially extremely powerful and rivals for the leadership of world communism.

In the 1960s, the ideological dispute had effects inside China. In what came to be known as the *Cultural Revolution*, there was an increasingly frenzied attack upon all forms of revisionism (see Glossary) Intellectuals and 'experts', who inclined to the supposedly-Russian ideas that there should be more emphasis on consumer goods and more cordial relations with the West, were attacked as fiercely as those who wished to preserve a small measure of private enterprise. Gangs of Red Guards, many of them youths, roamed the country. Schools and places of learning were closed for a time in 1967–8 to allow a complete rethinking of the educational curriculum and its purposes. In a period of great turbulence, the only anchor seemed to be in the little red books which appeared everywhere and which contained the *Thoughts of Chairman*

Mao Tse-tung. Supporters of Chinese traditions as well as of all kinds of westernization were rooted out and deprived of authority at all levels. The Communist Party was reorganized and men like Liu Shao-chi expelled from it. Like Lenin in his final years, Mao was anxious that the party should keep in touch with the masses. Above all, he wished to maintain contact with the young, the future upholders of communism. The party had too many bureaucrats who were losing that contact. But to the West it seemed that the hero-worship went beyond even Stalinist proportions as the land was filled with the rapturous retelling of the *Thoughts* of Mao.

Outsiders found it strange and frightening as countless millions of soberly and uniformly-dressed Chinese apparently abandoned themselves to a frenzy of revolutionary enthusiasm. It seemed even stranger that, apparently refreshed by the Cultural Revolution, the people could then settle down to work again and enter the 1970s with an amazing stability.

(d) Chinese Foreign Policy

Mao loudly preached revolutionary communism and his government constantly encouraged 'people's wars' against their oppressors. On the other hand, in foreign affairs as well as in internal matters, communist China remained an enigma. Western powers expected China to be aggressive and were sometimes puzzled when China did not match words with actions. Although other countries were less hostile, the USA stubbornly refused to recognize the new regime, maintained a fleet to patrol China's shores, supported Chiang in Taiwan and obstructed the admission of Red China to the United Nations. To the Americans, it was proof of Mao's aggressive intentions that he gave active support to North Korea in the Korean War (see Section 17.1(c)) and encouragement to North Vietnam at a later date; and it was the Korean War which prompted the USA rapidly to rebuild the strength of Japan and to set up SEATO in 1954. In practice, however, China has proved a remarkably peaceful power.

It may be argued that China attacked Tibet in 1950, occupying the east of that country and forcing the Dalai Lama to flee after an unsuccessful rebellion in 1959. In 1965, Tibet was given the status of a self-governing region of China. Tibet, however, was part of the Manchu Empire until 1911 and was regarded as part of China by the Kuomintang as well as by the communists.

In 1962, China briefly went to war with India, mainly over Ladakh and minor disputed areas on the ill-defined Indo-Chinese border. But, having won military success, the Chinese made no attempt to follow up their advantage and mildly withdrew from territory where they considered they had no legitimate claims. Nor did they seek to drive the British from Hong Kong or the Portuguese from Macao, although there was sometimes tension around these remnants of European empires.

Nevertheless, Mao's government kept up violent propaganda against the West and particularly the USA and it deplored the attempts of the USSR to improve relations with the capitalist world. It was, therefore, surprising that

1971 brought an apparent change of attitude both in Peking and Washington. Through the improbable medium of table-tennis matches, China showed a willingness to make contact with the West. It was a game in which the Chinese excelled and such was their new friendliness, it was suspected that they even, on occasions, deliberately allowed the West to win. The change of climate brought speedy results. The USA abandoned obstruction and China was admitted into the United Nations, shouldering aside the absurd pretensions of Chiang Kai-shek. President Nixon was courteously received in Peking, the beginning of some contact between the two nations and perhaps of a new realism in international relations, although it remained unlikely that suspicions on either side would die quickly.

15.4 North Vietnam

Ho Chi Minh served a long apprenticeship as a communist, much of it at some distance from North Vietnam which he eventually came to rule. His father was a nationalist who lost his job for opposing French colonialism, and Ho spent some time in Britain, Western Europe and at sea, before arriving in Moscow in 1922. He left Russia with Borodin to assist the Chinese Communist Party and then he went to encourage rebellion against the French occupation of Indochina. But it was not until 1941, when Japan invaded that area, that he set up a resistance movement called the *Viet Minh*.

The defeat of Japan, in 1945, at once revived the question of the future of French colonialism in Indochina (see Unit Sixteen). Ho declared that the eastern half of the area would be independent and he proclaimed the Democratic Republic of Vietnam, under his own Presidency. Even the French recognized him as the Vietnamese leader, for his politics and patriotic record were as popular as Tito's in Jugoslavia. But the French were not yet ready to abandon their authority in Indochina, especially to the communists, and it was not until they were routed at Dien Bien Phu in 1954 that they were persuaded to leave the area.

Like Mao in China, Ho and the Viet Minh had the support of the peasants. After 1950, the year in which China and the USSR recognized the Democratic Republic of Vietnam, they also received Chinese military supplies to ensure their survival. In 1951, the Viet Minh was reorganized into the Fatherland, or Lien Viet, Front, a popular and communist-based coalition which in due course became the undisputed government of North Vietnam. But, anxious to prevent communist expansion, the USA gave assistance to the French, spending over 1 000 million dollars in 1954 alone. Such spending failed to preserve the French Empire in Indochina, but, when the French withdrew, Vietnam was temporarily divided into two parts, at the 17th parallel. From this division developed the most prolonged confrontation and conflict so far to have occurred between the USA and the communists (see Unit Seventeen).

America intended to keep communism out of South Vietnam, but in North Vietnam Ho Chi Minh was supreme. With Pham Van Dong as Prime Minister and General Giap in charge of the armed forces as Minister of Defence, both of them long-associated with Ho in the struggle for liberation and communism, the government of the Democratic Republic proved remarkably stable. A new constitution of 1960 made little difference to either the system or the personnel of the government. Ho Chi Minh was re-elected President and the Communist Party continued to direct the development of the state. In spite of some peasant resistance and a crisis in 1956, when the government tried to effect social change too quickly, agriculture was organized into co-operatives. Industries were nationalized, although only Hanoi and Haiphong had extensive industrial areas. A thorough-going attempt was made to eliminate illiteracy and to develop education. But in spite of extensive aid from other communist countries, North Vietnam was still far from being a rich country and development was handicapped severely by the strain of the struggle for South Vietnam, particularly when, after 1964, the USA resorted to the bombing of the North. It seemed an unequal contest as the world's most powerful air force blasted the rail links, ports and industries of an underdeveloped state of less than 20 million people. But the bombing had no marked effect on the loyalties and determination of the North Vietnamese.

Ho Chi Minh died in September 1969, but the Communist Party remained in power. There was no doubt that North Vietnam was heavily dependent on aid from other communist powers, but the communists there were masters in their own country, subservient to neither the USSR nor to China. Their government had arisen, under the leadership of Ho, from the peasants of Indochina and from resistance to French colonialism. It was an American delusion that it was part of a Russian or Chinese plot to spread Marxism into lands reluctant to receive it.

15.5   Cuba

The Caribbean island of Cuba was liberated by the USA from the hands of Spain in a brief war in 1898. The island became a republic but American troops were needed until 1902, and again from 1906 to 1909, to create stability; American aid was necessary at frequent intervals to ensure solvency. Cuban presidents produced little but revolts and charges of corruption, and the election of General Machado in 1925 degenerated inevitably into dictatorship. A combination of Machado's terrorism and the Great Depression led to further unrest and, in 1933, the year that Hitler came to power in Germany, Cuba fell into the hands of Batista, an enterprising sergeant who secured control of the Cuban army.

Batista became a kingmaker. In the 1930s, he lurked behind a variety of incompetent presidents, pulling the political strings; he emerged in 1940, now with the rank of colonel, to secure his own election as President of Cuba until 1944. His regime had some of the trappings of fascism, although he introduced a constitution in 1940 modelled on that of the USA and declared war on the Axis powers. 1944 brought Batista temporary eclipse but, in 1952, he seized power again and for a time ruled by decree, securing election as President in 1955 as the only candidate. To mark his success, Batista issued an amnesty to political prisoners. One of those released was Fidel Castro.

Table 15.1   Communist powers outside Europe

Country	Population (est. 1972) millions	Main Export % of whole *(1969)	Exports Mainly To (% of whole) (1969)	Imports Mainly From (% of whole) (1969)
China	830	Textiles, metals (*)	Hong Kong c. 24% Japan c. 13%	Japan c. 26% West Germany c. 11%
North Korea	14	Metals 50% (1964)	USSR 62%	USSR 68%
North Vietnam	21	*	USSR, China } 85% East Europe	USSR, China } 85% East Europe
Cuba	9	Sugar products 85%	USSR 44%, China 9%	USSR 61%, China 7%
Chile†	9	Copper 76%	USA 17%, Britain 14%, Japan 14%	USA 38% West Germany 10%, Argentina 10%

* Not all figures available.
† N.B. Before election of Allende.

Castro wasted little time in resuming the revolutionary activities which had taken him to prison in the first place. At the end of 1956, he led an invasion of Cuba from Mexico, appealing to all those discontented with the rule of Batista. The invasion reduced the Castro faction to a dozen but guerilla headquarters were established in the mountains of the Sierra Maestra and support began to grow. Cuba was close to civil war and on 1 January 1959, Batista fled. Castro's guerillas occupied Havana, establishing a dictatorship of the Popular Socialist Party.

One of Castro's followers was Ernesto 'Che' Guevara: he was a Marxist who shared with Mao Tse-tung a faith in revolutionary peasantry. Under Castro, he worked on an agricultural programme to set up co-operatives and then, in 1961, became Minister for Industries. But he found administration dull and left Cuba in 1965 to continue the guerilla struggle in South America, meeting ambush and death in Bolivia in 1967. His brand of communism was one which turned its back on the power politics of the USSR, identifying with the poorest peasants whom he sought to liberate from the political and capitalist systems which existed in South America. Castro declared only in 1961 that he himself had long been a communist disciple of Marx and Lenin, and he then began to organize Cuba under a political system based on the United Party of Socialist Revolution, renamed the Cuban Communist Party in 1965.

At first, Castro's government had carried out a harsh purge of Batista's supporters. Elections were promised but not held and an attack was launched on capitalist enterprises, many of them American-owned. Castro was highly critical of the USA, whom he blamed for the inequalities of wealth which

But those behind cried 'forward!'
And those before cried 'back!'
And backward now and forward
Wavers the deep array

Fig. 15.3 An unfriendly comment from the New Statesman, *5 October 1962, suggesting that American business interests were pushing Kennedy into hostility to Castro's Cuba*

existed in Cuba as well as for the vice and corruption, not least the army of prostitutes in Havana. The USA hit back with a boycott of Cuban sugar, the island's basic export. Castro seized about 1 000 million dollars worth of American investments and, in January 1961, diplomatic relations were broken off by the USA. Already Castro was turning to the USSR and the communist world for help. The Soviet Union undertook to supply oil and buy Cuba's sugar. In 1972, Cuba became a member of Comecon.

But relations between the USA and Cuba deteriorated still further. In April 1961, Cuban exiles under Cardona launched an invasion of southern Cuba in the Bay of Pigs. The exploit had been supported by Eisenhower and was inherited by President Kennedy. The invasion was a fiasco. The exiles were routed and the United States government was quite unable convincingly to dissociate itself from the plot. An attempt to impose an economic blockade on Cuba only drove the island into even closer ties with the communist world. But when the USA detected Soviet rocket sites on Cuba in 1962, Kennedy acted vigorously and this time it was Russia who was humiliated: the missiles were dismantled and withdrawn (see Section 17.1(d)).

Thus Castro's Cuba became steadily communist, much dependent on the USSR although more in sympathy perhaps with the Chinese and Guevara's interpretation of communism. In 1962, Cuba was expelled from the Organization of American States, an association for inter-American co-operation (see Section 18.3). Castro's reply was to found, in 1966, the Latin American Solidarity Organization, to promote guerilla activities to undermine capitalism and the influence of the USA. Cuba became a constant thorn in the flesh of the United States, all the more aggravating for being less than a hundred miles off the coast of Florida. At the end of the 1960s, it became a favourite terminus for hijacked aircraft and a symbol of defiance for all who hated the USA. Castro, meanwhile, went on to confiscate the remaining American property in the island, nearly 3 000 million dollars worth in all.

Although an effort was made to promote industry, Cuba still relied heavily on sugar. Castro aimed to modernize and expand sugar production, setting an ultimate goal of 10 million tons, although the results at the end of the 1960s fell short of the targets. The National Institute of Agrarian Reform promoted the collectivization of agriculture. The public utilities were nationalized and, in 1968, all private businesses were taken over by the state. Efforts were made to develop the island's transport systems, to improve housing and expand the health services and priority was given to education, with the result that Castro claimed to have eliminated illiteracy. Above all, the regime befriended the poor, especially the negro and coloured Cubans. The status of women was raised and a particular effort was made to wipe out the vice which was deep-rooted in the country. The achievements of the regime were not inconsiderable but it remained totalitarian and undemocratic, although, from the outset, based on collective leadership and less on Castro personally than was popularly imagined. It brought stability in a land accustomed to political intrigue and it also had the distinction of being the first Cuban government really to rid the island of foreign domination, both political and economic. Even the

Fig. 15.4 Fidel Castro: a basketball game in Bulgaria during a tour of Eastern Europe, 1964. The bearded sportsman-politician became a symbol of defiance towards the USA

USSR was not permitted to control Cuban policies. Castroism was perhaps a not very orthodox form of communism but it seemed to be in many ways suited to the problems of Cuba.

15.6   Chile

Castro and Che Guevara firmly believed in the emergence of some kind of peasant communism in the states of South America through the revolutionary activities of guerillas. The results were frequently disappointing and Cuba remained for years the sole outpost of communism in the West. Many of the states of Central and South America were politically unstable. Most of them had large populations of poor people. But in some Latin and South American countries there was a tradition of army intervention to ensure the success of governments acceptable to the military; the poor themselves were often apathetic in matters of politics. Dictatorships were more common than democratically-elected governments and although some of them, from time to time, adopted socialist policies, poverty and illiteracy seemed likely long to remain. Although encouraged by the USSR and China, as well as by Castro, revolution made little headway. It was typical of South America that, in 1964, the army removed the president from power in Brazil to make way for a strongly anti-communist dictatorship and that, in 1966, the Argentinian president was similarly overthrown by an army coup prior to an attack on trade unions and the banning of strikes.

One country in South America, however, preserved some attachment to democracy and it was this country, Chile, which in 1970, by a narrow margin, elected a Marxist government under President Salvador Allende. All previous communist governments in the world had arisen out of upheaval—revolution, civil war or wartime dislocation. Chile did the unexpected, legally and peacefully electing to power a coalition of left-wing groups as a Popular Unity Government. Allende himself was a thorough-going Marxist, strongly supported by the Chilean working class. His first cabinet was a bizarre and fragile collection of representatives of the Communist Party, the Socialist Party (which in Chile was more extreme than the communists), the Social Democrats, the Action Movement of Popular Unity, Radicals and others. In opposition were the Christian Democrats who had formed an earlier government, in 1964, under Eduardo Frei, but who unlike the Christian Democrats of Europe were strongly committed to economic planning and development by non-capitalist means. To Europeans, Chilean politics were, therefore, rather strange. Almost all the parties seemed to lean to the left and the Communists were less extreme than the Socialists who tended to support Castroism. Chile could even find room for Independent Marxists, one of whom found a place in Allende's first government.

To South Americans also, Chilean politics were rather strange. Military and other dictatorships seemed to have been left behind in favour of a democratic power struggle between supporters of the working classes and reforming supporters of the middle classes. After 1964, Frei made a start on the setting up of peasant co-operatives and on confiscating the estates of large landowners, although he was anxious not to move too quickly and not to annoy the USA, who owned many of the copper-mining companies on which the Chilean economy rested. The Christian Democrats also, for all this apparent reforming zeal, remained a fairly middle-class party. Allende naturally intended to proceed more resolutely and quickly. When he came to power, he did not hesitate to nationalize the banks, copper and textiles and to redistribute the land more vigorously. In 1972, the powerful International Telegraph and Telephone

Company was dispossessed and reported to the United Nations for an alleged attempt to overthrow the Chilean government.

The *Popular Unity Government* faced many problems of which capitalist plots and the hostility of the USA were only a part. Allende's policies scared away private investment and made it difficult to sustain the rapid development which was essential for Chile to overcome poverty and illiteracy and to improve housing and the social services. At the same time, the government was an awkward coalition unable to rely on a firm democratic majority. Free speech and a free press remained and there was no reason, in 1972, to believe that the President's Marxism was likely to lead to a dictatorship. On the other hand, progress towards really revolutionary change was less rapid than the extreme left desired, and Allende found himself frustrated by middle-class opposition and threatened by revolutionary extremism. The latter began to express itself in the activities of the Movement of the Revolutionary Left (MIR), whereas the forces of conservatism seemed prepared to bide their time in the hope that Allende would lose the next elections and re-admit Frei to power. In spite of Chile's traditions of democracy and tolerance, civil war began to appear possible. The government survived, however, in the general election of 1973. Meanwhile, although Chile possessed valuable mineral deposits as a basis for industrial development and wealth, grave social problems remained. Allende told the UNCTAD Conference of 1972, which met in his country, that Chile still had '600 000 children who, for want of proteins in the first eight months of life, will never attain their full mental vigour'. It was about their future and about the future of unborn children that the political arguments raged.

In 1970, Allende had demonstrated that, at least in Chile, a communist-inclined government could come to power through the normal democratic processes which were so much prized in the West. The event provided food for thought among capitalists and communists. It seemed to strengthen the arguments of those revisionists who claimed that communism could succeed by methods other than violent revolution. But Allende's experiment was short-lived. In September 1973, his government was destroyed by the violent intervention of the armed forces and Allende himself died either by murder or suicide. There were plenty of arguments to excuse the action of the military although many of them were exaggerated. It was certainly true that inflation was rampant in Chile and that boycotts by small businessmen and transport-owners had done much to paralyse the country. But it could not be denied that, albeit on a minority vote, Allende had been elected and re-elected to power and that his supporters among Chileans were numbered in millions. He had also tried hard to appease the military leaders and even to admit them to a share in power. In the end, however, right-wing forces could simply not accept government by a Marxist and they wiped it out in a blood-bath.

Che Guevara believed that, in South America, communism could only be established by revolution. Allende believed that it could be established by peaceful means. Both died for their beliefs. The death of Allende was a serious setback for the revisionists and also for Chilean democracy. It also seemed likely to have world-wide repercussions.

A letter to the editor of the *Guardian*, shortly after Allende's death, summarized what some saw as being a major problem in the modern world:

Sir, I am a socialist and a democrat. I abhor the use of violence for political ends. Some of my socialist friends maintain that we will never be allowed to achieve socialism by peaceful means. What can I answer them now when they say 'Salvador Allende'?

Further Reading

Ayling, S. E.: *Portraits of Power*. Harrap (London, 1965)—Mao.

Bown, C.: *China 1949–75*. Heinemann (London, 1976).

Bruce, R.: *Sun Yat-sen*. Oxford University Press (London, 1969).

Jamieson, A.: *Leaders of the Twentieth Century*. Bell (London, 1970)—Mao.

Kennett, J.: *The Rise of Communist China*. Blackie (London, 1970).

Kuo, Ping-Chia: *China*. Oxford University Press (London, 1971).

Robottom, J.: *Modern China*. Longman (Harlow, 1967).

Rowe, D. N.: *Modern China*. Anvil (London, 1959).

Documentary

Breach, R. W.: *Documents and Descriptions, the World Since 1914*. Oxford University Press (London, 1966), Sections 18, 42.

Quotations from Chairman Mao Tse-tung.
   Foreign Languages Press (Peking, 1966); i.e. the *Thoughts of Chairman Mao*.

Tarling, N.: *Mao and the Transformation of China*. Heinemann (London, 1977).

Exercises

1. What elements are common to the communist states described in this Unit?
2. How does Chile differ from the other states described in this Unit?
3. In what ways is communism in China (*a*) similar to and (*b*) different from that in Russia?
4. Show how each of the following has been important in the history of China: Sun Yat-sen; Chiang Kai-shek; Mao Tse-tung.
5. Making use of this Unit, the references provided and the Index, how far would you agree that 'Communist China has proved a remarkably peaceful power' (see page 238).
6. How and why did two of the following states become communist: North Korea; North Vietnam; Cuba?
7. Study the reporting of Chinese affairs by the news media of your own country. Why is it necessary to be cautious in making judgments about modern China?
8. How do you account for the popularity with their countrymen of Ho Chi Minh and Fidel Castro?
9. Why has Che Guevara achieved widespread popularity?
10. Explain the dilemma referred to in the letter quoted above.

(See also **Appendix: Into the 1980s,** page 365.)

The End of Overseas Empires

16.1 Empires at the End of the Second World War

Italy's overseas Empire had been over-run and lost in the Second World War, just as Germany's was in the First (see Section 11.1). But the effects of the Second World War were much wider-ranging (see Section 10.5). States captured by Japan and then liberated were reluctant to return to European control. The Netherlands and France both met fierce resistance in South-East Asia, and in Singapore and Malaya Britain could only regain possession for a time. Imperialism was now unfashionable, bitterly attacked in communist propaganda and widely resented throughout the world. Almost everywhere nationalists were impatient for freedom.

The Dutch Empire in the East Indies collapsed with startling ease. The French floundered in Indochina and elsewhere and then tried in vain to construct a French Community. Britain abandoned her Empire rather more gracefully, constructing the Commonwealth instead. But by the end of the 1960s, almost all European overseas possessions had been surrendered; Portugal alone managed to continue to hold on to extensive territories in Africa, virtually as if nothing had happened.

16.2 The Dutch Empire

(a) Indonesia

Dr Sukarno declared Indonesia independent of the Dutch only two days after the surrender of Japan. His supporters were well-armed with weapons left behind by the Japanese. The Dutch government had problems in the Netherlands, now liberated from the Nazis, and was in no position to recover the East Indies by force.

Sukarno was proclaimed President of the Republic of Indonesia in 1945 and, when the Dutch tried to bargain, he refused to settle for anything short of total independence. Dutch troops arrived in 1946 but they were quite unable to topple the rebel regime. The Netherlands could only accept the independence of Indonesia at the end of 1949, under pressure from the USA and through the mediation of a United Nations commission. Sukarno agreed to a rather meaningless 'union' with the Netherlands but it was dissolved in 1954. The Dutch also kept possession of West Irian, a part of New Guinea, but their possession was hotly disputed and, in 1962, West Irian was placed under a United Nations administration and transferred to Indonesia in the following year. Meanwhile, in 1957, all Dutch citizens were expelled from Indonesia and their property confiscated, an ignominious end to an Empire which had lasted for well over three hundred years.

Indonesia remained under the leadership of Sukarno until 1967. He followed his confrontation with the Dutch by quarrelling with Malaysia in 1963. He had for some time resented the British possession of Sarawak and Sabah on the northern coast of Borneo, claiming that the entire island should belong to Indonesia. Britain had already agreed to the independence of Malaya and it now seemed sensible to link these countries with Malaya to create the Federation of Malaysia under the leadership of the Malayan Prime Minister, the football-loving Tunku Abdul Rahman. Sukarno regarded this as a British plot, to deprive him for ever of the total control of Borneo. He used guerillas to try to free Sarawak and Sabah and even sent parachutists into Malaya, in an effort to break up the Federation, but he was condemned in the United Nations and the world was unimpressed when he withdrew from UNO in protest in 1965. Malaysia had support from other members of the Commonwealth and from the USA and, in 1966, Sukarno abandoned the feud.

Meanwhile, Sukarno had become increasingly dictatorial. Indonesia consisted of some three thousand islands, many of which were resentful of domination by Java and the Javanese. Problems also arose from the activities of pro-Chinese communists and, in 1965, there were clashes between the communists and the army. Sukarno's authority dwindled. The army alleged that he himself encouraged the communists and, in 1967, he was forced to resign in favour of General Suharto. President Suharto began a purge of both

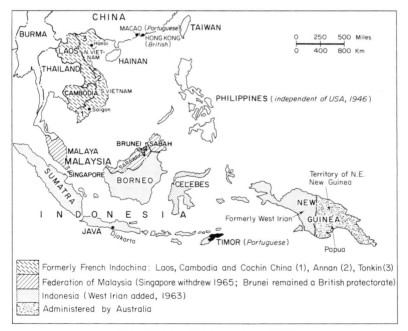

Fig. 16.1 South-East Asia in 1973

communists, unpopular for their atheism with devout Indonesians, and those of Chinese descent. Some fled and tens of thousands were killed, imprisoned or deported.

Substantial Chinese minorities existed in many of the countries of South-East Asia, where they were chiefly involved in commerce and business. Acquiring much wealth, they were obvious targets for working-class wrath. If, on the other hand, the Chinese remained peasants, they were suspected of being communist infiltrators. It was this situation which led to the anti-Chinese rioting in Singapore in 1969.

(b) The Netherlands West Indies

Nationalism was less advanced in Surinam and the Dutch islands of the Caribbean. After 1945, the Dutch had time to make new arrangements for the future. Self-government was conceded to Surinam in 1950. In 1954, Surinam and the islands were grouped as the Netherlands West Indies, with full control of their own internal affairs, but at the same time being constituent members of the Kingdom of the Netherlands. One advantage was that the states now became members of the EEC as Associated Overseas Territories.

16.3   The French Empire

(a) Indochina

It took rather longer to free Indochina from the French than to free Indonesia from the Dutch but nationalism was already well-established there in 1941 (see Section 6.3) and after 1945, the French had to contend with the Viet Minh (see Section 15.4). Indochina consisted of five states, only one of which, Cochin China, around Saigon, was technically a French colony. The others, Annam, Tonkin, Cambodia and Laos were protectorates under French supervision. The Viet Minh were particularly strong in Tonkin, around Hanoi, and it was their ambition to unite Tonkin, Annam and Cochin China in the independent state of Vietnam, a union already brought about to some extent by the Japanese before the Second World War ended. At first, the French seemed willing to accept the Democratic Republic of Vietnam which Ho Chi Minh proclaimed under the rule of the Viet Minh. But, like the Dutch in Indonesia, they wanted some continuing links with the area which the nationalists would not permit. Neither side would give way and at the end of 1946 fighting began.

By 1950, France was ready to concede self-government and to reduce the five states to three, Vietnam, Laos and Cambodia, provided that they remained in the *French Union*, which had been set up in 1946 to advise the French government on the management of the French overseas Empire. The French also now intended to make Vietnam subject to the Emperor, Bao Dai, formerly a puppet ruler in Annam. It took another four years of war to persuade them that such stop-gap measures were useless and that they must totally abandon Indochina. On 7 May 1954, the French army was forced to surrender to the Viet Minh after being besieged for many weeks in Dien Bien Phu. In France, the government was defeated and in July the new Prime Minister, Mendès-France, agreed to the independence of Vietnam, Laos and Cambodia.

All three states thus left the French Union. Cambodia, for a time, continued under the comparatively stable rule of Norodom Sihanouk who had inherited the throne in 1941. Laos had rather more difficulty, with a power struggle between the Pathet Lao, a communist-inclined group led by Souphanou Vong, and the nationalists of Souvanna Phouma. France agreed to withdraw under a settlement made at the Geneva Conference of 1954, which temporarily divided Vietnam between the communist North under Ho Chi Minh and the South under Bao Dai. Thus the stage was set for a new Vietnamese War which was to continue furiously in the 1960s with increasing American involvement (see Section 17.1(c)).

(b) Algeria

Algeria took up the struggle against French colonialism as soon as independence had been won by the nationalists in Indochina. In November 1954, the *Front de la Libération Nationale* (FLN), under Ben Bella, declared war on France. The FLN was handicapped by a lack of unity among the Arabs but above all it was opposed by the *colons* (French settlers in North Africa), who looked to the French government for effective assistance. A massive French army seemed unable to suppress the FLN: the military blamed the politicians and, in 1958, the army under General Salan rejected the authority of the French government. This helped to bring the Fourth Republic to an end. With the Fifth Republic led by de Gaulle (see Section 14.1) the colons looked forward to strong measures to put down the FLN.

In 1955 the United Nations had called for independence for Algeria, and de Gaulle showed no sign of using force to prevent this. In fury, the colons set up *L'Organisation de L'Armée Secrète* (OAS) to fight against Arab nationalism, demonstrating their anger with atrocities both in Algeria and France. But de Gaulle was intent on a settlement and agreement was reached with the FLN in March 1962. Algeria became independent a few months later, subject only to agreements for economic co-operation and to allow France the use of a naval base and weapon-testing sites.

The OAS continued for a time to splutter in protest but eventually they had to accept the inevitable. The struggle for liberation had been costly in human lives but the tide of nationalism was running with the FLN, not with the OAS.

(c) Morocco and Tunisia

France abandoned Morocco and Tunisia more readily than Algeria. French roots were less deep in these colonies and there was less opposition to independence from the colons. Independence was granted in 1956. In Tunisia, Bourguiba came to power, a veteran nationalist who, like Ben Bella, had been imprisoned in French jails. Such imprisonment was commonplace treatment for nationalists in both the French and British Empires and came to be regarded as an almost essential qualification for future leadership.

The French retreat from Morocco led Spain almost immediately to leave

Spanish Morocco (see Section 6.5). But Spain kept possession of the coastal province of Ifni until 1969 and remained even longer in the Spanish Sahara, an area rich in phosphates. African nationalists set up a new Liberation Front in 1972 to speed the Spanish departure.

(d) The French Union and the French Community

The Viet Minh and the FLN broke the spirit of French imperialism. In 1946, the Fourth Republic had established the French Union as a framework within which dependencies could move towards self-government while retaining connexions with France. Such ties were rejected in Indochina. In 1958, the Fifth Republic devised the *French Community*. Dependencies could have internal self-government, subject to some control of matters such as foreign policy and defence by the Community. De Gaulle was not inclined to press the matter of the French Community but he was realist enough to recognize that, by 1960, the time had come to grant independence to almost all of the remaining French possessions in Africa.

(e) Other French Possessions in Africa

By the end of 1960, France had granted independence to some fifteen states, including the former French Equatorial Africa and French West Africa, retaining possession only of French Somaliland, which, in 1967, was renamed the French Territory of *Afars and Issas* (see Fig. 16.2).

The divisions which European colonization had imposed on Africa were frequently artificial. After independence, experiments with unions such as the Mali Federation (of the Soudanese Republic and Senegal) made little headway, but looser groupings among African states became commonplace. Many of the former French states came to be known as the *Monrovia Powers* when they met with Ethiopia and other African states at Monrovia, in Liberia, in 1961. Eventually they created an Organization of Inter-African and Malagasy States as some sort of successor to the French Community. This gave rise to the *Organization of African Unity* (OAU), set up at Addis Ababa in 1963 to promote unity and solidarity throughout Africa (see Section 18.3). They put emphasis on the end of colonialism, especially in southern Africa where white domination remained, but real political unity remained distant. It was nevertheless a goal at which some African leaders like Nkrumah of Ghana aimed with enthusiasm.

(f) The Rest of the French Empire

Comparatively little of the French Empire remained after 1960. Some areas, such as French Guiana and Martinique, had become overseas departments of France in 1946. Pondicherry and other French outposts in India were smoothly transferred to the latter in the 1950s. The EEC had given France new interests and partners in Europe in the late 1950s and, after the final struggle in Algeria, France accepted that the age of huge overseas empires was past. In the end, France parted almost casually with her enormous possessions in Africa, the majority prepared for independence with only two years of self-government, a less careful preparation for the futures of former colonies than that undertaken by Britain. The ex-French states retained, nevertheless, a curious affection for France which the British sometimes thought undeserved. They also sought Associated membership of the European Community which brought them economic advantages.

16.4 The Belgian Congo

In contrast to the vast and sprawling French Empire, Belgium ruled little but the Congo (see Section 6.5). Until 1957, no inhabitant of the Congo was allowed to vote and even then only municipal elections were held, to appoint councils in the large towns. There was an almost total lack of preparation for future independence and no attempt was made to train the Congolese for future government. The Belgians were content to pursue economic development in the Congo and in particular to exploit its mineral resources. Yet with 150 tribes and a wide variety of languages, the Belgian Congo was likely, after independence, to be one of the most difficult states to govern in the entire African continent.

In the late 1950s, the Congo was caught up in the clamour for independence which was going on all around it, in French and British dependencies. African nationalist parties emerged, among them the Congolese National Movement led by Patrice Lumumba. In 1959, there were outbreaks of rioting, partly due to unemployment in the towns. The Belgian response was fast and foolish. At the beginning of 1960, a conference of African leaders was summoned and Belgium agreed to grant immediate independence, setting the date for the end of June.* Kasavubu became President of the new Democratic Republic of the Congo, Lumumba its Prime Minister. Almost nothing was done to anticipate the problems of those tribes and areas in the vastness of the Congo, which might wish for separate government. The first parliament had over fifty different factions and the rulers lacked experience. By the end of the year, the Congo was in chaos, having already experienced the dismissal of the Prime Minister, declarations of secession, an army coup and United Nations intervention.

The ending of the Belgian Empire in the Congo was thus the beginning of civil war (see Section 20.2).

16.5 The Portuguese Empire

(a) The Overseas Provinces

Portugal had no intention of granting independence to her colonies (see Section 6.5). Instead Portugal denied that they were colonies at all, classifying them as overseas territories and thus continuing to enjoy economic advantages

---

* Ruanda-Urundi, a Belgian mandate and trusteeship territory, was separated from the Congo and became independent in 1962.

from them. In 1961, Nehru's Indian government would have none of this and threw the Portuguese out of Goa and other outposts on Indian soil, by force. The Portuguese, with a stubborn refusal to accept reality, continued to believe in a Portuguese State of India although it no longer existed.

They did, however, continue to hold on to five provinces in Africa, one in Asia (Macao) and one in the Pacific (Timor). Macao lies next to Hong Kong on the coast of communist China. Its survival, with a population of less than 200 000, seems to be a tribute to the patience of Mao Tse-tung. The island of Timor, already partitioned between Portugal and Indonesia, seems an equally improbable overseas territory to hold indefinitely. But in the early 1970s, the most active nationalist resistance to the Portuguese was taking place in Africa.

(b) The African Provinces

Portugal's African provinces of Angola and Mozambique are among the larger states of the continent and part of the racial problems of southern Africa (see Unit Twenty-One). Her other three provinces, Portuguese Guinea, São Tomé and the Cape Verde Islands, are mere fragments, like Macao and Timor.

By the mid-1960s, Angola, Mozambique and Portuguese Guinea increasingly stood out as bulwarks of white supremacy as neighbouring states moved to independence. Portugal signed an agreement for economic co-operation with South Africa in 1964 and became closely involved in white efforts to maintain their power and privileges there and in Rhodesia. Resistance movements inevitably developed in all three of the Portuguese provinces. Fighting began in Angola in 1961, but the rebels were hampered by disunity. Disturbances spread to Portuguese Guinea a year later and the Mozambique Liberation Front (*Frelimo*) was founded under Mondlane, formerly a professor of anthropology. The scale of operations was not that of the Viet Minh in Indochina, but they tied down tens of thousands of Portuguese troops and won support from the Organization of African Unity. On the other hand, it was alleged in the early 1970s that Portugal was supported by white mercenaries, mainly from South Africa, West Germany and the USA.

Meanwhile United Nations observers investigated the affairs of Angola and Mozambique, and a commission of the ILO reported that labour recruitment in Angola was not in keeping with the international agreement on the abolition of forced labour.

(c) Why did the Portuguese Empire Survive?

Portugal's was the largest surviving European overseas empire in the 1970s. It was hardly significant, however, except for the possession of Angola and Mozambique, large but not heavily-populated states. Both Angola and Mozambique were still primarily agricultural, although Angola possessed minerals and industry was growing there. In both, the pace was slow and nationalism grew less quickly than in many of the more advanced areas of Africa. Portuguese authority was also reinforced by the strongly-rooted interests of the whites in South Africa and Rhodesia, which even countries like

Britain and France were reluctant to disturb. The Portuguese would claim additionally that their rule brought benefits to the provinces, thus discouraging mass dissatisfaction. But in the short term, the Portuguese Empire survived because the Portuguese were resolute in their refusal to abandon it. It seemed at least doubtful whether their resolution could continue to defy the growth of nationalism, which had brought independence almost everywhere in the one-time empires of the Europeans.

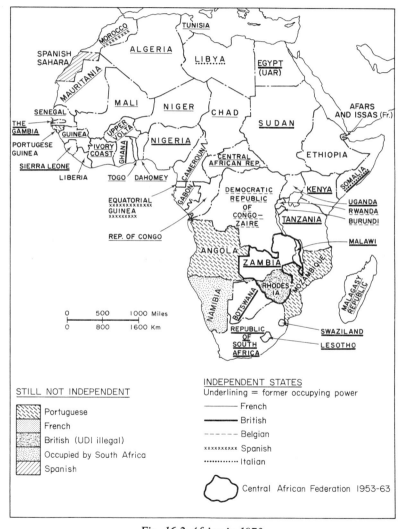

Fig. 16.2 Africa in 1973

16.6   Britain and the Commonwealth

By 1939 Britain had already made the British Commonwealth of Nations a 'white man's club', created from former colonies now known as *Dominions* (see Section 6.2). The Commonwealth stood the test of the Second World War and provided, in 1945, the foundations on which to build for the future (see Section 10.4). Britain prepared the colonies for total independence by progressive movement to self-government, sometimes too slowly to please impatient nationalists and sometimes too quickly to please conservative opinion at home. The task was enormous; it was impossible to please everyone or to achieve total success in creating sound and contented independent nations. But, by 1966, almost all the vast Empire had been brought to independence. Such goodwill remained that almost every new nation applied for, and achieved, voluntary membership of the Commonwealth.

The British Commonwealth of Nations became, in the 1950s, an *Asian–European Commonwealth*, a partnership between new Asiatic nations such as India, and Britain and the White Dominions. With a flood of new admissions after 1957, it became a *multi-racial Commonwealth*, a partnership of equals regardless of size, wealth, colour or creed. Only a few states dropped out. The Republic of Ireland detested any British connexion and resigned in 1949; Burma preferred not to join on gaining her independence in 1948. Britain admitted failure in Palestine in 1948 and abandoned her mandate there (see Section 19.1). In 1961, South Africa was virtually forced to resign from the Commonwealth, which condemned *apartheid* (see Glossary). Six years later, Britain gave freedom to Aden and that state too stayed outside the Commonwealth. The Arab world seemed to be the one area in which it had not proved possible to plant the Commonwealth ideal.

(a)   The Independence of the Indian Sub-continent

Independence for India could not be postponed after 1945 (see Section 6.2(c)). The election of Attlee's Labour government in Britain meant that the principle was readily accepted: the difficulty was to find a formula for independence, which would satisfy both the Indian National Congress under Nehru and Patel and the Moslem League under Jinnah. Only Gandhi was confident that goodwill could unite a single independent India in peaceful co-operation. The Congress Party wanted a united India but it could not win the confidence of the Moslems, who more and more rallied to the slogan, 'Pakistan or Perish' (a separate state of the sort advocated by the Moslem League for their religion).

The new Viceroy, Lord Wavell, called a conference at Simla but no agreement could be reached among the Indian leaders. Another commission from England sent by Attlee failed to find an acceptable solution. When Wavell invited Nehru to form a government in August 1946, as a prelude to independence, the Moslem League hit back, calling for demonstrations which quickly degenerated into violence and bloodshed, atrocities and reprisals. Only the British army and the peace-making of Gandhi prevented widespread civil war in the sub-continent. When Attlee called the Indian leaders to London, neither he nor they could produce an acceptable formula.

But Attlee could see no virtue in further delay. In March 1947, Lord Mountbatten, the last Viceroy of India, arrived in Delhi. He had been carefully chosen for his wartime popularity in the country and his task was to find a solution but, in any case, to bring British rule to an end in June 1948. Partition seemed the best answer: it would pacify the Moslem League and Mountbatten persuaded Nehru and the Congress Party to accept it. The final movement to independence was speeded up. In Britain, Attlee pushed the *Indian Independence Act* quickly through parliament and, on 15 August 1947, India and Pakistan became free nations. Both were admitted to membership of the Commonwealth at their own request.

The separation of Hindus into India and Moslems into Pakistan, however, was no easy matter. Violence flared up between the two as mass migrations began. In *The Times*, in September, it was estimated that 4 million people were already on the move. People were driven by religious frenzy to mass murder, both in the villages and in cities such as Delhi and Calcutta. Gandhi and Nehru both tried to halt the butchery but, in the Punjab alone (divided, like Bengal, when the boundaries between India and Pakistan were drawn), over a quarter of a million lost their lives and nearly 14 million became refugees. Neither Hindus nor Moslems felt that they could be safe if they remained on the 'wrong' side of the boundaries. The killing went on and, in the end, it even claimed the life of Gandhi, assassinated by a Punjabi refugee, a Hindu fanatic, who could not accept the preaching of tolerance to Moslems. Gandhi died in 1948. His death caused a great sense of shock, which at last helped to curb the bloodshed.

Fig. 16.3 Mohandas Karamchand Gandhi, 1869–1948

The new nations had problems enough to achieve economic development and social progress. India had nearly 400 million people, many of them desperately poor and often hungry. Pakistan had only a quarter of India's population but the state had been made in two parts, West and East Pakistan, a thousand miles apart. They were difficult to unite and the East, in particular, was never far from poverty. India speedily established a democratic system of government to which the prestige of the Congress Party gave some stability, and Nehru remained Prime Minister until his death in 1964. He was much respected both for his international statesmanship and for his reforming, socialist-inclined policies within India. Pakistan, on the other hand, experienced almost endless difficulties, searching for stable government. Jinnah, leader of the Moslem League, became Governor-General but lived only until 1948. The first Prime Minister, Liaquat Ali Khan, was assassinated in 1951, leaving the country with no one who could rule effectively. Inevitably, in 1958, democracy was suspended while General Ayub Khan tried to achieve a workable governing system. The turmoil was checked only temporarily and in 1971, Pakistan fell apart (see Section 20.5).

Meanwhile, in 1950, Nehru declared India* a republic, an example followed by Pakistan in 1956. In the past, the British Crown had always been Head of State in the Dominions but the Commonwealth took this new development in its stride, henceforth accepting republican members. When Ceylon† achieved independence in 1948, however, it was content to remain within the monarchy until well into the 1970s.

(b) Experiments in Federation

Britain experimented with *federations* in several areas (linking colonies under a sort of control similar to that in the USA). The results were always disappointing except in Malaysia. Such federations did show both Britain's carefulness in winding up the Empire and some of the problems which remained, especially in Africa, when great empires came to an end.

(i) **Malaysia.** Malaya gained independence in 1957, under the able Prime Ministership of Tunku Abdul Rahman, who ruled until his retirement in 1970. Britain was so impressed by his leadership that she agreed to transfer her remaining colonies in Borneo to a Federation under the Tunku in 1963. Brunei opted out, preferring to remain under British protection, but Sarawak and Sabah accepted membership of the Federation, as did Singapore. Abdul Rahman successfully resisted a long and bitter struggle with communist guerillas in the north of Malaya, against whom he received Commonwealth assistance from states such as New Zealand. He held the Federation of Malaysia together against the challenge of Indonesia (see Section 16.2) and he made considerable progress towards economic development, though he was unable to keep Singapore in the Federation.

The population of Singapore was mainly Chinese and although Lee Kuan Yew, Singapore's dynamic leader, readily protected the Malays there, as a minority, he was apprehensive of Malayan domination within the Federation. Singapore also favoured free trade but Abdul Rahman insisted on tariffs to protect new industries. Thus they parted company in 1965 and Singapore became an independent republic. The main British Empire in South-East Asia thus came to an end with the minimum of dislocation and gave way to the remarkably successful and stable rule of Abdul Rahman and Lee Kuan Yew.

* For the further history of India, see Section 22.2.
† Renamed Sri Lanka in 1972.

(*ii*) **The Central African Federation.** In 1953, Britain created a Federation of the colonies of Northern Rhodesia, Southern Rhodesia and Nyasaland, to prepare them for independence as one unit, which would have many economic advantages. This Central African Federation, however, was caught up in the conflict of interests which developed between white settlers and non-white Africans. The first Prime Minister of the Federation was Godfrey Huggins, a Southern Rhodesian with a firm belief in white rule. Black Africans had little opportunity for political activity in Southern Rhodesia (see Section 6.2(*d*)) but there were fewer whites in Northern Rhodesia and Nyasaland; there, National Congresses* were set up, to prepare for independence. In Northern Rhodesia (which the Africans called Zambia) the Congress was led by Kenneth Kaunda. In Nyasaland (which the Africans called Malawi), the Congress was led by Hastings Banda. Both were imprisoned.

Huggins retired and was replaced by Roy Welensky, but neither Zambia nor Malawi was prepared to accept the permanent rule of a white minority. Unrest among both African nationalists and whites—the latter rioted in the copper belt when an attempt was made to forbid racial discrimination in cafes —doomed the Federation. The British government sent two commissions, the Devlin Commission and the Monckton Commission, and their reports were gloomy. Macmillan, the British Prime Minister, was not prepared to hold the Federation together by force, so the Africans were allowed to set up parliaments in Malawi and Zambia. It was clear that there was overwhelming support for Banda and Kaunda, and the Federation was dissolved, in 1963.

Malawi became independent in July 1964, Zambia a few months later, both under governments which represented the will of the people. Southern Rhodesia, now known simply as Rhodesia, remained a British dependency. The whites were firmly in power there, denying political authority to the non-whites who heavily outnumbered them and, in these circumstances, Britain was unwilling to grant independence. When the whites seized it, with a unilateral declaration of independence (UDI) in 1965, Rhodesia became a problem for the whole world (see Section 21.3).

(*iii*) **The Federation of the West Indies.** The problem of the West Indian islands which Britain possessed was partly one of size. Few seemed large enough to stand alone, so in 1958 Britain brought about the Federation of ten of these islands. Britain was hopeful that the Federation could soon achieve independence as a unit. The larger islands in the Federation had doubts. There were arguments about the degree of central control and Jamaica and Trinidad feared that Britain was trying to saddle them with small and backward islands which could become a drain on their own limited resources. Jamaica voted to withdraw, Trinidad was unwilling to remain without Jamaica, and the Federation was abandoned in 1962.

Almost at once, Britain granted independence to both Jamaica and Trinidad which seemed large enough to survive alone. Although by no means free from economic and racial problems, they succeeded in establishing stable and
* Similar to the Indian National Congress.

reasonably efficient government for at least a decade. Under the Prime Minister-historian Eric Williams, Trinidad made her own link with the nearby island of Tobago. In 1966, Britain also gave independence to the smaller island of Barbados. But the future of the remaining small islands presented a problem. St Kitts, Nevis and Anguilla were already grouped in a union, but even the union was tiny and a rebellion in 1969 by Anguilla, not much more than an island village, showed that it was far from firm. In 1967, Britain devised a new arrangement, grouping many of the small islands as *Associated States*, which enjoyed internal self-government but left defence and foreign policy to Britain. About the same time, West Indian islands began to explore for themselves the possibilities of associations and, in 1968, they created the Caribbean Free Trade Area (*Carifta*) which was also joined by Guyana, the mainland state of British Guiana to which Britain had given independence in 1966 (see Section 22.4).

At least up to 1973, the ex-British states in the Caribbean and the remaining dependencies there had avoided the turbulence which had often overtaken Cuba and which continued to afflict Haiti and the Dominican Republic. Even Anguilla was pacified by a few troops and 45 policemen, who encouraged the children, in the true spirit of the Commonwealth, to play cricket. But it was likely that the period of adjustment after the passing of overseas empires would necessarily be a long one, as the islands sought to group themselves into viable units. The Federation of the West Indies may yet prove to have been a signpost to the future.

(c) The End of the Empire

1957, the year of Ghana's independence, was almost as important in the history of the Commonwealth as 1947, the year of India's independence. Ghana, under the leadership of Nkrumah (see Section 22.3) was the first British colony in Africa to become free under a non-white government. It was followed, in 1960, by Nigeria and then by a steady stream of African admissions to the Commonwealth, until only Rhodesia remained. In 1961, it was the turn of Sierra Leone. Then, in the same year, Britain wound up her mandate and trusteeship in Tanganyika which united shortly afterwards with Zanzibar to form Tanzania under the leadership of Julius Nyerere, one of the most remarkable leaders in Africa (see Section 22.3). In the years 1962 to 1964, independence was granted to Uganda, Kenya, Malawi and Zambia (see Fig. 16.2). Britain firmly accepted the principle of majority rule and government in all of them by Africans. Some African nationalists complained that independence was too long delayed and, in Kenya, Britain was involved in a particularly bitter struggle with the *Mau Mau* (a ferocious secret society sworn to mutilating and murdering in the 1950s). But the bitterness seldom lasted once independence was achieved.

The story was a similar one in other parts of the world and Britain steadily withdrew. Equally steadily, the new states joined the Commonwealth—Cyprus in 1960, Malta in 1964 and, later, Mauritius, Tonga and Fiji. Some dependen-

Fig. 16.4 Uganda's independence ceremony, 1962: the transfer of power to Milton Obote

cies however, preferred to remain under British control. Brunei had not wished to join Malaysia. Gibraltar welcomed Britain's continuing protection against Spain. Hong Kong seemed to thrive under the British, throbbing with vitality and pouring her exports into the British Isles. Other bits and pieces of the Empire seemed too small for independence, and Britain encouraged self-government while continuing aid and protection. Even Tristan da Cunha with a population of a few hundred had its representative council. When a local volcano erupted in 1961 the entire population was temporarily evacuated to Britain. Tristan da Cunha and other such fragments were all that was left of an Empire which once covered a quarter of the world; but there was now the Commonwealth instead.

(d) What is the Commonwealth?

The Commonwealth has hardly any machinery except for a Secretariat set up in 1965. Member prime ministers meet, usually annually, to exchange ideas. There are innumerable contacts at other levels, both professional and amateur, between educationists, defence experts, finance ministers, parliamentarians, journalists and technicians. But the organization is essentially one for voluntary co-operation. The Commonwealth is as reluctant as the United Nations to interfere in internal affairs and often as powerless to settle disputes, even between members. At the head of the Commonwealth is the British monarchy, still the symbol of association as laid down in the 1920s. Royal tours, therefore, often symbolize the Commonwealth connexion.

Attlee regarded the meetings of Commonwealth prime ministers as 'talk round a table between friends'. As the Commonwealth expanded, the numbers round the table grew and the talk was by no means always friendly. Britain was heavily criticized for her attack upon Egypt in 1956. Criticism of apartheid eventually drove South Africa from the Commonwealth altogether (see Section 21.2).

Each member was almost invariably careful to preserve its national interests, and it was a weakness, as in UNO, that hardly any member was prepared to place the common good first. Nevertheless, the Commonwealth was founded on mutual respect, and in spite of often enormous problems—political disunity, economic difficulties, poverty, and fierce internal pressures, resulting perhaps from racial tensions or tribalism—hardly any member abandoned a fundamental attachment to the values once thought British. Countries struggled to achieve workable democracy although for some, like Pakistan, it often seemed a distant goal. Sometimes plagued with corruption and even civil war, they reserved an ultimate aim of freedom and justice.

Much of the work of the Commonwealth greatly expands that done by the specialized agencies of UNO. Commonwealth scholarships and training schemes help the less-developed in education. Teachers, doctors, engineers and experts of all kinds provide varied help and strengthen international ties. It is easy to undervalue their achievements because it is impossible precisely to measure them. Prosperous nations sometimes see the poor only as a drain on their wealth and there are those who argue that the Commonwealth is little but a sham, but it is by no means uncommon for the poor members to help the even poorer. By 1964, India and Pakistan were able to give help on a small scale in Africa; Ghana helped the Gambia and Nigeria helped Tanzania. But, of course, it is the rich countries such as Canada and Britain who can offer the greatest assistance.

In 1967, the average annual income per head of the population was £692 in

Canada and £536 in Britain; in India it was £18, in Malawi £17. This was a gap, moreover, which threatened to grow larger in the last quarter of the twentieth century, as technological developments made the rich richer and left the poor even further behind. An infinite variety of schemes exist to wrestle with the problem, operated by organizations such as the Commonwealth Development Corporation (CDC), the Special Commonwealth African Assistance Plan (SCAAP) and the Colombo Plan, although this last is not limited only to members of the Commonwealth.

The world changed rapidly after 1945 and the Commonwealth evolved and adapted too. Britain's admission into the EEC in 1973 brought a new factor in Commonwealth relations with twenty developing nations of the association being offered associated membership of the EEC. Britain's membership of the EEC and her continuing concern over Commonwealth immigration have led to a change of attitude towards the Commonwealth by many British people. They suspect that the Commonwealth is sometimes used by black member nations against the interests of the white members. But in 1953, Queen Elizabeth II had made a statement of the *Commonwealth ideal*, declaring that, 'The Commonwealth bears no resemblance to the empires of the past. It is an entirely new conception, built on the highest qualities of the spirit of man: friendship, loyalty and the desire for freedom and peace.' When the British Empire passed, the Commonwealth took its place, trying, by no means always successfully, to create something of benefit to millions. It was a unique endeavour. No other great overseas empire left anything to compare with it. In spite of its weaknesses and lack of machinery, almost all of the former dependencies of Britain still wished, in 1973, to remain members of the association.

Further Reading

Caldwell, M.: *Indonesia*. Oxford University Press (London, 1968).
Hatch, J.: *Africa: the Rebirth of Self-rule*. Oxford University Press (London, 1967).
Hollings, J.: *African Nationalism*. Hart-Davis (London, 1971).
Jamieson, A.: *Leaders of the Twentieth Century*. Bell (London, 1970)—Gandhi, Nehru.
Kohn, H. and Sokolsky, W.: *African Nationalism in the Twentieth Century*. Anvil (London, 1965).
Pandey, B. N.: *The Rise of Modern India*. Hamish Hamilton (London, 1967), Chapters 5 and 6.
Watson, J. B.: *Empire to Commonwealth*. Dent (London, 1971), Chapters 6–11 and 14.
Wilson, D.: *A Student's Atlas of African History*. University of London Press (London, 1972).

Documentary

Brownlie, I.: *Basic Documents on African Affairs*. Oxford University Press (London, 1971).
Wallbank, T. W.: *Documents on Modern Africa*. Anvil (London, 1964).

Exercises

1. Why did European overseas empires come to an end so quickly after 1945?
2. How did the winding up of the British Empire differ from the winding up of the French Empire?
3. Why did the end of the Dutch Empire in Indonesia and the end of the Belgian Empire in the Congo lead to bloodshed?
4. Trace the history, from 1945 to 1954, of the ending of the Asian empires of Britain, France and the Netherlands.
5. With reference to Fig. 16.2, outline the main stages by which (*a*) France and (*b*) Britain withdrew from Africa. State briefly what principal problems they left behind.
6. What parts of Africa are still controlled by Europeans at the present time? How do you account for this survival?
7. How did the French wind up their Empire in various parts of the world from 1945 to 1960?
8. How and why did the British abandon India so rapidly in 1947?
9. What can one discover from current newspapers of the activities of African nationalist organizations against white supremacy in the continent? (Refer also to B. Cornwall, *The Bush Rebels*, Deutsch (London, 1972).)

(See also **Appendix: Into the 1980s,** page 365.)

International Relations: the Great Powers After 1945

17.1   The Cold War and Containment

(a) **Europe**

The emergence of the USA and the USSR as super powers, each supported by faithful blocs in Europe (see Units Twelve, Thirteen and Fourteen), quickly led to a state of tension which centred particularly on the boundaries between them. Yet for almost three decades, no territory changed hands and few lives were lost in the American–Russian confrontation. Their rivalry was a *Cold War*, fought mainly with propaganda and economic weapons. Each contained the other until gradually there developed something of an understanding between them. The basis for coexistence was an unwritten but apparent acceptance that, in Europe at least, neither side would trespass on the territories of the other. In part, this balance of power was achieved through fear, rooted in the destructive powers of the hydrogen bomb. From time to time there were crises, but one or other of the super powers always showed restraint. As time passed, a Third World War became more improbable. And in May 1972 an American President set foot on Russian soil, on a friendly visit for the first time since the Yalta Conference of 1945 (see Section 10.2).

The Cold War began in Europe. Stalin imposed Russian ideological and economic control on almost all the states which had fallen to the Red Army, including the eastern part of Germany. When Britain and the USA tried to consolidate capitalism and democracy in Western Europe, he then accused them of creating an anti-Soviet bloc. Almost everything that happened became subject to different interpretations on the two sides of the Iron Curtain (see Section 11.2(*b*)), until it became nearly automatic that East and West quarrelled about every point at issue.

The German Problem (see Sections 11.2 and 14.3) was the first bone of contention between them, a problem which flared dangerously at the time of the Berlin Airlift in 1948–9. By the time that the Soviet Union lifted the blockade of Berlin in May 1949, a variety of other disputes had already arisen and the USA had proclaimed and begun to implement the Truman Doctrine.

The Truman Doctrine (see Section 14.5), which became linked with the Marshall Plan, owed a good deal to the turbulent state of affairs in Greece, where two partisan organizations, one communist and the other monarchist, developed out of the resistance to the Axis invasion. By 1944, as the Germans retreated, Greece was near to civil war and Churchill sent British troops to assist an orderly return to normality (i.e. monarchy and free elections). In 1946, the Soviet Union appealed to the Security Council of the United Nations against the British presence. She alleged that the troops endangered Greece's 'national and internal situation'. Bevin heatedly declared that the charges involved 'the honour of my country and of the Commonwealth' and the Security Council took no action. The result was civil war as Greek communists tried to take control of the country by force.

The intervention in Greece was a financial burden which Britain, after 1945, was ill-equipped to bear. An appeal to the USA brought American dollars and the Truman Doctrine of March 1947. Truman undertook to 'support free peoples' against 'attempted subjugation by armed minorities or outside pressure'—in effect, to contain communism and prevent its further expansion. With American help, the British army remained in Greece until 1950, by which time something had been saved from communism although it was not necessarily democracy. By 1951, Greece had produced more than a dozen feeble governments and further incompetence and corruption culminated, in 1967, in a military coup. 'The Colonels' suspended the constitution, imprisoned political leaders, purged the universities and ruled by decree.

In 1951, meanwhile, Greece joined NATO and the Greek frontier came to mark the limit of communist expansion in the Balkans. The line of demarcation between East and West in Europe was to remain at least into the 1970s. Only when the Soviet Union evacuated eastern Austria in 1955 (see Section 11.1(b)), did any change occur in the territories held by communists and non-communists.

With NATO (see Section 14.5) and the Warsaw Pact (see Section 12.3), each side consolidated its grip. The German Problem remained unsolved, but central Europe was disturbed by only occasional flurries of activity. Content to have saved Greece, the West made no attempt to intervene in the affairs of the Russian satellite states or even to prevent the building of the Berlin Wall. The communist wall only emphasized the division of the city which, like the division of the whole of Europe, began to seem irrevocable but, at the same time, stable.

(b) The Middle East

A similar stability descended on East–West relations in the Middle East. In north-western Persia (Iran), the USSR tried to establish a communist regime under the Tudeh Party but withdrew after the matter was referred to the United Nations in 1946. Persia went on to suppress the Tudeh Party in 1949 but gave less satisfaction to Britain when, in 1951, Dr Mussadiq nationalized the oil industry. It was a costly blow to the Anglo-Persian Oil Company and to Britain's prestige. Mussadiq became the spokesman of hysterical anti-Europeanism. He was later arrested by his own countrymen and a compromise solution in 1954 gave British Petroleum 40 per cent of the shares of the National Iranian Oil Company.

For a time after 1945, the Soviet Union also brought pressure to bear on Turkey and endeavoured to set up joint Russo-Turkish control of the Dardanelles. But here, too, Russia was barred from making progress. Further south, in the disturbed area of Palestine, the USSR showed little interest at first but as the conflict between Jews and Arabs in the Middle East dragged on into the 1960s (see Section 19.1), the Soviet Union began eventually to develop closer ties with the Arab world. Such ties could be of advantage to Russia: the West depended heavily on oil from the Middle East; the Arab nations could provide a bridge for the USSR into Africa and Arab successes against Israel would embarrass the USA which supported that country. The Arabs had few successes, however, and by the 1970s Russia seemed to have doubts about the value of the Arab alliance.

In 1959, the *Central Treaty Organization* (CENTO) came into existence for joint security and defence between Britain, Persia, Turkey and Pakistan. It was built on the foundations of the Baghdad Pact of 1955, which had also included Iraq. The USA had taken part in some of the committees of the Baghdad Pact and, in 1959, made separate defence agreements with Persia, Turkey and Pakistan but without actually joining CENTO. CENTO was thus seen both in the West and the East as another barrier against communism, not fundamentally very different from NATO and SEATO.

(c) The Far East

The West soon discovered, however, that Russian communism was not the only communism against which to build barriers. The success of the communists in China and the downfall of Chiang Kai-shek caused considerable anxiety to the USA. The communists were also successful in North Korea and North Vietnam (see Unit Fifteen). From 1948, communist guerillas were active in Malaya, where a communist party had been banned since 1926 but where communism had gained popularity in resistance to the Japanese. Jungle warfare in Malaya caused a state of emergency which lasted until 1960 and, even after that, the communists were able to exploit both racial and economic discontents. Britain and members of the Commonwealth assisted in holding back communism in Malaya, but, elsewhere, the USA took on the main burden of resistance. Vigorous efforts were made to rebuild Japan in the image of the USA and to ring China with American bases and an American fleet. Chiang was protected in Taiwan and, in the *ANZUS Pact* of 1951, the USA gave guarantees to Australia and New Zealand. In 1954, the ANZUS Powers, together with Britain, France, Pakistan, the Philippines and Thailand joined together in the *South-East Asia Treaty Organization* (SEATO), for collective action against aggression and subversion. Even so, the USA thought it necessary to resort to force both in Korea and Vietnam.

(i) The Korean War (1950–3).
After the expulsion of the Japanese in 1945 (see Section 15.1) Korea was divided into two, communist north of the 38th parallel and non-communist south of it. South Korea had a considerably larger population than that of the North. The Americans hoped, by establishing a democratic constitution in the South, that free elections could eventually be held for the whole country and that the communists would be outvoted.

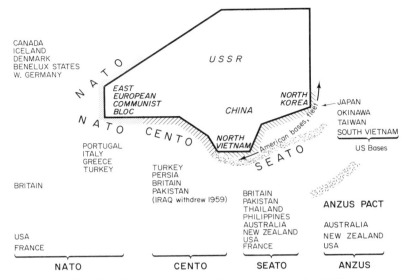

Fig. 17.1 The containment of communism in the 1960s

Both the USA and the USSR withdrew from Korea in 1948, leaving separate governments behind them in South and North. The National Assembly in the South left 100 seats vacant (out of 303) for representatives from the North. Kim Il-sung, the Northern leader, had no intention of filling them. While wrangling continued about the border between them, communists in the North trained an army of 130 000 men and launched an attack in June 1950. The South was unprepared and total defeat seemed imminent.

However, Kim had timed the invasion badly (suggesting a lack of that close association between Moscow and other communist governments which the USA always assumed to exist). The USSR was temporarily absent from UNO, in protest against the representation there of Chiang Kai-shek, and the United Nations were therefore able to brand North Korea as an aggressor and sanction the use of force against her. The United Nations forces were mainly American with some troops from Britain and fourteen other friendly countries. They were commanded by the American, General MacArthur. By September 1950, he had driven the communists back to the 38th parallel; but he continued to advance and the Anglo-American objective became the liberation and unification of the whole of Korea.

The conquest of North Korea took MacArthur's forces to the Yalu River on the border of China: they were driven back at a speed almost equal to that of their advance by the *Chinese People's Volunteers* (over 200 000 of them, suspiciously well-trained and resembling the Chinese Red Army). Before Christmas 1950, both sides were back at the 38th parallel. The USA seemed to be toying with the idea of discouraging the Chinese peasants with atomic bombs and Attlee hastily flew to Washington. Britain had already recognized the government of Mao Tse-tung in China and had no desire to become involved in a war with that country. Nor had the USA, although from the beginning of 1951 the Korean War became increasingly bitter. MacArthur again wished to try to invade the North but Truman dismissed him. Atomic weapons were not used.

The USSR now showed a readiness to encourage a settlement. The fighting went on in the area of the 38th parallel but truce talks were begun. They dragged on for two years while the bloodshed continued. Finally, an armistice was agreed in July 1953, leaving Korea divided at the 38th parallel. It also left the whole country devastated. Over 30 000 Americans and 4 500 of their allies had been killed. But it was the Koreans who suffered most. 70 000 South Koreans were killed in battle and nearly half a million others died as a result of the war. North Koreans suffered casualties on an even vaster scale, perhaps 4 million in all.

Neither North nor South Korea knew much of freedom after 1953. The communists remained in power in the North, in possession of most of the country's mineral resources and heavy industry, and Kim developed a regime almost Stalinist in its hero-worship of the leader. In the South, Syngman Rhee's regime fell in 1960 amidst complaints of repression and corruption. His successor, President Park, gave every indication of intending to be president for life.

The two Koreas were now separated by a demilitarized zone, an area fruitful of disputes with frequent charges by both sides about illegal fortifications. From time to time, armed clashes occurred. As in Germany, however, time brought a certain stability to Korea. Each side remained heavily-armed, a serious burden on peoples far from rich. In 1972, following the example of more prominent leaders in the world who were seeking improved relationships, Kim proposed a reduction of these forces and at last it began to seem possible that the two parts of Korea could draw together again. Unification would bring economic advantages. Koreans were, moreover, conscious of the growing strength of Japan and ideological differences began to seem less important in the face of the possible danger of more foreign domination. In any case, both Kim and Park now seemed to rule in similarly authoritarian ways.

(ii) **War in Vietnam: the American protection of South Vietnam.** Unfortunately, few of the lessons learned in Korea were applied in Vietnam where the communists were also in control of the North (see Sections 15.4 and 16.3). The French Empire in Indochina was wound up by the *Geneva Agreements* of 1954. These were made under the joint chairmanship of Britain and the USSR, in conference with France, China, the USA and the states of Indochina. It was agreed, temporarily, to divide Vietnam at the 17th parallel, the ceasefire line to be supervised by Canada, Poland and India. The reunification of Vietnam was to take place, through free elections (which the communists expected to win), in 1956.

In January 1955, the USA undertook the protection of South Vietnam

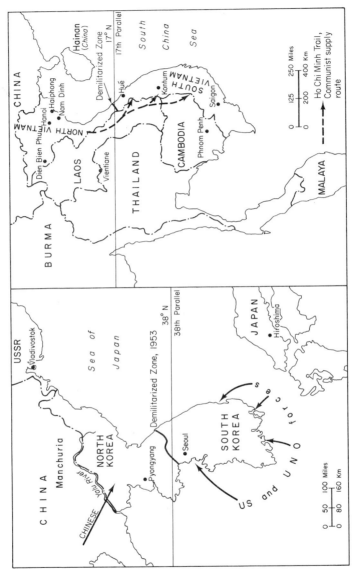

Fig. 17.2 (a) *The division of Korea;* (b) *The division of Vietnam*

which became a refuge for those fleeing from communism, and a republic was set up under the Presidency of Ngo Dinh Diem. He introduced a few reforms but did little to satisfy the peasants and stirred up considerable unrest.

The free elections were not held on the appointed date. Diem, who was a Catholic, antagonized the Buddhists, some of whom burned themselves to death in protest against his tyranny and corruption. South Vietnam badly needed government which was firm but just, for extremist organizations and vested interests were deep-rooted. Diem, in the end, lost the support even of the Americans and they abandoned him in 1963, shortly before he was murdered. But his regime had set South Vietnam on the road to civil war for the opposition formed the *National Liberation Front* in 1960.

The NLF was not exclusively communist. It aimed at the expulsion of foreign troops and the eventual unification of Vietnam and was, almost from the beginning, supported by North Vietnam. It became common to refer to the NLF, especially its military wing, as the Viet Cong. In 1963, the Viet Cong had about 25 000 soldiers. In 1966, the number had risen to nearly 300 000, about the same number of troops that by that time the USA had in Vietnam.

(iii) **Increasing American involvement.** The fall of Diem was followed by political confusion and military coups against the background of rising Viet Cong activity and increasing American involvement. President Kennedy first of all poured American 'advisers' into South Vietnam. With them came military equipment and then helicopters but, in 1964, an official American report estimated that the Viet Cong nevertheless controlled over 40 per cent of the villages of South Vietnam. Early in 1965, President Johnson began the bombing of targets in North Vietnam, assuming, perhaps wrongly, that the Viet Cong were actually under the control of Ho Chi Minh, the North Vietnamese leader, who could thus be persuaded to call off their rebellion.

Also in 1965, the government of South Vietnam fell into the hands of a National Leadership Committee led by General Nguyen Van Thieu. Thieu became President by disqualifying all likely rivals and appointed the air chief, Nguyen Cao Ky, as Prime Minister. The Thieu regime was an unconvincing advertisement for Western democracy, but the USA preferred it to the success of the Viet Cong. The USA also secured support from Australia, New Zealand and South Korea and the war in Vietnam escalated steadily. It was, however, a war which neither side seemed capable of winning. The North was blasted by American bombs but that appeared to make little difference to the Viet Cong or to the North Vietnamese forces, perhaps about 70 000 in 1968, who reinforced them. In 1968, in fact, the Viet Cong took the offensive and captured, for a time, 75 per cent of the main towns of South Vietnam and even parts of Saigon. This was in spite of opposition by three-quarters of a million men in the South Vietnamese army, half a million Americans and 50 000 of their allies. The South Vietnamese army suffered extensively from desertion but, even so, it was surprising that the vast military resources of the USA made so little impact, especially as supplies to the Viet Cong from the USSR, China and other communist countries were on a much smaller scale.

Fig. 17.3 American engineers check a road near Ca Lu in South Vietnam for Viet Cong mines in a regular morning routine before traffic may use the road

(*iv*) **Nixon and Vietnamization.** Johnson came under heavy criticism for the escalation of the war and the USA's failure to win it. In his memoirs, he later stubbornly defended his policies and persistence, almost glorying that 'the American people . . . knew Lyndon Johnson was not going to pull up stakes'. He had much less to say on the awkward leaks of Pentagon papers which cast doubts on the official reasons given by the US government for resorting to the bombing of North Vietnam in 1965. Before the Presidential election of 1968, however, Johnson agreed to stop the bombing of the North in return for the opening of peace talks in Paris. But the war went on and Richard Nixon, the new US President, found that the talks made little progress. Thieu and the NLF could not agree on a formula for fair elections in South Vietnam; the USA and North Vietnam could not agree on a formula for the withdrawal of foreign troops. Even the death of Ho Chi Minh, the founding father of North Vietnam, brought no change in the deadlock. Seeking desperately for a way out, Nixon announced a new policy towards the end of 1969— *Vietnamization.*

The central feature of Vietnamization was attractive: the South Vietnamese would take over the defence of South Vietnam. This would permit the withdrawal of American troops and, by the end of 1970, their numbers had been reduced by half. On the other hand, Nixon was not prepared to see the Viet Cong victorious, something which became increasingly difficult to prevent as American troops continued to leave. He thought the solution to this particular problem lay in cutting off the communists' supplies, so he resumed the bombing of North Vietnam (although this had not achieved much when Johnson was President).

The communists had not scrupled to use neutral territory in Laos and Cambodia to supply the Viet Cong, any more than the USA had scrupled to bomb it to try to interrupt the supplies. In 1970, an army coup in Cambodia overthrew Prince Sihanouk (see Section 16.3) and the new ruler, General Lon Nol, declared his intention of rooting out the communist bases in Cambodia. The communists seemed more likely to drive *him* out and in April 1970, Nixon announced a new American campaign, against the communists' Cambodian bases. They proved difficult to find and the campaign was brief.

The Viet Cong were able to start a new offensive early in 1972 despite the American search for their bases in Cambodia. They threatened Thieu's government on three fronts, around Hué, near the 17th parallel, around Kontum in the centre of South Vietnam and around Saigon in the south. But though many of the South Vietnamese troops showed more talent for rape and stealing chickens than defeating the communists, they could still rely on massive American supplies, the US Air Force and the optimistic eloquence of US military advisers.

Nixon still considered that supplies were the key to the problem. As it was not apparently possible to block them by bombing the North and the Ho Chi Minh Trail through Laos and Cambodia, the US Air Force now dropped mines, to seal the ports of North Vietnam through which many of the supplies arrived from the communist world. It was a strange prelude to Nixon's

Fig. 17.4 'If this boy of yours is real, how come we gotta wind him up all the time?' Doubts about Nixon's policy of Vietnamization—the Guardian, *3 May 1972*

long-heralded visit to Moscow (which took place in May 1972), at which it was hoped that East and West would reach a better understanding.

(*v*) **The effects of the war.** It is, of course, too early to evaluate the effects of the USA's intervention in Vietnam. One effect has certainly been to devastate the whole country, as Korea was devastated. Both sides fought ruthlessly and neither shrank from committing atrocities. The Americans no longer thought of nuclear weapons but their use of napalm, a clinging and highly inflammable jelly which turned men into human torches, raised world-wide protests. And the US Air Force's ready use of huge bomb-loads seems unlikely to have planted a love for Western democracy among the Vietnamese peasants.

The war also brought appalling effects in the demoralization of the towns, especially Saigon. The spending power of the Americans played havoc with the South Vietnamese economy and the passion of some American servicemen for drugs and women sowed considerable corruption. These were by no means firm foundations for Nixon's policy of Vietnamization.

What may be said with some certainty is that, by 1972, Vietnam was an embarrassment both to the USA and the USSR, and probably also to China. In the early 1970s, there were prospects of better relations between the USA and the communist world, encouraged by Brezhnev, Kosygin, Nixon and even Mao. But such considerations seemed to count for little with the Viet Minh and Viet Cong, smarting with a sense of gross injustice to Vietnam alongside which the convenience of the great powers mattered little.

The USA had first taken up arms in Vietnam under a belief in the 'domino theory', that if South Vietnam turned to the communists other states in South-East Asia would follow, falling like a row of soldierly dominoes. By 1972, the theory carried less conviction and America's involvement was widely regarded as a blunder. It may be argued that the war was not only a conflict between communism and capitalism but one between the rural and urban ways of life, between Chinese-style communism and Western industrialism. Americans had little understanding of the workings of a peasant economy and were slow to realize the need to gain support at village level. Only with the policy of Vietnamization was a real attempt made to do this.

(*vi*) **The ceasefire.** Meanwhile, the fighting in South Vietnam, American bombing of the North and, with interruptions, the peace talks in Paris, went on. In 1972, there was a new scandal in the USA when the Senate heard evidence of bombing raids by the US Seventh Air Force which had apparently some life of their own and went on, seemingly unofficially, when curtailment of the bombing was intended to further the peace talks. It was just one of the many incidents in the Vietnamese conflict which raised doubts about both the honesty and the competence of the administration in Washington.

North Vietnam's capacity to survive the enormous tonnage of bombs, far exceeding that dropped on Germany in the Second World War, was remarkable. It was said of Nam Dinh, the country's third largest city, that Johnson's bombing destroyed 60 per cent of the town and that, after rebuilding, Nixon destroyed 70 per cent. The damage to property was enormous and the use of anti-personnel bombs, exploding into lethal splinters, added to the pain and misery. Yet the North Vietnamese dispersed what they could of their factories, hospitals and population, worked furiously to repair the damage, adapted to the hardship and continued to support the Viet Cong. The continued withdrawal of American ground troops was small consolation for a land which suffered more than any other in the confrontation of the modern world between communism and capitalism.

At last, however, after yet more devastating bombing at the end of 1972, an agreement was reached to end the war. The ceasefire was arranged for the end of January 1973, although a good deal of fighting went on after that date. The US Air Force ceased its operations, prisoners-of-war were exchanged and a hesitant start was made in sorting out the problems left by the longest war of the twentieth century. Without enthusiasm, Canada, Indonesia, Hungary and Poland agreed to provide over a thousand truce supervisors. They were well aware that peace-keeping was likely to prove difficult for a long time to come. Eleven nations, including the four truce supervisors and the permanent members of the UN Settlement Council, were to try to bring about a lasting settlement in Vietnam. At the same time, a start was made on trying to settle the problems of Laos and Cambodia. Douglas-Home, the British Foreign Secretary, was realistic, however, when he observed that 'the history of Indochina gives little scope for easy optimism'.

(vii) **The cost.** It was estimated that nearly a million communists had died in battle, together with 180 000 South Vietnamese and nearly 50 000 Americans. Over 400 000 South Vietnamese civilians had perished. The numbers of civilian dead in North Vietnam remained unknown. At the ceasefire, the communists still held extensive areas of South Vietnam and, above all, the political future of Vietnam had still to be negotiated. North Vietnam claimed to have won 'a socialist victory'. The USA claimed to have obtained 'peace with honour'. Mankind could scarcely claim that anything had been achieved. The problems which remained when the French left Indochina in 1954 seemed as far from solution as ever. Meanwhile, a new crisis brewed in Cambodia. The communist threat to the government of Lon Nol grew and, for much of the summer of 1973, US bombers pounded that country too. Nixon was at last forced by Congress to call off the bombing. It seemed doubtful whether much had been achieved, and already there were ominous signs that fighting was spreading again in South Vietnam.

(d) The Caribbean

It came as a shock to the USA—intent on containing communism in the neighbourhoods of the USSR and China—when Castro seized control of Cuba (see Section 15.5). The shock gave way to angry alarm when, in October 1962, an American spy-plane discovered that Russian missiles were being positioned on the island. President Kennedy demanded their instant removal and imposed a blockade of Cuba to prevent further landings. Khrushchev tried

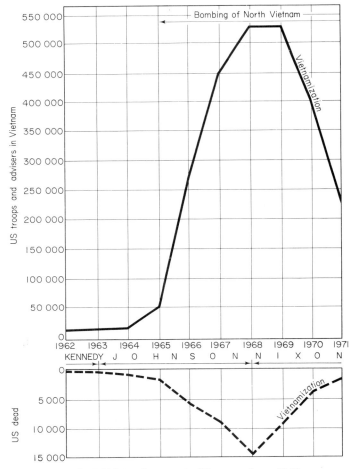

Fig. 17.5 US involvement in Vietnam, from 1962

to bargain, demanding the withdrawal of American missiles from Turkey as part of a package deal. The tension lasted almost a week before the Soviet Union gave way. Missile-carrying ships from the USSR turned back and Khrushchev ordered the missiles in Cuba to be crated and returned.

The Cuban Missiles Crisis was, perhaps, the moment when the USA and the USSR were closest to war. It ended in a complete victory for Kennedy and the humiliation of Khrushchev, helping to undermine his position in Russia. But Khrushchev had won a victory for common sense. Peace was preserved and a new telephone link was established to hold out the hope of the peaceful solution of future emergencies, the 'hot line' between Washington and Moscow. Both sides now placed the emphasis almost entirely on defence, and the will to war, if it had ever existed at all, became more remote. Even Castro followed up the Missiles Crisis with an agreement with the USA whereby he released the prisoners taken in the Bay of Pigs in exchange for food and medicine. Ten years later, he joined in the general involvement towards improved relations, by reaching a limited agreement with Nixon on hijacked aircraft.

17.2   Coexistence

(a) The Thaw

It is difficult to identify the exact moment at which the Cold War began to thaw. There was general relief at Stalin's death in 1953, but Khrushchev blew hot and cold, and deep suspicions of communism remained in the West. In the USA, suspicion of China went particularly deep and much bitterness was left on both sides by the Korean War. Events in Vietnam intensified the bitterness and not until the end of the 1960s did relations ease between the USA and China.

But in the meantime, Americans and Russians had apparently become content to coexist. The propaganda war was not much interrupted, but it was significant that the USA did nothing to assist the Hungarian rebels in 1956 and that in 1962 the USSR accepted that the USA had special interests in the Caribbean which must be respected. The super powers, though armed to the teeth, were beginning to behave with great caution although caution was not entirely new. Neither Stalin nor Truman had been a reckless man.

One of the first visible signs of a slightly less cold relationship between East and West came in the form of personal contacts. In 1955, Russia's leaders emerged from the Kremlin. Khrushchev and Bulganin talked to Tito in Belgrade and then travelled to Geneva for a summit conference with Eisenhower, Eden and Faure, the French Prime Minister. They talked about disarmament, but no major decisions were made and Eden's suggestion that Germany should be reunified was wildly optimistic. In the following year, Khrushchev and Bulganin spent over a week in Britain and, in 1959, Khrushchev went to America and met Eisenhower near Gettysburg. But in spite of continued bickering about Berlin and other problems, it seemed an appropriate time to call a second summit conference. After long discussions, it was arranged for May 1960, in Paris.

The summit ended in chaos even before it really began. Khrushchev arrived, determined to get an apology from Eisenhower for the activities of U-2 spy-planes which, although armed only with cameras, had for some time been flying over the USSR. One of them had been shot down over the Urals just before the summit conference was to open. Eisenhower had already stopped the flights but he refused to give the Russians the public declarations they required. Macmillan and de Gaulle were helpless spectators while Khrushchev called the summit off and cancelled Eisenhower's invitation to Moscow.

Before the end of 1960, Khrushchev had made a stormy appearance in the

UN General Assembly. The thaw seemed to have come to an end. Nothing was gained when Khrushchev met Kennedy, the new American President, in Vienna in 1961, and the Cuban Missiles Crisis in 1962 was yet another ungracious confrontation. Curiously, however, it suddenly helped to clear the air.

Although the 1960s opened inauspiciously with the summit fiasco in Paris and went on unpromisingly with the escalation of the war in Vietnam, the decade overall saw a considerable improvement in East–West relations. The thaw grew stronger with significant agreements about nuclear weapons (see below). The antagonism between Russia and China (see Section 15.3(c)) served to make international relations more complicated but, for a time at least, less dangerous. The USSR and the USA grew even more cautious, although they continued to elbow each other and struggle for position wherever there was instability. The USSR showed interest in Africa and Latin America and then developed links with the Arab world, especially Egypt in her long feud with Israel. At the beginning of the 1970s, Russia was also making progress in wooing India. But such connexions were inclined to fluctuate and many countries in the Third World were not anxious to tie themselves to either of the super powers. Many African states took offence at the manner of Russia's repression of Czechoslovakia in 1968, and the USA found that even such a well-established ally as Japan could sometimes be a highly-critical one. Both Russian and American embassies were often the targets for hostile demonstrations all over the world, providing them with some sort of common bond in unpopularity.

Moreover, China became increasingly outward-looking, forging links with Pakistan and, as the friend of the poor and a champion against white supremacy, gaining a foothold in Africa. Russia had helped Egypt to finance the Aswan Dam. China helped Tanzania with the Friendship Textile Mill and, in 1970, provided an interest-free loan and skilled assistance to build the Zam-Tan Railway, to enable Zambia and Tanzania to be more self-reliant in the face of racial divisions in southern Africa. China also had the advantage of appearing to ask little in return. The Chinese brought quantities of small red books with the *Thoughts of Chairman Mao* but they came to work, learning the local languages and asking for no special comforts or privileges. Neither of the super powers could create the same image and both of them found the Chinese activities worrying. This too gave them a new bond.

(b) Disarmament

No subject was debated more earnestly after 1945 than disarmament but nothing whatever was achieved until 1963. There were endless wrangles and, while they went on, the great powers conducted an arms race, especially in nuclear weapons. The USSR tried to catch up with the USA and, in 1952, Britain became the third nuclear power, successfully exploding an atomic device.

Neither the USA nor the USSR wished to sacrifice her own interests. Russia wanted to keep large ground forces but proposed a total ban on nuclear weapons and criticized American air and naval power. In this context, the Rapacki Plan for a nuclear-free zone in central Europe (see Section 12.3) was regarded by the West as part of a Soviet plot to tilt the balance in favour of the East, and it came to nothing. Eisenhower's proposal for 'open skies' was rejected by the USSR, in 1956, with the argument that it was an excuse for the West to spy on Russia from the air, under the pretence of inspecting the size of military forces. Scores of ideas for some reduction of armaments were lost amid these suspicions of the major powers.

Like the League of Nations, the United Nations began optimistically. The Security Council hoped to achieve some disarmament through its Military Staff Committee. In 1946, UNO set up an Atomic Energy Commission and, in 1947, a Conventional Armaments Commission but, in 1950, Russia withdrew from both. A new Disarmaments Commission was set up in 1952 and re-constituted in both 1959 and 1962, but none of this machinery could obtain results.

The first agreement, the *Test Ban Treaty* of 1963 was reached by the three nuclear powers at a meeting in Moscow. They agreed to cease testing nuclear weapons in the atmosphere or under water, with a view to limiting 'radio-active debris'. Other powers could sign the Treaty if they so wished and about a hundred quickly did so, but they did not include France and China who had joined the nuclear powers by exploding atomic bombs in 1963 and 1964 respectively. The original nuclear powers continued to test weapons underground.

Further progress was delayed by an argument about an American plan to create a single nuclear force for NATO which, the USSR objected, could lead to nuclear weapons in West German hands. The USA abandoned the plan and further lengthy discussion in the UN General Assembly, in the Disarmament Commission and between Johnson and Kosygin in America led to the *Non-Proliferation Treaty* of 1968. Its aim was to prevent the further spread of nuclear weapons. The USA, the USSR and Britain undertook not to transfer such weapons to other states and an attempt was made to offer greater security to non-nuclear countries against the nuclear powers, to discourage them from embarking on the manufacture of atomic bombs. It was a major weakness of the Treaty that, once again, France and China did not sign it.

In themselves, the Treaties of 1963 and 1968 accomplished little, but any agreement on restraint, however small, could become the foundation for further agreements. At the end of the 1960s, discussions began to try to find a way to cut back the development of missiles. These *Strategic Arms Limitation Talks* (SALT) took place in Vienna and Helsinki. Even the super powers were now beginning to feel the strain of the arms race. Intercontinental ballistic missiles and anti-missiles systems developed to the point of being staggeringly expensive, as well as terrifyingly destructive with their nuclear warheads. Technological changes also brought changed attitudes: arguments about U-2s and 'open skies' became irrelevant with the conquest of space and the use of satellites in orbit to observe rival countries.

By 1964, five nations possessed nuclear weapons and there were others for whom their manufacture was becoming a possibility. This again gave the super powers reason to pause. In their frenzied struggle, the one to outstrip the other, they were not only using their resources in an extremely costly rivalry but they were leading the world towards possible destruction. The Treaties of 1963 and 1968 and the SALT were the first, rather hesitant attempts to put on the brakes. It was still too soon to think in terms of a reduction of armaments, but at least an attempt was now being made to limit their future growth.

(c) Travelling Hopefully

The diplomatic travelling of Khrushchev and Eisenhower opened the way for new contacts between East and West. When Willy Brandt became Chancellor of the German Federal Republic he hoped to continue the thaw. His *Ostpolitik* (eastern policy) aimed to establish more normal relations across the Iron Curtain. By accepting existing frontiers, he hoped gradually to lead Germany and Europe away from the crisis atmosphere which had existed since 1945. The 1972 Treaties of Warsaw and Moscow were essentially non-aggression pacts, and they helped to make the German Problem less bitter (see Section 14.3). As relations improved between West Germany and Eastern Europe, so the Big Four were able to move towards more cordial relations over Berlin, seeking a less stark division in that city than the one which had existed since the building of the wall in 1961. A Four-Power Pact was signed to ease communications within the city and between West Berlin and West Germany. It also emphasized that West Berlin was not part of the Federal Republic.

The agreements about weapons in 1963 and 1968 and Brandt's travelling east of the Iron Curtain prepared the way for something less chilly than coexistence. By 1972, attitudes in Washington and Moscow—and perhaps even in Peking—seemed slightly less rigid. Although the confrontation continued in Vietnam, the admission of communist China to UNO at the end of 1971 (see Section 15.3(*d*)) opened up new possibilities in the Far East. It was too soon to anticipate more than the beginning of a thaw in the relations between the USA and China, but when Nixon went to Moscow in May 1972, more concrete agreements were expected than when he went a few months earlier to Peking.

The USA and the Soviet Union both had powerful positions to defend. Their interests would now best be served by agreements, defending their joint interests as great powers. The interests of the rulers of the USA and the USSR would also be served by agreements, for Nixon wanted to be re-elected as President and the Russians hoped to divert some spending from weapons to more popular consumer goods. Old-fashioned power politics were taking over from conflicts of principle.

So Nixon and the Russian leaders scribbled their signatures enthusiastically, piling up agreements. The most important one was the outcome of the SALT which, by fixing some limitations on missiles and their locations, would help to reduce costs in the future. (Each side, however, retained more than sufficient weapons to destroy the other several times over.) They also signed minor agreements about pollution and space research and created a commission to look into an expansion of trade between America and Russia. Again, the agreements in themselves were comparatively trivial, no more than a thin cover for the ideological differences between capitalism and communism, but their importance lay in providing a base for further pacts. When Nixon returned from Moscow, there was hope that a European Security Conference might follow, to build more understanding between the East and West in Europe. Brandt, Nixon, Gierek and Brezhnev had at least prepared the way.

Tension was thus easing in Europe. The situation in the Far East was more enigmatic. Apart from the problems of Indochina, there was still distrust between Moscow and Peking. The Russians, in 1972, still maintained massive forces within striking distance of China. The USSR and China had still to work out their future relationships as the world's leading communist states.

Further Reading

Bown, C. and Mooney, P.: *Cold War to Detente*. Heinemann (London, 1976).
Graebner, N. A.: *Cold War Diplomacy*. Anvil (London, 1962).
Hastings, P.: *The Cold War*. Benn (London, 1969).
Lancaster, A. B.: *From Containment to Co-existence*. Arnold (London, 1976).
Wint, G.: *Asia Handbook*. Penguin (Harmondsworth, 1969)—articles on Korea, Cambodia, Laos and Vietnam.

Documentary

Beggs, R.: *The Cuban Missiles Crisis*, Longman (Harlow, 1971).
Breach, R. W.: *Documents and Descriptions, the World Since 1914*. Oxford University Press (London, 1966), Sections 15 and 47b.
Snyder, L. L.: *Fifty Major Documents of the Twentieth Century*. Anvil (London, 1955), Document 44.

Exercises

1. What is the meaning of each of the following terms: Cold War; Containment; Coexistence; Confrontation; Crisis?
2. What evidence is there to support the argument that there was a *thaw* in the relations of the great powers in the 1960s? Why is it not possible accurately to date its beginning?
3. Explain how and why the Cold War developed and why 1953 may be regarded as an important year in the history of the relationships of the great powers.
4. 'The history of Indochina gives little scope for easy optimism.' What developments from 1954 to 1973 served to support this opinion?
5. Outline the history of attempts to achieve disarmament after 1945 and account for (*a*) the absence of progress before 1963 and (*b*) the limited progress from 1963 to 1973.
6. Did the USA save democracy in South Korea? Follow up developments after 1972 in South Vietnam and estimate what American intervention achieved there.
7. What developments have taken place in American–Russian and Sino-Soviet (Chinese–Russian) relationships since this book was written?

(See also **Appendix: Into the 1980s,** page 365.)

International Relations After 1945: Construction Outside Europe

18.1 International Trade

Not even rich countries could be complacent about trade after 1945. Essential imports could only be paid for by export earnings. This is a fact of economic life as important to Britain and the developed nations as it is to the under-developed. There was a general recognition that the high tariffs of the 1930s were no longer desirable. Soon after the war tariff reductions followed from GATT, the movement accelerating in the 1960s with the Kennedy Round (see Section 13.2(*e*)). But increasing unemployment and the difficulties of currencies such as the American dollar at the beginning of the 1970s threatened to bring a drift back to protective tariffs.

Meanwhile, the world recognized that increased exports offered the best means of obtaining wealth with which poor nations could finance their de-velopment. This led to the establishment, in 1964, of the *United Nations Conference on Trade and Development* (UNCTAD) and an *International Trade Centre*. Three years later, the United Nations set up an *Industrial Development Organization* (UNIDO) to promote industrialization. Such organizations were willing to discuss the problems of the poor, but it soon became clear that wealthy nations would not give them effective help if it meant subordinating their own interests.

One unfulfilled need was for international agreements on commodity prices (guaranteed minimum prices for the commodities on whose export poor nations often depended heavily): too often the poor were still at the mercy of the rich. Sometimes, they had to compete with synthetics, manufactured by the developed nations, and prices for commodities produced by poorer countries, such as tea, cocoa, copper and rubber, often fell alarmingly. Richer nations showed little inclination to do much about this, for they profited in such a situation. On the other hand, oil-producing countries such as Libya and Iraq were beginning to exploit the enormous needs of the wealthy for their produce, and to force up the price. OPEC (the Organization of Petroleum Exporting Countries), founded in 1961, was highly successful in protecting the interests of its members. They provided a lead and coffee-producing states, such as Brazil and the Ivory Coast, began to think about holding back their produce to bring about a fairer price. Similarly, the copper-producing coun-tries—Chile, Zambia, Zaire and Peru—began to discuss joint policies when, in 1972, the USA tried to seize Chilean copper shipments in protest at the nationalization of that nation's copper production.

Rich nations were inclined to howl in protest at such practices. Britain had already clashed with Persia over oil rights (see Section 17.1(*b*)) and a new conflict brewed with Iraq in 1972 on a similar issue. But Lady Jackson, a British speaker at UNCTAD III, pronounced a verdict which was perhaps not unfair on the relations between the rich and the poor, when she said: 'The profound, even heart-rending difficulties of the rich . . . are their excuse for doing next to nothing about the infinitely more real and heart-rending problems of the poor.'

By 1972 there was a general acceptance that international co-operation was more useful in the long run than the pursuit of selfish interests. Nixon and Brezhnev agreed to develop more trade between America and Russia, and attitudes were, in general, more enlightened than those of previous decades. Nevertheless, there were still fundamental problems to be solved in the relationships between the developed nations and those of the Third World; some of them were political (e.g. resulting from the East/West power struggle and racial problems), but many of them were economic, arising from the gulf between rich and poor.

18.2   International Aid

(*a*) The Problems of Development

Marshall Aid and similar schemes of assistance went a long way towards overcoming the problems of war-torn Europe, and improvements were soon evident on both sides of the Iron Curtain. But a huge gulf existed between the developed nations, growing ever more prosperous with the progress of technology, and the underdeveloped nations, whose progress often seemed painfully slow. The underdeveloped nations lacked capital, expertise and sometimes even the basic natural resources for industrialization and the rapid creation of wealth. After 1945, the gap between rich and poor grew ever wider. While many rich countries moved into the age of computers and space travel, many of the poor still grappled with the almost insuperable problems of famine, disease and grinding poverty. Although the average income per head of the population rose almost everywhere, it rose pitifully little in the states which were generally termed underdeveloped (see Table 18.1).

There was little difficulty in identifying the needs of the underdeveloped. In times of crisis (common in Asia and Latin America where storms, plagues and earthquakes could reduce millions to destitution), the need was for relief to deal with immediate problems. The more deep-rooted needs were for assistance with which to break away from poverty: capital and equipment with which to set up industry and power stations, through which to produce future profits; expertise with which to modernize agriculture and transport; schools in which to develop the skills essential to more advanced societies and to wipe out widespread illiteracy, and hospitals in which to conquer disease.

But the problem was not simply one of money, equipment and expertise. The rapid development of communications made the underprivileged societies aware of their disadvantages and eager for improvement. This imposed heavy burdens on national leaders, creating instability in some states but bringing

Table 18.1 Average income per head of the population (£s)*

	1958	1970	1976	Main Exports c. 1976 (% of whole)
Developed Countries				
West Germany	330	975	4 620	Machinery 29%
USA	880	1 630	4 600	Machinery 27%
Canada	620	1 075	4 300	Vehicles 22%
Australia	460	890	3 100	Wool 12%
Japan	120	630	3 100	Machinery 25%
Britain	425	700	2 200	Machinery 28%
Israel	260	610	1 500	Diamonds 33%
Developing (Third World) Countries				
Jamaica	130	190	600 †	Metals 66%
Syria	65	90	430	Crude oil 62%
Peru	70	100	320	Metals 44%
Zambia	47	98	250	Copper 91%
Sri Lanka (Ceylon)	50	56	120	Tea 44%
Kenya	29	43	120	Coffee 37%
Ghana	58	88	110	Cocoa 59%
Tanzania	20	25	85	Cotton 16%
India	27	30	80	Sugar 12%

† 1975

Income for 1976 reflects the effects of inflation, and a gap between the rich and poor which is tending to widen.

A Special Case: Japan
Average income per head of the population (£s):

1958, 120; 1963, 240; 1970, 630; 1976, 3 100.

Trade (1970):
   Main exports: machinery 23%; iron and steel 15%; vehicles 10%; textiles 9%; ships 7%
   Main export destinations: USA 31%; South Korea 4%
   Main imports from: USA 29%; Australia 8%
   Trade surplus: 157 000 000 000 yen

Population: 104 million

* Figures based on *Encyclopaedia Britannica* (converted from dollars etc.)

leaders of outstanding quality to the fore in others. Nyerere in Tanzania and Mrs Gandhi in India remained in power for many years carrying on the struggle against underdevelopment. In Asia, problems were often made worse by over-large populations, with more human beings to be fed than primitive agriculture and a hostile climate could manage to satisfy. Such states often possessed no mineral resources and they had to produce something which they could export and sell in exchange for much-needed machinery, vehicles and railway stock. Too often, however, the prices they could get for their commodities were desperately low. Those dependent mainly on one export, as

Ghana was dependent on cocoa, Ceylon on tea and Zambia on copper, found it impossible to rely on consistent prices or even on fair ones (see Section 18.1).

Such a situation required a more generous response than the rich powers were usually prepared to make. In the 1960s, the United Nations called upon the prosperous to provide 1 per cent of their national incomes. By the end of the 1960s, only Switzerland, France and West Germany were able to claim that they had exceeded this target. Britain fell a little below it, many other rich nations far short of it. But some progress had been made. Loans to the poor were usually free of interest, a step forward from earlier lending at interest rates which often entangled the poor in debts. Ghana, for example, entered the 1970s with an almost impossible load of debts, the result of earlier commitments to repay money at interest to the profit of the rich. Aid was now devoted to projects such as power stations, irrigation schemes, railways and factories which would create future wealth, rather than to prestige projects such as public buildings and little-used airports. The more enlightened countries had also ceased to attach strings to their aid, no longer seeking special privileges for themselves or compelling the poor to buy in certain markets. Even so, the rich were quick to complain of ingratitude when poor nations acted, for example in foreign policy, in ways that displeased them. They complained also when the poor appeared to waste their small resources in quarrels, military display and even conflict. For some reason, the developed powers appeared to expect a higher standard of conduct among the underdeveloped than they took for granted among themselves.

But in the 1970s, the gulf between the rich and poor continued to widen. States like Kenya and Tanzania, with desperately little to export, and others like India, with large populations, struggled almost in vain to catch up. Moreover, many were feeling the distorting effects of their contacts with the wealthier world. Development was not simply about the problem of obtaining sufficient international aid: it also concerned the transforming of society and the economy. In Ceylon and Ghana, unemployment among the better-educated became a difficulty in the early 1970s. In the West Indies, the attempt to boost income from tourism led to social strains with those still condemned to live in slums resentful of luxury hotels. In many parts of Africa, a gulf grew between urban and rural communities, a conflict between a Europeanized way of life and an African one. The transition from poor communities to the prosperity of industrialization called for the highest qualities of leadership as well as for generous assistance from the highly-developed.

(b) Aid

The assistance took many forms, from gifts and loans to the skilled advice of teachers, engineers and agriculturalists. Most of the developed nations set up aid programmes, although those involved in the Cold War found it difficult to dissociate aid from foreign policy. When the USA withdrew support from the building of the Aswan Dam in Egypt, the Soviet Union eagerly stepped in, hoping to win a new friend and influence the Arab world. It was easier for neutral countries like Sweden to approach international aid in a more impartial and humanitarian sense. This was also the objective of the UN specialized agencies (see Section 11.3, page 173), to which all members of UNO were expected to contribute.

Some countries had special interests. Colonizing powers like Britain already had ties with many underdeveloped nations in the Commonwealth which had had numerous arrangements for aid and co-operation (see Section 16.6(*d*) and Table 18.2). West Germany, after Hitler's persecution of the Jews, felt special obligations to Israel. Canada, partly through the Commonwealth connexion, took a particular interest in the welfare of the Caribbean.

But it was not only governments who were grappling with the problems of the underdeveloped nations. In Britain organizations such as *OXFAM*, *War on Want* and *Christian Aid* provided help. *Voluntary Service Overseas*, the *Peace Corps* in the USA and the specialized agencies of UNO provided an outlet for many individuals who wished to help. But governments inevitably bore the principal burden.

A few examples will illustrate the varieties of aid which have been given. In

Fig. 18.1 Contrasting ways of life in Karachi, Pakistan

1950, the Foreign Ministers of the Commonwealth devised the *Colombo Plan* to assist the development of South and South-East Asia; a Council was established to organize training, research, economic development and better health services. In addition to the developed states of the Commonwealth, such as Britain, Australia and Canada, the members of the organization include the USA and Asian states from Afghanistan to Japan, all engaged in co-operative development through the Council in Colombo, sometimes with the assistance of experts provided by UNO.

Less ambitious but vitally important was the *Indus Waters Project*. The partitioning of India in 1947 left disputes between India and Pakistan about the Indus basin waters. The International Bank came to mediate. The division of the waters between the two nations was agreed by a treaty in 1960 after which the Bank, with certain countries such as Britain, undertook to give financial help for irrigation works.

In 1958, a Conference at Montreal, in Canada, extended the ideas behind the Colombo Plan by introducing *Commonwealth Assistance Loans*. At the same time, an Education Conference was arranged to meet in Oxford in 1959, out of which *Commonwealth Scholarships* developed. Some years later, another Conference in Montreal brought together Commonwealth nurses and yet another at Toronto established a *Commonwealth Veterinary Bureau* which owed a good deal to the enthusiasm and professional interests of Jawara, the Prime Minister of the Gambia. These exchanges of expertise were just as important to the developing nations as Assistance Loans.

Table 18.2   Examples of international aid: the Commonwealth

In 1969 Britain made grants to members of the Commonwealth of almost £54 million (including spending on technical assistance) and loans of almost £69 million.

The Commonwealth Development Corporation had in hand over 170 projects, mainly in Africa, involving investment of over £150 million.

Commonwealth countries contributing aid through the Colombo Plan included Britain, Canada, Australia, New Zealand, India, Pakistan, Ceylon and Malaysia. Much of this aid took the form of technical assistance.

British Aid to Members of the Commonwealth 1964–9 (£s million)
Total Grants: 835
Total Loans: 862

Some receiving countries:

	Grants	Loans
Pakistan	9	91
India	11	345
Ceylon	4	16
Singapore	8	4
Ghana	9	14
Kenya	96	78
Tanzania	48	23
Zambia	34	8
Jamaica	23	13
Guyana	18	23

18.3   Regional Organizations

As old empires crumbled and many new nations emerged, the mutual assistance which it was possible to provide through United Nations agencies, the Commonwealth and organizations such as the Colombo Plan, was also extended through regional groupings. Groupings of European states, in the EEC EFTA and Comecon, for example, were matched by similar organizations elsewhere. They had a variety of aims, but common to almost all was the furtherance of economic development.

(a) The Americas

The *Organization of American States* (OAS) dated from 1948 but its roots went back to the late nineteenth century. Its members included most of the states of South and Central America and certain islands in the Caribbean, in addition to the USA, inevitably influential in the Americas. Ex-British islands also became members—Trinidad and Tobago, in 1967, and Barbados, in 1968. The aim was to achieve some unity of action in various fields, and to promote inter-American co-operation. In some ways, the OAS was like a regional United Nations Organization; its members set up machinery for arbitration and the peaceful settlement of disputes. But Cuba was expelled from the OAS in 1962 and there was some suspicion that the Organization was useful to the USA for influencing other American states.

In 1961, the USA sponsored the *Alliance for Progress*, bringing together many Latin American nations. Much of the finance (for the programme for economic co-operation and the target of annual growth) came from Washington. There was little doubt that one of the USA's motives in this Alliance was to prevent the spread of communism, but few organizations could completely divorce economics from politics and very few states were rich enough completely to stand aside from the great powers.

The *Organization of Central American States* (OCAS) was, however, more independent. It was set up in 1951 for economic and social co-operation between Guatemala and her neighbours. In 1960 the same states created the *Central American Common Market*, aiming at a common tariff and free trade. Less successful was the *Latin American Free Trade Association* (LAFTA) of the states in South America and Mexico.

(b) Africa

Diversity and size handicapped the *Organization of African Unity* (OAU). Its first members were the Monrovia Powers (see Section 16.3), several states such as Tanganyika, Uganda and the Sudan in East and North-East Africa, and five of the Casablanca Powers (Algeria, the United Arab Republic, Mali, Guinea and Ghana). Groupings such as the Monrovia and Casablanca Powers* were among the first attempts by Africans to create constructive unions for the

---

* One of the original aims of the Casablanca Powers, in 1961, was to create a common market.

future development of their continent. The OAU was more ambitious for it tried to bring together a large part of the vast African continent. Inevitably, it became caught up in the racial problems of southern Africa which caused further disunity. Nevertheless it was an attempt by Africans to manage African affairs, independent of the influence of richer and longer-established powers.

Britain had once considered an East African Federation. After independence, the three ex-British states in East Africa—Kenya, Tanzania* and Uganda—returned to the idea and, in 1967, set up the *East African Community*. Their aims were mutual economic assistance and a common tariff. In effect, much of the assistance in the early stages was likely to be from the more-advanced Kenya to her less-developed partners but the organization held out hope for the future. Kenya under Kenyatta and Tanzania under Nyerere were among the best-governed states in Africa but this Community too ran into problems. A coup in Uganda in 1971 deposed Obote in favour of General Amin and created, for some time, considerable tension between Uganda and Tanzania.

But Africa persevered with her experimental unions, facing up to the problems of the twentieth century like Europeans and Americans and meeting a reasonable measure of success in spite of the often enormous problems which came with independence.

(c) The Arab World

The Arab world struggled too. When the *Arab League* was founded in 1945, economic co-operation was only one of several objectives. Arabs wished to free their lands from foreign intrusions. The League loosely linked Egypt and

* Formerly Tanganyika and Zanzibar.

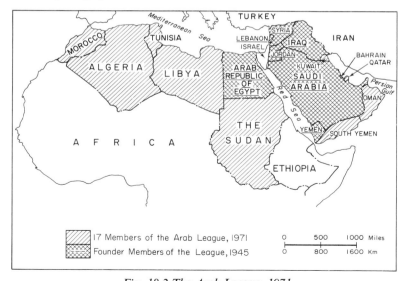

Fig. 18.2 The Arab League, 1971

states in the Middle East to hasten the departure of the French, who still held Syria, Tunisia and Algeria, and perhaps of the Jews who were continuing to settle in Palestine (see Section 19.1). The Arab League was initially sponsored by Britain, who sought to create a stable situation in the Middle East as a bulwark against communism and possible Soviet aggression. The French eventually gave up their possessions but the Jews created the state of Israel and the League was frequently to prove powerless and even divided in the face of their resistance. The League survived as a device for economic co-operation but it was handicapped by internal dissension (see Fig. 18.2).

Other Arab unions were even less successful. In 1958, Egypt joined Syria in the *United Arab Republic*, of which Nasser became President. The union was dissolved, at Syria's request, in 1961, largely because Syrians resented Egypt's assumption of a dominant role in the partnership. The UAR also tried, in 1958, to create a federation with Yemen under the title *United Arab States*—but that union also collapsed, in 1961. Even more brief was the union of Jordan and Iraq who tried to create a federation known as the *Arab Union*. It lasted for only two months, from May to July 1968.

Disunity presented many difficulties in the Arab world and though some of the Arab states were rich in oil, economic underdevelopment, political instability and the ever-present problem of Israel made for troubled waters in northern Africa and the Middle East, in which other nations inevitably came to fish. The sudden death of Nasser in 1970, in many ways the most outstanding leader of the Arab world, left little hope for the rapid solution of the many outstanding problems. Nevertheless, the Arabs persevered with the idea of unions. In 1971, a *Federation of Arab Republics* was set up, loosely linking Libya, Syria and Egypt, the latter abandoning its former name of the United Arab Republic in favour of the Arab Republic of Egypt. A year later, Nasser's

Table 18.3 The Arab world

Country	Population est. 1971 (millions)	Main export* % of whole	Exports* mainly to % of whole	Imports* mainly from % of whole
Morocco	16·0	phosphates 23%	France 37%	France 31%
Algeria	14·0	fruits 21% crude oil 64%	France 54%	France 44%
Libya	2·0	crude oil 99%	Italy 23%	Italy 23%
Egypt	34·0	cotton 40%	USSR 33%	USSR 14%
Lebanon	2·7	fruit/vegetables 13% machinery 10%	Saudi Arabia 16% Kuwait 10%	Switzerland 12% Britain 11%
Syria	6·5	cotton 40%	Italy 21%	USSR 8%
Jordan	2·5	phosphates 18% tomatoes 12%	Kuwait 14% Iraq 12%	Britain 14%
Iraq	9·5	crude oil 94%	Italy 29%	Britain 12%
Saudi Arabia	8·0	oil/petrol 93%	Japan 23%	USA 20%

* 1969

successor in Egypt, President Sadat, reached agreement with Colonel Gadafy, the Libyan Head of State, to create a new merger to come into effect perhaps in 1973, whereby Egypt and Libya would be merged into one Arab state.

18.4   A Special Case: the Reconstruction of Japan

(a) The American Occupation

The USA assumed almost exclusive responsibility for Japan's future after 1945, imposing an army of occupation under MacArthur and fashioning the Treaty of San Francisco (see Section 11.1) without a formal peace conference. The USA intended to plant genuine democracy in Japan and to demilitarize the country. Efforts to break up the *zaibatsu* (huge industrial combines whose businessmen, like the militarists, had often disrupted Japanese political life before 1939) were less successful. By the early 1950s, the zaibatsu had recovered and the army, too, made a comeback when the USA grew worried at the growth of communism in Asia.

Under the new constitution of 1947 Hirohito remained Emperor but he was no longer treated as divine. A parliament of two houses, both elected, and the principle of *ministerial responsibility* (the government being responsible to parliament rather than to the Emperor) established a more effective form of democracy than Japan had previously known. At first, it was intended that Japan would have no military forces but, in 1950, MacArthur introduced a constabulary which, like the people's police forces of Eastern Europe, soon came to possess tanks and grew into an army.

The occupation of the Japanese mainland ended after the signing of the Treaty of San Francisco but the USA retained Okinawa until 1972. The Americans continued to take a close interest in Japan and in 1960 signed a Security Treaty, guaranteeing her defence. American influence also set Japan on the road to economic recovery and considerable prosperity.

Nevertheless, resentment of the USA was not uncommon in Japan, frequently erupting among the country's turbulent student population. Sometimes it was a protest against too much Americanization, sometimes against the capitalist system and the pursuit of profit, and sometimes against nuclear weapons which had left terrible scars in Hiroshima and Nagasaki. The USA's insistence on keeping bases in Okinawa after 1972 was unpopular in many quarters and there were frequent protests against American involvement in Vietnam. In some ways, the results of American occupation in Japan were impressive but the occupation also left a degree of turbulence in its wake. Japan's cultural heritage was very different from that of the USA and American influence in the country could sometimes seem alien.

(b) Japanese Politics

But the constitution was successful. There were stable governments throughout the 1950s and 1960s. All had a bias towards conservatism and, after 1955, were based on a union of Liberal–Democrats, with Socialists as the Opposition. Violent battles between formidable Japanese riot police and determined demonstrators were by no means uncommon in the streets, but the majority expressed at the polls a general satisfaction with the state of their country, which was now geared to competition and private enterprise.

(c) The Economy

At least on the surface, the state of the economy was one explanation for their satisfaction. Japan continued to be the most industrialized nation in Asia, as she had been before the war, achieving a similarly remarkable rate of growth to the 'economic miracle' of the German Federal Republic (see Table 18.1). In spite of her lack of natural resources, Japan's achievements in shipbuilding, electronics and the manufacture of motor vehicles made her a fierce competitor in world markets. Improvements were made in living standards but the rapid growth of population continued to impose severe strains, especially in housing and the Japanese cities, where environmental problems were among the worst in the world.

Japan's successes could partly be explained in terms of dedicated hard work, modernization and heavy investment programmes. At the same time, she also avoided costly commitments in her foreign policy, concentrating her efforts to a large extent on internal development. Poverty was by no means eliminated, however, and Japan still remained heavily dependent on exports for her apparent prosperity. The startling economic progress of postwar Japan was achieved, therefore, at a high social cost. Heavy investment in capital goods has meant that social investment runs at a much lower level than in most Western democracies. Living conditions are bad. Wages, too, are low. The security benefits of the large industrial concerns go some way towards compensating for low state involvement. But this has been possible only because of the weak position of trade unions.

(d) Japan's Place in the World

Japan's geographical position also created difficulties. Trade with China fell dramatically after the Second World War and, in general, Japan's relationships with the communist world remained uneasy. Unlike states in Europe, however, Japan had no other neighbours with whom to make economic unions. Aid from the USA was for some time essential to her survival and recovery and American markets continued to be vital.

Close connexions with the USA made it difficult to have close ties with communist powers. Nevertheless, relations with the USSR were restored in the mid-1950s and Japan took care to avoid damaging involvement in either SEATO or the struggle in Vietnam. Admission to UNO was secured in 1956, but there was little to suggest that Japan wished to seek the pre-eminence in world affairs she had enjoyed before 1945. Her principal interests were now economic ones. In 1966, she took a leading part in planning an Asian Development Bank and, four years later, staged the international trade fair, EXPO 70, and seemed content with these peaceful pursuits. The country was no longer dominated by the militarists who had once dreamed of conquest and the Co-Prosperity Sphere.

Nevertheless, Japan's economic progress caused some misgivings. Her prosperity grew in the 1960s at a startling rate.* Her giant trading companies, the *sogo shosha*, skilfully cultivated markets throughout the world and their effects were felt in many ways. Apprehension about Japan's economic supremacy helped to drive North and South Koreans, in the 1970s, to consider reunifying their country (see Section 17.1(*c*), page 269). The strength of the Japanese yen and the great success of the country's exporters even caused anxiety in the USA and in Britain and resulted in the upward revaluation of the Japanese currency by almost 17 per cent at the end of 1971. And such was the momentum of Japan's economic upsurge that, in 1972, Japan was even seeking a new friendship with communist China, where markets were being won back. At last, the state of war between China and Japan, which had existed since 1937, was officially ended. Japan recognized the government in Peking and abandoned her support for Taiwan. It was too early to proclaim that Japan could now begin to monopolize the massive markets of China or that China could now begin to benefit from Japanese investment in her development, but the agreement between Tokyo and Peking seemed likely to bring about major changes in the alignment of powers in the Far East.

In a favourable political climate, the sogo shosha continued to flourish: in the early 1970s they handled about 60 per cent of Japan's overseas trade. Largest of them was the Mitsubishi Corporation whose profits increased in 1971 by over 11 per cent. It was partly the drive of these companies which lifted Japan from a comparatively poor country after the Second World War to become one of the prosperous nations. Rising from military defeat, it seemed that in 1973 the economic strength of Japan was such that even China could no longer afford to ignore her ex-enemy.

* Table 18.1 shows something of the rapid growth of Japan's wealth. Her rate of growth was one of the fastest in the world, over 8 per cent p.a. in the years 1953 to 1962, compared with $5\frac{1}{2}$ per cent in West Germany and 2 per cent in Britain.

Further Reading

Ayling, S. E.: *Portraits of Power*. Harrap (London, 1965)—Nasser.
Jones, D.: *The Arab World*. Hamish Hamilton (London, 1965).
Soper, T.: 'Western Attitudes to Aid', *Lloyd's Bank Review* (October 1969).
Storry, R.: *Japan*. Oxford University Press (London, 1965).
Tiedemann, A. C.: *Modern Japan*. Anvil (London, 1963).
Trade/Aid/Rich World and Poor World (publications of VCOAD—Voluntary Committee on Overseas Aid and Development).
Watson, J. B.: *Empire to Commonwealth*. Dent (London, 1971), pages 190–4 and Chapter 14.
'*What is British Aid?*' Foreign and Commonwealth Office (London, 1967).
Williams, B.: *Modern Japan*. Longman (Harlow, 1969).

Documentary

Breach, R. W.: *Documents and Descriptions, the World Since 1914.* Oxford University Press (London, 1966), Section 57.
Gibson, M.: *The Rise of Japan.* Wayland (London, 1972).
Zepke, N.: *The Hundred Year Miracle (Japan).* Heinemann (London, 1977).

Exercises

1. What do Tables 18.1 and 18.2 show about the problems of developing nations and their relationships with the rich?
2. Why have Arab states tried to form unions since 1945? How similar to their attempts have been the movements towards unity in Africa and in the Americas?
3. In what senses is it possible to regard Japan as *a special case*?
4. How would you define poverty (*a*) in Britain and (*b*) in the underdeveloped world?
5. Explain why trade is important to (*a*) Britain, (*b*) Japan and (*c*) the underdeveloped nations. What efforts have been made since 1945 to promote international trade?
6. Making use of this Unit and the Index, describe what has been done by the richer nations to assist the development of poor nations. What criticisms may be made of the richer nations in this field?
7. Outline the history of the attempts to create regional organizations since 1945 in *two* of the following areas: Europe; Africa; the Middle East.
8. Make a list of Japanese-made articles which you possess and which you can see in the shops. What points made in this Unit are illustrated by such a list?
9. What is the attitude of your present government towards aid to underdeveloped nations?
10. Nasser was a very popular President of the UAR. Why was this?

(See also **Appendix: Into the 1980s,** page 365.)

Confrontations Among the Lesser Powers

19.1 The Middle East

(a) The Independence of the Arab World

The Turkish Empire had been decaying for more than a century before 1918. Europeans moved in to take possession of Arab states such as Algeria and Tunisia, to build the Suez Canal and to establish control over Egypt. When the Turks were defeated in 1918, Iraq, Transjordan, Palestine and Syria were taken over by Britain and France as mandated territories. But Europeans could not hold these lands indefinitely in the face of Arab nationalism. By the end of 1946 Palestine was the last remaining mandate, but it posed a major problem.

Arabs thought that Palestine was an Arab state, destined to secure independence under an Arab government as Egypt had secured independence before the Second World War and Transjordan* immediately after it. All the Arab states faced problems. Egypt, for instance, went through a period of political upheaval in the 1950s, rejecting the monarchy of King Farouk in favour of a military regime under General Neguib, which set up a republic of which Nasser became President in 1956. The Egyptians resented the continuing presence of British troops in the Canal Zone and finally persuaded them to withdraw in 1955. A year later, Nasser nationalized the Suez Canal Company, claiming that a property in Egypt should rightly belong to the Egyptians. The Palestinian Arabs, however, found that their hopes of controlling Palestine constantly diminished rather than increased. For many years after the Second World War they had the support of other Arab states in their struggle, but the years brought them only disappointments until, by the 1970s, their plight seemed hopeless.

(b) The Palestinian Problem

Britain took over the mandate of Palestine in 1920, already faced with the problem of reconciling the interests of Arabs and Jews there. During the First World War, Arabs had been encouraged to fight against Turkey in return for a promise of eventual independence; but in 1917 Arthur Balfour had announced Britain's support for a 'national home for the Jewish people' in Palestine. For religious and historical reasons Palestine had a strong appeal to the Jews, whose World Zionist Organization rejected alternative suggestions. But

---

* Thenceforward known as Jordan.

Palestine had a religious significance for Arabs too, and they hoped to rule it independently of foreign control one day.

In the mid-1920s Jews were arriving in Palestine at the rate of 10 000 a year, encouraged by the British and the terms of the League of Nations mandate (see Fig. 19.1). This influx of Jewish settlers disturbed the Palestinian Arabs.

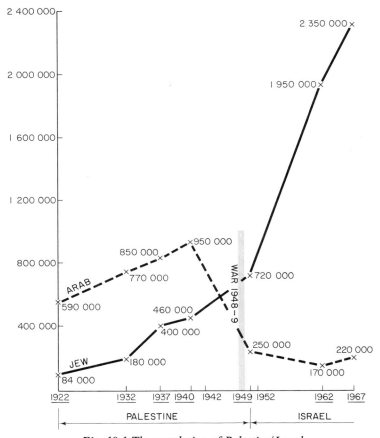

Fig. 19.1 The population of Palestine/Israel

Churchill, Britain's Colonial Secretary in 1922, tried to reassure them by declaring that 'a national home' for the Jews did not mean 'a national state'. Britain already seemed confused about her objectives and there was serious Arab rioting in 1929. A British attempt to restrict immigration led to Jewish rioting in 1933. But 1933 was the year in which Hitler came to power in Germany, and vicious Nazi persecution inevitably drove yet more Jews to seek refuge in Palestine. By 1937, Jews in Palestine numbered about 400 000; many of them were far more prosperous than the Palestinian Arabs and they bought up land, thus depriving the Arabs of what they considered to be their heritage. In 1936, the Arabs maintained a general strike for six months and in the following year, Arab guerillas took to the hills in what became known as the Arab Revolt. A pessimistic Report by the *Peel Commission* declared that the mandate was unworkable and recommended partition. The recommendation was rejected and warfare became more or less open, principally as an Arab rebellion against both the Jews and the British.

When the Second World War broke out, further attempts to solve the Palestinian problem were postponed. Nazi persecution and the war only increased the pressure of Jewish refugees and, meanwhile, the Zionists organized terrorist groups, among them the Stern Gang, and prepared for a confrontation. Illegal immigration continued, alarming the Arabs still further; yet, in

THE UNCOVERED WAGON

Fig. 19.2 A comment on the sad retreat of Bevin and Creech Jones (Colonial Secretary) from Palestine, News Chronicle, *28 April 1948*

1945, the United States put pressure on Britain to admit more Jews into Palestine. But the most serious postwar incident was the blowing-up of the King David Hotel in Jerusalem by Zionists. The hotel was a British headquarters and nearly a hundred people were killed in the attack.

Britain's mandate was due to expire in 1948, but in February 1947 Bevin asked the United Nations to take responsibility for the problem. A special UN Commission recommended partition and this was accepted by the General Assembly. Rather more than half of Palestine was to be given to the Jews, to form a Jewish state. The Arab powers condemned the plan and tried to refer it to the International Court but they were outvoted. Palestinian Arabs suffered a number of defeats at the hands of well-armed Zionists before the end of the British mandate, and then Egypt, Syria, Jordan and Iraq declared war on Israel, the newly-proclaimed Jewish state. Britain had managed to extricate herself from the Palestinian problem but, as had long been threatened, war flared up between Arabs and Jews in the Middle East.

(c) The First Confrontation

The struggle lasted from May 1948 to February 1949. The Arabs were defeated partly because their armies were badly co-ordinated, and partly because their leaders quarrelled among themselves about who should lead the Arab world. As a result Israel not only survived but actually increased her share of Palestinian territory (see Fig. 19.3). United Nations mediators brought an end to the war but not before Count Bernadotte had lost his life, murdered by Jewish terrorists in September 1948. His job as mediator was taken over by his deputy, Ralph Bunche. A million Arabs fled from Israel, homeless refugees. Neither side regarded the war as having settled anything; further fighting seemed unavoidable.

A *UN Truce Supervisory Commission* was still needed to police the frontiers. The city of Jerusalem was divided between Israel and Jordan. Israel claimed possession of the Gaza Strip, tolerating Egypt's presence there only as temporary, and frequent incidents occurred all round the borders of the Jewish state, which the Arabs refused even to recognize. In 1950, Britain, France and the USA issued a Tripartite Declaration, guaranteeing to preserve the existing

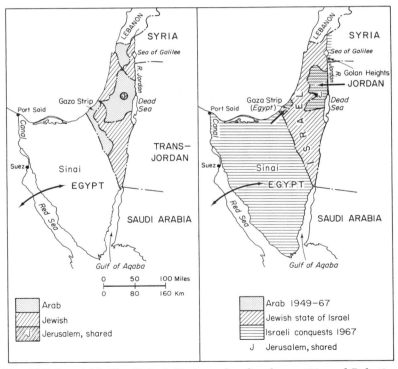

Fig. 19.3 Israel (a) *The United Nations plan for the partition of Palestine;* (b) *Israel after the war of 1948–9 and later expansion*

frontiers and to prevent either side gaining an advantage in armaments, but such a Declaration did nothing to solve the basic problem. A permanent settlement was not possible. Neither side was interested in constructive agreements and while the refugees rotted in temporary camps, both sides looked for a suitable opportunity to obtain a settlement through military success.

In 1955, Egypt secured arms from Czechoslovakia and the Soviet Union. This gave Nasser the confidence to step up the anti-Israeli propaganda and at the same time to nationalize the Suez Canal Company in July 1956. The stage was set for a renewal of the conflict.

(d) The Second Confrontation

Faced with the apparent threat of an Arab attack and angered by the closing of the Gulf of Aqaba to their shipping, Israelis invaded Sinai and the Gaza Strip towards the end of October 1956. The Arabs seemed powerless to stop them. On 5 November, Britain and France landed forces in the Canal Zone. Subsequent investigations revealed that the two powers had secretly conferred with the Israelis before the launching of the Jewish invasion of Sinai. They then issued an ultimatum to both Jews and Arabs to cease fighting and withdraw from the vicinity of the Suez Canal. When this was ignored by Egypt, the Egyptian air force was destroyed on the ground and British troops landed at Port Said.

Very few nations could see any justification for this action, despite Anglo-French anger over Nasser's nationalization of the Suez Canal Company, and their dissatisfaction over his friendship with the Soviet Union and the Egyptian encouragement of Arab nationalists in Algeria. Criticism was fierce and almost universal. Nehru of India voiced the disquiet of the Third World; the attack seemed to be reviving an imperialism more appropriate to the nineteenth century. Even the USA joined in the condemnation. The weight of hostile opinion in the United Nations forced Britain and France to accept a ceasefire within two days of their landing, and withdrawal less than a month later. Even at home, the British and French governments were vigorously attacked. On grounds of ill health, Eden resigned as Prime Minister of Britain at the beginning of 1957 and in 1958 de Gaulle returned to power in France to bring a new realism to French foreign policy and particularly to the country's relationships with the Arab world. The Anglo-French intervention also had the unfortunate effect of distracting world attention from Russia's suppression of the rebellion in Hungary which was going on simultaneously. Russia, posing as the friend of the Arabs and threatening retribution to the aggressors at a timely moment, was able to strengthen her position in the Middle East as a consequence of the ill-judged European action.

Anglo-French aims in the attack were threefold: to preserve oil supplies, to maintain freedom of navigation through the Canal, and to humiliate Nasser. Predictably, the reverse happened. The oil taps were turned off, block ships were sunk in the Canal, while Nasser was able to pose as the aggrieved underdog. United Nations troops quickly replaced the British and French, and once again an uneasy peace was restored in the Middle East.

It was clear that the Arabs were still no match for the Israelis but the confrontation settled nothing. A permanent solution to the Palestinian problem remained as distant as ever, and the United Nations forces continued to police Sinai, the Gaza Strip and the Israeli frontiers. They also removed the obstructions and reopened the Canal. By 1959 there were new quarrels, leading again to border incidents, with raids by Arab guerillas and reprisals by Israeli forces. The situation became particularly tense on the Israeli–Syrian border where the Syrians were able to shell the Jewish settlements from the Golan Heights.

(e) The Third Confrontation

Early in 1967, Syria stepped up the shelling and clashes in the air followed. In May, Nasser moved Egyptian troops to the Sinai frontier. Hussein of Jordan hurriedly patched up his disputes with Nasser, healing one of the splits which so often undermined Arab unity. Nasser requested the removal of United Nations peace-keeping forces from Sinai and the Gaza Strip, leaving U Thant no choice but to comply. Israeli shipping was again obstructed in the Gulf of Aqaba. Rashly, the Arabs again prophesied the imminent destruction of Israel and a third confrontation appeared to be at hand.

The Israelis appointed Moshe Dayan, their hero of the 1956 war, as Minister of Defence. He believed that attack was the best form of defence and on 5 June 1967, devastating raids were made on Arab airfields. Almost at once, Israeli troops tore into the Arab forces, driving the Egyptians back across Sinai, advancing to the Jordan River against the Jordanians and routing the Syrians on the Golan Heights. King Hussein capitulated on the third day; Syria and Egypt struggled until the sixth.

This time, the United Nations could not persuade the Israelis to give up their conquests. The Israelis now occupied Egypt as far as the east bank of the Suez Canal, and that part of Syria which included the Golan Heights. They intended to hold these territories until the Arabs accepted their permanent title to Palestine. The United Nations sent a new mission, this time to police the Suez Canal, but the Canal itself remained closed. Blocked by the debris of the Six-Day War, it had also become an uneasy frontier, but incidents continued on most fronts. The United Nations had to arrange a new ceasefire in 1970, and now Gunnar Jarring tried to find the basis for a settlement of the problem. But all parties to the dispute remained as adamant as ever (with the possible exception of Jordan), and even the death of Nasser, long the outstanding leader of the Arab world, made little difference to the entrenched attitudes. The major powers could do nothing to bring about a permanent solution.

(f) The Fourth Confrontation

Searching desperately for some way to injure Israel, Arab guerillas began to hi-jack aircraft. This gave them publicity but nothing more. In 1970, the Popular Front for the Liberation of Palestine hi-jacked four aircraft, including a British VC 10, taking them to Jordan where they were blown up. The world was horrified by this wanton destruction of property but showed little concern for the dispossessed Palestinian Arabs. Other outrages followed: in 1972, a suicide squad gunned down a hundred people at Lydda Airport, Tel Aviv, to prove the guerillas' absolute determination to continue their struggle. A few months later, the Black September group (a section of the Liberation movement) seized hostages among Israeli athletes at the Olympic Games in Munich. An ill-timed gun battle with the West German police resulted in the deaths of the hostages and five of the eight guerillas.

Fig. 19.4 'Young man! I am warning you.' A shrill protest from Douglas-Home, Britain's Foreign Secretary, as Moshe Dayan retaliates against the Arabs. Brezhnev (centre) *turns away, perhaps in boredom. Nixon* (next to the coach) *shows ineffectual alarm. Brandt and Pompidou* (extreme left). The Guardian, *15 September 1972*

These desperate actions aimed to draw attention to the Palestinians' dilemma, but they were condemned almost universally. Nothing seemed to bring the problem of Palestine nearer to a solution, and the world in general seemed only to wish that the problem would somehow go away. The Israelis now determined to hit back at the terrorists. Israeli jets struck at refugee camps and suspected guerillas bases, causing casualties far in excess of those at Munich. The intention was to discourage Arab governments from giving support and shelter to the Palestinians.

Meanwhile, in Jordan, Hussein had turned on the Palestinian guerillas, regarding Al Fatah, the Palestinian Liberation Organization, as a threat to his own authority and to his country's security. As time passed, Israel grew even stronger and the future of the Palestinian refugees became bleaker. Egypt showed little inclination to abandon their cause. A rift developed between Egypt and her Russian supporters, however, when in 1972, President Sadat sent home the Russian military personnel. It was a move which pleased Libya, where Colonel Gadafy was strongly anti-communist, but it was less popular in Syria, the other member of the Federation of Arab Republics (see Section 18.3 (c)), and caused yet again the sort of dissension which often handicapped the Arab world. It came as a surprise, therefore, when Egypt and Syria suddenly attacked Israel soon after the Third World meeting in Algiers in 1973, winning some early successes. The Arabs had Russian weapons. Israel was supplied by the USA and within weeks was able to turn the tide. For a moment it looked as if the new goodwill between Russia and the USA would vanish but Nixon and Brezhnev saw more advantage in co-operation. With the help of the United Nations, a ceasefire was arranged by the super powers and a determination expressed to find a solution to the problems of the Middle East.

It still remained to overcome the burning sense of injustice of the Arabs who suspected that the West had created Israel to atone for its own crimes against the Jews, creating it not at their own expense but at that of the Palestinians. The conflict between Jews and Arabs was a conflict between underprivileged peoples, a seemingly insoluble racial problem.

19.2   India and Pakistan: the Indian Sub-continent

(a) The Foreign Policies of India and Pakistan

The division of the Indian sub-continent was accomplished in haste (see Section 16.6(a)). It was unavoidable that there were points of detail still to be settled after the partition. The division of the waters of the Indus has already been mentioned (see Section 18.2). Another point concerned the sum of £44 million which Pakistan claimed from India as part of the independence settlement. Gandhi fasted and forced the Indian leaders to settle the debt but, shortly afterwards, he was killed and, although India and Pakistan had become fellow-members of the Commonwealth, there was now no one who could develop that friendship between them which had been one of the Mahatma's last desires.

Under Nehru, India was inclined to follow a neutral foreign policy, steering clear of commitment either to the West or to the communist powers. Pakistan joined SEATO and CENTO and, at least until well into the 1960s, leaned to the non-communist world. Pakistan would have liked to create a league of Moslem states and had strong sympathies with her co-religionists which extended to a refusal to recognize Israel. Nehru, on the other hand, carried into foreign policy something of the moral teachings of Gandhi, even when this involved strong criticism of India's friends. He angered the British by condemning their attack on Egypt in 1956, for he detested all forms of colonialism as much as he detested racialism and he never regarded the Commonwealth as anything but a partnership in which all members should speak as equals. At the same time, he sought to be constructive. He helped to mediate in the Korean War and in Vietnam in 1954, and he put Indian troops at the service of UNO to help to bring peace to Palestine, Cyprus and the Congo. He warmly supported the Afro-Asian Conference, held at Bandung in 1955, but they made less progress towards establishing a united Third World, aloof from the Cold War, than he would have wished.

In 1961, Nehru threw the Portuguese out of Goa, no longer willing to tolerate a European colony on Indian soil. Portugal refused to recognize the legality of his action but it was a comparatively trivial matter which did little to blacken Nehru's reputation as a statesman. A border dispute with China leading to a minor war in 1962 (see Section 15.3(*d*)) brought India some sympathy, especially from Britain and the USA, and tarnished Indo-Chinese relations which had previously been cordial. But India was never a belligerent state and her involvement in wars, especially with Pakistan, seemed oddly out of keeping with her role in international affairs since independence.

Yet Pakistan long regarded India as her principal enemy. The rivalry of India and Pakistan distorted, in time, the foreign policies of both. The Indo-Chinese border clashes helped Pakistan to see the possibilities of friendship with China, in spite of her earlier commitments to the West, and by the end of the 1960s, India was beginning to lean towards the USSR who showed more understanding of her problems (e.g. the emergence of Bangladesh) than did the USA. Thus Pakistan and India tended to line up on different sides in the Sino-Soviet dispute and, for both of them, the Cold War between West and East began to seem as irrelevant as Nehru had always argued that it was. Neither wished to become too deeply-committed to the major powers and, in truth, their attitudes were largely determined by the antagonism which existed between them, an antagonism which, after 1947, smouldered continuously in Kashmir.

(*b*) Kashmir

In theory at least, the princes of the Indian sub-continent were free, after independence, to join either India or Pakistan. Sir Hari Singh, the Maharajah of Kashmir had a freer choice than many of them for his state bordered both India and West Pakistan (see Fig. 20.5). Being Hindu, the Maharajah wished to join India but some 80 per cent of his people were Moslems whom tribesmen from Pakistan undertook to rescue. The disturbances brought troops from both Pakistan and India and, at the beginning of 1948, Nehru referred the dispute to the United Nations. A United Nations Commission arranged a ceasefire and prepared to settle the future of Kashmir through a plebiscite but at that point deadlock set in.

Kashmir had only about 800 000 Hindus in a population of over 4 million. There could be little doubt that the Hindus would be outvoted heavily. India, therefore, obstructed the plebiscite, frustrating even the attempts of Gunnar Jarring to mediate. Members of the Commonwealth were equally unsuccessful in resolving the deadlock and direct talks between India and Pakistan made no progress. Kashmir remained divided along the line where the ceasefire had been agreed.

Nehru died in 1964. Incidents multiplied in Kashmir until Pakistani forces crossed the ceasefire line and a brief war erupted in 1965 which the United Nations again quickly quenched. This time, the Soviet Union tried to mediate, calling Shastri (Nehru's successor) and Ayub Khan, the President of Pakistan, to a meeting with Kosygin in Tashkent. They met in January 1966, agreeing to withdraw their forces to the earlier line of division and to renounce force in the future settlement of the Kashmiri problem. Within hours of signing the agreement, Shastri was dead from a heart attack, but the agreement was honoured. Kashmir returned to its disruptive and economically damaging 'temporary' division, and the fundamental problem remained unsolved, as stubborn as that of Palestine.

Fig. 19.5 Pakistani stamp showing the areas disputed with India, 1960

(c) Bangladesh

The sub-divisions within the Indian sub-continent which seemed to offer a solution to the problems of 1947 turned out, in time, only to have created new problems. Pakistan always suffered from existing in two, widely-spaced parts, West Pakistan and the poorer East Pakistan. In the making of East Pakistan, however, the province of Bengal was divided so that Bengalis were to be found both on the Indian and East Pakistani sides of the frontier. This division took on a new importance when, in 1970, the often unstable political situation in Pakistan led to an open breach between the Western and Eastern parts of the state (see Section 20.5(c)). With a desperation bordering on the insane, President Yahya Khan, who had replaced Ayub in 1969, tried to preserve the unity of the nation by savagely suppressing the separatism of the East. Fleeing in terror from the armies of West Pakistan, millions of refugees poured into India to seek shelter among their fellow-Bengalis. In East Pakistan the butchery was almost unbridled. Bengalis committed atrocities against Punjabis from the West but they themselves suffered the most bloody vindictiveness.

The economic and social problems created by the stream of refugees threatened to overwhelm the Indian administration. The world was full of pious sympathy but the pleas of Mrs Gandhi, who had followed Shastri as Prime Minister of India, brought only a limited response. In any case, Indians and especially Bengalis were enraged by the ill-treatment of the East Pakistanis and, as the killing went on and the flood of refugees continued, Mrs Gandhi felt obliged to intervene. In December 1971, Indian forces invaded East Pakistan. Their objectives were clear-cut and they moved with speed and efficiency. The West Pakistani forces were no match for them. But India was not fighting a war of aggression. Mrs Gandhi's aims were to liberate East Pakistan from the forces of Yahya Khan, to restore law and order and facilitate the refugees' return to their shattered homes. The aims were accomplished and, although there were tremors in Kashmir and some disturbances on the Indian frontier with West Pakistan, fighting ceased when East Pakistan was free.

India's intervention was not universally popular. Nixon committed the USA to particularly fierce criticism, but China limited her encouragement of West Pakistan to little more than sympathy and the Soviet Union gave diplomatic support to Mrs Gandhi. There was now no hope that Pakistan could survive as a united nation and a separate government was established in East Pakistan, a new state known henceforth as *Bangladesh* (see Fig. 20.5). There were enormous problems of reconstruction and, for a time, violence continued to erupt between the Bengalis and a minority group of Biharis in Bangladesh, who were alleged to have collaborated with the West Pakistanis. West Pakistan, in addition to economic and political difficulties, had to overcome the shock of defeat, especially defeat by India, Pakistan's traditional enemy.

(d) The Simla Conference

There was, however, room for hope that a new harmony in the Indian sub-continent could eventually be built from the conflict. It could be argued that the action of the Indian army had cut short the killing. Mrs Gandhi now showed no great desire to exploit India's victory and in July 1972, Pakistan and India appeared to reach a promising agreement in conference at Simla, looking forward to the complete withdrawal of troops from occupied territory, the return of about 90 000 Pakistani prisoners-of-war, the acceptance of the *status quo* in Kashmir and the abandonment of the propaganda on both sides which had helped to keep alive Indo-Pakistani hostility since 1947. There was soon a setback, however, for President Bhutto of Pakistan refused to recognize Bangladesh and until that was done India refused to proceed to other agreements.

Meanwhile, in Kashmir, the Indians concentrated on the economic development of the areas they held and, as in Germany, the division began to seem almost permanent. The Indian sub-continent as a whole desperately needed stability. India, Pakistan and Bangladesh faced daunting internal problems without the added burden of international quarrels. The setbacks which followed the Simla Conference were disappointing but even so the outlook was perhaps more hopeful than in the Middle East. The sub-continent was an area where frenzied killing broke out from time to time with alarming ferocity, but it was also an area where the moderation of Gandhi continued to provide an inspiration and to influence the policies of the leaders of India. In 1973, a modest start was at last made on the resettlement of peoples in the wake of the recent conflict.

Further Reading

Jamieson, A.: *Leaders of the Twentieth Century*. Bell (London, 1970)—Nasser.

Janowsky, O. I.: *Foundations of Israel*. Anvil (London, 1960).

Watson, J. B.: *Empire to Commonwealth*. Dent (London, 1971), pages 68–74 and 95–116.

Documentary

Breach, R. W.: *Documents and Descriptions*. Oxford University Press (London, 1966), Sections 35, 37, 40.

Browne, H.: *Suez and Sinai*. Longman (Harlow, 1971).

Exercises

1. What information can you gather about the history of Palestine/Israel from Figs 19.1 and 19.3?
2. What problems still existed at the end of 1973 concerning (*a*) Israel and her Arab neighbours and (*b*) Kashmir?
3. Refer to Fig. 18.2—in what ways does it suggest that Israel might find it difficult to survive? How do you explain Israel's ability to survive?
4. Outline the efforts of the United Nations in both the Middle East and Kashmir (*a*) to stop the fighting and (*b*) to bring about a settlement. Why has it proved so difficult to achieve settlements?
5. How would (*a*) an Arab and (*b*) a Zionist have argued in 1948 that his people were entitled to the possession of Palestine?
6. Using this Unit and Unit Twenty-two, make a list of the problems which India has found difficult to solve since independence.
7. What is the present situation of the Arab refugees from Palestine?

(See also **Appendix: Into the 1980s**, page 365.)

Civil Wars—the Problem of Minorities

20.1 Minorities

The nation state, in the twentieth century, is something of a myth. Most states include minorities who, for reasons of race, religion and culture, differ in some distinct way from the majority of the population. Many large states, such as the USA, the USSR and India, are federations, which include people of many races. India has not even a common language. Even tiny states, such as Mauritius, may well have populations mixed in race, while the United Kingdom grew out of an earlier mixture of peoples which broadened further when immigrants arrived from the Commonwealth and elsewhere.

The presence of minorities can easily lead to problems, but few countries would now resort to the theories of racial purity which Hitler put forward in *Mein Kampf*. The world has become increasingly aware of the importance of harmony in race relations and of the need to deal justly with the grievances of minorities. Minorities may, indeed, have good reasons for complaint when they are treated as second-class citizens or if their lives and property are in danger. The twentieth century has already witnessed numerous savage conflicts, often resulting from the attempts of minorities to set up their own states through *secession*. This Unit examines some of the conflicts which have erupted in the Congo, Biafra, Cyprus, Bangladesh and Northern Ireland.

In many other states, however, the problem of minorities has given rise to little more than arguments about language and disputes about the structuring of education, with the majority making real efforts to meet the grievances of the minority. The extent of the minority problems depends on many factors, not least the size of the minorities and the depth of their grievances as well as on how the majority responds. In Britain, the Welsh and Scots have produced Nationalist Parties to promote their interests democratically, and, in spite of frequent controversies, there has been little threat of civil war in states such as Belgium, Canada, Australia and New Zealand, which all contain important minorities.

In recent years, minorities have been quick to resent unequal treatment and to suspect victimization, but it has also been the mark of intelligent statesmen to be quick to pay attention to genuine grievances, which are, of course, easier to resolve where the state has a tradition of stability. Sometimes, however, grievances have been deliberately cultivated to serve the interests of politicians, as the alleged grievances of Germans in the Sudetenland were cultivated and exploited in the 1930s by Henlein and Hitler. The creation of many new states has also, at times, led to trouble with minorities; and of course, new states have no tradition of stability. The withdrawal of Europeans from Africa frequently left states with boundaries which were artificial and with tribal rivalries which proved difficult to contain. In Nigeria, the Ibo tribe in the 1960s felt itself to be an aggrieved minority and tried to break free to set up the independent state of Biafra. In the early 1970s, there occurred ferocious conflicts in Burundi between the Hutu and the Tutsi, many of the former being massacred. At that time, civil war had long been raging in the Sudan. But the outside world paid little attention to Burundi and the Sudan. The United Nations showed no desire to repeat the intervention which it had undertaken in the Congo.

20.2   The Congo

The granting of independence to the Belgian Congo in 1960 (see Section 16.4) instantly led to civil war. The Congo contained a population of about fifteen million, divided into some 150 tribes: there seemed to be every likelihood of fragmentation. Areas such as Katanga, which were rich in copper and other minerals, were unwilling to share their wealth with the poorer parts of the country. The separatism of Katanga was encouraged by the Belgians, especially the *Union Minière*, who viewed with dismay the first Congolese government of Patrice Lumumba whose National Movement inclined to socialism.

Lumumba was of the Batatele tribe and other tribes, such as the Baluba of Kasai Province, had little enthusiasm for his rule. In July 1960, within two weeks of the declaration of independence, there was a mutiny in the Congolese army and Katanga and Kasai broke away (see Fig. 20.2). Belgium sent troops to protect Europeans and Belgian mining interests and Lumumba appealed to the United Nations. The Security Council did not wish the Congo to be broken up, for many other African states might follow suit. An emergency force was sent, but the UN troops had no authority to intervene in internal affairs. Lumumba, therefore, sought help from the USSR to crush Katanga. He was promptly dismissed by President Kasavubu, fell into the hands of the Katangese troops and was found dead early in 1961.

Katanga had found a leader in Moise Tshombe and, in South Kasai, Kalonji provided yet another authority. In September 1961 Dag Hammarskjöld, Secretary-General of the United Nations, was killed in an aeroplane crash while trying to mediate. His successor, U Thant, continued to work for the reunification of the Congo and matters came to a head when UN forces defeated the Katangese, at the beginning of 1963. The main problem now was to work out a satisfactory system of government for the Congo as a whole. The last UN forces were withdrawn in the middle of 1963 but the confusion in Congolese politics continued for most of the decade.

In July 1964, Kasavubu invited Tshombe to be Prime Minister of the Congo. He remained in power for little more than a year, faced with numerous rebellions against which he had assistance from Belgium, the USA and white mercenaries. The rebels lost ground but crops were destroyed in the fighting and there was a shortage of food. Tshombe was not popular in the rest of Africa where he appeared to be the tool of western capitalists, and he was dismissed in October 1965. At about the same time and not for the first time, the army, led by Mobutu, removed Kasavubu. Tshombe went into exile, was condemned to death in his absence and, in 1967, imprisoned in Algeria after his aircraft had been hi-jacked. He died two years later.

The government of the Congo was again reorganized under Mobutu. Katangese resistance was once again put down and, in 1968, with the assistance of the Organization of African Unity, Mobutu was able to clear his country of

Fig. 20.1 United Nations forces intervened in the Congo when civil war broke out in 1960

the white mercenaries who had helped to promote dissent and rebellion. European mines were nationalized, and with the restoration of order the Congo embarked on an economic recovery. In 1970, Mobutu was confirmed in office as President, and, a year later, the state was renamed Zaire, the original name of the Congo River. The first decade of independence had been a chaotic one but with the assistance of the United Nations and the intervention of the army, Zaire had survived and remained intact. With profitable exports of copper and diamonds it has a promising future.

20.3   Nigeria and Biafra

Nigeria was one of the largest British colonies in Africa. It was also one of the most advanced, being granted independence in 1960, second only to Ghana which had gained independence and admission to the Commonwealth in 1957. With a population of over 50 million and valuable minerals and oil in the Eastern Region its future seemed promising. Moreover Balewa, the first Prime Minister of independent Nigeria, soon established a reputation in the Commonwealth for being both capable and statesmanlike. But six years after independence, Balewa was murdered, and a year later, in 1967, the Eastern Region attempted to break away as the independent state of Biafra. A savage conflict developed between Nigerians and Biafrans which excited almost universal horror and gravely weakened the Nigerian economy.

Like most African states, Nigeria was made up of a mixture of tribes. The constitution was a federal one, like India's allowing regional governments in addition to the central one. But from the outset there was widespread dissatisfaction with the system, especially among the Yorubas of the Western Region and the Ibos of the Eastern Region (see Fig. 20.2). They alleged that the central government was too much dominated by the Hausas who dominated the Northern Region. The Yorubas, in particular, disliked the system under which Balewa was able to interfere in the Western Region, deposing and arresting the Region's Prime Minister, Awolowo, who had founded the Action Group to represent Yoruba interests. After that incident, the West was in almost constant disorder. Charges of corruption against the federal government became commonplace.

In January 1966, Balewa's government was overthrown in a military coup led mainly by Ibo officers. Balewa was killed, along with the Prime Ministers of the Western and Northern Regions. A military government under Aguiyi Ironsi was short-lived. Ironsi was assassinated and a new coup brought Gowon to power, an officer from the Northern Region.

Gowon hoped to secure agreement on a new constitution, but he could do little to stem the killings of Ibos, especially in the North where they were far from their tribal lands in search of work. The Ibos retaliated against Hausas in the Eastern Region and obstructed Gowon's attempts to produce a new system of government. They also found a leader in Colonel Ojukwu who, after a dispute about the oil revenues of the Eastern Region, declared that Region

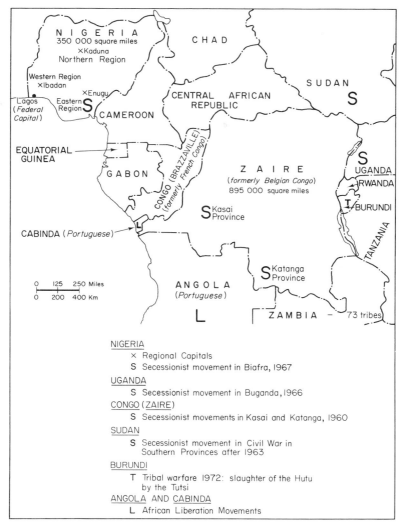

Fig. 20.2 Secessionist movements in West-Central Africa

independent in May 1967. The Ibos rallied to the new Republic of Biafra and war with the federal government of Nigeria began a few weeks later.

Biafra resisted for over two years but it was a state with few friends. In Africa, it was recognized by Nyerere of Tanzania and Kaunda of Zambia. Some arms were provided by France and Portugal, but the USSR favoured the Nigerian government and Britain followed suit with the argument that Britain could not allow the Russians to gain too much influence in Nigeria.

The Organization of African Unity did its best to mediate between the two sides and the world frequently expressed its horror at the sufferings the conflict caused, but the United Nations limited intervention to relief work. Civilian casualties in Biafra were even greater than military casualties for starvation and disease took a dreadful toll of the Ibos. Biafra was surrounded and squeezed but still its supporters resisted stubbornly, convinced that defeat would bring annihilation. The Biafrans did not surrender until January 1970. Ojukwu escaped by air and his successor, Major-General Effiong, capitulated. Only then could the massive relief which the Ibos desperately needed be brought to them.

Fig. 20.3 UNICEF distributes food to refugee children in Biafra. The United Nations did not otherwise intervene in the Nigerian civil war

The crushing of Biafra by the far superior forces at the disposal of General Gowon preserved the territories of Nigeria but it left a legacy of hatred and scars, of tribal warfare and separatism, which could scarcely be expected to heal quickly. In addition, Nigeria faced serious problems of unemployment and an alarming crime wave. Urgent action was needed to repair the economy.

Gowon embarked on a programme of reconciliation and personally visited the Ibo territories in 1971. The Ibos still made up nearly a fifth of Nigeria's total population and their rehabilitation called for great qualities of leadership and statesmanship. It was still Gowon's intention to base Nigeria's government on the federal system of *twelve states* which he had devised on the eve of the civil war but, for the present, military government continued, civilians being admitted only cautiously. Already, in 1972, the results seemed to be remarkable. Almost alone among African states, Nigeria moved into a healthy trading position. Internally, reconciliation made rapid progress and Gowon was also quick to repair Nigeria's relations with states such as Zambia which had recognized Biafra. He campaigned against corruption, the elimination of which was essential before civilian government was restored. Such was the quality of his leadership that, for the moment, most Nigerians were content. It still remained to be seen whether Nigeria could make a full recovery from the recent savage conflict and whether intertribal rivalries could finally be overcome, so that a fully democratic system could be restored. But for the moment, Nigeria was making considerable progress with every indication of being one of the most prosperous and important states in Africa.

Fig. 20.4 Wedding stamp, Nigeria. The state desperately needed the leadership of Major-General Gowon

For Africa as a whole, however, the struggle for Biafra, coming so soon after the civil war in the former Belgian Congo, served as a grim warning against the perils of tribalism (loyalty to one's tribe rather than to one's nation). The boundaries left within Africa by the Europeans were by no means ideal, but no practicable alternatives could readily be agreed.

20.4   Cyprus

Britain granted Cyprus her independence in August 1960. Most of the island's people are Greek-speaking but slightly less than 20 per cent are of Turkish descent. There had already been much conflict between the races, in some ways a continuation of the earlier struggle in the Balkans between Greek Orthodox Christians and Turkish Moslems which had been a feature of the *Eastern Question*; and from 1955 to 1959 Cyprus was in a state of emergency. British troops were trapped in a situation similar to that which had occurred earlier in Palestine: while trying to keep the peace between Turks and Greeks, they were also resented as a barrier to independence. Independence was granted when Sir Hugh Foot concluded successful negotiations with Archbishop Makarios, at a time when the island seemed to be comparatively quiet.

The way for independence was well-prepared. Makarios gave up his support for *Enosis*, a movement for the union of Greece and Cyprus which had always alarmed the Turks, and the new constitution provided for generous Turkish representation in the Cypriot government, police and civil service, and for the appointment of the Turkish leader, Dr Kutchuk, as deputy to President Makarios. Each race also retained the right to veto laws of which it disapproved. Unlike the Belgians in the Congo, the British only abandoned Cyprus when every effort had been made to give the island a stable future. Britain also allocated £12 million to help its future development, and Cyprus was admitted to the Commonwealth.

Cyprus also had the advantage of authoritative leadership. There was no doubt that Makarios alone had the authority to rule. He was always a distinctive figure at Commonwealth Conferences and throughout the 1960s he retained a considerable personal following.

Nevertheless, civil war broke out in Cyprus in 1963. The signal for its beginning was the attempt by Makarios to amend the constitution which so safeguarded both Greeks and Turks that it proved almost unworkable. A United Nations Peace-Keeping Force intervened in March 1964, and mediators tried to work out a new constitution. Incidents still occurred even after the ceasefire and in 1967 the situation was serious enough to bring about the threat of open war between Greece and Turkey. The danger was averted by U Thant and other UN mediators.

A year later, however, Turkish Cypriots elected their own provisional government, in effect partitioning the island. It seemed to be impossible to agree on a new constitution for the whole of Cyprus and the negotiations dragged on into the 1970s. Makarios was troubled by a revival of Enosis among Greeks. He obtained arms from Czechoslovakia with which to resist the pressure for a union with Greece, which could only antagonize Turkish Cypriots still further. But Makarios's own authority was challenged when General Grivas, once the leader of a pro-Greek terrorist movement, resumed his campaigning in 1971.

In spite of efforts in the United Nations and the Commonwealth, the problems of Cyprus therefore remained in 1973. Eight years of negotiation had achieved little. The island remained divided, an uneasy peace preserved by the continued presence of some 3 000 troops of the United Nations. Cyprus is therefore an example of a minority problem based on race, religion, language and history. Enosis is totally unacceptable to the Turkish Cypriots but it appeals increasingly to the Greeks the more the deadlock is prolonged.

20.5 Pakistan and Bangladesh

(a) Pakistan 1947–58

When the British abandoned their Indian Empire in 1947, Pakistan was created as a country whose future was always in doubt (see Section 16.6). A thousand miles of Indian territory separated West Pakistan from East Pakistan and the two parts had little in common but the Moslem religion. In the West, Urdu was the principal spoken language and wheat the main food crop. East Pakistan spoke Bengali and depended on rice, producing jute for export.

East Pakistan was itself created by dividing the Province of Bengal and even on a map the state of Pakistan looked unconvincing (see Fig. 20.5).

It took almost ten years to devise a system of government for Pakistan. The first Prime Minister, Liaquat Ali Khan, the deputy leader of the Moslem League, was assassinated in 1951 at Rawalpindi, by fanatics who were angered by his refusal to wage war against India. For seven more years, Pakistan persevered with a democratic system. No one now had sufficient standing to rule unchallenged as a democratic prime minister. The result was a sordid scramble for power among members of the Moslem League. Six prime ministers were appointed in the years 1951 to 1956 and then, when the new constitution of the Islamic Republic of Pakistan took effect, five more in the next two years. Corruption and incompetence threatened to tear the state apart. It survived largely because of the efforts of Major-General Mirza as head of state. In 1958, he suspended the constitution and proclaimed martial law: only the army now had the authority to hold Pakistan together.

(b) Ayub Khan

In October 1958, the Commander-in-Chief of the army, Mohammed Ayub Khan, took control as President. The squabbling politicians were pushed into enforced retirement for six years, while Ayub set himself to 'clear away the mess'. Like de Gaulle in France and, earlier, Kemal in Turkey, the new President intended to rescue his country from indignity and establish an effective system of government. He hoped that eventually there could be a return to democracy, but for the moment Pakistan was governed by a military dictatorship.

Ayub undertook an impressive programme of economic development, with Five-Year Plans for expansion and a vigorous attack on corruption and inefficiency. Pakistan soon saw the benefits of his rule in improved communications, the expansion of house-building, hydro-electric schemes and progress in the production of jute, carpets and leather goods. Agreement with India was reached on the waters of the Indus, although the problem of Kashmir remained and war briefly erupted in 1965 (see Section 19.2).

In that year, Ayub held a presidential election. He won a sweeping success in West Pakistan but did less well in East Pakistan, although even there he got a majority of the votes. It was impossible for him quickly to overcome the problems of flooding and famine which frequently affected Pakistan (especially East Pakistan) and in the later 1960s his popularity began to decline sharply. He intended to prepare the people for a return to democracy by a system of *Basic Democracy*, providing first for the election of local councils and then for the councils to send representatives to a central parliament. He would keep control of the country's government until Pakistan and its politicians developed experience. But by the end of 1968 discontent was widespread, particularly in East Pakistan whose governor was despised as Ayub's puppet, given to referring to the President as 'celestial light'. Ayub was now cultivating hero-worship among his subjects as Nkrumah had done in Ghana.

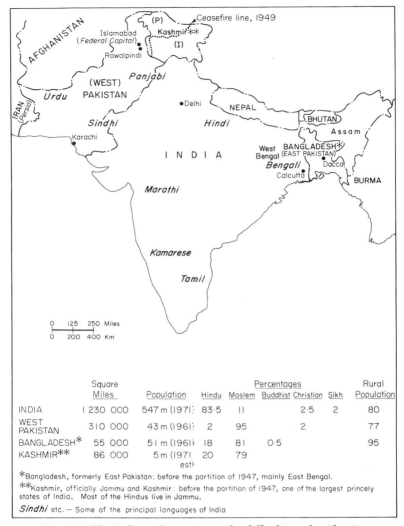

Fig. 20.5 The Indian sub-continent: the difficulties of unification

The suspicion grew that he had no intention of returning to democracy. The politicians, released from retirement, whipped up hostility to the President. There were charges of nepotism and corruption. The mullahs of the Moslem church criticized his lack of devotion to Islam. Communists alleged that Ayub favoured rich industrialists and landlords complained that he favoured the poor. Once more Pakistan began to seem unstable, its mixture of races and tribes suspicious of each other, the East bitterly resentful of the West.

Ayub declared that he would restore a fully democratic system and then retire. The army suspected that this would only produce chaos, so in March 1969 the Commander-in-Chief, General Yahya Khan, forced Ayub to resign and imposed martial law. Thus Pakistan once again had a military dictatorship, intending to rule, as Yahya declared, until stability had been restored and the country could return to democracy.

(c) Yahya Khan, Democracy and Civil War

Yahya kept his promise, launching a new economic Plan and preparing for elections in 1970. Civilian politicians set to work to win votes and although a devastating cyclone in East Pakistan caused delays, the long-awaited general election finally took place in December 1970. The election itself went off more peacefully than had been feared and few of the prepared hospital beds were needed, but the results of the election could hardly have been more disastrous.

The People's Party led by Zulfikar Ali Bhutto swept to success in West Pakistan. In East Pakistan, the Awami League led by Sheikh Mujibur Rahman achieved an even more convincing victory, winning 167 of the East's 169 seats in the Pakistani parliament and gaining an overall parliamentary majority. It was unlikely that West Pakistan would accept an almost wholly Eastern government and Bhutto announced that his party would boycott the parliament unless some formula for government were reached which would satisfy both West and East. Yahya's good intentions had merely created a dilemma.

One of the objectives of the Awami League was to remove East Pakistan from West Pakistan's control. The West would now not accept control by the East and President Yahya postponed the meeting of parliament. A visit by Yahya to the East achieved nothing and, on 26 March 1971, the explosion which had so long threatened occurred. Almost simultaneously, Yahya reasserted the authority of his military government over the whole of Pakistan and outlawed the Awami League, while rebel forces in East Pakistan proclaimed that country's independence as *Bangladesh*. The military government arrested Sheikh Mujib but civil war could now not be prevented.

Bengali refugees poured from East Pakistan into India, seeking to escape from the savage vengeance of West Pakistani military forces. This placed enormous strains on the resources of the Indian government.* Stories of slaughter and atrocities also came from East Pakistan. Frontier incidents occurred and tension mounted between India and Pakistan in the disputed state of Kashmir (see Section 19.2). In December 1971, India and Pakistan were at war. It took only two weeks for the Indian army with the help of the *Mukti Bahini* (the freedom fighters of Bangladesh), to complete the rout of West Pakistan's forces. Tens of thousands of West Pakistani prisoners were taken and before the end of the year Yahya Khan had been forced to resign. His place as President of Pakistan was taken by Bhutto while Sheikh Mujib was released from prison to take control of Bangladesh.

* The refugees were estimated to number 8 million.

(d) Division and Reconstruction

India's dramatic intervention thus ensured the separation of Bangladesh from Pakistan. Bengalis there were now no longer threatened with domination by the Punjabis of West Pakistan, although the latter would not yet accept the division of the country as permanent. Bangladesh emerged from the war with terrible problems. Much reconstruction was necessary and a grave food shortage threatened. Prices soared and it was clear that Sheikh Mujib would need all his skill if disillusionment were not to set in and further disturbances to follow. Tensions between Moslems and Hindus and between Bengalis and Biharis quickly revealed that, in itself, the creation of Bangladesh solved little. Like the whole Indian sub-continent, the country faced social and economic problems on a vast scale. Generous international aid was essential if Bangladesh were to rise above the wreckage of the war. Strong government and major social reforms were also needed, not least to deal with the millions of landless peasants and the ever-present threat of starvation to millions more.

In West Pakistan Bhutto's task was hardly less formidable. Work was begun on the framing of a new constitution but the authority of his People's Party was rather less secure than that of the Awami League in Bangladesh. There were, therefore, dangerous political problems still to be overcome. West Pakistanis, moreover, had suffered a grave blow to their pride in the recent war and considerable qualities of statesmanship would be necessary to lead them in the years ahead. West Pakistan had also to readjust herself to the outside world. China's friendship had proved of little value in the war and West Pakistan had received no effective help from anywhere else either. When Bangladesh applied for membership of the Commonwealth and was accepted, Bhutto announced Pakistan's withdrawal from that association but the gesture appeared to be an extravagant one, for Pakistan now had need of all the friends that she could get and faced a particularly difficult future. The country was now only a tenth the size of India and possessed few firm foundations, political or economic, on which to build recovery. Further disaster followed in 1973 when there were floods in the Indus valley, causing destruction on a scale vast even by Asian standards.

Indeed, the Indian sub-continent as a whole had need of active international sympathy, rather than apathy and indifference. Neither the Commonwealth nor the United Nations Organization did much more than dither when the conflict over Bangladesh was at its height. If the sub-continent were now to have a stable future, more positive attitudes would be needed to bring about economic prosperity and to encourage stability to grow.

20.6   Northern Ireland

(a) The Irish Problem continued

Lloyd George's efforts to solve the Irish problem (see Section 6.2(b)) left Ireland divided between the Free State, which later became the Republic, and

Northern Ireland. The latter remained within the United Kingdom, with a measure of Home Rule. About a third of the population of Northern Ireland was Roman Catholic; the majority was Protestant. When the Irish Republic withdrew from the Commonwealth in 1949, Britain passed the Ireland Act, asserting that 'in no event will Northern Ireland or any part thereof cease to be part of . . . the United Kingdom without the consent of the Parliament of Northern Ireland'. This Parliament, dominated by Protestants, was unlikely ever to consent to the reunification of all Ireland which many Roman Catholics desired. The Catholic minority in Northern Ireland also considered that they were treated as second-class citizens by Protestants. They were powerless to alter this situation by constitutional means. Such a situation was always potentially an explosive one, especially in a land accustomed to violence.

From 1923 to 1954, however, Ireland was comparatively peaceful. The Irish Republic refused to recognize the legality or the permanence of the arrangements made for Northern Ireland, and when De Valera became Prime Minister in 1932, he reaffirmed his hostility to the partitioning of the country. But Southern governments had problems enough, first in breaking completely with the British monarchy and the Commonwealth and then in establishing a degree of prosperity. In the North, the Protestant majority regularly confirmed its loyalty to the United Kingdom (and to the Conservatives and Unionists) in general elections.

It was the IRA (Irish Republican Army) which, in 1954, revived the issue with a series of outrages which continued for the rest of that decade. Extremists on both sides had never allowed old hatreds to die. Both in the Republic and in Northern Ireland, history was nourished with passionate care. Anti-Popery thrived in the Orange Lodges of the North where decorated walls and frequent processions commemorated triumphs of Protestant over Catholic long forgotten elsewhere. The outspoken sermons of Protestant preachers, ever fearful of the influence of Rome, also helped to turn the Protestant North into a stronghold of bigotry and narrow-mindedness, possessed of a *laager* mentality as stubborn as that of the Boers of South Africa (see Section 21.2). Genuine attempts at reconciliation between the two parts of Ireland and between Protestants and Catholics, undertaken from time to time by less-blinkered politicians such as O'Neill, Prime Minister of Northern Ireland in the mid-1960s, had little hope of success in such an over-heated atmosphere.

(b) Civil Rights and Near-Civil War

It was the concern for *Civil Rights*, which became fashionable in the USA in the 1960s and spread rapidly across the world, which served to plunge Northern Ireland into a state of near civil war. In 1968, Catholics in Northern Ireland complained bitterly of injustice, taking their case to the European Human Rights Commission. They made allegations of unfairness in the allocation of jobs and houses and in the arrangements for voting, embittered by their own inability, as a minority, effectively to alter the system, infuriated by the endless Protestant posturing and reminders about King Billy and the Battle of the

Fig. 20.6 A burnt-out bus used as a barricade during street fighting between Catholics and Protestants in Belfast, 1969

Boyne* and also inspired, no doubt, by those who still wished to bring about a united and republican Ireland. In March 1969, their protests developed into severe rioting. In the summer, petrol bombs and gunfire became commonplace in Northern Ireland's cities. The buses of Belfast became popular targets for hi-jackers, eager to convert them into prefabricated barricades and, with civil war threatening, the British government rushed troops to Northern Ireland. Although the British army had some initial success in quietening the rebellion, it soon entered a new phase and the Heath government found it necessary to suspend the government of Northern Ireland and the parliament at Stormont.

The British army found itself involved in another triangular struggle. Catholics fought Protestants and, in trying to keep them apart, the army found itself under attack as the symbol of the connexion with Britain which republicans hated. By early 1972, the toll of dead included over a hundred British soldiers. The Catholic resistance movement was supported by the IRA and another terrorist group, the IRA Provisionals. The Protestants, as the struggle went on, formed similar paramilitary forces. The government used the army, the police and the Ulster Defence Regiment, a well-armed supplementary police force. Although priority was given to re-establishing order and to halting the extensive toll of lives and property, the ferocity of the conflict continued to escalate until well into 1972 when an all-out drive by the British army to destroy the Catholic strongholds brought a measure of relief. The

* William III (Protestant) defeated James II (Catholic) on the Banks of the Boyne in 1690.

drift towards full-scale civil war, developing from the urban guerilla warfare, was checked for a time. The emergence of new and more violent Protestant organizations such as the Ulster Defence Association (UDA) soon suggested, however, that the respite was to be short-lived.

(c) Political Efforts

A political solution to the dilemma was not easily achieved although a programme of reform was begun. The government of Northern Ireland, under Faulkner, tried to broaden its support, before it was suspended, by including some Opposition members. It also accepted the principles of equal opportunities in employment and one-man one-vote in local government. A new system for allocating houses was worked out and the problem of provocation tackled in an Incitement to Hatred Act. But such measures did little to check the disorders for there was a fundamental Catholic distrust of a government so long dominated by Protestants and Unionists. Heath sent a minister from London, William Whitelaw, to try to devise a more acceptable system for Northern Ireland than that which had been provided by the parliament at Stormont.

Whitelaw faced exactly the same dilemma which had confronted Lloyd George. The only sensible settlement for Catholics was one which united the whole of Ireland under one government at Dublin. For Protestants, this was no solution at all, for then *they* would be a minority in a predominantly Catholic country. It was to avoid this that Northern Ireland had originally been created. In 1973, the gulf between Protestants and Catholics was still too deep for Ireland to be reunited. Progress towards a new system of government in Northern Ireland was still hesitant.

20.7 Solution by Tolerance

The world's mixtures of races and religions cannot easily be unscrambled. The boundaries of many states and the mixing of peoples are a result of the past and each generation must live with the problems it inherits. The consequences of these problems have already proved terrible for the Congo, Nigeria, Cyprus, Pakistan and Ireland. It is far from easy to find solutions to such problems. Unit Nineteen shows, in the case of the Jews, that the creation of new states for minorities offers no trouble-free way out. Nor is it easy to partition an island as small as Cyprus or to unite one the size of Ireland. Reconciliation between minority and majority can offer the only lasting solution to problems such as these. Events have already made reconciliation difficult to achieve for many of the states mentioned in this Unit. But it is worth noting that other states faced with similar problems have so far avoided painful confrontations, among them Zambia and Kenya, Guyana in the Caribbean, Malaysia and Singapore in South-East Asia, and India itself, which includes scores of minorities among its population of 550 million. Many have been fortunate in their leaders and in the tolerance of their peoples.

Religion by itself has rarely been a sufficient factor to cause bloodshed in the twentieth century. This is in sharp contrast to previous centuries where a man's conscience was often not his private property. In the examples discussed, religion played some part in causing the bloodshed. But economic and social problems were now more important in men's minds. Thus, just as the wealth of the Ibos was distrusted, so East Pakistan believed that West Pakistan was filching away its raw material wealth, and Catholics in Ireland believed that Protestants were monopolizing jobs and housing.

There is room for optimism here, for man has shown that he is able to overcome physical problems of need, given the will and the resources. But there are other causes of hatred between groups which are less easy to measure. Of these, race and colour have become the most significant during the course of the twentieth century. (See Unit Twenty-One.)

Further Reading

Elliott, F. and Summerskill, M.: *Dictionary of Politics*. Penguin (Harmondsworth, 1970).
Stephens, I.: *The Pakistanis*. Oxford University Press (London, 1968).
Wallbank, T. W.: *Contemporary Africa*. Anvil (London, 1964).
Watson, J. B.: *Empire to Commonwealth*. Dent (London, 1971).

Documentary

Breach, R. W.: *Documents and Descriptions, the World Since 1914*. Oxford University Press (London, 1966), Sections 30, 41.

Exercises

1. What do you understand by the term *minority*? What minorities can you identify in your own community?
2. What do you understand by *tribalism* in Africa?
3. Why have minority problems given rise in recent years to violent conflict in some countries but not in other countries which include minorities?
4. Explain how and why independence led to civil war in both the Congo and Nigeria.
5. How far can events in recent times in both Cyprus and Northern Ireland be explained simply in terms of religious intolerance?
6. Outline the main events in the history of Pakistan from 1947 to the present day and account for the emergence of Bangladesh.
7. What minority problems exist in Australia, Canada, New Zealand and Belgium?
8. Find out about the minorities and their problems in the USA (e.g. Red Indians) and the USSR (e.g. Jews).

(See also **Appendix: Into the 1980s,** page 365.)

Unit Twenty-One

Race Relations

21.1 The Question of Colour

The problem of the relationship between the different races of the world has become a prominent one since 1945. The question is often bound up with that of minorities (see Unit Twenty). Many newly-independent states have populations mixed in race and colour: it requires a measure of tolerance for them to live together in harmony.

Many states have worked towards harmonious relations based on tolerance. In the Commonwealth alone, African states such as Kenya under Kenyatta, Tanzania under Nyerere and Zambia under Kaunda, have all made progress in reconciling the interests of different races. The same is true of the multi-racial West Indian islands such as Jamaica and Trinidad and the mainland state of Guyana; of tiny states such as Mauritius and Fiji and of Singapore under Lee Kuan Yew. Sometimes the rulers of these states have been accused of using authoritarian methods, but they have given their countries sound government and, so far, have succeeded in avoiding racial confrontations such as those which will be considered later in this Unit. The racial mixture of each state varies, of course, and it is impossible in a book such as this to examine each in detail.

Perhaps the most important development in the twentieth century has been the unwillingness of traditionally-exploited races to continue to accept their lower status. In its simplest form, this has often involved a readjustment in the relationships of white and non-white. In Kenya, for example, European settlers have had to accept the independence of the state under a black African government and a change in the status of the African from servant to equal. Such adjustments have often been made fairly smoothly and the Commonwealth itself (see Unit Sixteen) was founded on the basis of this new respect of one race for another.

In states still dominated by white men, non-whites have begun to demand a similar equality, some taking their inspiration from Marcus Garvey who founded the Universal Negro Improvement Association and was deported from the USA in 1927. Garvey went to Jamaica where he continued his struggle to persuade those of African and slave descent to take a pride in their race and their culture and to throw off the habit of subservience. A popular slogan of the 1960s was 'Black is Beautiful', which extremists impatiently made aggressive in the *Black Power* movement while others, such as Martin Luther King, campaigned peacefully for *Civil Rights* and equality.

Few countries with mixed populations were unaffected by these changes of attitude, even those like Australia, which tried to keep out non-white settlers. Others, like the USA with a large negro population found race relations becoming a central issue in politics (see Section 13.2(*d*)). The agitation in Jamaica for the rights of non-whites showed the dangers of Black Power. Independent Jamaica already had a non-white government which had not, however, got rid of poverty and unemployment. To the supporters of Black Power there was something obscene in the contrast between the luxury hotels of the tourists and the hovels of the poor. Thus in Jamaica, as well as elsewhere, distinctions in colour also raised the problems of distinctions in wealth and opportunity. This underlined the importance of economic development as well as of race relations.

In many countries, governments saw the need for urgent action. The problem of colour and racial equality could seldom be isolated if it were to be tackled sensibly. But insofar as the world identified central issues of colour it did so, in the late twentieth century, first in relation to South Africa and then to Rhodesia.

Table 21.1   South and East African populations

	Estimated 1971 (millions)*
Black African Governments	
Lesotho	1·0
Swaziland	0·4
Botswana	0·7
Zambia	4·0
Malawi	4·5
Tanzania	13·5
Uganda	10·0
Kenya	12·0 (African 97·5%, Asian 1·7%, White 0·5%)
White Supremacist Governments	
South Africa	22·0 (African 70%, White 17·5%, Coloured 9·5%, Asian 3%)
Namibia	0·6 (African 84%, White 16%)
Rhodesia	5·5 (African 94%, White 5%)
Mozambique	8·5 (African 98%, White 1%)
Angola	5·5 (African 96%, White 3%)

* 99% or more African unless otherwise stated.

21.2   South Africa

(*a*) From Dominion Status to Apartheid

By the South Africa Act of 1909, Britain linked Cape Colony, Natal, the Orange Free State and the Transvaal in the Union of South Africa, to which was granted Dominion Status. The white settlers of Cape Colony and Natal were mainly of British descent but they were outnumbered by about two to one in the rest of the Union by Boers of Dutch descent. The whites formed only about a fifth of South Africa's total population, the great majority being of African descent, mainly Bantu of different tribes. But Britain transferred power to the whites and the first government took office in 1910 with Botha as Prime Minister.

Botha was succeeded by another Boer, Jan Smuts, in 1919. Botha and Smuts successively led the South African Party, the main opposition being that of the nationalists who were critical of South Africa's continued connexions with the British monarchy and the Commonwealth. Nevertheless, when the nationalists came to power under James Hertzog in 1924 the connexion was not discontinued. Britain was a valuable trading partner and a source of useful investment.

It was clear that the majority of Hertzog's white supporters had abandoned none of their traditional contempt for the non-whites when the Representation of Natives Act of 1936 removed the African voters of Cape Province from the common electoral roll and provided only a tiny representation in parliament for the non-whites, even then requiring that they must elect white representatives. No major party in South African politics believed in racial equality. Smuts was sometimes, quite wrongly, alleged by the nationalists to be 'soft on the *kaffirs*'* and when Hertzog joined forces with him in the United Party in 1933, diehard nationalists promptly formed a new right-wing party, the Afrikaaner Nationalists, under Dr Malan. Malan, even more than Hertzog and Smuts, was committed to the preservation of white privileges and supremacy. Indeed, the three leaders differed in their attitudes to the natives only in degree.

Hertzog resigned as Prime Minister in 1939, when parliament voted by a narrow majority to join Britain in war against Germany. Smuts took over and remained in office until 1948, but throughout the war there had been some sympathy in South Africa for the Nazis and Fascists, and white opinion moved steadily against Smuts when it ended. Smuts had always been an internationalist, an enthusiastic supporter of the Commonwealth and the League of Nations. Hertzog and other South African leaders had few interests outside their own country. This was the *laager* mentality, dating from pioneering days when white men sometimes found themselves surrounded by angry natives and forced to rely on their own resources and toughness. The world was changing after 1945 with new theories of racial equality, demonstrated by the British when independence was granted to India. In South Africa, such theories were alarming and, in the elections of 1948, Malan conjured up a vision of the 'Black Menace', and held out to white voters a lifeline. Their privileges and status could be preserved by *apartheid*. Malan was returned as Prime Minister by a small majority which the Nationalists then proceeded to consolidate.

Apartheid, the basis of which was the *segregation of the races* in South Africa, was not entirely new. There had long been separation with reserves for the Africans, but African communities had also developed in the towns, where their cheap labour was invaluable. Apartheid was intended to strengthen the

* A dismissive term for native Africans, mainly Bantu.

separation of non-white from white and to reinforce *baaskap*, white supremacy. How it would do so was probably not understood by many who voted for Malan in 1948 and, indeed, without black labour the South African economy could hardly prosper. Nevertheless, Malan seemed to offer a surer safeguard against the 'Black Menace' than did Smuts.

Fig. 21.1 South African prime ministers, 1910–60—Botha, Smuts, Hertzog, Malan, Strijdom, Verwoerd

(b) Apartheid in Practice

The Nationalists brought a vigour to the segregating of the races which undoubtedly pleased the white voters. In 1956, coloured electors (of mixed race) were removed from the common register and the parliamentary system further purified in favour of the whites. Successive elections strengthened the Nationalists and weakened the opposition of the United Party, giving ever greater authority to Nationalist prime ministers. Malan retired in 1954 in favour of Strijdom. He died in 1958 and was succeeded by Dr Verwoerd, who was shot by a white farmer in 1960. The farmer opposed apartheid and was declared mentally deranged. Verwoerd recovered only to be stabbed to death in 1966, and his successor was Johannes Vorster. Each of these Prime Ministers zealously applied and polished the principles of apartheid until white supremacy seemed invincible.

The pre-war *pass laws* were tightened and extended so that movement without authority became almost impossible for non-whites. Identity cards recorded the owner's racial group and almost everywhere the races were ruthlessly segregated. African children were educated separately from white children and at a lower level. African housing was apart from white housing. Where possible, jobs, especially those which carried responsibility, were transferred to whites and every effort made, as long as it did not damage the white man's prosperity, to move the non-whites into the reserves under the Group Areas Act. Asians, about 3 per cent of the South African population, were encouraged to return to India while the Nationalist government shrugged off the protests of the Indian government. An earlier Immorality Act was reinforced to prevent marriage and all sexual relations between the races. All resistance was dealt with ruthlessly, not least under the far-ranging Suppression of Communism Act, and when the Nationalists found the courts unco-operative they over-ruled them, creating a new and reliable High Court of Parliament.

The Nationalists took no account of the indignities suffered by non-whites, segregated even when visiting a post office. They asserted that the standard of living of Africans in South Africa was higher than that in other African states and that apartheid was of benefit to blacks. A central feature of apartheid was the creation of *bantustans* by Verwoerd: eight regions which would eventually become self-governing were set aside for the Africans. The first of them was the Transkei, where Chief Kaiser Mantanzima became Prime Minister, but he was less of a puppet than the Nationalists had hoped. He soon demanded that all whites should leave the Transkei and went on, in the early 1970s, to assert his intention to secure just and equal treatment for his people, for the original allocation of land was unrelated to the population of South Africa and the bantustans were to occupy only 14 per cent of the Union. The whites called Mantanzima's claim for more land 'ill-judged' and threatened to delay the Transkei's movement towards self-government if he persisted in it.

Effective resistance to the Nationalists was, however, almost impossible. In 1953, it was made a crime for native workers to strike. Political organizations like the African National Congress were powerless. When Chief Luthuli, a moderate and much-respected leader, tried to organize defiance of the segregation laws in 1952 he was deprived of his chieftaincy and a new law was introduced to impose flogging on those who wilfully broke existing laws. Yet the Africans were unwilling to resort to violence, even though all constitutional forms of protest were closed to them. They still sought to secure relief from oppressive laws by the tactics of Gandhi and, in March 1960, several thousand

Fig. 21.2 'Apartheid is better described as a policy of good neighbourliness'—
Dr Verwoerd. A not-untypical external comment on the system of apartheid,
Daily Mirror, *6 March 1961*

Africans assembled at Sharpeville to demonstrate against the pass laws and to invite arrest. The authorities sought to terrify them with low-flying jets and eventually the police opened fire, killing sixty-seven as the Africans tried to escape and demonstrating to the world the ruthlessness of the South African system. The further shooting of eleven African miners in 1973 in the course of a violent clash between workers and police at the Western Deep Levels mine in the Transvaal seemed only to emphasize the tensions in that system.

(c) South Africa's External Relations

Almost the whole of the non-white world condemned apartheid, with the exception of a few black African states such as Malawi, ruled by Dr Banda, who was well aware of his country's economic dependence on South Africa. South Africa's membership of the Commonwealth became increasingly embarrassing as that association grew more multi-racial. When the Nationalists made the Union a Republic in 1960 and broke off the connexion with the British monarchy, it was decided that South Africa must apply to members of the Commonwealth for its own continued membership. Verwoerd made his first journey overseas for over thirty years in 1961 to address the Commonwealth leaders in London. His arguments in support of apartheid made little impression but he refused all requests that he should moderate his policies. No other Commonwealth state expressed approval of apartheid, although Verwoerd undoubtedly had some sympathy from Australia and Britain. It was clear, however, that there could be no place for South Africa in a multi-racial association such as the developing Commonwealth, and Verwoerd finally withdrew his application. South Africa resigned, but was in effect expelled, from the Commonwealth.

Apartheid was frequently condemned elsewhere along with South Africa's continued occupation of Namibia (see Section 11.3(b)), where South Africa continued to rule, although making vague preparations for self-government. The Organization of African Unity, the communist powers, the United Nations Organization, all deplored South Africa's apparent indifference to criticism. In 1962, the UN General Assembly voted in favour of a resolution to sever diplomatic relations and impose an economic boycott, but although some countries took the necessary action it was ineffective. South Africa was not without friends, at least among certain white capitalist powers. Portugal, with colonies in Angola and Mozambique (see Section 16.5), had a vested interest in white supremacy in southern Africa. The USA, Britain and France condemned apartheid with words but stopped short of taking action. South Africa was well-armed and strategically-situated, perhaps a useful ally in a confrontation with communism, and the capitalist powers were willing to tarnish their own reputations rather than break openly with a blatantly racialist state run by whites of European descent. It was argued that South Africa was stable, with deposits of gold and diamonds more prosperous than many African states, and that apartheid would eventually be modified. Harold Wilson's government refused to supply arms to South Africa and some unofficial bodies in Britain tried to boycott South African goods, but the controversy raged mainly around sporting fixtures, resulting in cancelled cricket tours and South Africa's expulsion from the Olympic Games.

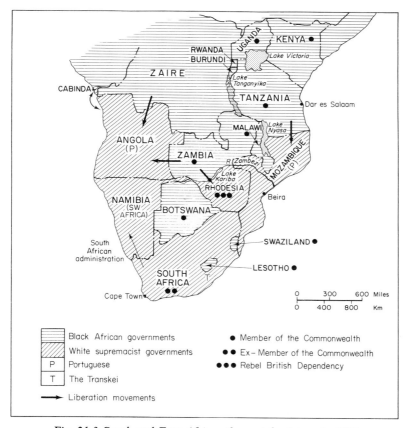

Fig. 21.3 South and East Africa: the racial mixture in 1973

The total segregation of the races has not been possible because of dependence on African labour but there is still little to suggest that its principal purpose is to do other than perpetuate *baaskap*. With the development of bantustans, however, and perhaps a more equal sharing out of the land, the lot of the non-whites may improve in the long term. But it is impossible to be certain that the generally tense and troubled race relations of southern Africa will not yet produce a confrontation of terrible proportions between the supporters of white supremacy and non-whites determined to break their grip. Already there are signs that apartheid is spreading into Rhodesia.

21.3 Rhodesia

(a) UDI

In 1963 Southern Rhodesia remained a British colony when Northern Rhodesia and Nyasaland gained independence (see Section 16.6). Britain could not transfer power in Rhodesia* to an African government because of the strength of the white settlers. On the other hand it was unthinkable that power could be transferred to a minority of whites in the 1960s, as had been done in South Africa in 1909. Although the whites were outnumbered by some sixteen to one they had in effect ruled Rhodesia since the 1920s. Power in Rhodesia had been shifting steadily to the right. The liberal Garfield Todd lost office as Prime Minister in 1958 after legalizing trade unions and increasing the number of Africans entitled to vote. His successor, Sir Edgar Whitehead, displeased the electors when he condemned racial discrimination. He was replaced by Winston Field, the leader of the right-wing Rhodesian Front, in the election of 1962. Field now demanded independence, rightly claiming that his country was in a more advanced state of development than either Northern Rhodesia or Nyasaland. Britain could see no alternative but to delay, for it was now accepted that power should be transferred only to the representatives of the majority. In the Rhodesian parliament, however, Africans were allowed, in effect, only 15 out of 65 seats and their political organizations, such as the African Congress Party, the National Democratic Party and the Zimbabwe African People's Union, had been banned. Field was forced to make way for Ian Smith, the new champion of the Rhodesian Front, in 1964. The whites expected that Smith would be tough enough to force the British to give way.

The principal difficulty in the way of independence was that under the existing constitution the African majority had no power to bring about any change in the system of government. Fewer than 250 000 whites, less than the population of Leicester, could retain supremacy in Rhodesia for ever. Douglas-Home, the British Prime Minister, made it clear that independence could not be granted without constitutional changes. Smith would not accept constitutional changes. The result was deadlock. A new British government elected later in 1964 made it clear that there would be no change in Britain's policy, although Wilson hoped that Smith would find a way to compromise. Instead, Smith talked of UDI.

UDI (a *Unilateral Declaration of Independence*) simply meant that if Britain was not prepared to grant independence, the Rhodesian Front would seize it, following in the footsteps of the Americans who had issued their Declaration of Independence in 1776, and the Irish when they set up their own illegal parliament in 1918. Britain had resisted with force on both occasions. This time, Wilson said that force would be used only if law and order were to break down in Rhodesia. The white police were unlikely to allow that to happen and Smith now saw little to deter him. On 11 November 1965, he declared the state independent, striking a blow, he said, for 'justice, civilization

---

* Southern Rhodesia, known henceforth simply as Rhodesia.

and Christianity'. It would be as independent as, say, Canada or Australia. But unlike Canada and Australia, Rhodesia's independence was illegal.

(b) The Struggle for Rhodesia's Soul

Smith's Government set out to reinforce the white man's supremacy, imposing censorship and banning meetings. Sir Humphrey Gibbs, Britain's Governor in Rhodesia, was isolated and powerless. African leaders such as Nkomo were put under arrest. There was uproar: the non-white world, already sensitive about apartheid in South Africa, clamoured for Britain to take action.

Economic sanctions were imposed on Rhodesia. Wilson maintained that the country was still a British colony and that it was therefore only a British problem. Outside interference would not be permitted, although the United Nations Organization helped with the boycotting of Rhodesian trade. Quick results were expected, but although Rhodesia suffered inconvenience and difficulties in disposing of her tobacco crops, Smith's Government showed no signs of weakening. It seems likely that the economic sanctions did far more damage to the economy of Zambia, Rhodesia's neighbour (formerly Northern Rhodesia), which tried honestly to implement Britain's policy, than to Rhodesia itself. Rhodesia found supporters in South Africa and Portugal, and in the scores of businessmen, in countries such as France, who preferred profit to moral conflicts about race and exploitation. Oil sanctions proved especially ineffective although the British navy mounted a patrol off Beira to close Rhodesia's pipe-line. This supply route was also Zambia's, heavily dependent on the Rhodesian railway system, and Zambia had to resort to obtaining fuel and other supplies by means of motor vehicles, bumping along ill-made roads through Tanzania.

Recriminations were commonplace. It was suspected that Britain was doing little more than play-acting although sanctions were annually renewed with great solemnity in the British parliament. Zambia and Tanzania, in due course, turned to China who offered to build for them a new railway, the ZamTan Railway, which was begun in the early 1970s. There was renewed pressure for economic sanctions against South Africa who was obviously helping Rhodesia, but capitalist powers declared these impracticable. Several times, the foundations of the Commonwealth were shaken by storms about the ineffectiveness of Britain's responses to UDI. Some African states declared their readiness to take part in an invasion of Rhodesia and in the late 1960s there were numerous clashes in northern Rhodesia between security forces, assisted by South Africans, and African *freedom fighters*. The whites of southern Africa came to regard the River Zambesi as their frontier against black Africa (see Fig. 21.3) and, inevitably, south of that line, Rhodesia drew closer to South Africa.

From time to time, new diplomatic initiatives were undertaken to try to reach a settlement of the dispute. The British government still argued that independence could be granted legally and sanctions lifted if the Rhodesian constitution were modified to permit, at least eventually, rule by the majority. Wilson met Smith in 1966 on *HMS Tiger* in the Mediterranean. Smith apparently agreed to terms but when he got back to Rhodesia, his government rejected them. In 1968, they met again at Gibraltar, on *HMS Fearless*. The terms offered by Wilson were considered to come near to a sell-out by many supporters of the African majority, but once again the Rhodesians rejected them. The Conservative government of Britain, elected in 1970, tried yet again. This time, Douglas-Home went to Rhodesia, producing yet another formula for settlement. Once again, there were charges of a sell-out, especially when the Rhodesian Front seemed willing to accept the deal. It was decided, therefore, that African opinion in Rhodesia should be consulted to determine whether the settlement was really acceptable. This task was undertaken by the Pearce Commission which could only report that black Rhodesians emphatically rejected the settlement, asserting a complete lack of confidence that the whites would ever be willing to admit them to power.

(c) Rhodesian Front Government

Since UDI, the Rhodesian Front had given them little reason to believe otherwise. Provisions for land tenure remained in force, a similar amount of land being allotted to over four million blacks as to less than a quarter of a million whites. Africans on 'white' land, such as the unfortunate Tangwena tribe, were driven from it, although the Tangwena for years stubbornly refused to be moved to the area allocated to them and Chief Rekayi declined to yield, in spite of the burning of their homes and the kidnapping of over a hundred of their children. In education, the gulf was widened between whites and non-whites and African primary schools were tribalized to promote disunity among the latter. In 1970, Rhodesia was declared a republic and the constitution revised. Whites and non-whites were completely separated on the voting lists, thus taking steps towards apartheid. A so-called Declaration of Rights strengthened the powers of the authorities to deal with resistance. Like South Africa, Rhodesia was subjected to a storm of criticism from outside and sometimes, especially from the churches, from inside; but the Rhodesian Front remained in control, apparently in no mood to authorize Smith to make concessions to British liberalism. They boasted of the figures of increasing white immigration, proof that many whites still looked eagerly for a privileged position in the world. But, like the white mercenaries who had plagued the Congo, many of the newcomers were unscrupulous fortune-hunters who would bring little credit to Rhodesia.

Moreover, the African population was growing steadily, all the more of a threat to white supremacy because of the high level of unemployment. Sanctions had not done the rapid damage which Wilson had once expected but undoubtedly they injured the Rhodesian economy and, in 1973, they were still in force despite the squalid manoeuvres of the USA which had lifted its embargo on Rhodesian chrome in order to secure cheaper supplies. There could be no guarantee that the whites south of the Zambesi would remain in their supreme position. Already they had the distinction of being almost universally hated. Already they had done much to embitter race relations throughout the world and to cause many disputes, for example between Nigeria and Britain. Of all the world's problem areas, southern Africa was the one which perhaps caused most anxiety in the United Nations Organization.

21.4   Britain: Immigration

(a) Immigration Controls

Easier and faster travel, and a greater knowledge and awareness of other parts of the world have had the effect, particularly since the Second World War, of increasing the rates of migration. Britain, as the mother country of the Commonwealth, became increasingly aware of this in the late 1950s when non-white immigrants were arriving at a rate of about 30 000 a year. This mass immigration of non-whites was almost totally unexpected. The possibility that the traditional British habit of going out to settle in Africa or to administer India could suddenly be reversed did not occur to the authorities in Britain. At first, immigrants were not even counted. But when 57 000 arrived in 1960 and 136 000 in 1961, many of whom had little knowledge of the English language, something like panic resulted.

The British economy needed the immigrants, to work in the transport services, the hospitals and on night shifts in textile factories. But Britain already had a shortage of adequate housing and problems soon arose over education, especially when immigrant children knew little English. Moreover, the government had no plans to disperse the immigrants and inevitably they crowded into the areas where they could find work and where they could find fellow-countrymen. The textile towns of Lancashire and Yorkshire and parts of the Midlands and London soon began to notice the substantial number of immigrants, if only because of the colour of their skins. Many of the British were shocked to realize that multi-racialism could also involve a mixture of colours.

The 1961 census showed that there were about two million people in Britain who had been born outside the United Kingdom. Only a third of them were from the Commonwealth, perhaps only a sixth members of the Commonwealth who intended to settle permanently. The population of Britain had increased by about two and a quarter million since 1951, but this was due less to migration (immigration was largely matched by substantial emigration) than to other factors, such as the lengthening of life. But there were howls of protest, based mainly on the fear that members of the Commonwealth, often faced with poverty and unemployment in their own countries, would become increasingly attracted to Britain as a land which offered hope, opportunity and stability.

In 1962, the Commonwealth Immigrants Act was passed which, for the first time, placed restrictions on the entry of immigrants into Britain from the Commonwealth. The Act was fiercely criticized both in Britain and elsewhere as being based mainly on prejudice against non-whites. Immigration restrictions are by no means uncommon in the world. Australia, Canada and New Zealand have imposed limitations principally against Asians and negro peoples. The USA has immigration restrictions, and South Africa also controls immigration, especially in relation to the occupations and skills of those seeking entry. It had long been Britain's boast that political refugees were always welcomed and members of the Commonwealth, who could afford to come, had received similar hospitality. However, in 1962 members of the Commonwealth were put into a special category.

They would only be allowed into Britain if they could obtain work vouchers from the Ministry of Labour or if they were closely related to earlier immigrants. In 1965, the annual ceiling for work vouchers was fixed at 8 500 although the actual number issued usually fell short of this figure. It meant that non-white immigration fell to about 50 000 a year, mostly the wives and children of earlier arrivals. Contrary to myths in common circulation, the immigrants were hard-working and made comparatively small demands on the resources of the British welfare state. Hardly any were old enough to qualify for old age pensions, although they often had need of the maternity services. It was in housing that immigration caused real difficulties, simply in adding pressure in an already unsatisfactory area.

(b) East African Asians

Britain soon blundered into a new problem which involved immigration from the Commonwealth. During the colonial occupation of East Africa, Britain had introduced into that area tens of thousands of Asians, most of them from India. When independence was granted to Uganda and Kenya in 1962 and 1963, the British government allowed these Asians, if they wished, to retain British citizenship. Many of them did so, suspecting that they might not be able to preserve their comparatively prosperous positions in the African states, for African governments were known to favour a policy of *Africanization* (extending the opportunities of native Africans). The Asians felt that, one day, it might be better for them to move to Britain or even to return to India.

Not unnaturally, there was dissatisfaction in Kenya and Uganda that thousands of the countries' inhabitants were able to combine foreign citizenship with comparatively privileged positions. The Asians, moreover, tended to remain apart from the Africans, discouraging intermarriage for example. General Amin, who overthrew Obote in Uganda in 1971, especially disliked their refusal to mix with other Ugandans. He had a great belief in intermarriage to unite tribes and races, and himself produced children through wives from six different tribes. In vain, he encouraged Afro-Asian marriages.

First in Kenya and then in Uganda, efforts were made to dispossess those Asians who had refused African citizenship. The aim was that Africans should take over their appointments and their businesses. By 1966, many of the Asians were clamouring for admission to Britain. It was now the turn of Wilson's Labour government to panic. Although it accepted Britain's responsibility in the matter, it was thought essential to control the flow of these new immigrants. In the first half of 1968, about 60 000 arrived from Kenya. There were perhaps as many again still in Kenya and almost as many in Uganda. It was decided to impose an annual quota for admissions in a new Immigration Act, in 1968. East African Asians could now not freely enter Britain even if they held British passports. The flow was to be limited to about 5 000 a year.

The situation reflected little credit on any of the governments concerned. In East Africa, the Asians were squeezed to hasten their departure. Those who arrived in Britain with passports but without the necessary authority under the quota system were promptly expelled or, in some cases, imprisoned. Once they had left East Africa, they were refused readmission. Complaints against Britain were made to the European Human Rights Commission and stateless Asians were shuttled about all over Europe. Some sought to return to India, involving the Indian government in the problem. Almost a hundred made an unlikely appearance in Jugoslavia. The change of government in Britain in 1970 made no difference to their plight.

The good sense of the leaders of Kenya, Tanzania and other African states with large minorities of Asians, took much of the heat out of the problem in the early 1970s; they allowed time for things to work themselves out under the quota system. But in 1972, a new crisis suddenly exploded in Uganda. General Amin made an apparently snap decision to expel all those without Ugandan citizenship from his country within ninety days. Britain seemed likely to face the sudden influx of perhaps another 50 000 non-white immigrants within three months (see Table 21.2).

In the event, other members of the Commonwealth came forward with offers of places for thousands of the refugees, among them India, Canada, New Zealand, Australia and Malawi. States outside the Commonwealth offered to help, including Sweden and Iran. And Amin's harsh policies were widely condemned: not only did other African leaders who faced problems similar to those of Uganda refuse to follow Amin's example; some gave new assurances to their Asian populations that they were under no threat and both Kaunda of Zambia and Nyerere of Tanzania roundly condemned the inhumanity of the Ugandan actions. The number of immigrants actually entering Britain proved to be not much more than about 20 000 although that total was enough to start new alarms in the country and to reawaken a measure of white hostility towards non-white newcomers. Once again it was clear that racial problems required careful handling. It was, however, significant of the growing care with which statesmen were treating racial problems that Amin found hardly any supporters and that a large number of countries rallied to help tackle the difficulties caused by the expulsion, even though many understood the justice of Africanization when such policies were carried out more sensibly.

In 1973, Britain's Conservative Government introduced another Immigration Act. It imposed further obstacles in the way of would-be immigrants from the non-white Commonwealth, making it clear that Britain would not admit another influx such as that from Uganda. East African Asians would again be admitted only in a trickle under a quota system. It seemed to many that this meant dishonouring the guarantees previously given to them.

Table 21.2 Migration

(a) *Commonwealth Citizens* probably in a position to qualify for British passports, 1972—mainly Asians. Except in Uganda, there was little to suggest that applications would be made and that immigration into Britain would result. (Foreign and Commonwealth Office Statistics)

(Uganda:	c. 50 000—About 20 000 sought entry to Britain, autumn 1972)
Malaysia	c. 110 000
Kenya	c. 50 000
Singapore	c. 30 000
India	c. 25 000
Tanzania	c. 20 000
Malawi	c. 6 000
Zambia	c. 6 000
Pakistan*	c. 3 000
Total	c. 300 000

(* including Bangladesh)

(b) *The British Census, 1971*
Population: 53 828 000
6% of the population in 1971 foreign-born, of which 2·3% were born in the new countries of the Commonwealth (including 0·6 West Indian and 0·6 Indian) and 1·3% were born in the Republic of Ireland.

(c) *Foreign Workers in Europe, 1972*

	millions	percentage of active population
West Germany	2·2	10·3
United Kingdom	1·5	6·0
France	1·3	6·3
Switzerland	0·8	28·0
Sweden	0·2	5·0
Belgium	0·2	5·0
Luxemburg	0·03	21·0
Holland	0·08	2·2

These figures do not include immigrants who have become citizens for permanent settlement, for example Holland took in c. 300 000 refugees from Indonesia.

(c) Race Relations

Net Commonwealth immigration into Britain was only 19 000 in 1969 and 7 000 in 1970. The non-white population was only about 2 per cent of Britain's total population; other European countries had much higher percentages (see Table 21.2), although the majority of their migrants were lighter in colour. The mixture of colours seemed to cause some particular anxiety in Britain and, in 1965 and 1968, legislation was passed in Britain to try to encourage harmonious race relations. These Race Relations Acts forbade incitement to violence and discrimination on the grounds of colour, first in public places such as hotels and then in employment, education and transactions involving property and finance. They set up a Race Relations Board to investigate complaints, to seek reconciliation and, if necessary, to take offenders to court. The results were, on the whole, encouraging. Even when unemployment soared to a million at the end of 1971, inevitably creating anxiety, race relations in Britain remained comparatively amicable.

Occasionally, however, prophets of doom were to be heard. One such was Enoch Powell, a Conservative MP who thought that great dangers existed in the presence of a million or so non-whites. Certainly, atrocious housing and other social problems occasionally led to disturbances between white and non-white, for example in Notting Hill, London, and Leeds. Hooligans sometimes resorted to 'Paki-bashing' (the mindless persecution of Pakistanis), attacking them with the same demented enthusiasm that they brought to the wrecking of British Rail's special football trains. Such incidents were isolated and untypical but served as a constant reminder that good race relations needed to be cultivated.

In the early 1970s, the conflict between workmen and employers in industry was often more bitter than that between the races; and no racial disturbances in England approached the savagery of the conflict in Northern Ireland. At the same time, however, non-white school leavers often had special difficulties in finding worth while employment and the housing problem continued to cause deep anxiety: there was certainly no room for complacency.

It may be argued that no problem is now of greater importance than race

Fig. 21.4 Support for Enoch Powell: a demonstration in Britain against Immigration

relations, especially between white and non-white. The greatest danger is that racial conflict often has no rational basis. Blind hatred is often more violent than hatred springing from economic or other tangible sources. It is certainly more difficult to heal, lacking any simple solution. It has been suggested that the problem of race relations will only be solved when the entire world is coffee-coloured, for colour differences provide an instant, visible means of distinction. The anxieties of many people, even unusually tolerant people, are also increased at times of economic and social difficulty. Frequently, therefore, racial groups have been made the scapegoat for problems which had, in reality, quite different causes.

The questions of minorities and of race relations have become closely linked in this century. It could be said that the white settlers of southern Africa represent a minority problem, just as do the Asians of East Africa. But a minority group only becomes a problem if it is oppressed or if it oppresses others. Invariably, such oppression springs essentially from fear. Strong guarantees, especially enforceable legislation, can play an important part in reducing fear of this kind.

Successful solutions can be expected only with the sort of foresight which produced the Race Relations Acts in Britain and the efforts of Kennedy and Johnson to bring equality to the negro in the USA. An opinion poll in Britain in 1972* reported that only 3 per cent of those interviewed found race relations the most worrying problem of the time. This was at once a tribute to the stability of such relations in Britain but also a glimpse of the near indifference of many people to the difficulties in Rhodesia and southern Africa. However, it was still a subject on which the world in general had strong opinions. Rhodesia was excluded from the 1972 Olympic Games because of the hostility of many nations to Smith's policies of white supremacy. Such hostility angered others, almost all of them white, who had sympathy with the Rhodesians. It was just one small indication of the gulf which still remained to be bridged.

Further Reading

Brookes, E.: *Apartheid*. Routledge & Kegan Paul (London, 1968).
Cornwall, B.: *The Bush Rebels*. Deutsch (London, 1972).
Field, F. and Hankin, P.: *Black Britons*. Oxford University Press (London, 1971).
Lane, P.: *A History of Post-war Britain*. Macdonald (London, 1971), Chapter 18.
Watson, J. B.: *Empire to Commonwealth*. Dent (London, 1971).

Documentary

Breach, R. W.: *Documents and Descriptions, the World Since 1914*. Oxford University Press (London, 1966), Sections 31–2.

Exercises

1. What is the meaning of each of the following terms: white supremacy; apartheid; racial discrimination; integration; the quota system?

* *Evening Standard*, 10 August 1972.

2. What do you understand by *economic sanctions*? Compare the effectiveness of their use against Mussolini and Smith's Rhodesia.
3. Explain the development of racial problems in southern Africa. Show what each of the following states has contributed to these problems: South Africa; Rhodesia; Portugal. Refer in your answer to Fig. 21.3
4. What problems arising from race relations has Britain had to face since 1960?
5. What parts are played by immigrants in the economy of your local community? What would be the effects of their withdrawal?
6. Refer to Table 21.1 and investigate further the mixing of races to which it refers.
7. What further developments have taken place concerning Rhodesia since this book was written?

(See also **Appendix: Into the 1980s,** page 365.)

The Struggle of the Emergent Nations

22.1 The Balance of Prudence

In his annual report to the United Nations General Assembly in 1972, Dr Waldheim, the Secretary-General, welcomed the 'balance of prudence' which now made the world's great powers cautious in their dealings with other great powers. At the same time, however, he felt it necessary to warn them that it was outdated to believe that a concert of great powers could keep peace in the world while ignoring the 'wisdom and importance' of the smaller states. In the early 1970s, few states outside Europe could approach even half of the annual income per head of the population of the United Kingdom or a quarter of that of the USA. But what these states lacked in wealth they made up in numbers. Since 1945, almost all of the great overseas empires of the past had been wound up (see Unit Sixteen) and, as a result, scores of newly-independent nations had been created, sometimes referred to as the *emergent nations*.

The leaders of many of these new states came together in Algiers in 1973. Their aim was to hold a summit meeting of the *Third World* (that is, the non-aligned nations which supported neither capitalists nor communists in the international power struggle). They were growing increasingly resentful of the arrogance of the great powers who so often ignored the lesser nations. They were aware that the recent improvements in American–Russian relations and the recent enlargement of the EEC were mainly for the benefit of the wealthy and had been undertaken with little regard for the rest of the world. Most of the emergent nations still feared exploitation and domination by the powerful and they felt keenly their own lack of influence. The ideas for a united Third World, once put forward by Nehru, were increasingly attractive. If the Third World could agree on programmes of united action, it would be less easy to ignore the new nations, despite the poverty of many of them. The driving-force for the meeting in Algiers came from India, Egypt and Jugoslavia and the leaders of the Third World assembled in large numbers.

The conference ended with an agreement to meet again, in 1976, in Ceylon, but there were few other hard-and-fast agreements. The Arab states had no difficulty in persuading the meeting roundly to condemn Israel, against whom economic sanctions were proposed and against whom there was a great bitterness born of sympathy with the Palestinian Arabs (see Section 19.1). But there were difficulties even over the definition of non-alignment. To Castro of Cuba, for example, it meant hostility to Western capitalism and friendship with the USSR, an interpretation much disputed by Colonel Gadafy of Libya. All of the emergent nations shared a deep hatred of imperialism and colonialism but there was no precise agreement on what these terms meant, and no complete agreement on which great powers were most to be blamed. Nor were they able to reach many agreements on how the Third World might best co-operate. In some ways, therefore, the conference was a disappointment. But, at the same time, the new nations gained confidence from the size of their conference and from the realization that at least some of their members possessed oil and raw materials which the great powers badly needed. When they dispersed, they were all even more determined to defend their independence.

The Algiers meeting and Dr Waldheim's warning were shots across the bows of the great powers. Small states no doubt made mistakes. Many of them were unstable and some of their leaders seemed, at times, to act emotionally, and in ways which exasperated others. In 1972, General Amin suddenly brought to a head the question of Ugandan citizenship and adopted harsh policies towards his country's Asians (see Section 21.4(*b*)). There was widespread condemnation of his actions and they caused particular annoyance to Britain where demands were heard that Uganda should be punished and aid suspended. Few indeed were prepared to defend Amin but the Third World had little sympathy in the matter with Britain. Heath's government had shown little sensitivity to the feelings of the new African nations. One of its first actions after taking office in 1970 had been to resume the sale of arms to South Africa, in defiance of a United Nations resolution, and it had then attempted to reach a compromise with Ian Smith of Rhodesia, causing further affront to black African opinion. Friendship with Portugal and a compromising attitude to the white supremacists of southern Africa caused great suspicion of Britain in the Third World, underlining the relevance of Dr Waldheim's warning. In large areas of the world such as Africa and Latin America, the great powers could no longer continue to arrange things just to suit themselves. In the 1970s, it was becoming vital that they should learn to pay attention to the wishes and ambitions of the underdeveloped nations.

The problems of underdevelopment and international aid have been considered (see Unit Eighteen). The following pages will examine the histories of just a few of the emergent nations.

22.2 India

(*a*) Nehru

After securing independence from Britain in 1947 (see Section 16.6), India was fortunate to have Nehru's uninterrupted leadership for seventeen years. The long struggle to achieve independence had strengthened the authority of the Indian National Congress, and Nehru's authority was unquestioned after the death of Patel, the leader of the party's right wing, in 1950.

He faced daunting problems. India was a vast state, with one of the lowest standards of living in the world. Although the average expectation of life was only thirty-two years in the early 1950s, its population of some 400 millions was rising fast. Many were illiterate and the country was difficult to unite, lacking even a common language. There were many minority groups and the partition of the Indian sub-continent left huge refugee camps, adding to the squalor of the slums in India's cities. Communications were often erratic and if the state was to be modernized the government would have to overcome deep-rooted religious traditions such as the socially-divisive *caste system* (see Glossary) and the age-old veneration of cows. In the short term, Nehru also faced the problem of establishing a new constitution and integrating into India areas formerly ruled by about 500 princes. The adoption of a democratic system in such a country seemed wildly optimistic. That India operated such a system with a great deal of success for more than a quarter of a century was a remarkable tribute to her statesmen and people. India became a republic in 1950. At the first election under the new constitution there were 176 million voters. The election was a gigantic undertaking but it confirmed Nehru and the Indian National Congress in power.

Nehru brought progressive socialist ideas to the task of government. He wished to unite and develop his state, to establish Western-style democracy combined with socialist economic planning, and to use his voice in international affairs in support of morality and an independent, unaligned Third World. He hated both imperialism and racialism and condemned them without hesitation whenever the occasion arose. He was thus distressed when Britain attacked Egypt in 1956 and by the intensification of apartheid in South Africa. At the same time, he welcomed the development of the Commonwealth as a multi-racial association and as a partnership of equals.

Fig. 22.1 Sikhs, one of India's minority groups, dance to their traditional instruments in Delhi

With a new Planning Commission, Nehru embarked on what he hoped would eventually effect both an industrial and social revolution in India. Such were the problems, however, that progress was painfully slow. Although by 1961 output had almost doubled, there were still jobs in industry for only 1 per cent of India's people and the rising population helped to cancel out almost any increase in the people's standard of living. An intensive programme to encourage birth control was begun in 1956 but its success was limited.

Nehru also made an attack on social problems. Women were given equal rights to property, and discrimination against untouchables was made an offence. The constitution laid down as an objective free and compulsory education for all children up to the age of fourteen, but when Nehru died in 1964

Fig. 22.2

the target had not been reached and the level of illiteracy remained alarmingly high. Even with foreign aid, India lacked the wealth to provide more than a fraction of the schools, hospitals and homes which were needed. There was a similar lack of capital for the necessary modernization of agriculture and great expansion of industry which alone could bring prosperity. Most of the foreign aid, moreover, was in the form of loans which had to be repaid, often at considerable rates of interest, imposing yet another burden on the republic.

Even so, there was clear evidence that India was making progress. Thousands of villages gained the benefits of electricity. New jobs were created. Cooperatives improved agricultural yields and irrigation schemes brought more stability at least to certain areas, although there was no hope of meeting all the natural disasters which afflict the country from time to time.

Nehru also won acclaim for his role in international affairs, in spite of difficulties over Kashmir, Goa and a brief war with China. He sought to mediate in the Korean War in 1951 and in Vietnam in 1954. Indians were quick to respond to the call of the United Nations for troops to intervene in Palestine, the Congo and Cyprus. Nehru's death was therefore mourned not only by millions in India but throughout the world. In many ways the founder of his country, he was also a statesman of great standing. He did much to establish the claims of the underdeveloped nations to be taken seriously in a world dominated by the super powers and the rich.

(b) Shastri

So firmly had democracy taken root under Nehru that India peacefully appointed a new Prime Minister on his death. The choice fell on the mild and unassuming Lal Bahadur Shastri who, like Nehru, had devoted much of his life to the service of India, spending nine years in prison for civil disobedience against British rule. He had held a variety of appointments under Nehru with particular responsibility for the laws against discrimination which were part of India's social revolution. The right wing of the Indian National Congress resisted his appointment as Prime Minister and, although he went to war with Pakistan over Kashmir in 1965 (see Section 19.2), they continued to deplore his willingness to seek reconciliation and criticized his decision not to make India a nuclear power.

Shastri, however, died suddenly in January 1966 and once again India had to choose a new Prime Minister.

(c) Mrs Gandhi

Many found the choice of Mrs Gandhi surprising. No country in the world faced greater problems than India whose government required strength and abilities far above the average. But Congress chose Nehru's daughter, Mrs Indira Gandhi, who would have to face male prejudice in addition to other problems. Ceylon had created a precedent by appointing Mrs Bandaranaike as Prime Minister in 1960, and Mrs Golda Meir later became the Prime Minister of Israel in 1969; but no woman in the world faced responsibilities as enormous as those of Mrs Gandhi. Nevertheless, her government was so competent that she was re-elected both in 1967 and 1971. Between these elections, she smashed the powers of the *Syndicate*, the group of party bosses who had long dominated the Indian National Congress. Many of them were professional manipulators who did not share Nehru's idealism and they tended to discredit politics in India. For some time it had been thought that the only unity in Indian politics was the predominance of the Indian National Congress in the face of a disunited opposition. By winning re-election in 1971, after the split in Congress between the Syndicate and herself, Mrs Gandhi underlined both the strength of Indian democracy and her own personal authority.

She had been active in Indian politics since 1938 and had been elected President of the Indian National Congress in 1959. By 1964, when she took office in Shastri's cabinet, she was a widow. A woman of tremendous energies and outstanding abilities, she was well-prepared by her father for the strains of the Prime Ministership.

Apart from the struggle with the Syndicate and India's deep-rooted social and economic problems, Mrs Gandhi faced many disturbances. Communism had already taken root in several parts of India. In 1967, West Bengal returned a communist-dominated government and violent rioting there led to a period of presidential rule. Such disturbances always threatened the unity of India and at the beginning of the 1970s there was a new threat from communist agitators armed with the *Thoughts of Chairman Mao*, a group known as Naxalites who spread into India from Nepal. Disorders were inevitable as long as India remained seriously underdeveloped. On the other hand, it would take generations of wise and patient government to overcome the country's social and economic problems. It was this wise government which Mrs Gandhi wished to continue.

Hindi was being developed as a common language to promote national unity. Economic planning continued but not without setbacks. The fourth Development Plan aimed to increase India's wealth at the rate of 6 per cent p.a., provide an additional 19 million jobs and raise average incomes over five years by about 25 per cent. Even if the aims were achieved, India would still be desperately poor but, in 1966, it was necessary to devalue the currency and, a year later, there was a grave food shortage with famine in Bihar. Natural disasters also continued to plague the state. In 1971, the coast of Orissa was struck by a huge tidal wave and thousands were killed in this one storm alone.

Many of Mrs Gandhi's policies were socialist. She nationalized the banks and, after the election of 1971, took over the management of general insurance. She wished to rule the country for the benefit of the people as a whole and not in the interests of privileged groups and her government aimed to achieve ambitious but realistic targets such as that in education, where it was intended to give all Indian children five years' schooling by 1975. People expressed approval of these policies in the election of 1971. Mrs Gandhi's supporters now held nearly 350 seats, having won more than 100, and the opposition was hopelessly divided with two bickering communist parties having the next largest representation, with some 25 seats each.

The flood of refugees from Bangladesh in 1971 and the war which then developed with Pakistan (see Section 19.2), however, imposed yet another serious handicap on India, but much of the world remained indifferent to her problems. For the first time, India began to turn to the USSR for friendship although, in continuing the Commonwealth connexion, Mrs Gandhi was still trying to maintain her father's policy of neutralism in the struggle between communism and capitalism.

22.3 Africa

The retreat of the Europeans from Africa in the years after 1945 led to the emergence of about three dozen newly-independent states in the continent. Even the comparatively prosperous ones, such as Ghana, were in fact wretchedly poor. Tribalism also plagued many of the new African states, threatened to tear them apart, and helped to bring about civil war in the Congo and Nigeria (see Unit Twenty). The problems of southern Africa (see Unit Twenty-one) and the presence of Asians in East Africa were further complications. The problems which confronted a group of African states, formerly in the British Empire, during their first years of independence will now be considered.

(a) Ghana

Ghana was the first British state in Africa to achieve independence, in 1957. It was created mainly from the former Gold Coast Colony and the one-time mandated territory of Togoland. The country's first Prime Minister was Dr

Nkrumah who also became its President when Ghana was declared a republic in 1960. Nkrumah was a socialist, eager to develop Ghana as a model for independent African states and also to advance the *pan-African movement* (creating links among African states to speed their development and increase their influence in the world). He was an enthusiastic supporter of the Organization of African Unity and, like Nasser in Egypt, was not unwilling to experiment in unions between his state and others. He formed, for example, a short-lived economic union with the former French colonies of Guinea and Mali.

Nkrumah, however, was a man in a hurry. Ghana embarked on a headlong programme of improvement which, although it had many beneficial results, plunged the country deeply into debt. His government, moreover, became increasingly dictatorial, built around a degree of hero worship which finally reached absurd proportions. He was removed from power by a military coup in 1966.

Ghana was unhealthily dependent on the exporting of cocoa, the production of which Nkrumah almost doubled. But the earnings from cocoa and other exports were not large and Ghana had few monetary reserves to fall back on. Nkrumah wished to give his people schools and hospitals and the higher standard of living which was common in Europe but this could be produced only by an industrial revolution. Industrialization, however, itself required vast sums of capital. This was Nkrumah's dilemma as it is the dilemma of all underdeveloped states. Rashly, he borrowed far more than Ghana could hope quickly to repay, until the country's debts amounted to almost £250 million, all the more embarrassing when the world price of cocoa fell steeply in the mid-1960s.

Some of Nkrumah's projects were nevertheless useful and sensible. The Volta River Project of 1961 would produce electricity and irrigate the land; linked to this scheme was an aluminium-smelting plant, begun in 1964. Nkrumah did much to justify his self-elected title of 'Founder of the Nation', with impressive developments in cattle-rearing, forest industries and fishing, in promoting village projects to improve water supplies and the environment, and in extending the social services. But there were also less creditable achievements. Money which Ghana could not afford was spent on prestige projects such as government buildings in Accra and a little-used motorway from Accra to Tema, and Nkrumah himself was soon being widely accused of extravagance.

He dealt harshly with his critics. In 1959, a Preventive Detention Act allowed the imprisonment of opponents without trial and, shortly afterwards, almost a thousand were lodged in jail. Even the President's own party, the Convention People's Party, was purged of dissent. In 1964, Ghana became a one-party state and all parties other than the CPP were disbanded. Although Ghanaians approved of the changes in a referendum and gave Nkrumah a personal vote of confidence, dictatorship and censorship were not what they had hoped for when Ghana became independent.

Nkrumah also had ambitions to play a major role in international affairs. He worked for improvements throughout Africa and took a keen interest in the affairs of the Commonwealth, deploring apartheid in South Africa but statesman enough to wish to persuade the South African government to moderate its policies rather than simply to drive that government from the Commonwealth. He also wished to develop Ghana's contacts both with the USA and the communist world and he travelled extensively. In February 1966, while Nkrumah was visiting China, his regime was overthrown. He was not allowed to return to Ghana and he died in exile in 1972.

Fig. 22.3 President Nkrumah with Russian technicians and politicians at a Russian Trade Fair in Accra

The coup which deposed the President was carried out by the army and the police who imposed the military dictatorship of the *National Liberation Council* led by Major-General Ankrah. Overnight, Nkrumah's supporters melted away. The CPP was outlawed but the Council declared its intention to return to democracy as soon as possible and meanwhile (like Ayub Khan in Pakistan) to build the foundations for stable, civilian government. Ghana also intended to pay her debts. Some independence was restored to the courts and many of Nkrumah's political prisoners released from prison, but reorganization was not without its difficulties and, in 1969, Ankrah resigned after charges of corruption and was replaced by Brigadier Afrifa. Nevertheless, a new constitution was painstakingly worked out and, in August 1969, elections were held which brought to power the Progressive Party led by Dr Busia. The National Liberation Council was dissolved a month later.

The restoration of democracy reflected considerable credit on Ghana's military leaders but many of the country's basic problems remained. There was almost no tradition of genuine parliamentary government. Nkrumah had argued, with some justice, that strong rule was essential in the face of tribalism and violence by those in opposition. Now Busia not only faced the problem of paying Ghana's debts but also a high level of unemployment and sharply rising prices. In 1971, he was forced to devalue the currency and impose restrictions on imports. Labour troubles led to the abolition of the Ghanaian Trades Union Congress and it became clear that parliamentary government was in difficulties. The end was not long delayed. In January 1972, a military coup led by Colonel Acheampong removed Busia's government from power. Although the World Bank had renegotiated the terms under which Ghana's debts should be paid, the burden remained crippling, eating up a third of the country's export earnings and, with heavy interest payments, showed few signs of diminishing. Like the National Liberation Council, Busia had honestly sought to repay the money but, with a population of only eight million and an economy geared mainly to the production of cocoa, Ghana faced an almost impossible task. It was to some extent the responsibility of these richer nations who were insisting on their pound of flesh, that parliamentary government again collapsed in the country.

(b) Kenya

Independence was granted to Kenya in 1963 and the state was declared a republic a year later. The economy was basically agricultural, heavily dependent on the exporting of produce such as tea, coffee and sisal, and the country possessed little industry and few mineral resources. There were racial problems to be faced, for in addition to Arabs, Asians and Europeans, Kenya contained a variety of African ethnic groups and many tribes with strong intertribal rivalries. The dominant tribe was that of the Kikuyu to which Jomo Kenyatta, the first Prime Minister and President, belonged and which in the 1950s had been closely associated with the *Mau Mau*, a terrorist society which had sought to speed independence.

Kenyatta recognized the country's need for firm and continuous government. He was unwilling to resort to the more extreme authoritarian methods of Nkrumah but he aimed to give Kenya stability and to develop racial harmony. For a time, one-party rule proved necessary, that of KANU, the Kenya African National Union. Kenyatta also thought it necessary to imprison his former supporter, Oginga Odinga, lest a parliamentary opposition should encourage separatism. In 1969, Kenyatta's hopes of building one nation received a major setback when Tom Mboya, one of the government's most gifted ministers, was assassinated. Mboya was a Luo, one of the few non-Kikuyu to have a share in power.

Kenyatta also faced problems with Asians who, at independence, had retained non-Kenyan citizenship. The President was determined that there should be opportunities for all who were Kenyan citizens regardless of race and tribe, and Europeans who had accepted Kenyan citizenship were favourably impressed with the fairness and competence of his government. On the other hand, his policies of Africanization, although stopping far short of Amin's in Uganda, made it clear that those who refused Kenyan citizenship could not hope to retain their privileges.

Kenya's stability was a tribute to Kenyatta's leadership. Economic targets were steadily achieved and, in 1972, the President was returned to power in elections, although not all of his supporters were successful. At that time, Kenya had avoided both the financial anarchy of Ghana and the separatist troubles of Nigeria and the Congo. Much progress had been made towards racial harmony. Kenyans had certain restrictions on their freedom but the nation had survived with the minimum of bloodshed and progress was steady. Kenyatta himself, however, was nearly eighty years old in 1972. He had the reputation of being one of Africa's most outstanding moderates. How firm were the foundations for national development and stability which he had laid in Kenya would only be seen after he was dead.

(c) Tanzania

Tanganyika achieved independence from Britain in 1961, uniting with Zanzibar in 1964 to form Tanzania. One of the poorest states in Africa, Tanzania had one great asset, the distinctive rule of Nyerere, much younger than Kenyatta and one of the twenty-six children of an African chief.

Tanzania faced similar problems to Kenya, with added strains which arose from being closer to the racial problems of southern Africa and bordering on Mozambique. Government was in the hands of TANU, the Tanzania African National Union. Nyerere ruled as President, providing for many years an administration which was stable, competent and idealistic. He was uncompromising in his condemnation of racialism and bold in his defiance of European vested interests. Whereas Kenya pursued broadly capitalist policies, Nyerere favoured socialism. It was not, however, the socialism of industrialized Russia; in many ways it was closer to that of Mao, as was perhaps inevitable in a country so dependent on agriculture. Underlying Nyerere's philosophy was a passionate belief in equality. His *Arusha Declaration* committed Tanzania to extreme austerity in which all, including members of the government, would share. There was to be no room in the country for nepotism and corruption and progress would be made largely by the efforts of Tanzanians themselves. Village projects such as those of Nkrumah in Ghana were encouraged. Nationalization was extensively practised and much of the economy managed by the National Development Corporation.

Progress was slow, for hardly any countries in the world were poorer than Tanzania and had further to travel. Nyerere's goal was not, however, simply a matter of economic prosperity. He intended to develop new attitudes, a sort of African socialism far removed from the competitiveness of European and colonial society. Tanzania became a haven for socialists from all over the world, observing and in some cases contributing to one of Africa's most exciting experiments. The nation had little help from outside, for Nyerere's uncompromising hostility to capitalists, financiers and the pursuit of profit frequently exasperated the richer powers. But perhaps no country could claim with greater justification to be attempting to build a new society. Without doubt, the driving force behind this remarkable undertaking was to be found in the cheerful but thoughtful Nyerere, once a schoolteacher but, from 1955, the dedicated leader of his people.

Fig. 22.4 Julius Nyerere: the encouragement of self-help and village effort in Tanganyika, 1962

(d) Zambia

One of Nyerere's closest friends was Kenneth Kaunda, who led Northern Rhodesia to independence in 1964 as the new nation of Zambia and became President of the Zambian Republic. Kaunda shared at least some of Nyerere's ideals as well as his detestation of racialism.

Kaunda hoped to build a state free from racial discord but, in addition to a multiplicity of tribes, he faced the problem of being Southern Rhodesia's neighbour, in the front line of the conflict between black Africa and the white supremacists in the south of the continent. Zambia was also much dependent on copper-mining and on the world price of copper, which accounted for more than 90 per cent of the country's exports. When the price slumped, as it did in 1971, the Zambian economy was in trouble. The nation's financial reserves fell rapidly and imports had to be cut back fiercely. In 1972, Zambia was struggling, denied fair prices for her output by the richer nations.

Unemployment, crime and violence added to Kaunda's problems although for years he struggled, like Kenyatta, to keep his nation united and to restrain intertribal rivalries. Like Kenyatta, he was also faced with the difficulties created by a breakaway supporter. In the late 1960s, there was a suspicion that Kapwepwe, the Vice-President of Zambia, was aiming to set up a breakaway group in favour of the Bemba tribe of the north. The President was forced to become increasingly authoritarian and, in 1973, he reluctantly turned Zambia into a one-party state, perhaps the only hope for preserving unity among the country's seventy-three tribes.

Kaunda's vigorous yet humane government still seemed to be the best guarantee, in the early 1970s, that Zambia could overcome its many difficulties. It had already provided an element of stability and Kaunda's personal reputation as a moderate of considerable ability was one of Zambia's most valuable assets. But future development would depend on many factors. Tribal separatism was an ever-present danger. Copper prices were of vital importance and the building of the ZamTan Railway was essential to the economy after Rhodesia's declaration of independence and the sanctions which followed it (see Section 21.3). It was also essential to overcome the nation's social problems and to develop a real sense of unity and purpose.

Like other African leaders, Kaunda was often abused by a hostile press in Britain and elsewhere, for it was far from being his intention to rule Zambia for the benefit of Europeans. Europeans in Zambia, like those in Kenya, who accepted that the days of privilege were past had little to fear. On the other hand, geography placed Zambia in a position where it was impossible to disregard the fact that many whites in Africa were determined to ignore the changes sweeping through the continent. Their stubbornness was a source of disruption throughout Africa, adding greatly to the difficulties of rulers who, like Kaunda, were trying to put their countries on the 'road to unity, peace and freedom' with an equal respect for all races and tribes. It seemed likely that African states would have need of rulers who possessed the personal qualities of men like Kaunda, Nyerere and Kenyatta, for many years to come.

22.4 Guyana

After considerable delay, when there seemed to be a danger that leadership in British Guiana would rest with the Marxist, Cheddi Jagan, Britain finally granted independence to the colony in 1966. The new nation was established with the name of Guyana, under the leadership of Forbes Burnham (who favoured capitalism) and the People's National Congress, who were now in a position to outvote Jagan's People's Party in parliament.

A more important difference between the parties, however, was that of race. Guyana's population was principally Asian, especially Indians, with some negro peoples of African descent. Asians made up about half of the population, Africans about a third, the remainder being Amerindian or of mixed race. It had been Guyana's misfortune that the earliest political parties had been founded mainly on the basis of race, creating problems similar to those which developed in Africa when political parties largely represented tribes. Jagan was of Indian descent, Burnham of African descent. Burnham tended to attract the votes of those of mixed race. Other areas of the West Indies had similar racial mixtures but, in Trinidad, Dr Williams had founded the ruling People's National Movement on a broader base. In the struggle of emergent nations to establish unity it was a grave handicap when political parties were closely identified with the interests of racial or tribal groups, a problem seen at its worst in the general election in Pakistan in 1971.

In Guyana, Burnham was returned to power in the 1968 election in spite of protests by Jagan about vote-rigging. Two years later, the state was declared a republic. The nationalization of the Demerara Bauxite Company in 1971 and the increasing concentration of financial control in the hands of Guyanese showed that the government was increasingly favouring the socialist policies to which many emergent nations turned. Guyana also sought closer relationships with the USSR and China and, in the West Indies, strongly supported the Caribbean Free Trade Area, perhaps with a view to establishing a Common Market. In 1972, Guyana joined Trinidad, Jamaica and Barbados in establishing diplomatic relations with Castro's Cuba in defiance of the wishes of the USA. Exports, mainly of bauxite and sugar, largely financed the country's imports and steady progress was made in electrification, the improvement of communications and land settlement. Like the governments of almost all emergent nations, the Guyanese government worked to expand education and the social services, conscious that such developments could only be spread over a lengthy period of time. Development had, moreover, to be geared to a rapidly-increasing population. But problems such as these were to be found in almost all the new nations. Even though Burnham's administration did much to achieve greater economic stability than had been achieved in the past, racial tension remained and the complete harmonizing of Africans and Indians still remained one of Guyana's most formidable problems.

22.5   Israel

The development of Israel had to take place against the background of disturbed relationships with the neighbouring Arab world (see Section 19.1). The government's aim was to make the state self-supporting but a high level of imports, unmatched by exports, called for considerable skills in management. On the other hand, Israel had an advantage over many emergent nations. Financial assistance came from Jews in many parts of the world and reparations were paid by West Germany, at about £14 million a year up to 1965.

Israel needed both capital and imagination to develop into a modern state, prosperous and powerful enough to resist hostile neighbours. A large part of the country was infertile desert and, although a profitable export trade in diamonds developed, Israel had to depend to a large extent on producing fruit and textiles and on developing the production of oil, discovered in the Negev. About a thousand co-operative villages (*kibbutzim*) were among the imaginative experiments of the Israelis, developing the lands of Palestine like pioneers. Water was supplied to the western Negev from the River Yarkon with a pipeline almost six feet in diameter.

Israel continued to have a small minority of Palestinian Arabs but the state was overwhelmingly Jewish and national unity was encouraged by the hostility of Arab neighbours. It was also encouraged by the government of David Ben-Gurion who gave Israel a solid start as the first Prime Minister. Ben-Gurion was born in Poland, founded Israel's Labour Party (the Mapai), but ruled for many of the years until he resigned in 1963 as head of a coalition

Table 22.1   The trading position of some emergent nations, 1970

Country	Population est. 1971 (millions)	Main Exports % of whole	Exports Mainly to % of whole	Imports Mainly from % of whole	Trade Balance: exports as % of imports
India	547·0	Jute manufactures 13% Tea 8%	USA 16% Japan 12%	USA 27% Britain 8%	93%
Ghana	8·5	Cocoa 64% Timber 8%	Britain 23% USA 18%	Britain 24% USA 18%	110%*†
Kenya	11·7	Coffee 29% Tea 16%	Britain 21% West Germany 10%	Britain 29% Japan 11%	54%
Tanzania	13·3	Coffee 18% Cotton 14%	Britain 22% USA 10%	Britain 21% China 14%	89%
Zambia	4·1	Copper 95%	Britain 26% Japan 24%	Britain 23% South Africa 23%	195%*‡
Guyana	0·8	Bauxite 34% Sugar 27%	USA 29% Britain 19%	Britain 31% USA 23%	99%
Israel	3·0	Diamonds 32% Fruit 16%	USA 19% Britain 10%	USA 22% Britain 16%	54%

* Trade surplus.   † Surplus but debts to be repaid.

‡ 1969, before the fall in price of copper which undermined Zambia's trading position.

(See also Table 18.1 : income per head of the population.)

government. No man did more than he to found and establish the Jewish state.

Ben-Gurion was succeeded by Eshkol, who had been born in Russia and, when Eshkol died, two years later, Mrs Golda Meir became Prime Minister. She had also been born in Russia. For a time she had served as Secretary of the Mapai and thus she continued the mildly left-wing government traditional in Israel since the state was founded. She also had to continue the delicate work of governing in such a way as to balance the demands for social improvement and economic development against the need to maintain strong military power for defence. In 1971, there was growing criticism that too little was being done for Israel's underprivileged, especially the oriental Jews, and that too much emphasis was being placed on foreign policy and defence. Such complaints were silenced when Israel was attacked by the Arabs in the Autumn of 1973. This new war and the constant need for a high level of military spending severely handicapped Israeli development. It was sometimes argued that Israel's own inflexibility after 1967 was a provocation to her Arab neighbours, but Mrs. Meir's government felt quite unable to risk reducing Israel's defences.

22.6   The Tight-rope

Almost every government in the emergent nations is walking on a tight-rope. From this brief consideration of a small selection of states in Asia, Africa, the West Indies and the Middle East, one can see that the emergent nations face formidable though varied problems. Their fundamental needs are to establish a working and stable system of government and to use whatever resources may be available to push forward social and economic development as quickly as possible. But they work under intimidating difficulties. They must try to satisfy the expectations of subjects to whom independence offered both excitement and promise. Often they must work with tiny resources, a serious lack of capital and a shortage of personnel experienced in administration, business, industry and almost every other field. Far more perhaps than in long-established countries, the quality of leadership is of outstanding importance in the emergent nations. This Unit shows that at least some of these nations have been especially fortunate in the choices they have made.

Further Reading

Ayling, S. E.: *Portraits of Power*. Harrap (London, 1965)—Nehru.
Jones, P.: *Kwame Nkrumah and Africa*. Hamish Hamilton (London, 1965).
Nussbaum, E.: *Israel*. Oxford University Press (London, 1968).
Watson, J. B.: *Empire to Commonwealth*. Dent (London, 1971).

Documentary

Breach, R. W.: *Documents and Descriptions, the World Since 1914*. Oxford University Press (London, 1966), Sections 27, 28, 33, 39, 57.

Exercises

1. Why is the progress of economic development slow in the nations mentioned in this Unit? Which of them may be expected to develop most quickly?
2. What does Table 22.1 reveal about the problems of emergent nations?
3. Compare Tables 14.2, 18.1 and 22.1. Explain why the gap between rich and poor nations has recently widened and may be expected to widen further.
4. Outline the history of India since independence, paying particular attention to (a) its political stability, (b) economic problems and (c) social problems. What do you consider to have been the outstanding achievements of India's governments?
5. Why has the history of Ghana been more turbulent than the histories of Kenya, Tanzania and Zambia since independence?
6. What problems common to many emergent nations can be illustrated by reference to Israel and Guyana? What less typical problems do these two nations face?
7. To which of the following nations could you refer in writing outline histories of underdeveloped nations similar to those in this Unit: Guinea; Jamaica; Malawi; Malaysia; New Zealand; Sri Lanka; Sweden?

(See also **Appendix: Into the 1980s,** page 365.)

Unit Twenty-Three
The World in the 1970s

23.1 The Major Powers

In the opening months of 1973, at least part of the world could again find room for a little cautious optimism. Relations between the USA and the USSR were better than at any time since 1945. There were visible signs of improving relations in Europe, springing from Brandt's *Ostpolitik*. Non-communist powers, among them Britain and France, at last recognized East Germany and a new hot-line telephone link was established between the two Germanies. Brandt had managed to reduce much of the tension in the German Problem and when talks between capitalists and communists opened in Helsinki, Germany no longer dominated the agenda. The task at Helsinki was to prepare the way for a conference on European security and co-operation. At the same time, talks were opened in Vienna to discuss the reduction of troops and weapons in central Europe. Immediate agreement seemed unlikely either in Helsinki or Vienna, but the talks themselves represented a further step away from the days of the Cold War.

Cracks had already appeared both in NATO and the Warsaw Pact but the gulf between capitalism and communism remained wide. Both sides now showed interest in reaching agreements, but it was unlikely that these would involve major changes in either Western or Eastern Europe. Nor was there any prospect of the early reunification of Germany. But both capitalists and communists now recognized that the frenzied search for ever-improving weapon systems could have ruinous economic results and that, if quarrels were pushed as far as nuclear war, there could be no victory for either side. Agreements without major sacrifices could therefore be advantageous.

The West was also establishing better relations with communist China. The arrival in Britain of a smiling Chinese ambassador held out the cheerful prospect of increasing friendly contacts, although China continued to be mysteriously remote from the western world, dedicated to paths of progress not easy to understand in industrialized, capitalist societies. As yet, only the first hesitant steps had been taken towards overcoming the barrier of suspicion which existed between the West and China. There was also mystery about Sino-Soviet relationships, with occasional ominous rumblings from the borders between China and Russia. To the outside world, serious divisions seemed to exist between the two largest communist powers. China remained a predominantly agricultural country, closer than either the USSR or the USA to the emergent nations. Already there was speculation that the capitalist/communist division, so prominent in the world after the Second World War, was now giving way to another major division, between the countries rich in advanced technology and those which were poor and underdeveloped. That such a split coincided closely with the split between the white and non-white worlds offered little comfort.

Such optimism as there was was, therefore, cautious. The world was perhaps on the threshold of stabilizing, if not exactly solving, one problem (that of the relationships between the super powers, between capitalism and communism), but the future would surely hold other problems. For the moment, however, China had been admitted to UNO; ambassadors were being exchanged; there were increasing contacts across the Iron Curtain in Europe; the admission of the two Germanies to UNO was close at hand and even the isolation of Cuba was breaking down as governments in the Caribbean and Latin America, led by Guyana and Trinidad, began to recognize Castro. These were hopeful signs of a new realism in international relations.

At the same time, the major powers were not without anxieties. Many of them faced troublesome economic and social problems. The struggle to hold back inflation was widespread. There were troubles with international currencies, involving increasingly frequent adjustments to the values of the US dollar, the Japanese yen, the pound and the currencies of Europe. Many countries were anxious about their exports, fearful that a confrontation over world trade between the USA, the European Common Market and Japan could not long be avoided. The USA seemed likely to lead a movement towards tariffs and protection unless some lasting adjustment could be made to international exchange rates. Nor was the USSR free from economic difficulties. Agricultural yields had often been disappointing, the standard of living lower than the communists would have wished.

Economic problems often added fuel to social problems. Almost everywhere the underprivileged raised their voices in protest. Red Indians as well as negroes protested in the USA. Jews protested in Russia. The aborigines protested in Australia. The students remained turbulent in Japan, and Britain endured a series of bitter industrial disputes, merging with more dismal trade figures and yet another state of emergency at the end of the year.

23.2   The Third World

In spite of their anxieties, the major powers nevertheless grew richer. A much larger number of people in the world were concerned not with the problems of prosperity but with the problems of poverty and underdevelopment. It was especially difficult to break free from poverty in many parts of Africa and in the Indian sub-continent.

Bangladesh survived a year of separate nationhood, but the year ended with serious shortages of food, the result of poor harvests which also affected India. Sheikh Mujib remained a popular ruler: he was again returned to power in March 1973, with a landslide victory. But he had done little to overcome his country's many problems. Many of the problems were beyond immediate solution. At best, it was thought impossible for Bangladesh to produce sufficient food for her population before about 1976 and the population was continuing to grow at an alarming rate. Other problems were political.

Non-Bengalis were still being victimized, the government was frequently accused of corruption, and robbery and murder became almost commonplace.

In West Pakistan, Bhutto had strong support in the Punjab but he too failed to solve his country's outstanding problems and force was used to hold the nation together. Reforms were few and ineffective and dissent, in provinces other than the Punjab, raised fears of a new civil war. Without political stability, real economic progress was impossible. Over a year after the downfall of Yahya Khan, political stability was by no means secure in Pakistan. Bhutto still felt unable to risk further antagonizing the opposition by recognizing Bangladesh, the first essential if Pakistan's relations with India were to be improved and the prisoners of the recent war to be returned.

Under Mrs Gandhi, India continued to have much more political stability than her neighbours. Mrs Gandhi took pride in the fact that her country survived as 'a free democratic nation'. But economic progress was handicapped by the rising population and the world-wide inflation. A break in the monsoon in 1972 wiped out India's food stocks. At that time, the government calculated that there were still over 200 million Indians living in dire poverty. The new economic plan for 1973 required huge sums of capital even to begin to better their lot. Finding that capital itself presented enormous difficulties but it was essential that such plans should succeed if India were ever to achieve even the minimum standards of prosperity. Growth in the early 1970s was disappointing, falling from 7 per cent in 1969 to below 3 per cent in 1971. Such a low rate of development could hardly keep living standards as they were, with the population continuing to increase towards 600 million.

Elsewhere in the world, population pressures were seldom as great as in the Indian sub-continent, but scores of underdeveloped nations faced similar problems in getting together the capital with which to finance expansion and to provide even the basic necessities for all of their people.

23.3   An Age of Violence

Already, by 1973, the 1970s threatened to set new standards as a decade of violence. The ceasefire which officially ended the savage killing in Vietnam brought little peace to that land: unofficial, but just as deadly, the killing went on. The terrible atrocities of the war in Vietnam had established new records in the story of man's inhumanity to man, all the more degrading as the world's richest nation used its air power to pulverize mercilessly the cities of North Vietnam. Alongside the raids of the B-52s, the numerous other atrocities of the 1970s seemed almost insignificant. Yet together they made a dismal picture of intolerance and barbarism.

The Middle East was still one of the most unsettled areas. The Jews shot down an Arab airliner, killing nearly all its passengers, and Israelis continued to raid neighbouring territories to kill guerillas and destroy their bases. Arabs sent letter-bombs by post, hardly discriminating in the victims they killed. Embassies and diplomats were seized, the latter held as hostages and sometimes murdered. Atrocities and reprisals became merged in a grim pattern of cruelty, leading to yet another Arab–Israeli war in October 1973.

Vicious killing also continued in Northern Ireland where explosions and murders became almost daily occurrences. Violence was hardly abated in Bangladesh and other parts of the Indian sub-continent. There were outbreaks of killing in black Africa and disturbances in the West Indies. Even Bermuda was not too remote to be affected and the British governor there was murdered. All over the world, in West Germany, the USA and the developed nations no less than in the emergent nations, the urban guerilla became a familiar figure in the early 1970s.

Nations showed little enthusiasm for a united front against such terrorist activities. Only to their enemies were the guerillas known as terrorists. Their friends regarded them as freedom-fighters, for the roots of the troubles lay in the many problems which the world had failed to solve. Almost nothing had been done to bring justice to the dispossessed Palestinian Arabs, to solve the Irish problem, to settle the futures of Kashmir and Cyprus, to guarantee any sort of future at all to the people of Vietnam and the rest of Indochina. Indeed, hardly any single government could claim with honesty that it had achieved justice and fair shares for all of its subjects. Too often, for reasons of power politics, even the great powers seemed only too willing to condone injustice.

In 1973, southern Africa remained both a problem area and an area towards which the great powers decided their attitudes more on grounds of convenience than on grounds of morality. In spite of frequent controversies, South Africa showed few signs of departing from the policies of apartheid. Around South Africa, other white supremacist regimes remained in power. They were hated by most of the non-white world and reviled by the communists. At the United Nations, they were constantly protected by west Europeans and the USA, preserved as a bulwark against communism, black Africa and non-European civilization or simply as a source of economic profit. An explosion in Africa at some time in the future began to seem increasingly likely. The increasing activities of black African guerillas in northern Rhodesia and in Portugal's colonies suggested, as many had long prophesied, that this area was destined to experience growing violence.

Except for the token renewal of sanctions, still often evaded, nothing effective was done to save the white Rhodesians from themselves. Smith's government moved steadily towards apartheid and tyranny. Collective punishments (imposed on communities without the need to search out individual wrongdoers) were one example of the growing harshness of Rhodesian law. The silencing of Peter Niesewand, a respected journalist, by arrest and secret trial was another. Smith's policies led to a new dispute with Kaunda which further disrupted the economies of both Zambia and Rhodesia. Members of the Commonwealth were quick to offer economic assistance to Zambia and efforts were made to tighten the sanctions against Rhodesia, but the Rhodesian problem, like the problem of southern Africa as a whole, had long been something which much of the world preferred to ignore. Events may yet show that they have been neglecting a time-bomb.

Of course, Rhodesians could claim with justice that there were similar and worse examples of tyranny in some black African states, not least in Uganda where Amin went on shamelessly persecuting the Asians. But such injustices, wherever they were committed, only added to the probability of further violence in the violent 1970s. Amin's policies provoked skirmishes with Tanzania and threatened to undermine the East African Community.

Moreover, political violence was matched by criminal violence. Many cities in the USA became notoriously unsafe after dark, some parts of them unsafe even in daylight. Law-abiding citizens often fell victim to 'mugging', the term often used to describe the activities of thugs who carried out robbery with violence. Few countries in the world were free from rising crime figures and hooliganism. Violence was nothing new in the twentieth century but never had it seemed so widespread and never had it shown itself more frequently in the form of apparently senseless cruelty and destructiveness.

23.4   The Human Environment

Not only was man doing violence to man in the 1970s; there was a growing awareness that he was also doing violence to his environment. In 1971, the population of the world was approaching 3 750 million and it was growing at about 2 per cent a year. This growth was itself a reason for anxiety, but at the same time there was concern about the ways in which human beings were polluting their environment and using up the earth's resources.

(a) Population

The most rapid expansion of population was occurring in Asia. Already, in the 1970s, over half of the world's people were Asians, living on about a fifth of the world's land surface. Such was the rate of increase that from about 2 000 million in 1973, Asia's population was likely to rise to nearly 3 000 million by the late 1980s. India's population was growing at 2·6 per cent a year and seemed likely to reach about 800 million by 1985. Birth control programmes so far achieved only limited success. The birth rate, in the early 1970s, was 42 per 1 000 of the population, the death rate 17 per thousand. The rate at which India's population was expanding was by no means the fastest in the world— it was higher than that of any country in Europe but lower than that of many

Fig. 23.1 India's campaign to reduce the birth rate, 1966

states in the Middle East and of some states in Africa—but it was a grave threat to India's future development and her efforts to break free from poverty.

In general, the population of countries already wealthy grew more slowly, but hardly anywhere was population actually diminishing. With increasing wealth, the rich countries could support a growing population although discomfort seemed likely in areas already densely-populated. The annual increase in population in the USA and the USSR was only about 1 per cent a year. In Britain and many parts of Europe it was below 1 per cent. The main problems here were not the problems which arose from feeding the hungry but those which arose from crowded urban living. In Africa, there was room for expansion. Population growth rates were generally higher and it seemed probable that by 1985 Africa's population would for the first time exceed that of Europe. It was essential, however, that African states should outstrip their population growth with economic growth if they were ever to achieve prosperity. But in India and many other parts of Asia, all the problems combined. Cities such as Calcutta were already dreadfully overcrowded; reserves of land were dangerously low and economic problems such that even a large part of the existing population lived in misery and poverty from which it became increasingly difficult to escape as the population expanded. This was a dilemma to which the world had no immediate solution in 1973.

The growth of population in areas such as India, Pakistan and Indonesia threatened to combine with economic and social discontents to undermine political stability. There were also fears that, just as population pressures increased Japan's aggressiveness in the 1930s, the changing balance of the world's population might cause international problems in the future. The Russians half-suspected that China might wish to expand into the underpopulated areas of the USSR. Africa and Latin America were likely soon to outstrip in manpower Europe and North America. Non-whites already outnumbered whites and the gap was certain to grow wider. The implications of these changes were yet only dimly perceived in 1973.

(b) Pollution

The rich nations sometimes regarded the rapid growth of population as a problem mainly for the poor about which they would prefer to remain ignorant. It was nevertheless a fact, in the early 1970s, that a child born in the USA was likely to consume during his lifetime twenty times as much as a child born in India, and that he would contribute about fifty times as much to the pollution of the environment. In 1972, a conference of over a hundred nations met in Stockholm to discuss environmental problems. It was a belated recognition of the fact that man was steadily destroying the 'air, water, land, flora and fauna' around him and rapidly consuming some of the earth's most important resources.

(i) **The problems.** Technological progress was much to blame for the damage to the environment. Industrial plant consumed large quantities of fuel and raw materials. Industry also produced suffocating smoke and poisonous gases and deposited dangerous and unsightly waste in rivers, in the sea and on land. Developments in nuclear power not only produced deadly radioactive fall-out when weapons were tested but also such dangerous by-products that nuclear power stations were introduced far more slowly than had been expected. By the 1970s there was great anxiety about the relentless march of technology. Poisonous discharges into rivers upset the balance of nature and killed fish. Dangerous deposits on land, for example of cyanide, threatened immeasurable hazards to the future generations, adding to the concern felt by present generations about the use of pesticides on crops and their effects on human and animal life. Even the seas became increasingly contaminated, a dump for all manner of waste produce and endlessly polluted by oil. Holiday resorts cried out in alarm as oil, sewage and growing amounts of rubbish floated on to their beaches, but the greatest danger lay in the possibility that the seas would become more and more hostile to life until the oceans became as dead as was already the case with many rivers in the industrialized countries.

For millions who lived in cities, smog (a suffocating mixture of smoke, fumes and fog) was already a serious hazard. To the fumes produced by industry and crowded dwellings were added the exhaust gases of countless motor vehicles. Diseases such as bronchitis and lung cancer took a heavy toll of city dwellers and the impure air drove some of them to wearing masks and even to seeking refreshing breaths of oxygen in order to survive. Tokyo and Los Angeles seemed to present a bleak picture of the fate in store for cities everywhere if steps were not urgently taken to restore fresh air to the people.

Meanwhile, the world became anxious about future supplies of vital commodities such as oil. In spite of the discovery of new oil fields, for example under the North Sea, petroleum products were by no means certain to outlast the twentieth century. Utterly dependent on their motor vehicles, the citizens of the developed world viewed the prospect with alarm. As oil began to grow more scarce it also began to grow more expensive, raising questions which could prove serious for the economies of all nations. Technological development itself was often extremely costly. By 1973, many of the world's airlines were in financial difficulties, facing mounting costs as aircraft grew more sophisticated. Few felt able to afford the purchase of Concorde, the Anglo-French supersonic airliner; the probable costs of operating Concorde with even more expensive fuel raised new doubts about technological advancement and supersonic flight.

Concorde had already aroused criticism. There was growing concern not only about the pollution of the air, water and land but about the noise which went hand in hand with development. The roar of traffic, aircraft and of all kinds of machinery and the spreading plague of transistor radios made people sensitive to new sources of disturbance. Supersonic flight seemed likely to be banned over considerable areas of the earth.

(*ii*) **The search for solutions.** It was against this background that the conference met in Stockholm to discuss environmental problems. The underdeveloped nations were as interested in environmental problems as the wealthy nations. They had no intention of accepting any solution which involved calling a halt to development which alone would enable them to escape from their poverty. But they were well aware of the problems which uncontrolled development had already created. Some of the African states were already taking great care to preserve wild life, so often threatened with extinction since the invention of the gun and the growth of markets for ivory, skins and furs. They were willing to contribute to the general care for the environment but they insisted at the same time on their right to attempt to catch up. The British representative in Stockholm expressed what must be the general aim for both rich and poor, when he said: 'We believe that the pressing need is to create more of the right kind of wealth and to use it much more wisely: to clean up rivers, to quieten engines, and above all, on a global scale, to get rid of poverty, illiteracy and disease.' There would be no abandonment of development, no retreat from technology, but the conference sought to lay down the guidelines for a co-operative effort simultaneously to protect the environment.

No master-plan could be agreed. The problems were too big for immediate solution and the nations were often in disagreement. China wanted to place the blame for pollution on 'the plunder and aggression of imperialism and colonialism' and suggested the total abolition of nuclear weapons. When neither proposal was accepted, China refused to sign the rather vague Declaration in which the members of the conference expressed their intention to protect and improve the environment and guard against the exhaustion of 'the non-renewable resources of the earth'. Neither China nor France was willing to cease testing nuclear weapons in the atmosphere. Japan insisted on reserving the right to hunt whale, indifferent to the survival of the species. Other countries, too, safeguarded what they considered to be their special interests.

But the conference was not a failure. Problems were recognized which the world could no longer ignore. There were a number of specific agreements on the protection of plants and animals, on monitoring the atmosphere and the seas and on surveying the earth's resources. But it would be left to governments to carry them out, subject perhaps to a Council of Environmental Programmes if the United Nations could agree to create one. Before the end of 1972 some further limited progress was made when over fifty nations agreed not to dump in the sea certain categories of waste.

It seemed reasonable to hope that such agreements would multiply. In the late twentieth century, the world was changing rapidly and many of its problems were too big for nations to solve individually. The great powers were in a mood for agreements in the early 1970s. Too often, however, they would not make agreements in any way hurtful to themselves. It was at least encouraging that at Stockholm they had met to discuss the problems of mankind and to recognize that there existed 'only one earth'.

Further Reading

Jenkins, I. M. L.: *Science and Technology*. Hamish Hamilton (London, 1966).
Jones, C., Gadler, S. J. and Engstrom, P. H.: *Pollution: The Population Explosion*. Dent (London, 1972).
'Population Growth' (Folder), VCOAD Education Unit.
Richardson, R. (ed): *Learning for Change in World Society*. World Studies Project (London, 1976).

Exercises

1. Why were the great powers 'in a mood for agreements' in the early 1970s?
2. In what ways was the rapid growth of population in the second half of the twentieth century important?
3. What do you understand by *environmental pollution*?
4. Explain the improvements which took place in the early 1970s in the relationships of the great powers. On what issues is there still division today (*a*) between the USA and the USSR and (*b*) between China and other major powers?
5. Explain why there was increasing concern about the environment at the beginning of the 1970s. What action has been taken to deal with environmental problems?
6. List the environmental problems which exist in your community. What action is being taken to deal with them?
7. Oil began to grow 'more scarce' and 'more expensive' (page 362). What facts illustrate the truth of this statement?
8. In what ways have the agreements mentioned in Units Seventeen and Twenty-Three been extended since this book was published?

(See also **Appendix: Into the 1980s,** page 365.)

Appendix: Into the 1980s

It was with apprehension rather than confidence that the world entered the 1980s. Far from slackening, the speed of change in the modern world seemed only to accelerate. In the short time since this book was written, the late 1970s had already seen many upheavals; and the *Guardian* cartoonist Les Gibbard expressed a common fear that the world's 'Destination' in the 1980s was 'Unknown'. Neither the British downstairs passengers on Gibbard's bus, nor the international statesman travelling upstairs, could view the 1980s with much enthusiasm. Already an economic crisis was almost universal. The 'Energy Crunch' had brought rises in the price of oil which were beginning to reflect its growing scarcity. Inflation was widespread, and it was often accompanied by recession and soaring unemployment. Even the USA faced formidable economic difficulties, and the plight of many Third-World nations

'Good luck Kid—and by the way, there don't seem to be any brakes!'

was desperate. Economists debated whether Keynesian solutions were any longer appropriate to the many-headed problems of capitalist economies, and there was a revival of the philosophy that governments should play a much smaller part in economic and social management. Milton Friedman was one of the principal spokesmen for this doctrine of non-intervention, though the non-intervention was to be accompanied by tight control of a country's money supply, to curb inflation. Those governments which practised this monetarist theory – like the Conservative government headed by Margaret Thatcher which came to power in Britain in 1979 – worked to reduce government spending and, at least in the short term, a harsh economic climate and further increases in unemployment seemed inevitable. In the late 1970s unemployment in Britain had already almost reached the dismal levels of the inter-war years, though it now went hand-in-hand with persistent inflation. For a time pressure on the pound caused its exchange rate against the dollar to drop to around 1 : 1.60, towards the end of 1976. The weakness of the dollar then caused the pound to recover to a rate of about 1 : 2.00 dollars in the autumn of 1978. Almost at once, however, Britain faced a new problem. North Sea oil, which seemed likely to make the United Kingdom almost self-sufficient in oil in the 1980s – at least for a time – created artificial confidence in the pound. Its exchange value climbed well above 1 : 2.00 dollars. This added to the problems of selling British exports, thus increasing unemployment and creating severe balance-of-payments difficulties (compare Table 13.2 on page 211).

Britain was only one of many countries which wrestled with the problems of a world economic order which was now seriously out of balance. But the world faced political upheavals too. The long struggle in Vietnam ended with a communist victory which was quickly extended to Laos and Cambodia, but there was little peace in Indochina after the withdrawal of the US forces. A brief conflict occurred between Vietnam and China; and there was another conflict between Vietnam and Kampuchea (Cambodia), where the excesses of the Khmer Rouge under Pol Pot brought the country near to paralysis and starvation. There were wars and upheavals too in many parts of Africa, though some progress was made towards transferring power to black Africans in the states where white supremacy had flourished. The Portuguese empire collapsed in the mid-1970s, and the independent states of Angola and Mozambique rose from the ruins. With these states now under black leadership there was a sudden new urgency about the problem of Rhodesia. Black nationalists stepped up the guerilla warfare against the white-minority régime there. This in turn triggered off new diplomatic efforts to arrive at a settlement, with the result that black rule was at last introduced and Britain found it possible to make a grant of legal independence in 1980.

Dramatic changes also occurred in the Middle East. The Yom Kippur War of 1973 led to energetic diplomatic activity, some limited measures of agreement, and a bold initiative for peace by President Sadat of Egypt. But relations between Israel and its other Arab neighbours improved hardly at all and, meantime, there were new crises in the Lebanon. Another crisis erupted in Iran. After a Moslem uprising against his western-dominated government, the Shah of Iran was driven into exile in 1979. A Moslem religious leader, the Ayatollah Khomeini, in turn went back to Iran from exile, inspiring his countrymen to a revolutionary and anti-western fervour, one result of which was the seizure of the US embassy in Teheran by radical students, and the holding in captivity for over a year of some fifty American hostages. The students hoped to force the USA to ensure that the Shah returned to Iran, to stand trial for crimes against his people. Negotiations achieved little at all, and in desperation early in 1980 the US government resorted to economic sanctions against Iran and to a military raid which failed dismally. It was President Carter, successful in the American presidential election of 1976, who had to wrestle with this dilemma, and he had problems too in Afghanistan, next door to Iran. Towards the end of 1979 Afghanistan was invaded by Russian forces. The West regarded this as an act of naked aggression, though the Russians claimed that they had been invited to assist the Afghan government against sedition. The Russians were also worried by the upsurge of Moslem religious enthusiasm which was occurring in Iran and were anxious, perhaps, to prevent any similar development in Afghanistan, which might unsettle the substantial Moslem population of the Soviet Union. The result increased tension in international relations so much that a revival of the East–West Cold War seemed likely in the 1980s.

Meanwhile, many countries experienced changes of leadership. Richard Nixon was disgraced in the USA, and the Republicans lost the presidential election of 1976. Mao Tse-tung died that year, and a new generation of leaders took control of China. In the Soviet Union there was growing speculation in the late 1970s as to how long Brezhnev might continue to rule, and as to who would succeed him. President Tito, another veteran leader, died in 1980, amid speculation as to Jugoslavia's future. Other veterans also died, among them Franco, Haile Selassie, Chiang Kai-shek and Archbishop Makarios. Some rulers were deposed – some, such as Amin of Uganda, without regrets. In India Mrs Gandhi and the Congress Party were defeated in the general election of 1977, amid a storm of protest that she had abandoned democracy, resorted to emergency rule, and even used compulsory sterilization in an effort to check India's rising population. But Mrs Gandhi made a remarkable return to power when public opinion swung in her favour and she won another general election in 1979. In Britain Mrs Thatcher also won a general election in 1979, ousting Callaghan's Labour government and becoming Britain's first woman Prime Minister.

In the sections which follow we shall look at the principal developments which have occurred in world affairs since the beginning of 1974. The sections are arranged to correspond with the postwar Units of this book.

Unit Eleven

The *United Nations Organization* continued to grow in size with the admission to membership of more newly-independent states. Mozambique and Surinam joined in 1975, Angola a year later and, in 1978, membership exceeded 150 with the admission of Dominica, a former British island in the West Indies. The Organization also set up a new specialized agency, the World Food Council, to tackle the problem of feeding the poorer nations. The USA and the major powers were sometimes disconcerted by the growing number of emergent nations in the UN. Though the countries of the Third World seldom worked in close harmony with one another, they could at times unite in opposition to the richer nations who often seemed unsympathetic to the plight of the poor. The Afro-Asian countries were especially hostile to South Africa and to Israel. In 1974 the UN General Assembly voted temporarily to suspend South Africa's membership, critical not only of the continuance of apartheid but of South Africa's continuing hold on Namibia. In the following year South Africa itself defiantly boycotted the General Assembly in retaliation. Meanwhile, a UN resolution was passed which equated Zionism with racism, and the USA often found itself embarrassed in the face of fierce Afro-Asian criticism of its Israeli ally. The great powers generally found that they could no longer easily get their own way in an association where Americans and Europeans might now be outnumbered (see page 341).

On the other hand, the non-aligned movement of emergent nations who wished to steer clear of the rivalries of the great powers, found itself in difficulties towards the end of the 1970s. A deep split developed in the movement between those countries such as Cuba, which argued that non-alignment actually meant alignment with the socialist countries, including the Soviet Union, and others such as Jugoslavia, which aimed to keep an equal distance from both the Soviet bloc and the US capitalist bloc.

Unit Twelve

Brezhnev increasingly imposed his personal stamp on the *Soviet Union* as the 1970s went on. Kosygin remained the Soviet Prime Minister until 1980, but Podgorny resigned the presidency in 1977. Brezhnev's authority seemed undisputed, however, and he was personally associated with the new constitution which in 1977 replaced that drafted by Stalin in 1936. The new constitution did little to change the Russian system of government. But there seemed in some ways to be movement away from the comparatively liberal years of Khrushchev's rule. Stalin's tyranny was no longer denounced, and civil liberties seemed to be under a greater threat. Attention centred on Russian dissidents and their counterparts in eastern Europe, for example in Czechoslovakia. Some of these dissidents made themselves the spokesmen for Human Rights, and they embarrassed the communist authorities by keeping up a running commentary on the failures of the latter to carry out the agreements on Human Rights, which had been reached at Helsinki in the Conference on Security and Co-operation in Europe in 1975 (see Section 23.1). The western world strongly supported the dissidents' stand and it was sometimes argued that western opinion helped to shield the dissidents from savage punishment. In fact trials were held, and at least some of the dissidents such as Yuri Orlov were imprisoned. The communists regarded the dissidents as capitalist lackeys, and the apparent enthusiasm of President Carter of the USA for civil liberties in the Soviet Union and eastern Europe perhaps did more to embitter than to ease the situation.

Russian economic development was handicapped by a disastrous grain harvest in 1975, but there was come recovery in later years. Eastern Europe made considerable economic progress during the 1970s, and both the Soviet Union and its satellites expanded their trade with the outside world. The political and economic organization of the communist states cushioned them to some extent against the economic problems which beset the western world, but there was nevertheless evidence in the late 1970s that some problems were being shared. Inflation began to affect east European economies, such as that of Hungary. Moreover, the Russians were forced into a more urgent search for new supplies of oil with which to supply the needs of the communist bloc. Oil prices were raised, though countries such as Cuba still received Russian oil at prices well below those of the world generally. By western standards, communist states still expanded their supplies of consumer goods only modestly, and they continued to practise the close control of their economies – to avoid unemployment, for example, partly by the direction of labour. But East Germany seemed to be just one of the countries of eastern Europe which had begun to achieve marked increases in its standard of living.

At the time of the suppression of dissent in Czechoslovakia in 1968 (see Section 12.4(c)), the 'Brezhnev Doctrine' proclaimed the right of socialist states to intervene where an established socialist system was in danger of being overthrown. The 1970s were comparatively quiet in eastern Europe, and Brezhnev had no need again to invoke his Doctrine. It seemed nevertheless to have begun to be accepted that the east Europeans could pursue their own socialist roads to communism. Under President Ceausescu Rumania especially insisted on this degree of independence. The Rumanians led other east Europeans in increasing trade links with the West, almost 10 per cent of Rumanian exports in 1976 going to West Germany, half as much as went to Russia. Ceausescu also showed some inclination openly to criticize Russian foreign policy, especially when Afghanistan was invaded. At times it seemed that Rumania was threatening to follow in the footsteps of Tito's Jugoslavia, in pursuit of some sort of non-alignment. Meanwhile, however, Brezhnev was by 1976 seeking to improve Russian relations with Jugoslavia, and there were even moments when Russia's relations with Albania seemed likely to improve. Albania became disenchanted with China during 1978, finding lesser men in control there after the death of Mao Tse-tung, but Albania was in any case of little significance in international affairs. Greater uncertainties in 1980 concerned the future of Jugoslavia, after more than thirty-five years of personal rule by Tito; and the future course of events in the Soviet Union, when the time should finally come for Brezhnev to retire. Only Stalin had dominated Russian affairs longer than had Brezhnev, and it remained to be seen whether Brezhnev could arrange for power in the Soviet Union to pass to one of his own nominees.

Unit Thirteen

There was considerable political turmoil in the *USA* in the years 1974–6. In 1974 American politics were dominated by the Watergate Scandal (see Glossary). President Nixon was pressed relentlessly to produce the tapes of conversations in the White House, and it was confidently expected that these tapes would reveal the extent of his own complicity in the Watergate break-in. Arguments about the production of the tapes led to accusations that Nixon was engaged in a 'cover-up', and further murky details came to light about the President's private life, including matters of tax evasion. Impeachment seemed extremely likely and, to escape this final indignity, Nixon resigned in August 1974. Gerald R. Ford, who had only recently replaced the disgraced Agnew as Vice-President, now found himself in office as President, and he lost at least some of the sympathies of the American public when he promptly granted Nixon a full pardon. The affairs of Watergate and of the tapes had discredited Washington politicians generally. Rumours abounded, and even Henry Kissinger, the energetic Republican Secretary of State (for Foreign Affairs), only narrowly escaped involvement. Nor were these the only scandals. There was increasing anxiety in the USA about the activities of the Central Intelligence Agency (CIA).

A new presidential election was due in 1976 and Ford seemed certain to face problems in seeking to retain office for the Republicans. The Democrats had already won sweeping victories in the mid-term elections of 1974. The Republican difficulties were now made even worse by economic crises. In common with many other countries the USA was grappling with inflation, the energy crisis and recession. Ford had had only limited success in trying to curb rising prices and rising unemployment. Jimmy Carter, the Democrat candidate for the presidency, had plenty of targets to attack, and he also made much of his own previous remoteness from the corruption in Washington. A peanut-grower from Georgia, he appealed to anti-Washington sentiment but, in the event, Ford did remarkably well, winning 48 per cent of the popular vote. Carter was nevertheless elected, and Table 13.1 on page 202 may now be extended as follows:

1976	Carter (D)	297	241	D

The USA now had a Democrat President as well as a House of Representatives in which the Democrats were dominant

Carter showed a particular commitment to the solution of international problems. Cyrus Vance replaced Kissinger as the Secretary of State, and Andrew Young was made US Ambassador to the United Nations. Young was a campaigner for civil rights, and as a Negro found no difficulty in identifying with the aspirations of black Africans and with many of those in the Third World. His appointment was popular with black Americans, but his enthusiasm sometimes ran ahead of his tactfulness. His habit of stepping on diplomatic toes made him the delight of newspapermen and cartoonists, but Carter felt obliged to dismiss him in 1979. Although care was taken to ensure that his

A cartoonist's view of the diplomatic progress of Andrew Young

replacement was also black, it seemed likely that Carter would lose black votes when he sought re-election in 1980, for forcing from office so popular an ambassador.

Continuing economic problems dogged Carter's presidency, and opinion polls soon showed that many Americans were disillusioned with their new leader. Too often the White House now gave the impression of fumbling incompetence, although there were some successes in foreign affairs. Carter played a major part in building reconciliation between Egypt and Israel, he continued to improve America's relations with China, and he negotiated a treaty whereby the USA would eventually withdraw from controlling the Panama Canal. But his interest in civil rights and moral causes helped to undermine relations with the Soviet Union and, by 1980, he seemed to be presiding over the rebirth of the Cold War. While he struggled to deal with the crisis in Iran (see page 367), he bitterly condemned Russian actions in Afghanistan and demanded a boycott of the Moscow Olympics. His outspokenness seemed at first to win back some popular support, but by the spring of 1980 Carter badly needed some tangible successes if he were to make sure of re-election to the presidency. He suffered further setbacks when Vance resigned after the unsuccessful raid on Iran, and when it was revealed that the President's brother Billy Carter, had been involved in financial dealings with Libya. In November 1980, Carter was heavily defeated in the presidential election by the Republican, Ronald Reagan.

Britain meanwhile went fron one economic crisis to another. 1974 began with a state of emergency and, as a result of the energy crisis and industrial disputes, a three-day working week. Edward Heath went to the country in a general election, but the Conservatives were defeated. Harold Wilson returned to office as Prime Minister at the head of a minority Labour government, which won a tiny overall majority in October 1974 in a second election – the first time since 1910 that Britain had two general elections in a single year. Wilson retired in 1976 and leadership of the Labour government passed to James Callaghan. Electoral defeat had sealed the fate of Edward Heath, and the Conservatives replaced him as leader with Margaret Thatcher. It was Mrs Thatcher who therefore led the Conservatives to victory in the next general election of 1979, when Labour suffered unpopularity with the voters as the result of economic difficulties and renewed industrial unrest.

Wilson, Callaghan and Denis Healey, the Chancellor of the Exchequer from 1974 to 1979, made some progress in dealing with the immediate economic crises, but the late 1970s were difficult years. Before the tide was turned inflation reached an annual rate of over 20 per cent. In the mid-1970s there was a large balance-of-payments deficit, and unemployment climbed ominously. The pound also sank for a time (see page 366). In an effort to curb inflation, the Labour government worked out a 'social contract' with the trade unions, part of which made provision for the control of wage increases. But the contract worked imperfectly, and the government had again to impose a pay policy. Although this and other measures began to bring improvements after 1977, there were still a million and a quarter unemployed and inflation remained high enough to fuel demands for greater wage increases than the government wanted. The result was a series of industrial conflicts in the winter of 1978–9. Labour's claim to some special expertise in handling industrial relations suffered a serious setback. It was argued that North Sea oil, the first of which had been brought ashore in 1975, might at last give Britain a chance to achieve economic health in the 1980s, and Callaghan dearly wanted to win the election of 1979. But the voters were embittered by strikes and by the struggles of the 1970s, and they again demanded a change. The Conservatives promised a change of direction (see page 366), but the 1980s nevertheless opened with inflation again rising to an annual 20 per cent, unemployment exceeding two million, further balance-of-payments problems, and now unprecedentedly high interest rates too.

The state of the economy was inevitably the dominant theme in British affairs in the 1970s and early 1980s. Much of the Labour legislation was concerned with economic reorganization, including the nationalization of ship-building. Britain's weak competitive position in world markets lay at the root of the country's problems: investment and productivity were comparatively low, and production costs comparatively high, and no government since 1945 had apparently been able to make any real breakthrough in curing this underlying weakness. Yet most British people had enjoyed a steadily rising standard of living since the late 1940s – prosperity, it was alleged, which had not fully been earned. The Labour governments of 1974 to 1979 also concerned themselves with social measures. In education strong encouragement was given to the movement towards comprehensive schools. The Sex Discrimination Act of 1975 aimed to promote more equal opportunities for women, and another Race Relations Act in 1976 the more equal treatment of

Britain's ethnic minorities. There were further developments of the social-security system, with a more elaborate arrangement for earnings-related pensions, and child benefits to replace the earlier family allowances. In response to the rise of Scottish and Welsh Nationalist parties, an attempt was also made to introduce regional parliaments in Scotland and Wales but, at least for the time being, these came to nothing.

The furious arguments which raged in the late 1970s about Home Rule for Scotland and Wales, and the industrial conflict which erupted from time to time, seemed part of some general unrest in British society. The high level of unemployment threatened a return to the 1930s, with some areas of the United Kingdom deep in depression. Social disorder increasingly worried the authorities, and there seemed to be a general escalation of violence, both by criminals and by hooligans. Race relations continued to cause anxiety. Many of the unemployed were non-white, and it was particularly difficult for non-white school-leavers to obtain work. West Indian youngsters grew especially resentful of a society which seemed to condemn many of them to sub-standard housing in the inner cities and to dismal prospects for advancement. The British were shocked by a sudden outburst of violence in Bristol early in 1980, in an area with little history of racial conflict. There was still intermittent argument about the immigration laws, though others were more concerned with the promotion of equality and tolerance, and with constructive efforts to build a multicultural society in a Britain which now had permanent and substantial ethnic minorities. Yet race relations in Britain were far from being acrimonious. Small extremist groups like the National Front nevertheless preached racial hatred with a bigoted frenzy which many found reminiscent of pre-war fascism. Indeed an Anti-Nazi League came into existence to combat the activities of the National Front. Disastrous election results showed that the National Front held little appeal for the majority of British voters, and the party was unable to win a single parliamentary seat in the general election of 1979. On the other hand, the level of lawlessness in Britain was such that the new Thatcher government felt it necessary to exempt the police from the widespread cuts in public spending which were part of the new economic policy of the early 1980s.

Unit Fourteen

Western Europe faced economic problems similar to those of the USA and Britain. The German Federal Republic coped with them with considerable success, but Italy, like Britain, struggled. The Italian Communist Party remained strong, and seemed several times to be almost within reach of winning control of the Italian government. But Italy faced ruthless extremist groups, well to the left of the Communist Party, as well as a continuing neo-fascist movement on the extreme right. Europe, like the rest of the world, was prey to innumerable acts of violent brutality, and Italy had rather more than its share of such outrages. In 1978 the Red Brigade gloried in the kidnapping and murder of Italy's veteran statesman, Aldo Moro and, in the following year, the island of Sardinia won special renown as a place for kidnapping and holding to ransom. French and West German politics remained more stable than those of Italy, where it was sometimes difficult to form any government at all, and which in 1980 had its forty-third government since 1943. Pompidou died in April 1974 and Giscard d'Estaing was elected as French President, narrowly defeating the left-wing François Mitterrand. Giscard had formerly been the Minister of Finance. A month after Pompidou's death, Willy Brandt resigned as the Chancellor of West Germany, following the discovery on his staff of an East German spy. The Social Democrats remained in power, and Brandt was succeeded by Helmut Schmidt. Both Giscard in France and Schmidt in West Germany remained in power during the rest of the 1970s, providing a continuity which few other west European states could match.

The *EEC* could produce no dramatic solutions to the economic problems of its members. EEC affairs were often uneasy, and Britain in particular seemed to have doubts about the benefits of membership. Wilson's government went through the motions of renegotiating the transitional arrangements under which Britain had taken up membership. Only minor changes were secured, but these were approved by the British people in a referendum in June 1975. Sixty-seven per cent of those who voted preferred to remain within the EEC. By the late 1970s, however, disillusionment was widespread, and the turnout of British voters was almost derisory when the first elections to a European Parliament were held in 1979. By that time Britain was at the end of the transitional arrangements, and the full contribution had to be made to the EEC budget. The British complained bitterly that they paid the largest contribution, though all the members of the EEC except Italy and Ireland were producing greater wealth per head of population than was the UK. EEC imports flooded into Britain, and there was little evidence that Britain gained any similar advantages in exporting to Europe. Thatcher's government came to power in Britain determined to seek some reduction in Britain's payments to EEC funds. The French in particular were unsympathetic, and the haggling was sometimes acrimonious. Meanwhile, the EEC was slow to settle urgent problems such as that of Europe's fisheries, and the British fishing industry faced such competition that it declined sharply. The EEC had nevertheless signed the Lomé Agreement in 1975, undertaking to assist 46 countries of the Third World with investment-aid, guarantees concerning commodity prices, and trade preferences in European markets. There were some grounds for optimism in this concern of the wealthy for some of the poorer nations, but the Brandt Report in 1980 showed that far more was still needed to bridge the wealth gap between North and South (see Unit Eighteen below).

Unit Fifteen

China introduced a new constitution in 1975 and then another in 1978. They both left power with the National People's Congress, the State Council and, above all, with the leadership of the Communist Party. That of 1975 reaffirmed support for the guiding philosophy of Mao Tse-tung, but it allowed Chinese workers to pursue some small-scale free enterprise. Almost at once, it seemed that Mao began to plan a new campaign against revisionism and to look forward to a second Cultural Revolution. He died, however, in 1976. Chou En-lai had also died earlier in the year. Chou, China's veteran and moderate Prime Minister, might well have succeeded Mao had he lived. Another veteran, Chu Teh, also died in 1976. There had long been interest in the traditional struggle among the leaders of the Chinese Communist Party between moderates and radicals, and now that interest quickened. Mao's widow, the actress Chiang Ching, led the radicals, and seemed likely to benefit from the deaths of moderates such as Chou and Chu Teh. But her influence was nevertheless resisted, and a new generation of Chinese leaders outmanoeuvred Chiang Ching and the radical 'Gang of Four' she led. By the end of 1977, Mao's mantle fell on Hua Kuo-feng, who was elected Chairman of the Communist Party, having already succeeded Chou as Prime Minister. Teng Hsiao-ping was Vice-Premier, though by 1980 it began to seem that Teng was more influential than Hua. Teng had been reinstated after earlier disfavour, and the triumph of the moderates seemed to be confirmed in the new constitution of 1978, which made more references than usual to individual freedom and to legal rights in China.

China showed an increasing interest in trading links with the West, and in improving diplomatic relations with Europe and the USA. Hua travelled extensively, and further diplomatic and commercial missions to China were welcomed. In 1978 China at last signed a peace treaty with Japan, more than thirty years after the Second World War had ended, and Japan, too, scrambled for the new markets which seemed to be about to open up in China. In 1979 Carter at last gave full recognition to the rule of the Communist Party in China, and China seemed to have few remaining enemies at all except for the Soviet Union. Some cautious attempts were made to improve relations between Peking and Moscow, but they continued to suffer setbacks. China fought a brief war with Vietnam in 1979, regarding Vietnam by this time as a Soviet satellite, and the Chinese vigorously condemned the Russian aim of 'hegemony' when Soviet troops moved into Afghanistan later that year. Such anti-Russian postures delighted the Americans and Margaret Thatcher, whom Moscow had long ago dubbed the 'Iron Lady' for her hostility to the Kremlin, but there were nevertheless those in the West who warned of the danger of putting too much trust in the 'China card' in the international poker game. China developed in ways which seemed pleasing to the West during the 1970s, and it was now China which seemed more easily to co-exist with the USA than did the Soviet Union. Great-power relations continued nevertheless to be triangular – the USA, the Soviet Union and China at the three corners. There could be no certainty in the light of the history of the postwar world that cordial relations between any two of them would be long-lasting.

Taiwan remained independent of China. The death of Chiang Kai-shek in 1975 and the improvement in relations between China and the USA weakened Taiwan's diplomatic position, but there seemed no immediate threat from Peking to the island's security. In the meantime, Taiwan was increasingly successful in marketing its exports, achieving, like *South Korea*, above-average growth in spite of international economic problems. *North Korea*, on the other hand, seemed to be plagued with uncertainties about the succession to Kim Il-sung whose health caused anxiety, and the North Korean economy seemed less buoyant.

Cuba too had economic problems, partly the result of continuing over-dependence on sugar and some poor yields. Castro's government continued to make use of strict economic controls, and the Soviet Union continued to help support the Cuban economy. Castro showed no inclination to change the direction of his social revolution within Cuba. Abroad, Cuba began to win more acceptance among its neighbours. Guyana and the English-speaking islands of the Caribbean took the lead in the mid-1970s in resuming economic and diplomatic relations with Cuba, and the Organization of American States lifted its boycott of Cuban trade. Some patchy improvement also occurred in Castro's relations with the USA. American senators and businessmen visited Havana and, in 1977, American tourists were again allowed to visit Cuba. President Carter nevertheless remained deeply suspicious of Castro. The Caribbean and central America showed various indications of swinging to the left. A number of right-wing governments were toppled, for example in Grenada and Nicaragua, and the influence of Castroism continued to worry Washington. In spite of Cuba's own problems, Castro continued to pledge aid to less prosperous countries and to challenge established conventions. Showing perhaps less interest in Latin America than in the days of Che Guevara, Castro turned instead to Africa, where his activities again embarrassed the USA (see Unit 16 below).

Chile remained firmly under the control of the military junta which had overthrown Allende, and General Pinochet showed few signs of relaxing his repressive regime. Pinochet and Castro seemed to represent the opposite extremes in the affairs of Latin America and the Caribbean. Although there was nothing democratic about Pinochet's Chile, there was no doubt which the USA preferred. Chile's economic system remained capitalist and, with American help, the junta made some progress towards curbing Chile's roaring inflation and towards developing the economy. Pinochet's regime was detested almost universally in left-wing circles, however. Memories of 1973 remained strong and, in countries such as Britain, the question of dealings with Chile was always likely to spark off fierce controversy.

Unit Sixteen

European colonial empires had already largely disappeared by 1974. Much of what was left disappeared in the later 1970s. Newly independent nations joined the United Nations Organization, as did Surinam, which became independent of the Netherlands West Indies in 1975. Those which had been British also joined the Commonwealth, whose membership exceeded forty in 1980. Among the new members were Papua New Guinea (previously a Trust Territory in the charge of Australia), the Seychelles, the Solomon Islands, Dominica and Kiribati (formerly the Gilbert Islands). Many such new nations were comparatively tiny, but more important states were still emerging from the decolonization of European empires in Africa.

Africa was affected by changes in Europe. The death of Franco in 1975 led to extensive change in Spain, where the monarchy was restored in the person of Juan Carlos and a general election was held in 1977. The Falangists were decisively rejected, and Spain at last had a new democratic government. The future of the *Spanish Sahara* was less straightforward than the expected grant of independence, however. Spain had ceded the territory to Morocco and Mauritania in 1976, and the guerillas of the Polisario Front fought to liberate their country from both of these neighbouring states. Here too, it seemed, the Europeans left problems to their former African subjects. Rather more successfully, the French withdrew from the Territory of Afars and Issas, which became independent in 1977 as *Djibouti*. The French nevertheless continued to intervene in the affairs of many of their former African colonies, and even in those of Zaire (see Unit Twenty below).

Portugal meanwhile also withdrew from empire. Salazar's retirement opened the way for political change in Portugal itself (see Section 14.4). His successor, Marcello Caetano, preserved some stability until he was overthrown by a coup in April 1974. Events then moved rapidly. There was a sharp movement to the left, and free elections were eventually held in 1976. In the meantime, African nationalists were quick to take advantage of the Portuguese confusion. Antonio de Spinola, briefly in power in Portugal in 1974, promised freedom to the African colonies, and Portuguese Guinea was quickly set free as *Guinea-Bissau*. In 1975 *Mozambique* achieved independence under the presidency of Samora Machel, the culmination of the long struggle for freedom by Frelimo, and the beginning of an attempt to build a Marxist state in Mozambique. The *Cape Verde Islands*, *Sao Tomé* and *Principe* were also set free.

Angola too received independence in November 1975, but – like the Congo in 1960 – Angola plunged into civil war. It was not clear to which group of African nationalists the Portuguese should transfer power, and the Portuguese themselves had not prepared for a transfer in the way that the British usually tried to do. Control of Angola was now disputed between the MPLA (Popular Movement for the Liberation of Angola), the FNLA (National Front for the Liberation of Angola) and UNITA (National Union for the Total Independence of Angola). The strategic position of Angola attracted foreign powers like a magnet (see Fig. 21.3). The Soviet Union backed the MPLA, whose leader, Agostinho Neto, had Marxist sympathies, and Castro of Cuba sent troops to help the Popular Movement. The FNLA and UNITA joined hands to resist Neto. The USA, with the support of Zaire, encouraged the FNLA and, for a time, even China showed interest, favouring UNITA. Refugees, many of them white, sought to flee from the confusion and conflict; and since Angola bordered Namibia, the South Africans became involved, partly seeking to protect the refugees, partly aiming to prevent the conflict spreading southwards, and partly hoping that Neto would be defeated. The future of Angola was not clarified until well into 1976, when the MPLA proved victorious and it was generally recognized that Neto was the president of the new republic. There were new uncertainties, however, when Neto died suddenly during 1979.

The collapse of the Portuguese empire transformed the map of southern Africa. Regimes sympathetic to Marxism both in Mozambique and Angola increased the pressures on white-minority rule in Rhodesia, and the tide of black nationalism flowed nearer to the bastions of white privilege in Namibia and South Africa (see Unit Twenty-one below). But nothing remained of the Portuguese empire by the end of the 1970s except for Macao on the coast of China. The Portuguese left another problem behind in the south Pacific, however. Timor gained its freedom from Portugal but was promptly claimed, and indeed invaded, by Indonesia.

Turbulence in Africa continued in the wake of the withdrawal of the Europeans, and it was undoubtedly made worse by the ready supply of arms which the great powers were ever ready to sell, and by the intrigues of foreign powers in African affairs. Nowhere was this more clear than in the *Horn of Africa*, where conflicts grew into serious warfare during 1977. The Soviet Union had for some time cultivated the friendship of Somalia, strategically placed at the entrance to the Red Sea. The Russians then sought influence in Ethiopia, where the overthrow of Haile Selassie in 1974 opened the way for a movement to the left and for radical change. The socialist-inclined Colonel Mengistu came to power in 1977, and Russian advisers were welcomed. Conflict developed between Ethiopia and Somalia, however. The latter claimed much of the Ogaden Province of Ethiopia, alleging that many of its inhabitants were Somali. Somalia broke away from the Soviet Union, while Russians and Cubans developed yet stronger ties with Ethiopia. The Ogaden war was fought fiercely, and both sides made extensive use of Russian weapons. But Somalia could not prevail against the Ethiopians with their outside advisers, and the Somalis had little option but to sue for peace. The problem was hardly settled, however. Having lost its influence to the Russians in Addis Ababa, the USA began cautiously to consider some counter-balancing influence in Mogadishu, the capital of Somalia and, meanwhile, skirmishing in the Ogaden went on. The Soviet Union also had influence in the Yemen, at the other side of the mouth of the Red Sea, and the West generally was concerned about all developments in an area lying close to the West's supplies of oil. Ethiopia faced another problem and that too concerned the outside world. Eritrea, once an Italian colony, had been merged in Ethiopia in 1962, but Eritrean guerillas demanded independence. Again Russians and Cubans supported Ethiopia, but it proved far from easy to suppress the rebellion. The Horn of

Africa remained dangerously unstable at the start of the 1980s and, in the West's view, Russian involvement there was part of the general ambition of the Soviet Union to extend its influence southwards and to threaten, so it seemed, the world's oil routes.

Unit Seventeen

Changing circumstances in *South-East Asia* led to the abandonment of SEATO in the later 1970s. The USA had lost a good deal of its prestige in Vietnam, and the American withdrawal in 1975 from Vietnam and Indochina doomed SEATO to extinction. To some extent, its place was taken by the Association of South-East Asian Nations (ASEAN), within which Indonesia, Malaysia, the Philippines, Singapore and Thailand had begun to develop co-operation among themselves in the late 1960s. ASEAN was not primarily an anti-communist alliance, however though it was not until the mid-1970s and late 1970s, respectively, that China and the Soviet Union ceased to regard it as such. ASEAN existed as a regional association to further the interests of its members without necessarily being closely linked with the USA.

The ceasefire of 1973 had little meaning for *Vietnam* (see Section 17.1 (*c*) (*vi*)). Thieu's regime in South Vietnam was unable to cope with further communist pressures, and the US policy of Vietnamization began to look like surrender. Nixon left Ford to complete the American withdrawal and, though Ford tried to prop up Thieu with money and supplies, Thieu resigned in April 1975. Saigon fell to the communists that same month, and the Viet Cong quickly took control of the whole of South Vietnam. In 1976 the two halves of Vietnam were united in a single Socialist Republic. The new Republic was admitted to UNO in 1977 after some opposition from the USA and, a year later, Vietnam joined Comecon, its membership sponsored by the Soviet Union but criticized by some east European governments.

Communists also took control of the rest of Indochina. The Khmer Rouge, the communist organization in *Cambodia*, seized Phnom Penh even before Saigon fell to the Viet Cong. Sihanouk was restored to power in Cambodia, but events moved swiftly. The Khmer Rouge came under the authority of Pol Pot. Sihanouk was ousted and Cambodia was renamed Kampuchea. Pol Pot now presided over a fanatical and savage attempt to build a communist republic so primitive that not only were efforts made to purge it of all capitalist and bourgeois influences, but even of almost everything (except weapons) which belonged to the twentieth century. City dwellers were driven off to work on the land. Phnom Penh was depopulated and fell into decay. China encouraged this social revolution, but relations between Kampuchea and Vietnam deteriorated rapidly. Border conflicts and ideological argument escalated, and the Vietnamese invaded Kampuchea towards the end of 1978. Pol Pot and his forces retreated, and only then were the full horrors of his regime exposed. Its vast cruelties seemed at least to match those of the Nazis in Germany, and even now Pol Pot continued to wage guerilla warfare against the invaders. The Vietnamese set up a new communist government in Phnom Penh under Heng Somrin, but the outside world remained suspicious. It was widely assumed that the Vietnamese were acting under Russian instructions, and that Soviet influence was being extended. Like China, many western governments went on maintaining that Pol Pot was Kampuchea's rightful ruler. China launched a brief attack on Vietnam to register its displeasure. Meanwhile, Kampuchea plumbed the depths of misery. The country had been torn apart by the Pol Pot regime, coming on top of earlier upheavals. The people were starving, and it took time to plant and grow new crops. The Russians poured in aid and the West too, albeit hesitantly, sent relief supplies. Yet the 1980s opened with a continuing severe crisis, and it seemed likely that it would take years for Kampuchea to recover, even if there was a period of political stability.

Laos also became communist at the end of 1975, with the Pathet Lao in complete control. Laos was in urgent need of economic development, and it looked for assistance to Vietnam and the Soviet Union. The USA also sent food supplies in 1978 when Laos faced a threat of starvation. Three decades of conflict in what had once been French Indochina left a legacy of social and economic problems throughout the area, and all the new regimes faced difficulties of reconstruction. American policy in Indochina had ended in total defeat, but a flood of refugees from Vietnam and Kampuchea showed that communist rule was not welcomed universally. The middle classes in particular resented it, but many of the refugees were also of Chinese origins, fleeing as much for ethnic as for political and economic reasons. The ASEAN states meanwhile began tentatively to establish relations with the new governments of Indochina, though it seemed that the transition in the area to stability and prosperity was likely to be a lengthy one.

Détente was a word used increasingly in the 1970s to describe the improving relations between the great powers – similar to what Khrushchev had called 'peaceful co-existence'. The conference on Security and Cooperation in Europe at Helsinki bore fruit in 1975 (see Section 23.1). The USA, Canada and thirty-three European nations signed a charter which was the outcome of Brandt's *Ostpolitik* (see Section 17.2 (c)). They agreed that the European frontiers in existence since the Second World War should be 'inviolable', and they thus accepted the *status quo* in Germany. They also agreed to pursue economic and cultural links, and to recognize certain fundamental Human Rights. They would further explore ways of settling international disputes, and meet again in 1978. The new Conference met in Belgrade, but it was promptly soured by arguments about Human Rights. Carter, with the support of the West, alleged that Human Rights were still not respected in Russia and eastern Europe. Brezhnev accused the West of trying to interfere in the East's internal affairs. Little was achieved, though a further meeting was arranged for 1981.

It seemed doubtful whether much real progress had been made during the 1970s after all, and American-Russian relations remained fragile. There had been moments of optimism. Nixon again visited Moscow shortly before his resignation. The USA recognized East Germany, and East-West trade increased. But tension lurked below the surface. When the USA sold grain to the Soviet Union in 1975, an attempt was made to force the Kremlin to permit free emigration in exchange; and thereafter the USA frequently tried to use grain supplies to extort concessions from the Russians. Co-operation in space exploration led to the Apollo–Soyuz link-up in 1975, and progress was made in succeeding years, though slowly, in a new round of Strategic Arms Limitation Talks (SALT). When a new SALT treaty was agreed, however, Carter found the American Senate unwilling to ratify it, and the Russian invasion of Afghanistan at the end of 1979 caused American-Russian relations quickly to deteriorate further.

China shared the US hostility to the new Russian move. American relations with China, indeed, had seemed to improve more consistently during the 1970s than American relations with the Soviet Union (see Unit 15 above). Ford went to China in 1975, and Kissinger, the world's most industrious negotiator while the Republicans were in the White House, laid good foundations for future American-Chinese accord. Carter and Vance built on these foundations, while persistent distrust of Moscow provided cement for them. Meanwhile, the world had another nagging worry. India exploded an atomic bomb in 1974 and, though the Indian government insisted that it had no intention of stockpiling nuclear weapons, the manufacture of such weapons was clearly within the capability of a growing number of governments. The super powers themselves went on amassing weapons of destruction – both nuclear and chemical – and the SALT achievements and earlier agreements such as the Non-Proliferation Treaty provided only flimsy safeguards against the further spread of armaments which could one day destroy the human race.

Unit Eighteen

Economic problems seemed more immediately threatening, however. In the mid-1970s, a large part of the world faced inflation, recession and an energy crisis. Oil prices were raised by OPEC (see Section 18.1), and there was growing realization that oil supplies would one day run out. Other prices rose too, forcing rich and poor alike to pay more for their foodstuffs and raw materials The industrialized countries raised the prices of their manufactured goods but, as purchasing power declined, so too did sales. Unemployment became widespread. There was a slight recovery in the late 1970s, but the 1980s again opened with a deepening recession. Both rich and poor searched desperately for solutions to economic crises. Towards the end of 1975, an economic summit meeting was held by the leaders of the USA, Britain, West Germany, France, Italy and Japan, and they met again in 1978, this time with Canadian representation. Such summits seemed likely to be a feature of the modern world, but they had only a limited impact by 1980. The main concern of such summits was to restore the developed world to economic health, as the basis for any wider settlement of economic problems. The world as a whole had still to tackle the widening gap between the richer nations of the northern hemisphere and the poorer nations of the southern. The need here was for what was called in the 1970s a North-South dialogue. The size and urgency of the problem were the subject of the Brandt Report of 1980, the report of a commission headed by Willy Brandt and of which Edward Heath was a member. The Report recommended action to assist the poor to achieve prosperity not only in the interests of justice and humanitarianism, but because customers in the Third World seemed the best guarantee of the prosperity of the developed world itself, where men and machines stood idle for want of markets for their output.

Meanwhile, attention centred on oil. Many countries searched for new supplies. Britain and neighbouring countries intensified their drilling operations in the North Sea. In 1975 work was begun on an Alaskan pipeline to bring oil from the Arctic to the rest of the USA. A limited attempt was also made to cushion oil consumers against some of the effects of the price rises. A UN emergency fund was set up, with the co-operation of the IMF and oil-producing nations, and the latter gave some more direct assistance to the poorest countries. The Islamic world issued the Declaration of Lahore in 1974, and set up a committee to help the poorer Moslem states. The Lomé Agreement provided some help to states which had the sympathy of the EEC (see Unit Fourteen above). But such agreements only scratched the surface of the problem. Many poor countries such as Jamaica were reduced almost to bankruptcy, and the position of others remained precarious. Even nations such as Japan which could afford to pay the higher prices for oil, sometimes found it difficult in the 1970s to obtain supplies of it, and fear grew that by the end of the century supplies might well be near to exhaustion. In the meantime, however, the oil producers much increased their income. Nations such as Nigeria as well as the Arab producers benefited, although over-dependence on oil production could itself produce problems when the economy was imperfectly balanced.

Japan weathered the storms. It went on accumulating balance-of-payments surpluses, and the yen remained strong The Liberal-Democrats survived the election of 1976. Takeo Fukuda became Prime Minister, followed in 1978 by Masayoshi Ohira. Yet Japanese society continued to be plagued by unrest. Unemployment rose, but it was turbulent students who continued to be the most disruptive. There were regular violent protests against the siting of Tokyo's new airport, though it was finally opened in 1978.

The following details of the Japanese economy, which relate to 1977, can be compared with those on page 284, which relate to 1970. Even allowing for inflation, they show the continuing impressive achievement of Japanese business.

Average income per head of population: 4 300 (£s)

Main exports: machinery 25%; vehicles 19%; iron and steel 15%; ships 10%

Trade:
    Main export destinations: USA 25%; South Korea 5%
    Main imports from: USA 18%; Saudi Arabia 12%; Australia 8%
    Trade surplus: 2 532 000 000 000 yen
Population: 114 million

In 1979–80, however, even Japan had a balance-of-payments deficit.

Unit Nineteen

The Middle East again embarked hesitantly on a search for more lasting peace after the Yom Kippur War of 1973 (see Section 19.1 (*f*)). This time the USA took a direct interest. The ubiquitous Kissinger practised shuttle-diplomacy (see Glossary) in a vigorous effort to reconcile Arabs and Israelis. The first priority was to separate Arab and Israeli forces and to get UN peace-keeping troops between them. There was agreement at Geneva in 1975 on new lines of demarcation between Egyptians and Israelis in the area of the Suez Canal, and the USA agreed that American civilians would monitor an early-warning system in Sinai, to discourage future conflict there. In the same year normal traffic flowed again through the Suez Canal, when the waterway was cleared of wartime debris. It took rather longer to bring about disengagement in the Golan Heights, but there too Syrians and Israelis were eventually separated.

The problem was still far from being settled, and incidents continued to occur. The border between the Lebanon and Israel was particularly uneasy. Palestinian guerillas in the Lebanon were a standing provocation for the Israelis and the latter several times attacked their bases in 1974 and 1975. Such raids played their part in reducing the Lebanon to civil war in 1975. A tangled conflict between the Palestinians and Christian militias became a battle for political control between left and right and also a religious war between Moslems and Christians. Syria intervened and eventually Arab League forces arrived in the Lebanon, to try to restore peace. The Israelis launched another attack in 1978, however, bent on supporting the Christians and on wiping out the Palestinian bases in south Lebanon once and for all; and yet another UN force was raised, to continue into the 1980s to try to keep apart the Palestinians and Israelis. The Lebanon suffered acutely. The various conflicts produced extensive devastation, and the Lebanese economy was much disrupted.

Meanwhile, there was a dramatic shift in Egyptian policy. The friendship between Egypt and the Soviet Union ended in mutual recriminations, and President Sadat turned instead to the West. Nixon visited the Middle East, and Sadat himself visited the USA in 1975. Two years later, Sadat launched a bold new initiative. In November 1977 he visited Jerusalem, a lonely and improbable figure as the following cartoon shows. He was condemned by President Assad of Syria, by the Palestinians and by Gadafy of Libya. There had already been skirmishing on the Egyptian-Libyan border, and in the eyes of the Arab world it was treachery even to admit the existence of Israel. At the same time, Sadat risked rebuff at the hands of hard-line Israelis. He was given a cautious welcome by Menachem Begin, whose Likud Party had only recently ousted the Labour Party from power in Israel, but Begin himself nevertheless had a reputation as an ardent Zionist who had been something of a 'Hawk'.

Begin returned Sadat's visit and was welcomed in Cairo. The two men bargained. Moderates on both sides hoped they might reach a settlement, but there were many others who feared a sell-out. Begin's difficulties with Israeli critics were small, however, compared with Sadat's unpopularity in the Arab world. In 1978 the initiative seemed to be running out of steam, but new life was breathed into it by President Carter of the USA. Carter invited Sadat and Begin to Camp David, and the framework of an Egyptian-Israeli peace treaty was mapped out. Sadat was offering Israel full recognition, the first by any Arab nation. In return, the Israelis were to evacuate Sinai, part of their conquests in 1967. But Sadat also hoped to persuade the Israelis to leave the Gaza Strip and the West Bank of the Jordan, to secure a homeland for the dispossessed Palestinians (see Fig. 19.3). Begin and Moshe Dayan, his Foreign Minister, gave ground only slowly. A start was nevertheless made on implementing the Egyptian-Israeli Treaty which had been signed in March 1979. Israel began handing back Sinai. But there were misgivings when Begin failed to stop the planting of new Jewish settlements on the West Bank. In 1980 the future of the Treaty still hung in the balance. The apparent reluctance of Israel to begin withdrawing from the West Bank embarrassed both Sadat and Carter, and it further infuriated the Palestinians. Sadat has paid a heavy price for his pursuit of peace, and his unpopularity in the Arab world and among Moslems increased when, in 1980, he offered sanctuary to the deposed

Shah of Iran (see page 367) who died soon after settling in Egypt. Sadat persevered along the course he had chosen, however, though he could do little now but wait for the Israelis to show that they too had a genuine desire for reconciliation, and would make concessions to the Palestinians.

Unit Twenty

President Mobutu remained in power in *Zaire* throughout the 1970s. In 1977 and 1978, however, he faced new uprisings in Katanga (known now as Shaba, since European names had been abolished in Zaire). The uprising of 1977 was supported by Angola, where the MPLA remembered Mobutu's encouragement of the FNLA at the time of Angola's independence (see Unit Sixteen above.) It was suspected that it was also supported by Cuba and perhaps the Soviet Union, since Mobutu was close to the USA. The rebels' main aim was to break free from Zaire, and their rising was therefore a continuation of the earlier Katangese secessionist movement (see Fig. 20.2). At the same time they complained bitterly of Mobutu's government, especially of his authoritarianism. In spite of controlling a large army, Mobutu found it difficult to contain the rebellion, and he needed the support both of Morocco and Egypt. A new invasion of Shaba was launched from Angola in 1978. This time whites were massacred in Kolwezi, and the French and Belgians sent troops to the area. The rebels were forced to retreat, and an uneasy peace was restored in Zaire. The incidents showed not only the tribal unrest which continued to plague many African states, but how difficult it was for Africans to settle their own affairs without foreign meddling. The French began to talk of mounting some sort of military fire-brigade, to deal with outbreaks of violence in Africa, and they were soon involved again elsewhere, for example in Chad. Unit Sixteen (above) has already shown Cuban and Russian involvement in African affairs. The Organization of African Unity still fell short of being able to achieve real stability in the African continent, and it was still embarrassed by the frequency with which outsiders meddled in African affairs. In the late 1970s the prestige of the OAU seemed indeed to decline.

Nigeria faced two main problems in the later 1970s. One was political: Gowon was overthrown in July 1975, but the coup was followed by another when the new President, Murtala Mohammed, was killed during 1976. Control of the military government passed to Olusegun Obasanjo, and it fell to him to begin the promised return to democratic civilian government. Elections were held in 1979, but it remained to be seen whether Nigeria could make a successful transition back to parliamentary rule, or whether it might again plunge into political confusion. Much seemed likely to depend on the economy, and the second problem was that of creating a balanced economy with a fair distribution of prosperity. As a member of OPEC, Nigeria gained from rising oil revenue. But comparatively few Nigerians were employed in the oil industry, and the bulk of the population still earned a living in agriculture. Its size, oil and comparative stability nevertheless made Nigeria one of the most important states in Africa, which the major powers were anxious to court, and which was a leading member of the recently-formed Economic Community of West African States.

Cyprus meanwhile plunged into more trouble. Makarios was overthrown in July 1974. Nikos Sampson, his successor, made a brief and unsuccessful attempt to achieve the aims of *enosis*, and to unite the island with Greece. Turkish Cypriots offered fierce resistance. With the help of Turkish troops, they seized much of the north of Cyprus and put to flight almost a quarter of a million Greek Cypriot refugees. British and UN troops helped to check the fighting, but there now existed in effect two Cypruses. Turkish Cypriots claimed about a third of the island where there would be no more talk of *enosis*, and immigrants from Turkey strengthened the Turkish sector. Makarios was restored to the leadership of the Greeks and, after his death in 1977, Spyros Kyprianou became the Greek President of Cyprus. Turkish Cypriots looked for leadership to Rauf Denktash, however. Time and again the UN extended the term of the peace-keeping forces in the island, and hoped that the wounds might eventually heal. The Greeks made remarkable progress in reviving the economy of southern Cyprus, but the north depended heavily on economic support from Turkey.

The upheaval of 1974 not only divided Cyprus: it also weakened NATO. Greece and Turkey for a time hovered on the brink of war over Cyprus. The USA blamed Turkey rather than Greece for the crisis, and suspended supplies of arms. Turkey explored better relations with the Soviet Union in the late 1970s, and the effectiveness of NATO in the Mediterranean began to seem questionable.

Paksitan came under military rule again in 1977. Bhutto had made some headway in improving the country's economy and, after the loss of Bangladesh, he had contained further secessionist movements. Early in 1977 he won an impressive electoral victory. But there were noisy complaints of corruption, and serious civil disorders followed. Bhutto was arrested, and General Zia-ul-Haq took control. Two years later Bhutto was executed for alleged crimes against his people. *Bangladesh* fared little better, and there too military rule was established. Sheik Mujib (Mujibur Rahman) was murdered in 1975, less than four years after his release from prison to lead Bangladesh to freedom. Further assassinations occurred and General Ziaur Rahman emerged as the new President. 1978 brought new strains to the country's fragile economy when there was a sudden influx of Moslem refugees from Burma, but many were eventually repatriated, and assistance from Arab oil producers helped Bangladesh to grapple with its still enormous economic difficulties.

Northern Ireland continued to prove that it was not only developing countries which suffered from upheavals. 1974 began with an experiment in power-sharing and government by a coalition which included Catholics as well as Protestants. It lasted only until May of that year, when the economy was paralysed by a widespread strike brought about by Protestant extremists. Prime Minister Wilson saw no alternative but to reimpose direct British rule, since the bombings and killings continued. British troops went on with their thankless task of trying to keep the peace, and they suffered steadily mounting casualties. A woman's peace movement tried in 1976 to bring some sanity to Northern Irish affairs, protesting against the almost daily barbarism, but it had little effect on the hardliners on either side. Protestant extremists rejected compromise, and Catholic extremists still sought to achieve union with the Irish Republic by terrorism. There was little support for another call for strikes in 1977 in protest against the alleged weakness of the British government in dealing with the IRA, but extremists such as Ian Paisley continued to win massive support from Protestant voters in elections to the Westminster parliament. Such extremists also continued to obstruct all efforts to devise a system of self-government for Northern Ireland which would protect the minorities from self-interested Ulster Unionism. What the hardliners wanted was a simple restoration of the system which Ulster Unionists had previously dominated, and which had brought on the disorders at the end of the 1960s. And that was something no British government was prepared to tolerate. There was no end in sight to the problems of Northern Ireland at the start of the 1980s, and meanwhile Northern Ireland remained the poorest area of the United Kingdom, with the highest level of unemployment. It was also the area on which British governments spent the most money per head of population.

Unit Twenty-One

South Africa came under increasing pressure from the critics of apartheid following the collapse of the Portuguese empire (see Unit Sixteen above). The Nationalists were returned to power in the election of 1974 with an increased majority, but there were unprecedented protests by black South Africans in 1976, when many African townships, and especially Soweto, flared in revolt. The police struck back with violence far in excess of that used at Sharpeville. South African whites claimed that some progress was being made to soften the rigidities of apartheid, especially after Vorster resigned as Prime Minister in 1978 and Pieter Botha came to power. But the blacks still suffered indignities and hardships. They complained in particular of inadequate educational opportunity, as well as of exclusion from politics. Organizing protest was always difficult and Steven Biko, the founder of the Black Consciousness movement and an advocate of peaceful resistance, followed the numerous earlier African leaders into detention. He died of brain injuries while in police custody. Government investigators alleged that nobody was criminally responsible for his death, but this did little to quieten the allegation that murder had been committed.

The outside world was not much impressed by claims that apartheid was being softened. Opinion remained fiercely hostile, especially in the non-white world. Many countries boycotted the Olympic Games of 1976, in protest against the participation of New Zealand, which had insisted on playing rugby with South African whites. The world also ignored the granting of 'independence' to the Transkei in 1976 and to Bophuthatswana, a collection of six scattered units, in 1977. These were the first of the bantustans to be given their freedom, but the world refused to believe they were anything more than puppet-states, established to suit the convenience of South African whites.

Namibia also brought continuing criticism of South Africa. SWAPO guerillas stepped up their nationalist opposition to South African rule there, and UNO continued to demand freedom for the former mandated territory. It was a major shift in South African policy to begin to discuss such freedom, and South Africa negotiated with a UN commission of which the USA, Britain, Canada, France and West Germany were members. South Africa had its own ideas, however, about the future of Namibia. It intended to keep control of the port of Walvis Bay, and it hoped to set up an acceptable African government from which SWAPO would be excluded. The whites therefore set up the Turnhalle Talks with Namibian parties who seemed likely to make concessions, but this internal settlement – like that which Smith attempted in Rhodesia (see below) – found little favour in the outside world. South Africa was clearly fighting a delaying rearguard action, but its days of authority in Namibia seemed to be numbered. Attempts to win friends in Africa had met only limited success, though for a time they included Liberia until President Tolbert was overthrown and murdered there in 1980. Meanwhile, even France, with reservations and exceptions, began to apply the international ban on the sale of arms to South Africa.

Rhodesia too was much affected by the collapse of the Portuguese empire in Africa. Machel and Frelimo now encouraged Rhodesian guerillas to attack Smith's white-minority regime from the east, while attacks were also stepped up from Zambia to the north. China and the Soviet Union supplied arms, and Smith found little sympathy in the world at large for his increasing problems. The death toll in the guerilla war mounted. Economic sanctions had had only limited effect on Rhodesian whites, and the Bingham Report in the late 1970s revealed something of the extent to which they had been broken, even by the British. But Smith found it harder to deal with the guerillas, and now international pressure too began to increase. The USA finally decided to impose sanctions on Rhodesian chrome, and the energetic Secretary of State, Dr Kissinger, arrived in Africa to try to conjure up a settlement.

Only one settlement was possible: that power in Rhodesia should be transferred from the whites to the overwhelming majority of blacks. This was demanded by the Front-Line Presidents of Rhodesia's neighbours – Kaunda, Nyerere, Neto, Machel and Seretse Khama of Botswana. And it was the resolute aim of the guerilla leaders – Joshua Nkomo, the veteran leader of Rhodesian nationalism whose forces operated from Zambia, and Robert Mugabe, allegedly a Marxist whose forces operated from Mozambique. Both had suffered detention and hardship at the hands of Rhodesian whites, and they came together in the Patriotic Front (PF) for their country's liberation. Kissinger extracted from Smith a declaration of intent, but all the details for a transfer of power remained to be worked out. Ivor Richard, Britain's ambassador to the UN, presided over a conference at Geneva at the end of 1976 to tackle this problem. But Smith played for time, and used the divisions between Rhodesia's black leaders to postpone any real progress. Apart from Nkomo and Mugabe, there were others such as Bishop Abel Muzorewa and Ndabaningi Sithole who claimed to speak for the blacks, and it was by no means clear to whom power must be transferred.

Smith's aim was at least to ensure the exclusion of the PF. He therefore sought to bypass outside opinion by setting up an internal settlement. By early 1978 he was introducing a transitional period with a sort of apprenticeship for black ministers, serving under the guidance of ministers of the Rhodesian Front. This would lead to a new constitution and elections. Muzorewa, Sithole and Chief Chirau co-operated, hoping to win power in the absence of the PF. Elections were in fact held, and Muzorewa took over from Smith as Prime Minister. The outside world remained highly sceptical. The Front-Line Presidents condemned the settlement, and the PF simply continued the guerilla war. Though Muzorewa now demanded the granting of legal independence, the British refused it. Meanwhile, Britain had a new Foreign Secretary in David Owen after the sudden death of Anthony Crosland, and in America Cyrus Vance had replaced Kissinger when the Ford presidency ended. Owen and Vance insisted on further concessions, enthusiastically supported by Andrew Young. They had made little headway when the Labour Party lost the British general election of 1979, and the Conservative Lord Carrington arrived as Foreign Secretary at the Foreign Office.

The Commonwealth Conference of 1979 met in Lusaka, Zambia. Margaret Thatcher attended as well as Carrington, and the Front-Line Presidents ensured that Rhodesia was at the top of the agenda. The result was the Lancaster House Conference in London later in the year, where Carrington worked hard to bring about a real settlement of the Rhodesian problem. The PF was involved as well as Smith and the internal black leaders, and months of tough negotiation produced a breakthrough. A new constitution was agreed, reserving twenty seats for whites in a Rhodesian parliament of 100. The PF agreed to stop the war. Muzorewa surrendered power in Rhodesia to a British governor and, under British supervision and with Commonwealth help, new elections were held in Rhodesia early in 1980. Carrington had prepared the way, and Lord Soames proved an effective governor, but it was the PF guerillas who had brought things to a head. Rhodesian blacks recognized as much. They gave an overall majority to Mugabe, while Nkomo won all the seats among the Ndbele people. The other black leaders were routed. There was no doubt but that Mugabe was now the people's chosen leader, and he was quickly installed as Prime Minister. Zimbabwe, the African name for Rhodesia, became independent in April 1980, and the fourteen years of the UDI came to an end. Mugabe began his rule in statesmanlike fashion. Nkomo was given a seat in his cabinet, and ministries were also found for representatives of moderate white opinion. Mugabe preached reconciliation and moderation, and the whites who had long feared his rule as likely to lead to some sort of Marxist purge or to anarchy, found themselves having to re-examine the prejudices which had done so much to sustain Ian Smith and the Rhodesian Front. Zimbabwe would undoubtedly face many difficulties in the coming years. Not only had past bitterness to be set aside and racial harmony built, but the country's whole economy revived, too. The election of 1980 had also shown an uneasy division on tribal lines, with the Ndbele solid for Nkomo and the Shona equally solid for Mugabe. Such a division would need skill and goodwill in nation-building, and there were many problems of resettlement and employment for those whose recent years had been spent in ferocious civil war. There was something like general astonishment at the successful beginnings which Mugabe's government made in tackling these daunting problems, and it was perhaps only in what had been a British colony that years of strife and bloodshed could lead in the end to what seemed a remarkable atmosphere of tolerance and moderation. A British gift of £75 million, in instalments – a small sum considering the task that lay ahead – helped to launch Zimbabwe as an independent nation.

Unit Twenty-Two

The *emergent nations* generally suffered grievously from the economic upheavals of the 1970s. The rising prices of oil and of the manufactured goods of the developed countries were seldom matched by increases in the value of the exports of the poor. Yet the countries which were chosen for consideration in this Unit fared better than many of their neighbours. They enjoyed comparative political stability and, where governments changed, they did so peacefully. It seemed for a time, however, that democracy was coming to an end in *India*. The recent undemocratic practices of Indira Gandhi (see page 367) brought her humiliation in the general election of 1977, and legal proceedings were instituted against her. The fate of Bhutto in Pakistan (see Unit Twenty above) perhaps served as a timely warning to the Indians, however, and the disillusionment with the new government which came to power in India in 1977 – an anti-Gandhi coalition, led at first by Morarji Desai – soon swung opinion back in Mrs Gandhi's favour. Above all, Indians continued to believe in democratic elections rather than in coups and dictatorship. Congress rule had given the country thirty years of stability from 1947 to 1977, and its achievements were not inconsiderable. On the other hand, it seemed that the Nehru 'dynasty' had grown corrupt and harsh under the enormous pressures of governing a country with so many pressing economic and social problems. Desai's Janata government represented a search for something better, but that too crumbled under the pressures, and masses of voters swung back in 1979 to the Congress (Indira) Party. Some questioned whether Gandhi might not again abuse her authority and persecute the opposition for their obstructiveness to her policies. But India was still a democratic country – the largest in the world – at the start of the 1980s.

African countries seldom managed the luxury of any choice of political parties. Even those which avoided military dictatorships, such as Amin's in Uganda, were normally one-party states. But *Ghana* persistently sought a return to democracy. Early in 1978 Acheampong promised elections within two years, but he resigned later in the year in favour of another military leader, Fred Akuffo. In 1979 Ghana again set out on the road to another experiment in democratic government. *Kenya* remained stable despite the death of Kenyatta in 1978. He was succeeded by the Vice-President Daniel Arap Moi, and Kenya remained firmly committed to the capitalist world and to by no means unprosperous private enterprise. *Tanzania*, on the other hand, continued to pursue the socialist goals of Julius Nyerere. Critics alleged that Tanzania was in deep economic difficulties, made worse by problems caused by Amin of Uganda. Border disputes escalated into open warfare, and Nyerere joined hands with Ugandan rebels to rid Africa of a regime whose cruelties and bombast had been almost universally despised. There were pious complaints that the Tanzanians were interfering in the affairs of another state, but it was a comment on the disunity of the world and of Africa itself that it was left to one of the world's poorest nations to liberate the Ugandans from a bloody tyranny. It confirmed yet again, however, that Nyerere would not allow his ideals for Africa to be compromised by the grotesque image of the continent projected by Amin. Nyerere also played a major part in bringing about a settlement in Rhodesia (see Unit Twenty-One above), as did Kaunda of *Zambia*, whose country had suffered severely during the economic dislocation of the years of the UDI. Zambia also suffered from the fluctuating prices obtainable for its copper exports and from shortages of maize. The birth of Zimbabwe at last produced more normal conditions in central Africa and eased Zambia's lines of communication. Kaunda had weathered the storm, and Zambia was one country which could look forward to the 1980s with greater optimism. If fair prices for Zambian copper could also somehow be guaranteed, the future might indeed be less dismal than the past.

Guyana entered the 1980s with growing criticism of the leadership of Forbes Burnham. It was alleged that he grew increasingly authoritarian. He had also pursued a variety of socialist policies which seemed close to those once advocated by Cheddi Jagan. Guyana drew closer to Castro and, in 1978, it became an associate member of Comecon. Burnham had also helped to found the Caribbean Community and Common Market in 1973, however, forging closer ties with the English-speaking Caribbean. The early progress of the Community was promising, but West Indian economies were hard hit by rising oil prices and dissension between its members erupted, reminiscent of the ill-fated West Indies Federation. Only Trinidad, itself an oil-producer, managed to maintain a reasonably healthy economy into the 1980s.

Israel at last turned away from rule by the Labour Party in 1977. Golda Meir had resigned as Prime Minister in 1974, after criticism of the country's unreadiness in the war of the previous year. Her successor, Yitzhak Rabin, was handicapped by dissension within the Party, and high taxes helped to lose him popularity. The voters turned to the more right-wing Likud, and Begin came to power. Few voters could have expected that Begin would soon be responding to the peace overtures of Sadat of Egypt (see Unit Nineteen above). Not all of his supporters approved, and there was perhaps greater enthusiasm in Israel for the frequent punitive raids which went on being launched against Palestinians in the Lebanon. Begin, like Sadat, was nevertheless awarded the Nobel Peace Prize in 1978.

Unit Twenty-Three

At the start of the 1980s the USA and the Soviet Union remained the world's only real *super powers*, the awesome accumulation of their weapons now further increased by fast developing technology and by the neutron bomb, capable of killing people while leaving property intact. China, whose population was now around 1 000 million, commanded growing attention and had begun to be spoken of as at least a 'great' power. The simple division of the world between East and West, communist and capitalist, seemed no longer to apply, however, and relationships between the USA, the Soviet Union and China had grown more complex (see Unit Seventeen above). Most of western Europe still adhered to the USA and to NATO, and there were signs in 1980 that the members of the EEC were beginning to try to put together a common European policy towards a number of international problems. President Carter demanded European support for his efforts to secure the release of American hostages in Iran (see page 367), and he also expected west Europeans to share his hostility towards Russian activities in Afghanistan (see page 367). He found a firm supporter in Mrs Thatcher, but it was far from easy to get west Europeans generally to speak with a single voice. A revival of the Cold War between West and East seemed nevertheless to be coming about, with China apparently closer to the West than to its former Russian ally on many occasions. The Chinese opposed Neto in Angola and supported Mobutu in Zaire and, like the Americans, were highly critical of Russian ambitions in the Horn of Africa and in Indochina (see Units Sixteen and Seventeen above). Peking repeatedly warned the world against an alleged Russian desire for 'hegemony', claiming Russian policy in Afghanistan in 1979–80 as further evidence of it. Russia's Afghan policy embarrassed Castro of Cuba. It was sometimes argued that Moscow used Cuba, for example in its dealings with Africa, as a sort of bridge between the industrialized Soviet Union and the developing Third World, which might otherwise feel closer affinity with the peasant-based society of China. But it seems unlikely that Castro saw himself merely as a pawn in great-power politics. He nevertheless linked what he saw as Cuba's mission to liberate less emancipated peoples with a loyalty to the Soviet Union – so much so that there was some strong objection in 1979 to his chairmanship in that year of the non-aligned movement (see page 368). The unpopularity of Russia's Afghan policy helped further to damage Castro's image among emerging nations.

The political manoeuvring of the major powers took place in the 1970s against a background of mounting economic crises, the worst effects of which were often felt by the poorer nations of the *Third World*. It was always a struggle for such nations to balance their trading accounts, let alone to advance the standard of living of usually growing populations. A continuing worry was the instability of commodity prices, such as those of copper on which Zambia relied so heavily and of cocoa on which Ghana depended. The following Table, which can be compared with Table 22.1 on page 353, shows that some developing nations such as India and Guyana managed in spite of the difficulties to make small improvements in their trading positions. But there was often little continuity from one year to the next. In 1977, for example, Guyana again had a substantial deficit on its international trade.

The trading position of some emergent nations

Country	Population est. 1976 (millions)	Main Exports % of whole	Exports Mainly to % of whole	Imports Mainly from % of whole	Trade Balance: Exports as % of Imports
**India	615·0	Sugar 12% Tea 6% Jute manu- factures 6%	USA 13% Japan 11% USSR 10%	USA 25% Iran 9%	100·5%
*Ghana	10·3	Cocoa 59% Timber 8%	Britain 15% USA 11%	USA 16% Britain 15%	102%
**Kenya	13·8	Coffee 37% Tea 12% Petroleum products 12%	West Germany 13% Britain 11%	Britain 19% Iran 17%	81·5%
**Tanzania	15·6	Cotton 16% Coffee 13%	West Germany 14% Britain 13%	Britain 12% Kenya 11%	77%
*Zambia	5·3	Copper 91%	Britain 22% Japan 17%	Britain 20% USA 12%	71%
*Guyana	0·8	Sugar 50% Bauxite 24%	Britain 28% USA 23%	USA 30% Britain 22%	103%
**Israel	3·6	Diamonds 33% Chemicals 10%	USA 18% West Germany 8% Britain 8%	USA 22% Britain 16%	42%†

* Trade figures, 1975; ** Trade figures, 1976.
† Israel's bill for imports is high because of the import of armaments.

There was little respite in the late 1970s from the *violence* and barbarism which so disfigured the world. It was not confined to confrontations between armies, regular and irregular. Few countries escaped the activities of assassins, arsonists, bombers and the ruthless bully-boys who, with or without official approval, preferred force to argument in pursuit of their aims. The broken bodies and the corpses of their victims bore regular witness to the savagery of the modern world, and there seemed no reason for optimism that the 1980s would see any lessening of such violence. Urban terrorism was now a characteristic of many societies. Organizations such as the IRA, the Italian Red Brigade, and the anarchists of West Germany known as the Baader-Meinhoff Group were only some of those who stained the 1970s with blood. Hi-jacking aircraft had continued at a reduced pace, but kidnapping and holding to ransom took its place. The 1980s seemed certain to produce yet further variations on these melancholy themes. Violent crime, quite apart from that which claimed for itself a political motive, also seemed to be on the increase, and parts of many large cities in one country after another grew less safe and less civilized by 1980 than they had been for many generations past.

A good deal of lip service was paid to mankind's *environmental problems*. The Caracas Conference of 1974 debated the Law of the Sea but produced few specific results. Not much was done to preserve fish stocks or to curb pollution. Oil spillages regularly fouled the oceans, and Japan and the Soviet Union remained insensitive to the need to conserve the world's shrinking whale population. There was concern about the rapid decline of the earth's resources generally. The developed world especially consumed vast quantities of fuel and raw materials, and as the human population of the earth expanded relentlessly, beyond the 4 000 million mark, there was also anxiety about endangered species of livestock. The World Population Conference in Bucharest marked World Population Year (1974) with declarations of concern about 'the urgency of the global crisis'. As human beings increased in number, so they tended to consume even more, not just to meet their basic needs but from a greed for luxuries and for profits. Anxiety about ivory-poaching in parts of Africa to supply demand in the richer nations was just one of the areas of concern about what might not survive for future generations to inherit. Others expressed alarm about the spread of nuclear power stations in those countries able to afford them. There too, it seemed, was a hazard for the future, and opposition in some cases, for example in Austria, came near to paralysing the development plans of governments which blandly claimed that such plant was sure to be 'safe'.

It would be misleading, however, to end this survey on a wholly gloomy note. At no time in history has greater awareness existed of the problems facing mankind, and at no previous time have such vast armies of people been at work in tireless efforts to bring about the betterment of the human race. Their constructive work seldom captures the newspaper headlines, except when there is some splendid achievement such as the near-eradication of smallpox, or some dramatic new initiative such as those of Sadat of Egypt, the women's peace movement in Northern Ireland, and the relief workers in Kampuchea. But the work goes on, even so. Much of the protest in the modern world is both constructive and peaceful. The media may inevitably be drawn more readily towards confrontation and disruption rather than towards co-operation and construction, but it should not be forgotten that, in spite of the world's many miseries, many millions neverthless enjoy a standard of living and quality of life undreamed of by earlier generations.

Glossary

Amnesty The granting of forgiveness, a pardon, usually to political offenders.

Apartheid South African system for separating the races.

Appeasement Reaching agreement by negotiation and conciliation. In the late 1930s it came to be identified with giving way to aggressive powers.

Arbitration The settlement of disputes through the verdict of a third party.

Autarky A plan for economic self-sufficiency in Nazi Germany. Germany would not be economically dependent on other nations.

Authoritarian Not liberal; usually applied to a government which imposes strict discipline and represses its opponents.

Autocracy Absolute rule by one man, a dictatorship.

Bolshevik Party Part of the Russian Socialist Democratic Party which believed in working as a dedicated organization to bring about a Marxist revolution; followers of Lenin. Members of the party were known as *Bolsheviks*. The party later changed its name to the Russian Communist Party.

Bourgeoisie The middle classes.

Caste Hereditary class in India, its members socially equal and united in religion. Usually linked with occupation and the means of livelihood. Exclusive, having little contact with those outside the caste. The term is often applied to the over 2 000 divisions of Hindu society. The four main divisions are into priests, rulers and warriors, traders and farmers, and artisans. Those outside these divisions are *untouchables* (see below).

Centre Middle-of-the-road, usually of political parties. Neither extreme socialists nor extreme conservatives.

Coexistence A state of international relations in which rivals tolerate one another. Neither seeks to bring about the downfall of the other although dislike remains.

Cold war A war fought with propaganda and economic weapons, stopping short of military confrontation, as between the USA and the USSR after 1945.

Containment The building of alliances to prevent expansion by a rival power.

Coup d'état A sudden and illegal change of government; a seizure of power.

Curzon line The proposed Polish–Russian frontier put forward by the British in 1920.

Democracy Rule by the people: a system of government which permits some effective control to the masses.

Desegregation The ending of *segregation* (see below).

Dictatorship　Rule by a dictator, similar to *autocracy* (see above).

Dominion　Term used to describe the first independent members of the British Commonwealth of Nations, e.g. Canada. *Dominion status* was defined in 1926. The Dominions were free from British control but retained a connexion with the British monarchy.

Franchise　The right to vote.

Guerilla　A fighter engaged in irregular warfare, often as a member of fairly small bodies resisting authority. *Guerilla warfare* is often associated with resistance movements using hit-and-run tactics and resorting to sabotage. *Urban guerillas* operate in towns.

Indemnity　Often used for a sum of money, a sort of fine, required by one country from another after war. See *reparations*.

Independence　Freedom. The freedom granted to former colonies when the mother country gives up control of them.

Integration　Merging together; the merging together of peoples of different race into one society.

Lebensraum　Living-space, elbow room. The areas which Nazi Germany claimed were necessary for Germany's development. Such areas were often rich in economic resources.

Mafia　Robber bands which originated in Sicily—a criminal organization.

Mandates　Mandated territories. Areas placed under the control of selected powers by the League of Nations, so that they could be prepared for *independence*. Some of them remained to become UN Trust Territories at the end of the Second World War, e.g. Tanganyika.

Ministerial responsibility　The responsibility of government ministers to parliament. Ministers must answer to parliament for their actions. This is regarded in many countries as an essential part of a system which is democratic.

Nation　Loosely, an independent country.

Nationalism　Pride in one's country, enthusiasm for the country's success. Nationalism may take various forms, e.g. a campaign to free one's country from foreign control; a campaign to make one's nation united and strong; a campaign to make one's country supreme over others.

Nationality　Belonging to a nation. The citizens of France have French nationality.

Nation state　An independent country made up to a large extent of people of one *race* (see below).

Nationalization　Converting into national property, placing under state ownership, e.g. the nationalization of railways, making railways the property of the nation instead of the property of private owners.

Pact   An agreement, a treaty.

Partisans   Fighters for freedom, freedom-fighters: see *guerilla*. A term used during the Second World War, e.g. in Jugoslavia.

Plebiscite   A vote by people in a given area on a particular question, e.g. the inhabitants of the Saar on the future of that region.

Proletariat   The working masses.

Protection   A system of *tariffs* (see below) to protect home industries against foreign competition. The opposite of *free trade*.

Race   A group of persons of common descent, perhaps of a distinctive ethnic stock. People of different races may be found in one nation, e.g. in the USA, the USSR, Guyana. In a *nation state*, one race may be expected to be predominant, e.g. Norwegians in Norway.

Radical   Enthusiastic for major change, for reform.

Reactionary   Backward-looking, desiring to put back the clock; opposed to change.

Referendum   Direct consultation of the people, similar to a *plebiscite* (see above).

Reparations   Compensation for injury and damage. Similar to an *indemnity* (see above) but compensation rather than a fine.

Republic   A state without a monarchy.

Reserves (gold/foreign currency)   Gold and foreign currency available within a state to pay for its imports and to support its own currency. For example, if Britain possesses large reserves of gold and US dollars, there is likely to be more confidence in the value of the pound.

Revisionism   Theories which depart from the teachings of Marx and seek to 'revise' (amend) them. The term is often used by those who believe violence is necessary for communism to succeed in order to denounce those who argue that communism may be achieved by non-violent means.

Sanctions   Penalties, methods with which to put pressure on nations which commit unpopular acts. *Economic sanctions* (e.g. against Rhodesia in the 1960s) involve restrictions on trade. *Military sanctions* (e.g. against North Korea in 1950) involve armed action.

Secession   Separation, breaking-away. Within any union (of states or races), one part may favour secession.

Segregation   Separation, usually imposed. The authorities may wish to segregate different groups of people. See *apartheid, desegregation*.

Separatism   A movement in favour of breaking away, usually of *secession*.

Shuttle-Diplomacy   Diplomacy conducted by one mediator 'shuttling' between the various parties to a dispute. A style of mediation favoured by Henry Kissinger, American Secretary of State 1971–77, in the Middle East, southern Africa and elsewhere.

Soviet   A council, committee. Often thought of as being revolutionary as a result of the development of soviets in Russia in 1917.

Suffrage   The right to vote.

Tariffs   Taxes on imports. See *protection*.

Totalitarian   Permitting no rival parties, e.g. the totalitarian regime of the Nazis in Germany.

Tribalism   Loyalty to the tribe often in preference to loyalty to the nation.

UDI   Unilateral Declaration of Independence. The declaration of *independence* without the permission of the mother country.

Untouchables   Those outside the main divisions of the Indian caste system. (See *caste*.) Usually associated with menial tasks and under-privilege.

Watergate   Headquarters of the Democrats in the 1971 US elections. Charges against Republican burglars escalated into a series of scandals which involved many officials around President Nixon. So many examples of dishonesty and corruption were uncovered that there were demands for Nixon's resignation or even his impeachment. In the course of the investigations, the Vice-President, Spiro Agnew, resigned (1973).

Welfare state   A state with comprehensive social services and social security system, for example in health, education and national insurance against sickness, unemployment and old age.

Zionist   A supporter of the colonization of Palestine by the Jews. The World Zionist Organization was founded in 1897.

Bibliography

Further Reading has been suggested at the end of each Unit. The following books will be found useful on the period as a whole.

Purnell's *History of the Twentieth Century* (originally issued in weekly parts)
Keesing's Contemporary Archives.

Documentary Collections

Bettey, J. H.: *English Historical Documents 1906–39.* Routledge & Kegan Paul (London, 1967).

Breach, R. W.: *Documents and Descriptions, the World Since 1914.* Oxford University Press (London, 1966).

Lane, P.: *Documents on British Economic and Social History*—Book 2, 1870–1939 and Book 3, 1945–1967. Macmillan (London, 1968).

Snyder, L. L.: *Fifty Major Documents of the Twentieth Century.* Anvil (London, 1955).

Wallbank, T. W.: *Documents on Modern Africa.* Anvil (London, 1964).

Wroughton, J.: *Documents on British Political History*, Book 3, 1914–1970. Macmillan (London, 1972).

Sketch Map Books

Perry, D. G. and Seaman, R. D. H.: *Sketch Maps in Modern History, 1789–1970.* Murray (London, 1971).

Richards, I., Goodson, J. B. and Morris, J. A.: *A Sketch Map History of the Great Wars and After.* Harrap (London, 1965).

Sellman, R. R.: *A Student's Atlas of Modern History, 1485–1971.* Arnold (London, 1972).

Collected Biographies

Ayling, S. E.: *Portraits of Power.* Harrap (London, 1965).

Jamieson, A.: *Leaders of the Twentieth Century.* Bell (London, 1970).

National Histories

Cobban, A.: *A History of Modern France*, Vol. 3. Pelican (Harmondsworth, 1970).

Hill, C. P.: *British Economic and Social History, 1700–1975.* Arnold (London, 1977).

Nove, A.: *An Economic History of the USSR.* Allen Lane (London, 1969).

Seaman, L. C. B.: *Post-Victorian Britain.* Methuen (London, 1966).

Sherlock, P. M.: *West Indian Nations.* Macmillan (London, 1973).

Spear, P.: *A History of India.* Vol. 2. Pelican (Harmondsworth, 1970).

Thomson, D.: *England in the Twentieth Century*. Pelican (Harmondsworth, 1970).

Watson, J. B.: *The West Indian Heritage*. Murray (London, 1979).

The Commonwealth and Emergent Nations

Watson, J. B.: *Empire to Commonwealth, 1919–1970*. Dent (London, 1971).

Miscellaneous and Reference

Barnett, Correlli: *The Collapse of British Power*. London (Eyre Methuen, 1972).

Brandt, W. et al: *North-South: A Programme for Survival*. Pan (London, 1980).

Charlesworth, M.: *Revolution in Perspective*. Lowe (London, 1972).

Davidson, B.: *Discovering Africa's Past*. Longman (London, 1978).

Elliott, F. and Summerskill, M.: *A Dictionary of Politics*. Penguin (Harmondsworth, 1970).

Moore, W. G.: *The Penguin Encyclopaedia of Places*. Penguin (Harmondsworth, 1971).

Palmer, A. W.: *A Dictionary of Modern History, 1789–1945*. Penguin (Harmondsworth, 1964).

Palmer, A. W.: *The Penguin Dictionary of Twentieth Century History*. Penguin (Harmondsworth, 1979).

Rayner, E. G., Stapley, R. F. and Watson, J. B.: *Evidence in Question— International Affairs Since 1919*. Oxford University Press (London, 1980).

Rodney, W.: *How Europe Underdeveloped Africa*. Bogle-L'Ouverture Publications (London, 1972; reprinted 1976).

Walters, F. P.: *History of the League of Nations*. Oxford University Press (London, 1960).

Wint, G.: *Asia Handbook*. Penguin (Harmondsworth, 1969).

Wiskemann, E.: *Europe of the Dictators 1919–1945*. Fontana (London, 1970).

Index